M000305724

Wellington's Redjackets

Wellington's Redjackets

The 45th (Nottinghamshire) Regiment
on Campaign in South America and
the Peninsula, 1805–14

Steve Brown

FRONTLINE BOOKS

WELLINGTON'S REDJACKETS
The 45th (Nottinghamshire) Regiment on Campaign in South America
and the Peninsula, 1805–14

This edition published in 2015 by Frontline Books,
an imprint of Pen & Sword Books Ltd,
47 Church Street, Barnsley, S. Yorkshire, S70 2AS.

ISBN: 978-1-47385-175-7

Printed and bound by CPI Group (UK) Ltd, Croydon, CR0 4YY
Typeset in 10/12 point Palatino

For more information on our books, please email: info@frontline-books.com,
write to us at the above address, or visit:
www.frontline-books.com

Contents

Foreword

'Observe this regiment – how well they look! They have been
with me the whole time. They have gone through everything –
what fine fellows!'
*The Duke of Wellington during the final inspection of the 3rd
Division, 13 June 1814.*

Wellington's Peninsular Army was filled with many illustrious regiments
whose deeds have been enshrined in the history and folklore of the Napoleonic
Wars. Included among them are the 95th Rifles, the British Guards, the Buffs
and the Die-Hards. Yet in the 'fine fellows' quote mentioned above Wellington
was not referring to any of these, but to a regiment that is remembered by few:
the 45th Foot. What makes the 45th Foot stand out above the rest is that it was
one of four regiments to fight in the Peninsular War from the very beginning
until the very end. The regiment landed in Mondego Bay, Portugal, on 1 August
1808 and only returned to its barracks in Ireland in July 1814, after the first
abdication of Napoleon.

During the six years that the 45th Foot served in the Peninsula, it would gain
fame among its fellow soldiers. It would fight in almost every battle and siege
Wellington commanded at, except for the sieges of Burgos in 1812 and that of
San Sebastian in 1813. The 45th Foot, which only ever had its 1st Battalion
serving in the Peninsula, would receive an incredible fourteen Peninsular War
battle honours for its colours. Only two other units would receive more: the
5th Battalion 60th Rifles would earn sixteen, and the 95th Rifles would earn
fifteen. Yet those numbers can be a bit misleading. The 5th Battalion 60th Rifles
never operated as a battalion in the Peninsula, instead having its companies
sent piecemeal to different brigades – thus having the opportunity for at least
one of its companies to take part in a battle; while the 95th Rifles had three
battalions serving in the Peninsula.

But the battle honours do not tell the whole story of this remarkable regiment.
When the 45th Foot arrived in Portugal in 1808, there were over 650 officers and
men present with the colours. Over the next six years, 1,800 men would serve

with the 45th in the Peninsula. The harsh campaigning, battles, sickness and disease took its toll. After the initial deployment in 1808, periodically men would go out as replacements to bring the regiment up to strength. On 25 April 1814, despite receiving over 1,000 replacements over the years, the 1st Battalion 45th Foot could only muster 279 effectives. During those six years it took numerous casualties, with over 540 men killed or dying of sickness and disease. Many were sent home broken in body from wounds and disease.

The casualties among its officers were even higher, for they believed in leading from the front. Twenty-five of the 123 officers who served with the first battalion in the Peninsula would be killed in action or die from their wounds, while another thirty-seven would be wounded, many of these multiple times. Of the six lieutenant-colonels who would command the battalion in the campaign, two would be killed in action, one would die from his wounds, a fourth would be wounded and captured, while the last battalion commander, Lieutenant-Colonel Leonard Greenwell, had been wounded five times prior to assuming command in May 1814. During the siege of Badajoz in April 1812, out of thirty-five infantry officers present in the 1st Battalion, three would be killed, three who would die of their wounds, and another nine would be wounded. This was a staggering forty per cent casualty rate for one battle.

The Rolls of the Military General Service Medal provide a testimony to the many years the regiment served in the Peninsula. The medal was first issued thirty-three years after the end of the Peninsular War, in 1847. A soldier who fought in any of the twenty-eight battles covered by the award was eligible to receive it; the only stipulation was that he had to still be alive. For many, the medal came too late. However, for others, it was long overdue recognition of their valour on the battlefield. Of the twenty-eight battles named, twenty were fought in the Peninsula. For each battle the soldier fought, he could receive an appropriate clasp on the medal.

Over 26,000 medals were awarded, 278 of them going to the 45th Foot. But the regiment stands out not because of the quantity of medals issued, but the number of clasps awarded. Two soldiers earned fifteen clasps, meaning that they had fought in fifteen of the twenty major battles of the Peninsular War. One of the recipients was from the 45th Foot – Private James Talbot. Of the thirteen soldiers who received the medal with fourteen clasps, five were from the 45th Foot. Eleven of the forty soldiers awarded the medal with thirteen clasps served in the 45th Foot, while twelve veterans of the 45th Foot were among the seventy-seven soldiers who earned twelve clasps. The regiment had over twenty per cent of the longest serving soldiers in the Peninsular War.

Why this distinguished regiment is not better known is something of a mystery. Perhaps it is because only one private soldier had his memoirs published. Whatever the reason, Steve Brown has brought to life this valiant regiment and the soldiers who served in it.

Robert Burnham
Editor, *The Napoleon Series*

Introduction

The first battalion of the 45th (or the 1st Nottinghamshire) Regiment of Foot was one of the hardest-fighting and longest-serving units in Wellington's Peninsular Army, being one of the few regiments to serve continuously from the fresh-faced landing at Mondego Bay in August 1808 until the war-soiled remnants sailed home from Pauillac in July 1814. The 45th fought at nearly every major engagement in the Peninsular War, and formed one-third of a famous brigade in Lieutenant-General Thomas Picton's Fighting Third Division, alongside its old friends the Irish 88th Connaught Rangers and the Scottish 74th, the Assaye Tigers; Wellington's equivalent perhaps to the American Civil War era Iron Brigade.

Sir Charles Oman's classic study *Wellington's Army* contains an extensive Regimental Bibliography. Nearly every regiment which participated in the long and sanguinary Peninsular War is represented therein, with some receiving disproportionate representation - the 43rd Foot have four references, the 95th Rifles eleven - but the 45th Foot has none. History is written by the victors; and by the survivors. The 45th left few diarists, and only one memoirist, a roguish cobbler's son from Kilmarnock named William Brown,[1] who left an entertaining tome entitled *The Autobiography, or Narrative of a Soldier* in 1829. Although Brown claimed to be 'an unlettered mechanic' and a 'rough untutored soldier', his book contains many prosaic passages concerning his escapades, and a compelling account of the sack of Badajoz. Parts of it are so erudite and lyrical that one almost wonders how a cobbler's son could have contrived it. The only problem for a historian is that Brown spent so much time away from his battalion, either sick or on detached duty, that fully half, or maybe two-thirds of the book tells us little about what the 45th actually did. According to William Brown's reckoning, some 3,300 men served in the 1/45th during the War.[2] I have been unable to verify the exact number, but deaths, desertions and men sent home during the war totalled nearly 1,100; close to a hundred were taken prisoner of war, and many never returned; in addition there were the 574 survivors present at Cork after arriving home in 1814; so perhaps 1,800 is closer to the mark. I felt that, unlike Victorian or early twentieth century histories which only talk in terms of officers and 'other ranks,' the men of the 45th, from serjeant-major[3] down to drummer should have at least an equal voice. All of the officers and staff who served in the regiment at this time do appear, all 120 or

ix

so of them, to a lesser or greater degree, but that is done primarily to show the regimental system at work; seniority, promotion, purchase, supersession, leave of absence, the whole box and dice. Unlike the other ranks, officers could apply for home leave if they felt unwell or had urgent matters at home, so the large number reflects coming-and-going as much as sickness or death. The other ranks, however, were there until death or disablement took them.

The 45th Regiment of Foot was an organisational entity with a single entry in the Army List of the time; the sub-division of the regiment was the battalion, of which the 45th had two (after 1804). The intent behind the creation of second battalions was that they would stay at home and act as a trainer of new recruits and feeder of said recruits to the first battalion on service. In reality, shortages of troops meant that many second battalions went on service themselves, although the second battalion of the 45th (or 2/45th in shorthand) stayed at home for its entire existence. In the interests of readability the first battalion in the Peninsula is generally referred to throughout simply as the '45th' in the text, unless some distinction needs to be made with the second battalion. Generally other units are referred to by their full, though shortened, title, i.e. 1/88th Foot.

The sub-division of a battalion was the company, of which every British battalion had ten. In the field these were generally referred to by the commander's name (i.e. Captain Cole's Company) and assumed seniority within the battalion by the relative seniority of the company commander. This is a difficult concept in the historical context, since firstly, company commanders changed often, and a new commander brought a shuffling in the order of seniority; and secondly, a company would still be known by a commander's name even when he was not present, sometimes for lengthy periods. Luckily for pay and administrative purposes (and for researchers!) each company was allocated a number, which did not alter for the entire period; and although this numbering was rarely used in the field, I have generally favoured using this company number in the text as a way of maintaining continuity across the seven year period, but have left the company commander's name in play whenever necessary to achieve historical flavour.

A short note regarding place names: British accounts of the time use the early nineteenth-century versions of geographic places, usually names suitably anglicised for British ears. I spent considerable time reconciling some of these places (sometimes without success) to names on modern maps, but ultimately decided to use the archaic version in the text to maintain the period flavour, nonetheless having provided a contemporary version in brackets if necessary to hopefully allow the modern reader to follow the course of events on current maps.

I am indebted to Cliff Houseley, the Museum Trustee at the Museum of the Mercian Regiment (Worcestershire & Sherwood Foresters Collection) in Nottingham for approval to quote copiously and reproduce images from the Regimental Annuals. Thanks go out also to Ron McGuigan for his very detailed review comments, ensuring I maintained a degree of scrupulous accuracy in all matters related to the British Army of the period; and to Bob Burnham for his encouragement and generously agreeing to write the Foreword. Thanks also to Andrew Bamford for his input related to strength figures for the battalion between

1808 and 1814. I could not have completed this task without the hours put in by my father Roy at the National Archives in Kew, a long way away from me in Melbourne but luckily only a few hours' drive from his home in Shropshire. Any misinterpretation or misrepresentation of the information is mine alone.

Hopefully in these pages the reader will find a documentary version of what it was like to be a British soldier in the years 1807 to 1814, and why the regiment – both literally and as a concept - mattered so much.

Notes on Sources

There are four sources which were consulted more than any other in the preparation of this book. In alphabetical order (to be fair) the first was William Brown's *The Autobiography, or Narrative of a Soldier*, published in 1829 and to my knowledge the only first-hand account of the war by a serving soldier of the 45th. Brown avoided mentioning names for many of the incidents he recalled (or at least, the editor struck them out), however he left sufficient clues to enable me to reconstruct the events and individuals concerned by reference to the muster rolls and Army Lists.

The second was James Campbell's *A British Army, As It Was, - Is, - And Ought To Be* from 1840, in which the author, despite the generalised title and intent of his book, could not help but bring his experiences as a company commander and brigade-major serving with the 45th into play at frequent intervals, providing the most useful account from a serving officer of the battalion.

The third, and most heavily consulted, was Henry Carmichael Wylly's monumental (and hard-to-find) *History of the 1st and 2nd Battalions the Sherwood Foresters (Nottinghamshire and Derbyshire Regiment)* from 1929. I have avoided quoting directly from this work but it formed an excellent source of information, particularly in terms of overall chronology, movements, strengths, locations, and rosters of officers present. It is the book that kept this story on track, and is generally not noted as a source in the descriptions below simply because to do so would be repetitive and tiresome, as it informed every single chapter. Like most regimental histories of its era, Wylly almost completely ignores the other ranks (except to refer to them simply by that collective title) which left ajar the door to create this new and hopefully more representative work, with the other ranks having as much consideration as the officers.

The fourth source was perhaps the most useful in fleshing out the story – the *Regimental Annuals* produced by the Sherwood Foresters between 1909 and 1938. These contain all manner of minutiae from the regimental archives (including some otherwise impossible-to-find portraits) which have enabled this work to hopefully develop some depth and were particularly useful in completing the biographies of serving officers.

---

[1] For the avoidance of doubt, no relation to the present author, who can nonetheless claim his Browns as Nottinghamshire coal-miners some generations distant.

[2] Brown.

[3] I have used the early 19th century spelling of 'serjeant' throughout for Napoleonic flavour.

List of Maps

Part I

The Early Years

Chapter 1

1741-1804

The celebrated 45th Regiment of Foot – the 1st Notts, the Hosiers, the Fire-Eaters, the Old Stubborns – did not start life with any of these titles. There had been an earlier 45th Regiment, being one of ten Marine regiments raised during the war between Britain and Spain in 1739. In the ensuing two years new line infantry regiments numbered 44 to 60 in seniority were raised for action against the French. The peace of Aix-la-Chapelle in 1748 saw no further immediate need for the Marines, so they were disbanded and the line regiment numbering was shuffled up to fill the vacant slots; the 56th Regiment thus became the 45th Regiment of Foot in 1741. The other, less formal titles and nicknames came later.

The 45th Regiment of Foot went overseas for the first time in 1755, to British North America. The force under General Wolfe which captured Quebec in 1759, thus ending French rule in the region, included the Grenadier Company of the 45th. The regiment saw much service in Canada, gained its first battle honour, 'Louisbourg' and returned home in 1765. The next ten years were spent in Ireland. In 1771 it was anything but a regional English county regiment, having (at inspection on 30 May that year) some 176 Scotsmen to 138 Englishmen and seventy-one Irishmen in the ranks. The regiment served in America from 1776 to 1778 during the War of Independence, and returned to England in November 1778 with a strength of less than one hundred across all ranks.

Regimental Colonel of the 45th, Lieutenant-General William Haviland[4] was notified by a circular from Horse Guards dated 31 August 1782 that his regiment had officially been re-designated the 45th (or 1st Nottinghamshire) Regiment of Foot: 'His Majesty having been pleased to order that the 45th Regiment of Foot which you command should take the County name of the 45th or 1st Nottinghamshire Regiment, and be looked upon as attached to that County.'[5]

The regiment remained at home until March 1786 when it sailed from Monkstown in southern Ireland for the West Indies to fight the French for the possession of the islands. These were horror years; yellow fever,

1

malaria, a poor diet and hostile slaves made the islands the most mortal of any Army posting. Fever alone killed over 40,000 before the turn of the century.

In April 1794 the regiment (or what remained of it: six officers, two staff, seventeen serjeants, ten drummers, eighty men, thirty-four wives and children) sailed from Grenada for home (via Barbados) and landed at Bristol in late June. After a month or so they sailed for Guernsey where, within months, fervent recruiting brought the strength back up to 625 rank-and-file, virtually all raw recruits.

On Christmas Day 1794 they again embarked for the West Indies – although the original destination was Corsica – under the command of Lieutenant-Colonel Oliver Nicolls, with his nephew Lieutenant Jasper Nicolls on the roster strength. Barbados was reached on the first day of April 1795, before they sailed on for Martinique. At the time of arrival on Barbados the 45th was inspected by local commander General Vaughan and described as 'totally unfit for service in any climate'.

By June 1796 the battalion's numbers were so low that the regiment was forced to receive 421 volunteers from six regiments being 'drafted out' prior to returning to England – in the main sickly, homesick men from the 8th and 15th Regiments of Foot who were perhaps deemed misfits and malcontents by those unit's commanding officers. The following month the 45th were dispersed on tedious garrison duty on Dominica, The Saints, St Christopher's and Martinique. Thirteen officers died in 1797 and 1798 without seeing a shot fired in anger. It is no surprise that subalterns keen for promotion toasted each other with 'a bloody war and a sickly season!'

After five years of terrible losses – almost entirely to sickness – the regiment was ordered home in May 1801; 203 men had been given to other regiments in the West Indies, leaving twelve officers (with newly-appointed Lieutenant-Colonel William Guard commanding) and 153 men to return to Nottinghamshire and rebuild. The survivors sailed from Basseterre on 4 May 1801; other than five months in England in 1794, the regiment had served in the West Indies for fifteen years.

The bulk of the 45th arrived at Portsmouth on 5 July 1801. One of the transports, the *Windsor*, contained Captain William Gwyn, fourteen non-commissioned officers and sixteen privates of the 45th. Also aboard were 150 French prisoners of war. On the third night of the voyage the *Windsor* lost contact with the rest of the convoy. The following night the officer-in-charge of the guard and some sentries went below to call his relief, when the French prisoners overpowered the remainder of the guard, seized the arms chest, secured the rest of the soldiers, took over the ship, and ordered a course be set for Boston. Once there the 45th men were released (on the very same day the rest of the battalion landed at Portsmouth) and after a few weeks in captivity, they returned to Plymouth in October 1801 via Halifax aboard the store ship *Camel*.[6]

Upon landing at Portsmouth on 5 July 1801 the regiment moved around the south of England as home-based garrison battalions tended to do – Hilsea, Horsham, Winchester, and then Portsmouth again.

Whilst they did so the preliminary articles of peace were signed in London on 1 October 1801 between the French ambassador and the British foreign minister. Britain's new Prime Minister Lord Addington was, unlike his predecessor William Pitt the Younger, weak and conciliatory towards Napoleon and the French First Consul took advantage of this to gain the upper hand at the peace table. Amiens was chosen for the signing of 'A Treaty of Universal Peace'. The papers were signed in the town hall of Amiens on 27 March 1802, but the Treaty of Amiens was no cause for celebration. Under the terms agreed, Great Britain had to hand over most of its recent conquests, including islands in the West Indies and the Mediterranean, whilst France was to give up Naples and restore Egypt to the Ottoman Empire. Great Britain could not long survive without the trade these conquests guaranteed, and so the blueprint for further hostilities was created. The treaty was destined to be short-lived.

On New Year's Day 1802, nearly six months after returning from the West Indies, the regiment strength of the 45th stood at only seventeen officers and 154 other ranks. From Portsmouth they sailed on 5 April 1802, bound for Ireland, with even lower numbers, and arrived at Kinsale on 14 April. Little did they know they would not see England again (albeit only briefly) until 1806 - and after that, not again until 1837.

After a brief sojourn in Fermoy they occupied Kinsale Barracks on 6 July. At this place they received a large number of enlistments.[7] Ten weeks after arriving at Kinsale, on 16 September 1802, Lieutenant-Colonel William Guard married 21-year-old Margaret Letitia Coxon, daughter of the late Major Michael Coxon of County Durham, and niece to the Right Honourable Lord Kinsale, at the tiny parish church in Ballymartle. Had it been a whirlwind romance? Quite possibly. Would it last? We shall see.

The 45th marched to Limerick in February 1803, where they were stationed until June 1804. The 45th was divided (as were all British infantry battalions) into ten companies. In 1803 the nominal establishment (authorised strength) of the 45th was set at 847 other ranks (privates and corporals), so about 84 men per company, commanded by a captain. Each company was further sub-divided into two platoons (42 men in each, commanded by a lieutenant or ensign), and each platoon divided into two sections (about 21 men in each, commanded by a serjeant or corporal). This strict adherence to structure was vital to both parade-ground and battlefield evolutions of the troops; every man needed to understand where he slotted into the military machine. Interior management and discipline of a company, often referred to in contemporary accounts as 'interior economy', was viewed as a measure of an officer's abilities. Officers were required to be the brains, the serjeants the brawn. 'No serjeant is ever to give the word of command or put the men through any motions when the officers of companies are on parade: every order is then to proceed from the officer commanding the company,'[8] stated a general order of the period.

The British Army was the most intensively trained of the time, and company exercises comprised 25 separate march movements, plus 14 exercises of arms, all to be practised daily. The Drill Manual required that 'the greatest precision must be required, and observed, in their execution'.

Such precision and execution applied equally to the deportment of the men when away from the parade-ground; complaints were made against patrols of the 45th, particularly on the Patrickwell and Dublin roads, 'getting into orchards and taking away apples and committing other depredations'. Any soldier detected in so unmilitary a practice could depend upon being severely punished. Some sentries were also observed in the unsoldierlike practice of leaving their arms in the sentry-box and walking about without them. 'Such nonmilitary practice is positively forbid, and in future will meet with exemplary punishment.'[9]

'Severely punished' and 'exemplary punishment' were not things to be taken lightly in the early nineteenth century British Army. The average private lived in fear of being lashed (whipped) for the slightest infraction, but much was expected of the non-commissioned officers and junior commissioned officers also.

The Peace of Amiens had imposed an uneasy sixteen-month truce into the conflict which had started in 1793, but normal service was resumed on 16 May 1803 when Great Britain declared war on France. More men would be needed to conduct this war – especially since the new French Emperor had declared an intention to invade England.

On 6 July 1803 the 'Defence of the Realm Acts' were passed, one for England and Wales and one for Scotland, each being 'an Act to enable His Majesty more effectually to raise and assemble … an additional Military Force, for the better Defence and Security of the United Kingdom, and for the more vigorous prosecution of the War'. The Act stipulated how many private soldiers must be raised by volunteering or by ballot in each county and also detailed those exempt from the ballot.[10] Nottinghamshire and Derbyshire brought forward more volunteers than their quota required, although some counties fell well short. Many, many of the positions created at ballot were filled by substitutes, but exemptions regarding age or number of children did not apply to men who were substitutes.

The Colonel of the 45th, General Cavendish Lister, received a letter from Horse Guards dated 8 August 1804, advising him that His Majesty had been pleased to direct that a second battalion to the regiment under his command should be formed, from the men to be raised under the authority of the late Act of Parliament, styled the Defence Act, from the County of Nottingham.[11] The headquarters of the second battalion was set at Mansfield in Nottinghamshire, and a party of officers, non-commissioned officers and men left the 45th (now the first battalion) at Ballyshannon in Ireland for that place to form a nucleus of the new unit. The second battalion (or 2/45th in short-hand) was placed on the Army Establishment on Christmas Day, 1804, with an official establishment of 38 officers, 23 serjeants, 22 drummers and 400 rank-and-file.[12] Establishment was a theoretical ideal not matched by the actual numbers however, and recruiters had to resort to all sorts of means to get civilians into red coats, occasionally even straying into illegal territory.

Second battalions thus raised were for home service, but the men, when trained, were induced by bounties to transfer to the first battalion. The 2/45th was destined to see neither overseas nor active service, but fulfilled a valuable role in recruiting, training and feeding drafts[13] of men to the first battalion whilst on service. Therefore its role cannot be understated.

---

[4] A regimental colonel was usually a general officer who was responsible for the overall administration of a regiment, not necessarily involved in every detail but having the final say on all matters concerning events such as promotion.

[5] 1928 Regimental Annual, pp.1-2.

[6] Dalbiac, p.20.

[7] Some of these enlistments may have been men from the recently discharged Nottinghamshire Militia, who were disbanded at Newark and Retford at the start of May 1802, receiving one month's pay as gratuity. The regiment was re-formed in early 1803.

[8] ibid.

[9] ibid.

[10] House of Commons Parliamentary Papers (HCPP) online.

[11] Wylly, pp.110-1.

[12] ibid, p.111.

[13] In more modern times we would say 'replacements'.

Chapter 2

A Secret Expedition

After leaving Limerick in late 1804, the 1/45th marched to Ballyshannon where it sent a cadre of officers and NCOs to the new second battalion; in return, in May and June 1805, it received 175 volunteers from the Irish Militia. This gift of resource was a milestone for two reasons – it was the first significant draft of militiamen ever received by the regiment; and the first large single draft of Irishmen, who would dramatically alter its regional and demographic mix.

On 18 July the new-look battalion marched to Enniskillen, and from there to the Curragh of Kildare where it camped with 15,000 other troops under the command of General Lord Cathcart, the then-commander of His Majesty's forces in Ireland. A fortnight later it marched to Fermoy, and later Cork, where on 28 December the men embarked to join the expedition under Lord Cathcart assembling off the Sussex Downs, aimed at recapturing Hanover from the French. After three years of dreary garrison duty in Ireland, it looked as if action was afoot.

On arrival in the Downs it was obvious that the news of Napoleon's victory over the Austrians and Russians at Austerlitz on 2 December had changed everything. The destination was altered and the battalion was disembarked at Deal and Ramsgate in mid-January 1806, marching first to Deal Barracks, then to Brabourne Lees Barracks, also in Kent, and then to Shorncliffe Barracks under the command of Major-General Rowland Hill. Here they were instructed in the drill system of Sir John Moore, Britain's foremost trainer of infantry and the rising star of the Army.

So impressed was Moore by the 45th's bearing that he suggested to Lieutenant-Colonel Guard that he report his battalion 'fit for immediate or any service'; A far cry from Vaughan's 'totally unfit for any service' report of 1794.

From Shorncliffe the men marched to Portsmouth, and boarded ship on 27 and 28 July bound for 'foreign service, destination unknown'. The second battalion was at the time stationed in Chelmsford in Essex, and provided twenty volunteers to the first battalion; but they were brought up to strength by the receipt of a motley draft of 204 untrained recruits from the general infantry depot at Cowes.

After some muddle and delay in the best army fashion – sailed to Torbay, sailed to Plymouth, re-landed on 3 September, camped at Bichley and Buckland Downs, then sailed to Falmouth - the battalion finally boarded transports in late September and bobbed in Falmouth Harbour whilst other regiments, and finally the commanding officer, arrived. Nobody had any idea about their destination; they were 'engaged on a secret expedition'.

They sailed from Falmouth on 12 November, forming part of a task force under Brigadier-General Robert Craufurd,[14] a 38-year-old jet-black-haired Scotsman with a scowl and permanent five o'clock shadow, but an inspirational leader of light troops. The fleet of forty transports was escorted by eight men-of-war under the command of Commodore Robert Stopford, RN. The 45th were distributed amongst six transports.

The first part of the passage was rough. The *Lady Delaval*, with one company aboard – No.3 Company with Captain Douglas, Lieutenant Brinsley Purefoy and Ensign Theo Costley supervising – went through such adventures that Costley later wrote 'we had such a narrow escape of our lives in the Bay of Biscay'[15] and lost one man through an accident on 18 November. The transport *Fame* carrying men of the 45th under the command of Major Gwyn was praised by the brigade commander as being the model of 'minute regularity and perfect cleanliness' and he recommended all officers commanding transports to go aboard this ship to see for themselves how it should be done.

Three weeks later they were at Port Praya in the Cape Verde Islands, where they remained some weeks as a labour force to build small batteries and field-works in the harbour. The flotilla sailed south on 12 January 1807 and reached False Bay at the Cape of Good Hope at five o'clock in the morning of 19 March, where four days later the battalion was put ashore twice for exercise and a searching inspection by Brigadier-General Craufurd.[16] Certainly the shore leave was necessary to get the muscles in the men's legs working again – they had been aboard ship for six months.

Was the Cape their final destination? Were they bound for the East Indies? New South Wales? Java? Then orders arrived which changed the destination of the expedition. They sailed from the Cape on 6 April, stopped briefly at the tiny island of Saint Helena for six days to take aboard fresh water, and arrived at the mouth of the Rio de la Plata (River Plate, separating modern Argentina and Uruguay) on 27 May. Due to a severe gale they put back out to sea and did not reach their ordered destination of Montevideo until 14 June, when the expedition joined the force already assembled there under the command of Lieutenant-General John Whitelocke.

The battalion had been aboard ship for 267 days. No wonder the men were happy to disembark from their six transports on 28 June, although they still had little idea where they were or who they were to fight. In fact, they were in South America to try and wrest the colony of Rio de la Plata from Britain's newest enemies, the Spaniards. Major-General William Carr Beresford had succeeding in capturing the city of Buenos Aires with a tiny force in June 1806 (news of which reached England in September that year) but had been forced to surrender to a reinforced Spanish relief force a month later. Outraged, Horse Guards had immediately dispatched an expeditionary force to conquer Buenos Aires a second time. Unwisely, they had ignored the old military tenet of never reinforcing failure.

On 16 June 1807 the expeditionary force was brigaded, and the 45th was placed in Robert Craufurd's 4th Brigade alongside the 36th (Herefordshire), 47th (Lancashire) and 88th (Connaught Rangers) Regiments of Foot. The pairing with the 88th was a serendipitous one, and the start of a relationship that would continue until 1814. Lieutenant James Campbell of the 45th was appointed brigade-major[17] and Lieutenant Charles Costley of the 45th to the staff of Major-General John Leveson-Gower, the expedition's second-in-command. On 19 June the regiment was back aboard ship bound for Buenos Aires on the other side of the River Plate. Captain Æneas Anderson's No.10 Company was left behind at Montevideo as part of the 1,300 man garrison to secure the British supply lines.

On landing at Ensenada de Barragon on 28 June, the force was re-organised again, and eight companies of the 45th were placed in the 3rd Brigade under Colonel the Honourable Thomas Mahon (alongside the 6th Dragoon Guards, 9th Dragoons and 40th Foot), whilst the Light Company under Captain Leonard Greenwell was detached as part of a composite light battalion in Craufurd's new Light Brigade. The intelligent and energetic Captain James Dawes Douglas of the 45th (a Royal Military College student) was made aide-de-camp to General Whitelocke.

The expeditionary force lumbered north, the Light Brigade advancing well ahead of the column, and found a force of about 1,000 Spanish and twelve cannon blocking the road beyond a ford on the River Chuelo at a place called Passa Chica. Craufurd ordered the light companies to advance, and the 45th had the advantage of a clear narrow lane to run down to reach the guns first. Seeing the leading elements coming, a Spaniard shot Captain Greenwell in the neck from three yards away, and then calmly threw down his fired musket and drew an ornate sabre to do battle with the advancing Lieutenant George Bury of the 88th; but the shooter was promptly bayoneted by a following Light Company soldier. Private Timothy Riordan of the Light Company was killed in the skirmish, and Lieutenant Alexander Martin assumed command of the Light Company as Greenwell was carried to the rear. This was to be the first of Greenwell's many wounds.

Whitelocke's force reached the village of Reducción just outside Buenos Aires on 1 July, the men tired and exhausted from three days of wallowing through thick mud with insufficient supplies. Whitelocke considered the likelihood of getting supplies greater from the city of Buenos Aires than from his own ships and so advanced again at two o'clock in the morning of 2 July. Major Gwyn and Ensign John O'Donohoe of the 45th were left behind 'on command' of a garrison of sick men plus a troop of the 9th Light Dragoons. The other eight companies of the 45th tramped on towards the suburbs of the city, crossed the river and were halted 'in front of Mister White's house' on the south side of the city in the pouring rain at three o'clock in the afternoon of 3 July.

Argentine Roasting

On 4 July orders were issued for the assault on the city, to occur the following day. The force was to advance in thirteen small columns from west to east, from the inland corral overlooking the city down to the Plate, and to link up at the public buildings near the water's edge. The 45th was to form the twelfth and thirteenth columns (on the right flank) immediately to the left of the light battalion (which contained Lieutenant Martin's company) and to advance 'left in front' (the left wing of each half-battalion to lead the way) and to occupy the Residencia de Barbones, the Governor's residence.

The force assembled in the (appropriately named) Corrales de Miserere at the western end of the city at daybreak on Sunday 5 July, an elevated spot which afforded them some view over the slumbering city as far as the River Plate, some two miles away. The panorama was of a block-grid of low sturdy buildings, many with rooftop parapets, studded with distant landmarks such as the citadel, cathedral and convent.

Whitelocke's plan of attack was based upon a faulty map and the assumption that the Spaniards would flee on their approach, if they hadn't already; the eight avenues down which they were to attack appeared deserted. Leaving Ensign John Connor behind to guard the knapsacks and the sick men, the 45th took up their start positions. Guard commanded the seventh column, the companies of Captains Bridge, Smith and Drew, with the Grenadier Company under Captain John Payne in the rear. His second-in-command, Major Jasper Nicolls, commanded the sixth column on Guard's left, the other four companies of the 45th. 'Having previously occupied the roads by which we were to enter the town, I moved forward at daybreak' Guard later wrote.[18]

Apparently the advance to the Residencia was relatively unopposed, save for parties of horsemen who occasionally galloped across their path, sent to gather information perhaps. After proceeding for about three quarters of a mile, the columns met together, a consequence of the junction of the two roads. Acting under orders, Guard's column made a considerable detour to the right, meaning that they did not reach the Residencia until three or four minutes after Nicolls's left wing column; Guard found Nicolls in the act of breaking open the doors of that building. The loss so far had been 'trifling', losing three men killed. 'Hearing a considerable firing on our left, I desired Major Nicolls to make the necessary arrangements for the occupation of the Residencia, and acquainted him that I would take the grenadier company with me, and reconnoitre the position of Brigadier General Craufurd's brigade, and return to him immediately.' Guard moved forward with his four companies, and 'recollecting three of them, left a company in each', the Colonel later recorded.[19]

Major Nicolls was a career soldier with a fine family military reputation. The son of General Gustavus Nicolls, Jasper was born at East Farleigh, Kent on 15 July 1778, educated at Dublin University and acquired an ensigncy in the 45th Foot (of which his uncle was lieutenant-colonel) in May 1793, aged fourteen. He spent the first eight months of his military career on leave, waiting for the regiment to return from the West Indies (it returned a skeletal wreck in early 1794), killing time by spending a year on recruiting duty in Ireland. In November 1794 he purchased a lieutenancy and went with the regiment to the West Indies. During seven years in the pestilential islands, he served fifteen months as paymaster, did two stints as judge advocate, and served as an aide to his uncle, who commanded on Grenada and was made major-general in 1796. Jasper purchased a captaincy in November 1799 at the age of 21, continued as paymaster and returned home in May 1801. Eight months later he accompanied his father to India (who was assuming the post of commander-in-chief, Bombay) as an aide and military secretary. Never having seen action, he volunteered to join Major-General Wellesley's expeditionary force in the Mahratta War, and commanded a company of the 78th Foot for three months, serving at the actions at Argaum and Gawilghur. On 14 July 1804 Jasper purchased a vacant majority in the 45th Foot and returned immediately to England, and then joined the regiment in Ireland.

Nicolls had with him that day in Buenos Aires four companies under Captains Lecky and Coghlan, Lieutenant O'Flaherty and Ensign Persse. 'I possessed myself, in a very short time, of all the adjoining houses of consequence, and cleared all around me of armed bodies, though much annoyed at times by snipers. I waited with anxiety the return of Lieutenant Colonel Guard, or some orders from General Craufurd,' Nicolls later recorded in his diary. Guard was off towards the river with his four companies and had not returned. 'The Calle being occupied in great force by the enemy, I judged it consonant to my orders to protect the right flank of our army, by stationing my own companies in the Residencia, which is a very large building, and completely commands the principal retreat of the enemy in this quarter.' At about noon, he noticed 'a union was hoisted on a large building seven or eight hundred yards in our front' (presumably towards the river) but towards this he did not advance; to his 'great mortification' that colour was lowered at about three o'clock in the afternoon 'and has not flown in our view since'.[20]

On his way back to Nicolls, Lieutenant-Colonel Guard returned by the street by which his men had entered the town, and turning to his right came into one which led directly towards the great square. His column had proceeded about thirty or forty yards, when they came to a large house, which he thought would be prudent to occupy with a small detachment. On unsuccessfully trying to break down the door he sent back his adjutant, Lieutenant James Campbell and a few privates to Nicolls at the Residencia to obtain some tools that were left there.

Campbell had just returned when he was joined by a picquet of the regiment which had entered the town with the light battalion. The officer commanding this detachment brought General Craufurd's orders to charge down the street with the grenadier company, supported by the detachment.[21] Guard brought forward his Grenadier Company, the pick of his battalion, under Captain John Payne, with his subalterns Lieutenants William Moore and William Grant; Adjutant James Campbell and Surgeon William Tonry joined them.

In the ranks of the grenadiers were men who would survive this day and serve for long periods in Portugal and Spain in years to come. Senior NCOs included men such as Serjeants Richard Condon and Samuel Eves, an immensely tall former tailor from County Cork; and Corporals Robert Atchison, William Elliott, Richard Streater and Hugh McTeague, another giant [22] from County Fermanagh. Amongst the Grenadier Company's four drummers and fifers was William Hannon from County Galway, who had volunteered from the militia five years earlier. Lest the reader think the entire company was Irish, the ranks contained many Englishmen and even a few Scots – Private Joseph Norman from Edinburgh was one of the latter. Private Ralph Foss, a strapping Yorkshireman, Private Jeremiah Looney from County Kerry and Private James Nixon from County Fermanagh were three men who would survive the campaigning to 1814. Six of the other ranks had served in the Army for fourteen years or more, and thirteen for seven years or more; it was the most veteran company in the battalion.[23]

With Guard at their head, the grenadiers braved the advance into the centre of the city, where the action was the hottest. At first they met with no opposition other than two discharges from a heavy piece of ordnance which was posted at the upper end of the street. As they advanced, they found the tops of the houses crowded with the enemy, 'and they opened a smart fire of musketry on us as we passed'. About half a mile farther along, with the men considerably out of breath, and stalled due to the intensity of the small arms fire from the houses, they drew off to a street on their right. Seeing Colonel Denis Pack with some of his light battalion approaching towards the church of San Domingo, Guard crossed the street to consult with him, relying on his local knowledge for guidance (Pack had been a PoW in the failed 1806 campaign). Pack told Guard that it was impossible to reach the square without great losses. Guard returned to his grenadiers, and found General Craufurd, with several companies of light infantry, riflemen and a field piece in the same street as his men.[24]

The Light Company under Lieutenant Martin had advanced with the left wing of Craufurd's attack in the centre and were forced to fall back to the Convent of San Domingo, where riflemen from the 95th kept the Spaniards at bay. Martin's sole subaltern was Lieutenant John Robinson; ensigns were not permitted to serve in the flank companies, being considered too junior for the handling of elite troops. The serjeants were all dependable veterans; Alexander Adie, Lawrence Walsh and James Yates would serve through the Peninsular War, and beyond.

Their brigadier, Robert Craufurd, had spent a considerable portion of the morning in the convent in ignorance about what was happening in other parts of the city. He later stated, 'Had I been aware of the general state of affairs, I should probably have thought it right to retreat to the Residencia in which at that time I should have met with no opposition.' But he did not think himself justified in abandoning the post which he had gained so near to the enemy's principal defences. From the top of the convent he saw the Union Jack flying on the heights of the bullring, or Plaza de Toros.[25] This presumably was the same colour as that sighted by Major Nicolls at the Residencia.

By mid-morning, the assault was falling to pieces. All the left-hand assault columns had been surrounded and rendered immobile. Between eleven o'clock and mid-day a Spanish officer with a flag of truce came to the convent sent by General Liniers to inform the defenders that all their attacks had failed, 'that the 88th Regiment and many others were prisoners and to summon me to surrender to which I gave the most perempory [sic] signal'. It was quite evident that they were the only troops remaining within the town, surrounded by a great body of the enemy's forces that had been disengaged by the cessation of fire in all other quarters.[26] Craufurd obviously did not realise at the time that the 45th were still holding out, undefeated, on the right flank. Despite the disaster all around them, Guard and Nicolls were undaunted; Guard in the street near the church, and Nicolls at the Residencia.

The action was hot in the street near the convent. All the houses close to the gates had been occupied by the enemy, and they pressed forward in the street to take the remaining field piece, a three-pounder on the outside of the gate commanded with great boldness by Captain William Dann Nicolls of the Royal Artillery, Major Jasper Nicolls's youngest brother.

When the attackers threatened to swamp the gun crew, they were charged by Lieutenant-Colonel Guard and his grenadiers of the 45th, assisted by a part of the light infantry commanded by Major William Trotter, who was killed. Grenadier commander Captain John Payne of the 45th was shot through the breast, and a large part of this force killed or wounded in an instant, but the gun was saved.[27] Lieutenant-Colonel Guard conspicuously distinguished himself in this charge; two musket-balls passed through the blade of his sword, one struck the handle, a ball stuck in the top of his steel scabbard, and another musket-ball went through his hat. But it came at a cost – Captain John Payne was wounded, and his deputy Lieutenant William Moore seriously wounded in the leg. Serjeant Condon was wounded, as were nine privates; five privates were killed, and one, Private James Martin, went missing.[28]

The writing was on the wall – Craufurd and his light companies were completely surrounded, and there could be no break-out. This must have been a bitter blow to the hard-fighting Scotsman. 'Nothing now remained possible but to confine ourselves to the defence of the convent ...' he wrote. By four o'clock in the afternoon he was of opinion that 'a retreat, surrounded as they were in every direction by six or seven thousand men with many guns, occupying all the houses and streets in the vicinity of the convent, was utterly impracticable and that the enemy had it perfectly in his power to annihilate the detachment if we continued there until the night set in.' He consulted Lieutenant-Colonels Pack and Guard and Major Norman McLeod of the 95th, and seeing no possible option, held out a flag of truce and after finding no other terms could be obtained, surrendered the remnants as prisoners of war.[29]

The captives included Craufurd, Guard and the wounded Captain Payne. Major Nicolls and his four companies of the 45th were still holed up at the Residencia, and another two in surrounding houses.[30] These men slept with loaded muskets at their sides but were not disturbed during the night. They were on guard well before daylight on Monday 6 July, and Nicolls recorded in his diary in the early afternoon that Whitelocke's aide Captain Samuel Ford Whittingham, 'arrived with the Grenadier Company of the 40th Foot under Captain John Gillis from the reserve at about one o'clock in the afternoon; and whilst in communication with Major Henry Tolley of the 71st Foot and myself, the discharge of a cannon announced the approach of the enemy, which was soon confirmed by messages received from the advanced post under Captain George Drew'. Within ten minutes Nicolls formed his companies and charged the guns in column of sections, and sustained little loss in capturing the two brass 6-inch howitzers. They also secured the limbers and then 'leisurely retired to the Residencia'.[31] The cannons had been spiked (put out of action by driving a nail into the touch-hole) by the Spanish, but by drilling the nails out, Nicolls hoped to use them against their original owners. Despite the bad news undoubtedly brought by Whittingham, Nicolls remained bullish: 'The men have behaved like Britons, and your Excellency may rely on it, will continue to do so.'[32]

The garrison at the Residencia received a messenger under a flag of truce in the late afternoon on 6 July, bearing a note from Major-General Leveson-Gower (Whitelocke's second-in-command) that hostilities were suspended until further orders. Lieutenant James Campbell arrived at the Residencia on the morning of 7 July with the news that Brigadier-General Craufurd and the Light Company had been captured at the convent. The men had not eaten in 48 hours, and so in the afternoon, Captain William Smith (who it seems spoke some French and Spanish) was sent out under a flag of truce to demand provisions; as he cautiously proceeded down the eerily quiet streets, the bells of the cathedral rang out to advert all to the fact that the preliminaries of peace had been signed. Nicolls's men continued to garrison the Residencia until early on 8 July, when Captain David Lecky arrived with a message from Brigadier-General Craufurd to join the remainder of the defeated expeditionary force at the Retiro, the great fort overlooking the Grand Plaza. They marched out through the gates at ten o'clock 'with their colours flying, fixed bayonets, and drums beating' accompanying the captured four pieces of artillery, and proceeded down the crowded streets to the western side of town (without being molested by the population), to find that a substantial part of the first seven columns had been taken prisoner.

Whitelocke had signed a treaty with the Spanish commander General Liniers the evening before; the force would evacuate the city and return to England at the earliest possible opportunity. Nicolls's success on the right flank was perhaps the only signal event in the whole sorry mess. Brigadier-General Samuel Auchmuty later said to him, 'I congratulate you, sir, very sincerely on your success: had all the posts been maintained as yours, the town must have been ours'.

Set At Liberty

The British prisoners were released by the Spanish on 8 July. The 45th camped by a church on the edge of town. Adjutant of the 45th, Lieutenant James Campbell wrote a letter to his brother in Ayrshire the following day: 'I had the misfortune to be taken prisoner with the grenadiers of the 45th ... The 45th was the only one that kept his [sic] position in the city. They took from the enemy four cannon, and are particularly mentioned in General Orders ... We are all, in consequence of the negotiations, set at liberty. It was with difficulty that the inhabitants could be kept from putting us to death when we were in their power. We are much indebted to General Liniers, the Spanish commander, who did everything in his power to save us.'[33]

Admiral Jacques Antoine Marie de Liniers et Brémond was a 54-year-old Frenchman in the service of Spain, who had lived in the country for thirty years and had the absolute trust of the local government. He seems to have been a humane man who believed wars should be fought hard, but with civil conclusions. Despite being set at liberty, Campbell was experiencing the deprivation that British soldiers would commonly experience in the ensuing six years. 'I beg you will excuse this, as it is written in the fields outside the town, in the open air, to which the army have been much accustomed since we landed, as well as to want of provisions and every other comfort.'[34]

He must have written this as the regiment was waiting to board ship, as embarkation commenced that day; however the 45th did not actually board until 12 July. The three-day hiatus afforded an opportunity for the soldiers to become sightseers; many walked around the local bull-ring and admired the capacious villas along the river frontage. On the day of embarkation, Major Nicolls asked Captain William Smith to remain behind as a hostage (a certain number of hostages being one of the conditions of the treaty). Smith plainly balked at the idea since he sailed with the regiment that afternoon.

Once back at Montevideo at noon on 15 July the force was reorganised; the 45th boarded the transports on 20 July and sat at anchor until 9 September, during which time Private Andrew Carr fell overboard and was drowned on 22 July. Incredibly, on 25 July about 70 reinforcements under the command of Lieutenant Robert Hardiman from the second battalion arrived, just in time for the 45th to transfer a number of men to other regiments in the expeditionary force on 24 July; 77 privates and one drummer to the 87th Foot, 86 privates to the 47th Foot, and 7 privates to the 89th Foot. Major Nicolls referred to them as 'our Isle of Wight vagabonds' suggesting that the opportunity was taken to rid the regiment of most of the 204 untrained recruits taken on strength at Cowes, men judged a dead-weight rather than an asset.[35] Major Nicolls was called back to Buenos Aires on 4 August, as one of three 'hostages' to be swapped with the Spanish as guarantee for the correct execution of the terms of the treaty. On arrival he found that he was actually no longer required and sailed back to Montevideo on 13 August.[36]

Some 41 women accompanied the 670 remaining men for the 7,500 mile journey home. Captain William Smith expected as much discipline at sea as on land. His diaries are full of instructions (in today's parlance we might judge it micro-management) for the subalterns and men of numbers 4 and 10 Companies waiting to sail aboard the *Hercules* transport:[37] 'Speak to the non-commissioned officers regarding their very negligent manner in not putting a stop to irregularities among the men the moment they perceive them,' he recorded on 18 August. 'The recruits to be drilled every day when the companies march round the deck,' he wrote two days later, presumably referring to the 70 newly-arrived reinforcements. And two days after that: 'Tailors and shoemakers to attend parades and bring with them the work they have done the day before. When the men march round the decks the drums and fifes will play half an hour to each company, fore and afternoon. Officers to fall in with their companies … When the guard, watch or any party fall in, the officers and non-commissioned officers invariably are to be the first on deck, without which alertness and regularity cannot possibly exist.'

The last troops boarded ship on the morning of 9 September and the fleet of 80 ships set sail at ten o'clock. They did not make the open sea until four days later. The journey home was otherwise uneventful; en route the officers organised a subscription for the relief of widows and disabled men, and some £80 was raised. Unfortunately the wounded Lieutenant William Moore, his right leg recently amputated, died on the way and was buried at sea.

The now veteran but much-reduced 1/45th arrived in the harbour at Cork on 27 December 1807 and disembarked three days later; other than three weeks ashore at Buenos Aires, the battalion had been aboard transports nearly eighteen months. Major Nicolls returned from the Buenos Aires fiasco as arguably the only senior officer with an enhanced reputation. He stepped ashore at Cork in December 1807 to find that he had been given a lieutenant-colonelcy without purchase in the Royal York Rangers, a bittersweet reward for a man who had spent his entire career in the 45th and loved the regiment deeply. His breadth of military and administrative experience would have been invaluable to the 45th in the Peninsula, but alas fate led him elsewhere. He used the promotion as a stepping-stone to gain command of the 2/14th Foot, which was part of Baird's force in Spain and eventually part of Moore's force in the Corunna campaign. He went to Walcheren with the 14th later in 1809 and served there on the staff. He ultimately climbed the Army ladder in India, serving in Nepal, then making it as far as Commander-in-Chief Madras in 1838 and Commander-in-Chief in Bengal from 1839 to 1843, siring a son and eight daughters along the way. He died a lieutenant-general at Goodrest Lodge, Reading, on 4 May 1849.[38]

The 45th marched into the New Barracks at Cork that night, with 31 serjeants, 21 drummers and 626 rank-and-file. But if they thought a good stretch on dry land at home awaited them, they were dead wrong.

---

[14] Himself an ex-45th man, as was the other brigadier in the South American expeditionary force, Samuel Auchmuty.

[15] Wylly, p.114.

[16] Many of the dates are derived from Major William Smith's diary and extracts from the 1929 Regimental Annual, pp.169-70.

[17] Brigade-major (or major of brigade) was effectively the chief staff officer of a brigade. In true perverse British Army fashion, a brigade-major was usually a lieutenant or captain.

[18] Wylly, p.120.

[19] ibid.

[20] 1926 Regimental Annual, p.253.

[21] ibid, pp.249-50.

[22] Giant is a relative term in an early nineteenth century context – anyone six foot tall was lofty well above the norm.

[23] WO12/5726.

[24] 1926 Regimental Annual, p.250.

[25] Verner, Vol. 1, p.110.

[26] Verner, Vol. 1, p.111.

[27] ibid.

[28] WO12/5726.

29   Verner, Vol. 1, p.111.

30   Captain Coghlan's No.2 Company and
     Captain Smith's No.4 Company.

31   1926 Regimental Annual, p.254.

32   ibid.

33   National Library of Australia, 19th
     Century British Newspapers Online.

34   ibid.

35   WO12/5726; Wylly, p.130.

36   Wylly, p.130.

37   Smith's diary extracts are as per the 1929
     Regimental Annual, pp.171-5.

38   Biographical details based upon article
     in 1928 Regimental Annual, pp.283-4.

Part II

The Peninsula

Chapter 3

Portugal Bound

The first battalion of the 45th enjoyed a peaceful sojourn in Cork after their return from South America. Life went on within the battalion in the usual way; men joined, men moved up (or down) the promotion ladder, men departed. Captain George Purdon Drew was promoted to Oliver Nicolls's vacant majority in January, and Lieutenants John O'Flaherty and Edward Scott were promoted to captain. It was a time when many people who will feature in the Peninsula story joined the regiment as ensigns; John Tyler, James MacPherson and Ralph Ousely, the last of whom immediately went off to the new Royal Military College at Great Marlow, where fellow officer Captain James Dawes Douglas was already a student.[39] Lieutenant Marcus Dalhunty received the appointment of paymaster (William Birch Brinley had been unceremoniously dismissed by Horse Guards whilst at sea) and John Boggie was appointed surgeon in the 45th on transfer from the 28th Foot, in place of Surgeon William Tonry who died in June.

The last days of peace were spent at Midleton (about 13 miles east of Cork) and later at Cork Barracks, enjoying the remarkably warm early summer, the hottest the men had experienced in Ireland. That something was afoot was obvious by the number of regiments marching into Cork, and the ships arriving in the harbour; but the 45th had received no orders, so routines continued as normal. But Viscount Castlereagh, the Secretary of State had written to the newly-promoted Lieutenant-General the Honourable Sir Arthur Wellesley on 30 June 1808, to state that 'two additional battalions, at present cantoned in the neighbourhood of Cork, the 36th and 45th, consisting of about 1,200 men, have been ordered to embark, and join your force'.[40] The force referred to was eight battalions of infantry and four companies of the green-coated 95th Rifles, ear-marked to accompany Wellesley to conquer (of all places) Mexico and Venezuela. This hare-brained scheme was tempered somewhat after the Buenos Aires debacle, and the troops made available for other uses. Recruiting detachments, men discharged after South America and sick left at home rendered Guard's battalion much weaker than at establishment. Luckily, the Local Militia Bill, recently enacted, permitted men to volunteer from the Irish Militia into the British Army.[41] Thus the 45th received its share – 167 Irish militia volunteers to boost the numbers.

And so, with little notice, a large number of new men in the ranks, and no particular idea where they were going (or for how long), the 1/45th packed its kit and marched down to the Cove of Cork where a variety of ships sat at anchor. There was considerable muddle in the harbour. Wellesley wrote to Castlereagh on 7 July to say that the promised 3,000 tons of shipping for the infantry had not arrived, and that the transports were much too crowded.[42] The extra transports eventually arrived, but the troops must have endured several days of loading and unloading the cramped ships whilst those in charge worked out the best arrangement. The 45th lost two men to sickness or accident just whilst floating at anchor – Private Simon Prescott on 7 July and Private Patrick Noonan two days later.

Insufficient transports were not the only problem. Wellesley wrote the same day to Lieutenant-General John Floyd, commanding at Cork, to complain that camp equipage for only 8,000 men had been provided for the army about to sail, and that he did not have it in his power to make the necessary issue to the 36th and 45th regiments. Camp equipage for another 1,500 men was soon rustled up and delivered over to the quartermaster-general's department at Cove.[43] The quartermaster-general (or QMG) was the officer in charge of stores and supplies for the Army in a particular theatre. In Ireland at this time it was Major-General William Henry Clinton of the 1st Foot Guards, the eldest surviving son of General Henry Clinton of American War of Independence fame, and later a field commander of some note. Wellesley's concerns that the Army had been insufficiently supplied would be a constant theme all through the coming campaign.

William Guard and his Staff

Overseeing the loading of the 45th onto transports (hopefully including their new camp equipage) was 35-year-old Lieutenant-Colonel William Guard. Born at Honiton in Devon, William purchased an ensigncy in the 45th Foot in June 1789 aged sixteen, and a lieutenancy seventeen months later. In February 1791 he joined his regiment on the island of Grenada where it did little but wither away from disease. Guard then joined Sir Charles Grey in his expedition against the French garrison on Martinique, during which he developed an interest in light infantry tactics. In September 1795 he purchased the rank of captain (one day junior to his good friend, William Gwyn) but on 15 November 1797 leap-frogged over five captains senior to him on the Army List by purchasing a vacant majority.[44]

On 3 October 1799, at the age of 26, he purchased the vacant second lieutenant-colonelcy of the 45th and commanded the regiment on its return to England in 1801. He was physically unimposing, being short and quite rotund, but had a commanding manner and was well-respected by his peers. First in Ireland, then in South America, and finally in Portugal, this 'fat, round little man' exerted an iron control over his battalion.[45]

Noticeably absent from Lieutenant-Colonel Guard's life at this time but no doubt clouding his thoughts were his wife Margaret, and his children, Susie, William Junior, and baby John, who were all in Guard's hometown of Ottery St. Mary, Devon, where Margaret was preparing to face the music for some indiscretions of the previous year. William Guard had brought a case against a certain Charles Hodge, which had excited considerable interest in the town; the damages were laid at £10,000, a vast fortune for the time. The court records tell us that 'in November, 1806, the regiment being ordered to Buenos Aires, the Plaintiff was obliged to accompany it; his wife could scarcely be prevailed on to remain at home, and nothing but the positive orders of the Commander-in-Chief hindered her from sharing with her husband the dangers of the campaign, Lieutenant-Col. Guard having embarked at Plymouth, his disconsolate Wife came to reside, during his absence ... near the friends of her husband. Here her acquaintance with the Defendant first commenced.' The inevitable then occurred: 'A child was the consequence of this amour. On Lieutenant-Colonel Guard's return from abroad, a correspondence took place between him and his wife, in which she acknowledged her guilt, upbraided herself for the levity of her conduct, which had brought her into this stare of disgrace, and sent to her injured husband all the letters of her paramour.'

The Jury consulted a short time, and returned a verdict of £3,000 against Hodge.[46] Poor Lieutenant-Colonel Guard turned out to be unlucky in love and war, as we shall see. No doubt £3,000 eased his pain somewhat, but it would be a long time before he could spend it. It was an astronomical sum, nearly ten times his annual salary, and nearly the amount needed to purchase a lieutenant-colonel's commission in the Army. William Guard had purchased his (or at least, had to pay the difference between the sale of his major's commission and the cost of the lieutenant-colonelcy) from the retiring Bryan Blundell in October 1799, leaving the vacant majority to be purchased by Captain William Howe Delancey.[47]

No doubt also present on the quayside at Cork were the battalion's two majors, both very experienced men. The senior major was William Gwyn, a 34-year-old Londoner who had joined the regiment back in 1788 aged fourteen, and spent virtually the first fifteen years of his career in the West Indies, with only one six-month break back in England in 1794. He had fought with Sir Charles Grey on Martinique, St Lucia and Guadeloupe, spent two years as an assistant engineer on Dominica and a year as a prisoner-of-war aboard the *Windsor*. Always one month senior to Guard as a lieutenant and captain, he and other poorer captains had seen Guard purchase a vacant majority in November 1797 and thus leapfrog six places on the seniority list. The British Army would need men like Gwyn where they were going.

One month junior to Gwyn in regimental seniority was second major Andrew Patton, aged 37 from Clatto in Fifeshire; of a long military pedigree, he had served with the famed 92nd Highlanders in the Irish Rebellion, at the disastrous campaign in the Helder in Holland in 1799, and against the French in Egypt in 1801, the last of which had almost completely destroyed his health. Both knew the junior officers and men well; in turn, the men greatly respected them.[48]

Assuredly present also – because his job title demanded it – was the adjutant, Lieutenant James Campbell, a 21-year-old Scot from Ayrshire. He was undertaking a demanding job for such a young man; as adjutant he was the commanding officer's personal staff officer, responsible for the day-to-day administration. An adjutant was habitually the busiest man in the regiment; his work was never done. A 1782 book had this tongue-in-cheek advice for the new adjutant: 'Whenever the colonel or commanding officer is on the parade,' it advised, 'you should always seem in a hurry, and the oftener you run or gallop from right to left, the more assiduous will you appear: laying your rattan now and then over the head, or across the face, of some old soldier, for being stiff through infirmity, will get you the character of a smart adjutant … And lastly, and most importantly when on parade; should you make a mistake in telling off a division, shift the blame from your own shoulders, by abusing the serjeant or corporal of the division; and when, at any time, there is a blundering or confusion in a manoeuvre, ride in amongst the soldiers, and lay about you from right to left. This will convince people that it was not your fault.'[49]

This last was a tactic unlikely to fool the battalion's senior non-commissioned officer, Serjeant-Major Oswald Pilling, a Lancastrian in his early thirties from the tiny hamlet of Goosnargh, just north of Preston. Pilling would have been most certainly distinguishable on the dock by his jacket, scarlet like the officers rather than the brick-red of the men, with four enormous white chevrons on his right upper arm, a crimson waist sash, and a gold-capped walking stick. Whether he had the customary serjeant-major's withering stare, strut and bawl is lost in the mist of history, but he was plainly a literate man, and survived the war to become a field officer himself, something that happened infrequently but was ultimately possible for the common British soldier – contrary to society mythology.

The regimental surgeon, 29-year-old John Boggie from Edinburgh, and his two assistants, John Mousdale and Robert Chambers, would have been busy checking that their vital equipment was correctly stowed. The 45th were lucky to have Doctor Boggie; he was anything but an amateur saw-bones. He had commenced his medical career under the tuition of Messrs. Ball, Wardrop and Russell of Edinburgh aged 16, studying anatomy, chemistry, medical theory, surgical procedure, midwifery and clinical medicine for three years, before graduating a year early at the age of 20. Having passed an examination at the Royal College of Surgeons in London he was appointed hospital mate at Harwich. From there he went to Egypt with the army and was appointed assistant-surgeon in the 28th Regiment of Foot in January 1801. He served with them through campaigns in Hanover in 1805 and Copenhagen in 1807 before transferring to the 45th in October 1807, shortly before the first battalion's return from South America. Whilst in the service of the 28th he had developed remedies for the ophthalmia then raging amongst the 28th Foot in Sussex and Kent – which brought him to the attention of the Inspector General of Army Hospitals – and spent much of his later life engaged in medical research.[50]

Another with a vital concern that his records were securely stowed would have been the battalion paymaster, Lieutenant Marcus Dalhunty. He was an Irishman, and it was his job to ensure that the pay serjeants in each company made the correct payments to their men each month (or when the necessary funds were available), and to look after other battalion expenses generally. As paymaster, he was exempt from doing military service in the field, even that of sitting at courts-martial; his appointment being effectively of a civil nature, and one for which Dalhunty had had to provide two sureties of £1,000 as proof of his competence and trustworthiness. Other ranks joked that everything in the Army was late – supplies, reinforcements, rations – but pay, never; at least not when stationed at home. They could rely upon being paid on the 25th of each month no matter the bungling around them. The campaign and years ahead would fail (and often fail catastrophically) to live up to this expectation. As regimental paymaster Dalhunty took rank after the most junior captain, but was paid more (fifteen shillings a day – nearly the same as a major), with the same baggage and forage money as was allowed to captains without companies. He was also allowed a clerk[51] who ranked and received pay as a serjeant, and £20 per annum for stationery and postage.

The battalion quartermaster, Edmund Thresher, one of the red-faced prisoners from the *Windsor* incident, was, like most quartermasters, a former NCO, having been promoted from quartermaster-serjeant on Christmas Day 1798. He had overall responsibility for the ordering and distribution of equipment and consumables within the battalion. The quartermaster was not to do any duty except that of quartermaster whilst the regiment was on actual service. His primary duty was to take care of the ammunition and stores of the regiment, to attend to all deliveries of stores, and to prevent frauds from being committed against the public service.[52]

Army wives were permitted, but their travel with the Army was strictly regulated. The Regulations and Orders for the Army stipulated that when a regiment embarked for active field service, the number of soldiers' wives to be permitted to accompany it was limited to six per company. To the remaining wives of soldiers not permitted to embark with their husbands, a 'rate of allowance' was granted to enable them to proceed to their homes during the absence of their husbands on service; but nothing at all for subsistence.[53] Since the wives had no idea where the men were going, or for how long, both staying and going were decisions fraught with uncertainty. For the sixty wives who had drawn a 'to-go' ticket, ahead lay an unknown adventure in a foreign land, living with the men under any conditions, often earning a little extra doing the washing and mending. The muster rolls do not tell us the names of the wives on campaign (since for the Army to record them would suggest some form of accepted responsibility) however we can only assume that the 45th took along a normal complement – six wives per company. Those unlucky enough to have drawn a 'not-to-go' ticket were consigned to a primitive existence (more often than not close to the barracks), living on whatever their husbands could afford to send home.

Portugal Bound

James Dawes Douglas was born on 14 January 1785, the eldest son of Major James Sholto Douglas of the Black Watch, a cousin of the Marquis of Queensberry. With such a military pedigree, it was natural for him to be gazetted an ensign in the 45th Foot on 10 July 1799 at the age of fourteen. Thanks to the purchase system, less than a year later he was a lieutenant, and was a captain commanding a company at the age of seventeen-and-a-half. He served some time as an aide-de-camp to General Sir James Duff at Limerick, where a fellow aide and lifelong friend was future Peninsular War historian William Napier. He attended the Royal Military College at Great Marlow and served as a staff officer during the Buenos Aires expedition. He was mentioned in dispatches, and as a young officer on the rise, looked forward to his next assignment.[54] Captain Douglas received an appointment to Wellesley's quartermaster-general's staff in mid-1808 and arrived at the dockside to find the staff transport delayed. He went back into Cork that night to see an old friend, only to arrive back at the quayside the next morning to find that his ship had just sailed. He jumped aboard another ship and eventually arrived at his destination before his allotted vessel.

Days went by with no departure. Wellesley wrote in frustration to Castlereagh on 10 July: 'I see that people in England complain of the delay which has taken place in the sailing of the expedition … it was only yesterday that the 20th dragoons arrived, and the ships to contain the 36th regiment and a detachment of the 45th, which arrived yesterday evening and embarked.'[55] This last statement may refer to the last of the 167 militia volunteers for the 45th, and there is every possibility that some joined the battalion still wearing their old militia uniforms.

The fleet sailed at last at three o'clock in the morning on Tuesday, 12 July 1808; presumably the left-behind wives and sweethearts had long since returned to Cork. Also left behind but with much work to do in the coming years was the second battalion in Nottingham under Lieutenant-Colonel the Honourable John Meade, supported by Majors Francis Frye Browne and George Purdon Drew, and their network of recruiting serjeants; Serjeant Thomas Garner in Stafford, Serjeants John Bates and Edward Davis in Nottingham and Serjeant Nicholas Bowring in Preston.[56] Second battalions were conceived as feeder units for the first battalion, a stable at-home recruiting and training depot. The system worked both ways, since it gave first battalions in the front line somewhere to send unfit or worn-out men.

The sailing took a little over two weeks, but luckily the weather was perfect. Transports were vessels built specifically to carry troops, and so were functional rather than the three-masted sailing ships of romantic imagination; squat, ugly, crowded, the holds dark, damp and revolting. Officers' horses occupied some holds, to further add to the olfactory experience. Smoking – the soldier's favourite pastime – was not allowed below decks, so the men spent as much time as possible on deck, either being detailed off to help the sailors, drilling, being entertained by musicians in the ranks, or performing amateur theatricals. They left their red coats in their knapsacks and wore coarse cotton smocks on deck and shirt-sleeves when below-decks. It was too windy for shakos up top and too stooped for headgear below. The few wives on board shared their husbands' cramped accommodation – if a five foot long by eighteen inch wide berth could be called accommodation – and subsisted on a half ration, thin victuals indeed. Parades were at nine o'clock in the morning and half an hour before sunset. Lights went out at eight o'clock every night and all had to be up before six in the morning. Some placed bets as to where they were going; south by all accounts, so perhaps back to South America to deal with the Spanish. The battalion considered itself undefeated at Buenos Aires.

The fleet arrived off the coast of Portugal, near the mouth of the River Douro on 24 July, and the men learnt their intended destination for the first time, although the officers had guessed it by the fairly small size of their advanced pay allowance, which suggested a short transit. Most were none the wiser; in the days before easy continental travel, Portugal was a closed book. Most could only imagine that it must be like Spain, which meant it must be like the River Plate, which they remembered only too well. But they were here to fight the French, not the Spaniards, who were now suddenly their allies rather than enemies.

On Tuesday, 26 July they were seventy miles south, at Mondego Bay, heaving and rolling in the heavy swell. The weather was too rough to land, so they spent their time helping to bring up their arms from the hold, cooking provisions and admiring the nightly illuminations in their honour from the inhabitants of the small coastal town of Figuera da Foz.

Captain Douglas suddenly found himself placed in a position of some responsibility. 'On the 31st of that month received an order to commence disembarking the Army next morning,' he later wrote. 'It was suggested by some of the party that I should wait upon Sir Arthur Wellesley, state our inexperience and request more detailed instructions.' Douglas did not like this suggestion and obtained a boat from the line-of-battle ship in which he had embarked, and proceeded under charge of a lieutenant of the ship to select a place of landing. Having accomplished this, he made a sketch of the spot and narrowly escaped being drowned on the bar of the Mondego. In returning, he made his report to Wellesley, and received orders to land one-third of the force the next morning.[57]

The 45th were part of the first brigade to sail in longboats through the choppy Atlantic swell towards the south side of the mouth of the Mondego River on Monday, 1 August 1808 – in seas so rough that several longboats capsized, and about twenty sailors and riflemen were drowned.[58] On landing they were greeted and had flowers thrust into their lapels by tanned Portuguese holding colourful parasols against the sun; guarding the landing were 400 Royal Marines in red coats and black top-hats. Once formed, the brigade marched six miles south through plains of soft white sand 'hot enough to almost to have dressed a beefsteak'. This was hard work after three weeks aboard ship. The battalion muster-strength as they assembled in a pine grove just outside the village of Lavos was 35 officers, 40 sergeants, 37 corporals, 22 drummers and 614 privates. In addition there were 21 sick men in the camp and another 72 had been examined and sent off to the 'hospital' for treatment by staff doctors, perhaps suffering from heat-stroke or blisters.

Although not a Nottinghamshire man – Guard was born in Devon – he had a profound pride in his men. In the attack on Buenos Aires they had been lions; losing fourteen men killed, Captains Leonard Greenwell and John Payne, four sergeants and forty-one other ranks wounded, and one man missing. A third officer, Lieutenant William Moore, had died of wounds on the way home. Honourable mention was made of Guard's conduct in Whitelocke's dispatches; but the kind words of a disgraced commander had not make up for the sting of defeat, and surrender.

One facet of warfare for which Guard had a taste was light infantry tactics, having commanded a composite light infantry battalion in 1804. He keenly wanted to equip his regiment's caps with bugle-horn badges and green tufts, and rename them the 45th (Sherwood Foresters) Regiment of (Light) Infantry. Alas Horse Guards paid no mind, at least not until many years after his death, the regiment becoming Foresters in 1866, but even then only as 'heavy' infantry.[59] There is a story – and it is probably apocryphal, or at least based only in part on truth – of the 45th being brigaded with two Irish Regiments in Kent. The time was probably June or July 1806, before departure to South America. Hearing the 87th and 88th addressed by their commanding officers as 'Prince's Royal Irish' and 'Connaught Rangers' when called by their commanding officers to snap to attention, Guard puffed out his chest and commanded 'Nottinghamshire Hosiers! Attention!', at which point the officers, then the sergeants, then the corporals, and finally the other ranks progressively burst out into laughter. Given that the vast majority of Nottingham men in the ranks were ex-hosiers or framework knitters, it was not inappropriate.[60] Another version has Major-Generals Rowland Hill and Arthur Wellesley present, at which the latter stepped up to what would in more recent times be the microphone, and declared: 'Good luck on your expedition. I wish I was going with you.' This latter scenario was no doubt a misty-eyed embellishment from a post-Peninsula journalist, but might contain microbes of truth. Luckily Wellesley did not go to South America, for he might have been tarred by Whitelocke's residue, not gone to Portugal and the events of 1808 onwards might have looked very different.[61]

Lavos

On 3 August, the force commander published one of his first General Orders. The order of battle of the Army was to be two deep, and beginning from the right, comprise Major-General Ferguson's brigade, then Brigadier-General Catlin Craufurd's brigade, then Brigadier-General Fane's brigade on the left. There was to be a howitzer and three pieces of cannon attached to each of the brigades of infantry. The 9-pounder brigade was to serve under Major-General Ferguson, and the remainder of the artillery to be in reserve.[62]

Two deep lines were still a relatively new innovation, the British Army having used the continental system of three ranks until about 1801 (and the 1807 Drill Manual still referenced company manoeuvres in three-deep line). But at least with two ranks, every man could discharge his musket, not just the first two ranks of three.[63] Battalion drill was ordered and before long Serjeant-Major Pilling and the serjeants had the ten companies of the 45th parading in the boiling sun at the camp-ground near Lavos, two miles inland from the landing beach and four miles south of Figuera, practising their evolutions, especially the large draft of new militiamen. In camp the 45th got their first sight of their commander-in-chief, Lieutenant-General Arthur Wellesley. Never having served under him, he was a complete unknown to the battalion; all they knew is that he had served in India for many years, and had made a reputation for himself at Copenhagen. They liked what they saw – fortyish, lean, vigorous, dressed in a blue coat and wide-brimmed hat against the sun; crisp, concise orders; seemingly pragmatic over dogmatic. He was slightly taller than average, with a quiet but hoarse voice, a roman beak for a nose and a commanding way of addressing people. He rode everywhere at speed and required his staff to keep up, one of whom was one of their own: Lieutenant James Dawes Douglas, now assigned as Deputy Assistant Quartermaster-General. Douglas was keeping close to his new mentor. 'During the operation of landing, which continued five days, Sir Arthur said to me on one occasion, "I see you never make a difficulty." But that there was something of trick in all this must be confessed. The day before the Army was to advance, riding with him along the lines he said, "And, pray, how are all these tents to be got on board again?" I answered at once, "There can be no difficulty, sir; you will order carts into the lines and the men will strike and pack the tents." How it was done, I never knew.' Douglas later admitted that 'this appears to have been the critical point of my military life, which gained me the friendship of the great man.'[64]

By now the men knew: the Spanish were now allies. Twelve months ago they had been old and bitter enemies, sniping at the 45th from rooftops in Buenos Aires. The Portuguese, on the other hand, had been allied to Britain since the fourteenth century, a strange union bound by a common strength in maritime commerce, a voluminous trade in port wine and a mutual suspicion of the Spaniards. The Emperor Napoleon, in his desire to hurt Britain commercially by cutting off her Continental trade markets, needed to bring Portugal – effectively the last open market – to heel. However Portugal had been neutral throughout the wars of the revolution and empire. Not for much longer. In July 1807 the French ambassador in Lisbon had demanded that the Prince Regent, the corpulent forty-year-old João Maria José Francisco Xavier de Paula Luís António Domingos Rafael, close Portuguese ports to British ships. With his mother, the insane Queen Maria the Pious, lying screaming and drooling in a hospital bed at Queluz, the Prince Regent stalled for time as effectively between two fires; agreement to this demand would see the Royal Navy blockade Portuguese ports.

Napoleon had lost patience in October 1807 and sent an expeditionary force commanded by one of his oldest friends, the rash and temperamental Général de Division Jean-Andoche Junot, across the Pyrenees with 25,000 mostly second-line troops. This force became strung out along the line of march and 1,500 exhausted Frenchmen arrived in Lisbon on 30 November 1807 to find the royal family already over the horizon, transported to Brazil in a fleet shepherded by the Royal Navy. The rest of Junot's force eventually caught up, and even this meagre force was sufficient to conquer a country with no leadership and a small, poorly-equipped army.

Although the men in the 45th probably did not know all of these details, it is fair to assume that the senior officers were apprised of the strategic situation, and slowly the reasons for their presence on this hot and sandy shore would have percolated down to the lower ranks. 'Portygul' was a country most would have known absolutely nothing about, save for perhaps passing references to port wine and oranges.

The 45th were redistributed to the 5th Brigade on 7 August, commanded by Brigadier-General James Catlin Craufurd, called 'Cat' or 'Catlin' by his friends, a tall sandy-haired Scotsman in his early thirties, son of the Governor of Bermuda, a man utterly devoted to his wife and family; he had left five small children behind in England. The 45th's companions were the 50th (the West Kents) and Craufurd's old regiment, the 91st Highlanders.

Whilst at Lavos, news arrived – cheering news – for every man in the British Army: powdered hair and queues had been abolished. An order from Horse Guards dated 20 July 1808 advised that His Majesty had been graciously pleased to dispense with the use of queues until further orders. 'His Royal Highness desires the commanding officers of regiments will take care that the men's hair is cut close in their necks in the neatest and most uniform manner,' the order went on, 'and that their heads are kept perfectly clean by combing, brushing, and frequently washing them.'[65] Within a short time, there was probably not a queue left in the 45th; every barber and butcher (presumably because of a facility with knives and scissors) in the ranks would have been pressed into service, snipping the eleven-inch powdered queues away, brushing out the grease and powder. Without warning, the order had saved each man an hour's labour in his day. Consistent with practices in other regiments, the discarded queues were probably either burnt on campfires or buried in a mass grave.

A Column of Route
Anyone wanting to understand the British Army of this period should start at any Army List, since the army mirrored British society, and the Army Lists explained the stratification to a tee. Every list started with a complete summary of all the field-marshals, generals, major-generals, colonels, lieutenant-colonels and majors in the Army, in order of seniority, so that all could understand who was superior or inferior to whom. These men were the military equivalent of the high-born and wealthy, even if the officers themselves came from humbler origins.

Thereafter followed a regiment-by-regiment summary, again in order of seniority; all officers studied the published Army List every month to understand where they resided in terms of regimental seniority, and to see how far and fast they were moving up the pecking order. The captains, lieutenants and ensigns were the equivalent of local squires and the middle-class, and young officers often a military version of earnest young men about town. And just as they did in civilian society, these men ruled the working-class other ranks, men with (perhaps) a trade but little education or opportunity. The other ranks expected to be commanded by the class of men that made up the regimental officers, and these men in turn expected to be commanded by the military version of the upper classes.

British regiments frequently exhibited excellent *esprit de corps* not because of loyalty or higher ideals, but because the British military system inherently made sense to even the greenest new recruit. A regiment quickly became a home away from home, where everyone knew where he stood, who was superior and who 'inferior'. The British Army was the ultimate civil service.

Order of seniority was more than important to any officer; it ruled his life. In sentimental terms a Briton did not join the Army; he joined a regiment, and in so doing, joined the Army. However this was more true for other ranks (who generally stayed loyal to their selected regiment) than officers, who regiment-hopped around to take advantage of vacancies arising. Vacancies could be filled by the principle of 'dead man's shoes' without purchase, or a young gentleman could purchase a step-up in rank from another, thereby providing the departee with a deposit for his step-up, or a neat retirement fund. Often cited as class elitism, the Purchase system was in fact similar to today's senior employees buying a share of their own company, hoping to get a nest-egg back (at least) when they leave or retire. New officer positions created by death or the expansion of a battalion could be had without purchase simply because there were no departees to pay. Thus more than two-thirds of promotions were gained without purchase.

'Regimental rank' determined how high or low an officer ranked within their regiment, this could differ from their rank in the Army. This anomalous situation could arise when an officer was granted promotion in the Army for meritorious service or gallantry and was given a step in rank by a brevet warrant, but his rank in his regiment remained unaltered.[66] Thus a captain in a regiment could be a brevet major in the Army whilst within his regiment he was still uniformed and paid as a captain, but could be detached to fulfil a major's responsibilities with the Army whilst on campaign. Andrew Coghlan and David Lecky were two such captains who also held the brevet of major. The date one became a lieutenant-colonel (in the regiment or the Army, either way) determined an officer's future career once and for all, since he suddenly found himself on the end of a long list of senior officers shuffling forward, awaiting their turn to be brevetted colonels, or promoted to major-general, lieutenant-general and finally general. But any brand of general when not on campaign was paid at his highest regimental rank (which could be as low as major) rather than brevet rank.

Contrary to a popular romantic view of the nineteenth century British Army, there were no blue-blooded 'toffs' in the officer corps of the 45th; in fact there were relatively few in any regiments save the Household Cavalry and the Guards. Just about all the officers were what we would today describe as 'middle-class'. Greenwell, Milnes and Ousely were, it is true, sons of landed gentlemen, but Dawson was a provincial inn-keeper's son, and Burke a failed theological student with some rudimentary training at a seminary in Spain. The Scotsmen in particular, men such as Patton and Urquhart, tended to come from middle-class military heritage; Patton was the son and grandson of career officers, and Urquhart the son of an ordnance-master. The upper classes made up less than three percent of British officers in the Peninsula; the war was largely fought and won under the direction of middle-class men such as those in the officer ranks of the 45th.

It was before dawn on the morning of Wednesday, 10 August 1808. The battalion staff assembled in the tiny hamlet of Lavos. It would be another hot day, as it had been every day since landing. Of the thirty-five officers in the battalion, five were unavailable for duty – a fairly typical situation in the Army on campaign at time. Lieutenant-Colonel Guard had two chargers, the majors and adjutant one apiece. The other ranks could only rely upon one pony – 'shanks'.[67]

Baggage conveyance was organised, as most of the officers had trunks and portmanteaus that had to be loaded aboard the scrawny local mules. The men were lightly loaded to ensure a rapid march, their knapsacks having been sent back aboard ship, which the men viewed as a godsend. The timber-framed knapsacks normally contained mess tin, blanket, dress coat, white off-duty jacket, two shirts, spare pair of boots, two pairs of stockings, razor, brushes, stick and comb, spare buttons, pen and paper, pipe clay, bread and beef.

The timber frame was uncomfortable and would end up as firewood; the men would find ways to gradually discard all but the most essential items. Instead they carried greatcoats, a spare shirt, a spare pair of shoes and four days' supply of bread in slung canvas forage bags. Each man had only one uniform coat and one pair of trousers – or trowsers – the wear of which was evened by wearing them four ways; front, reversed, inside-out, and devil take the hindmost.

In addition to this, each foot-slogger carried his best friend: 'Brown Bess', his India Pattern musket, fifty-five and a quarter inches long, ten pounds of mass-produced iron and steel from the lowest bidder, virtually unchanged in design since 1722. Behind his right hip sat a black leather ammunition pouch and sixty rounds of ball cartridge; behind his left his seventeen-inch triangular section bayonet in a scabbard, the white canvas forage bag and canteen, painted steel-blue and showing the soldier's company number. One canteen would be never enough during an Iberian summer.[68]

The ten companies fell in arranged in column of companies as the pale orange dawn light gave their excited faces an unearthly glow. The 20th Light Dragoons formed in a compact mass at the head of the column, followed by the artillery. The infantry brigades formed up and follow as the expeditionary force moved south, the 45th at the head of the 5th Brigade. Their goal for the first day was Lugar, twelve miles to the south.

At their head rode Lieutenant-Colonel Guard, a rotund little man on an immense horse, in a fine red tailored jacket with a dark green cutaway lapel and cocked hat worn sideways. Alongside him rode his senior major, William Gwyn. Behind these two marched the Grenadier Company, followed by the other nine companies. They probably marched in a column of route four files wide; three files wide columns did not become the norm until 1810 as a pragmatic response to the narrow Iberian roads. Each company would therefore have been four files wide by about fifteen ranks deep, split into two platoons of about seven or eight ranks apiece. The company commander marched at the right front of the company; his lieutenant at the front of the rear platoon; and the ensign or junior lieutenant at the rear. The serjeants were posted at the corners of each platoon, to keep an eye on alignment, and on stragglers. Contrary to what one might expect, the drummers marched at the rear. Behind Guard rode the Adjutant, Lieutenant James Campbell, whom we last met at Cork; and Surgeon John Boggie, also mounted. Behind and on foot would have been the men of the band.[69]

The Grenadier (or No.6) Company – usually composed of the tallest men in the battalion – held the first post of honour when arrayed on the parade-ground or battlefield, the right flank, and also led the column of route. The grenadiers were differentiated by their white shako plumes and 'wings' (shoulder pads). Fairly typically for the era, this company was numerically the strongest in the battalion. Contrary to popular myth, the Colour Party marched behind the first company, not at the head of the column. We do not know who carried the colours this particular day; normally it would have been the two junior ensigns (John Tyler and Hill Phillips) but such requirements were not mandated in the King's Regulations, and the guardianship of the sacred flags may have been determined rather by practicalities such as physical strength, or by place in a roster system. Whoever carried them, they were shadowed by four serjeants from the ensigns' own companies.

Behind the grenadiers came the first of the battalion or 'centre' companies, No.1 commanded by the senior captain, 38-year-old Andrew Coghlan from King's County in Ireland, a captain for thirteen years and impatient for promotion.[70] Thirdly marched the No.10 Company of Captain Aeneas Anderson. He was a diligent diarist who had accompanied Abercrombie to Egypt in 1801 and published a book about his experiences. The fourth company was No.4, that of Captain (and Brevet-Major) David Lecky, an Ulsterman and former captain in the late Londonderry Regiment who acquired a commission in the 45th in 1804 after many years on half-pay. He would prove one of the stalwarts of the regiment in years to come. At the rear of the first division trailed the heavy baggage, probably transported on primitive Portuguese carts that would have driven the men mad with the constant high-pitched squealing of ungreased timber axles.

The left wing (or second division) of the battalion then snaked behind. At the head was the junior major, Andrew Patton. The leading company was the No.3 Company of Captain William Smith, whom we have met previously; he was to be one of the outstanding officers of Wellington's army, conscientious to a fault yet bold on the battlefield, admired by fellow officers and men alike. Behind came Captain Francis Drew's No.8 Company – Drew was the youngest of four Irish brothers in the Army, three serving with the 45th - he would be destined to be a short-timer, not for health reasons, but rather due to a falling out with a superior officer, and a court-martial. The last two centre companies were those of Captains Douglas and Lightfoot. James Dawes Douglas we have already met, on the staff; he was destined to be the only man in the battalion eventually to become a full general, but not through service in the 45th. The last of the centre companies was No.9, commanded by Birmingham native Captain Thomas Lightfoot, old at thirty-three to be a junior captain, but who would go on to high rank after being the only 1808 captain to serve throughout the entire war.

At the rear marched the Light Company (No.5), men trained to fight in open skirmish formation and invariably the best shots in the battalion, whose uniforms were distinguished by shoulder wings and green plumes. The Light Company held the second post of honour, the left flank when in line of battle; being on the flank also made it easier from them to break away from the battalion when fighting in skirmish order. The Light Company was fortunate to have as its commander Captain Leonard Greenwell, the 27-year-old third son of Joshua Greenwell of Kibblesworth in Durham. He was a 45th man through-and-through, having being commissioned into the regiment as an ensign in August 1801. He received his first wound at Buenos Aires, and would receive four more in years to come. Buglers William Jordan and John Thompson gave the trumpet tones of command that would carry a greater distance than the rattling timbre of drums.

Not present with the battalion would have been Quartermaster Edmund Thresher and Quartermaster-Serjeant Francis Tinkler, since their roles required them to be out ahead of the column, selecting billets and supply sources for that night's rest stop.

The lieutenants had between seven years and eighteen months service in the rank, fairly typical for the time. The seven ensigns present were, as one would expect, freshly-minted – none had been in the Army more than thirteen months. Only two, Charles Barnwell and John Tyler, would serve through the entire war; Barnwell as the battalion's future adjutant and Tyler as ADC to Lieutenant-General Sir Thomas Picton. An ensign tended to join the Army at sixteen (although there were plenty of instances of boys joining at an earlier age) and became official the day he received a commission from the King. Every officer was allowed one manservant, the proviso being that the man must not be a non-commissioned officer. William Brown was later to be one such manservant (for which the contemporary slang was 'bone-polisher', as in cleaning the officer's cutlery), and he described the role as 'often attended with such extra fatigue and toi'. Despite Brown's moaning, manservants were relieved of certain other regimental duties which tended to make up for the hardships.

Most of the officers of the 45th were Buenos Aires veterans. Not counting the tedious sea journey, the action in that campaign had been over

35

and done within a matter of weeks. If somehow they could have learnt the final casualty rate for officers, the cumulative Butcher's Bill as presented in April 1814, they would certainly have shivered in dread. Of the officers who ultimately reached the rank of lieutenant-colonel, five out of six would be killed or wounded; also five out of six majors; nineteen out of thirty-one captains; twenty-six out of fifty lieutenants; and eight out of thirteen ensigns. The battalion would lose seven commanding officers in action before the war was over.[71] Being an officer had its disadvantages.

---

[39] Captain Douglas had curtailed his studies to go on the South American expedition.

[40] *Wellington's Dispatches*, Vol. 4, p.20.

[41] Some 7,355 Irish militiamen had volunteered into the line by early 1808.

[42] *Wellington's Dispatches*, Vol. 3, p.24.

[43] ibid.

[44] WO65, Army List for 1797.

[45] Guard's biography is based upon his own hand-written service record in WO25/745.

[46] This court newspaper extract was found at 19th Century British Newspapers Online.

[47] Delancey was Wellington's future Quartermaster-General at Waterloo.

[48] Officer biographies were sourced from Phillipart and the WO25 series.

[49] Grose, Advice to Officers of the British Army, pp.48-9.

[50] Boggie's biography is based on his service record in WO25/3905.

[51] Paymaster's clerk Serjeant John MacLauglin, who did not accompany the battalion from Cork. A replacement was found from the ranks.

[52] James, The Regimental Companion, p.248.

[53] General Regulations and Orders for the Army.

[54] Douglas' biography is based on his memoirs in the 1938 Regimental Annual, pp.216-7.

[55] *Wellington's Dispatches*, Volume 4.

[56] Based upon WO25/1275.

[57] 1938 Regimental Annual, pp.216-7.

[58] Only Fane's brigade – the 1/36th, 1/45th, 5/60th and 1/95th – landed the first day; the rest of the force landed on succeeding days.

[59] The 45th became the 45th (Nottinghamshire - Sherwood Foresters) Regiment in 1866 and the 1st Battalion the Sherwood Foresters (Derbyshire Regiment) in 1881. But Guard was long dead by then.

[60] The Hosier story is as quoted in Dalbiac, p.45.

[61] Wellesley was a very junior major-general in 1806, so there is no good reason why he would have been asked to give such a speech. In any event he was not partial to giving them.

[62] The orders are as published in General Orders for 1808.

[63] This was important, as we shall see. The French stuck to three ranks until the bitter end.

[64] 1938 Regimental Annual, pp.216-7.

[65] General Orders, 20 July 1808.

[66] Brevet commissions were confined to grades from captain to lieutenant-colonel. The brevet conferred rank in the Army, but not in the regiment. However determination of seniority when handing out higher commands was based upon army rank.

67 Shanks' Pony; foot-slogging.

68 General descriptions of soldier's attire and equipment are based upon Haythornthwaite, pp.43-74.

69 Officer details in this section are based upon data taken from various WO25 series sources.

70 Andrew Coghlan held the brevet of major in the army but ranked as a captain in his regiment.

71 Although one of these COs was actually killed serving with his old regiment before he could take up the new command.

Chapter 4

Men of the 45th

Amongst the 732 non-commissioned officers and other ranks were men who would earn up to fifteen clasps to their Military General Service Medal, the highest for a county line regiment.

The NCOs were, as the saying went, the backbone of the regiment. All four serjeant-majors eventually serving with the battalion would be commissioned as officers before the war's end. There were thirty-seven serjeants with the battalion in August 1808, collectively having an average of about eight years' service per man. One of the oldest was George Richardson, forty-three, a former weaver from the hamlet of Benburb in County Tyrone, whereas one of the most junior was Robert Thomas Elliott, a 21-year-old from Stanage in Derbyshire who had only held the rank for six months, having been made corporal shortly before the attack on Buenos Aires. A fair percentage had had prior military experience before joining the 45th, many in the Nottinghamshire Fencibles and Militia. Another particularly good source of men had been the Northumberland Fencibles, of which a large group had joined the 45th in Athlone on the disbandment of the Fencibles in August 1802.

The thirty-seven corporals were generally younger, mostly aged between 23 and 28 years old, with an average of six years' service. Nine had more than seven years' service with the colours and one, Corporal Campbell Kelly, over sixteen years, having joined the 45th as a drummer-boy. Some had been spotted as possible NCO material and elevated to corporal rank quite young, such as William Orchard and Peter Robins, who had been given the two stripes some years earlier, aged seventeen and eighteen respectively. Corporals were generally serjeants-in-waiting, but there were some who were happy to dwell in the intermediate rank, at least having the benefit of a musket to fire rather than the nearly useless serjeants' pike.

The life of an NCO was precarious; one slip and a man could be back to private immediately. Promotions tended to occur on the 25th of each month to fit in with the Army's pay cycle, and a reliable private might find himself promoted straight to serjeant over the heads of long-serving corporals. More often than not, anyone so promoted was transferred to another company, the theory being that a new NCO would have more authority over relative strangers than his immediate circle of friends.[72] If ever a serjeant was unavailable due to other duties or sickness (a common occurrence during the war) a corporal could be delegated to perform his duties, with the temporary title of lance-serjeant; and a reliable private could be asked to step into a corporal's shoes as a titular lance-corporal. This latter rank did not officially exist at this time in any regiments other than the Foot Guards, who used the award of a single chevron; the archaic term was 'Chosen Man', but only the Rifles still used this nomenclature in 1808.

Contrary to myth, the drummers were mainly not boys, although many started that way. Thomas Griffiths, aged twenty-eight and from Stepney in London, was 'born in the Army'[73] and had joined the 45th as a drummer-boy aged seven; the regiment was always his home. John Mackey had been born in the 49th Regiment on Barbados and joined the 45th as drummer in 1799, aged ten. Tall sandy-haired Richard Carlton, a 23-year-old from Frome in Somerset, likewise joined the 45th aged nine and had drummed the 45th through the streets of Buenos Aires in 1807. They had to learn the various drum-patterns for use in service – nine patterns for in the field, ten patterns for drill in barracks. But the drummers had three other roles besides that of timekeepers and signallers: first, as inflictors of punishment – each drummer was expected to keep a cat-of-nine-tails within his knapsack – second, as orderlies in the officers' guard-room; and third, to assist the wounded in battle. None were sought-after tasks.

Each company provided one or two bearded pioneers, men with axes and leather aprons for construction or destruction of obstacles. By tradition, these were the only men in the battalion permitted not to shave, although this rule became lax when on campaign. The French on the other hand, who liked their soldiers hairy, encouraged mustachios in all ranks and beards for their grenadiers.

The regimental band was small, but augmented by the battalion's twenty drummers, they probably made up in rhythm what they may have lacked in melody. The band was led by Private Joseph Morgan, a former professional musician from Doneraile near Cork. Alongside him, four privates tootled and parped a collection of army favourites – *Hearts of Oak*, *The Lincolnshire Poacher*, *The Walls of Old England*, *Brandy-O*, *Johnny's Gone for a Soldier*; not to forget the old favourites *Rule Britannia* and *The British Grenadiers*. And of course, for special occasions, *God Save the King*. The musicians played their parts from memory, to arrangements pieced together by Joe Morgan himself, so there was no guarantee they would play selections in the same key or tempo as neighbouring bands when on the march or at parade.

The other ranks were mainly aged between eighteen and forty, with an average age of about twenty-four. Most of the men were veterans of Buenos Aires, and perhaps one in twenty had served in the West Indian campaigns at the close of the previous century. The Englishmen came from all over, but a distribution map of their birthplaces would show a high concentration around Nottinghamshire, Derbyshire and Leicestershire. Areas that feature strongly in the 'enlisted at' column of their attestation records include Northumberland, and Preston in Lancashire. There were plenty of Irishmen, even before the 167 militia volunteers joined at Cork. Over a third of the battalion was from the sister kingdom, slightly higher than the army average for an English county regiment. Nearly six men in ten were English, the vast majority coming from within a fifty-mile radius of Nottingham; the battalion therefore was more representative of its county title than most, and would proudly remain that way until the end of the war. Only five percent of the men came from other places, including drummer John Mackey from Barbados. Of Scots, there were less than thirty, mostly lowlanders from the Borders. A rare highlander was Serjeant Alexander McIntyre in Captain Coghlan's company, from Croy in Inverness-shire. Welshmen were even fewer, less than a handful.[74]

Thirty-five men in the battalion had served in the Army for more than fourteen years. Although the ten companies were more or less equal in numbers, the experience was not so evenly distributed. The companies of Captains Douglas and Milne each contained seven privates with over fourteen years' experience, whereas Captain Greenwell's light company had only one such man. Captains Coghlan and Lightfoot had twelve and fourteen seven-year veterans apiece, while Captain Lecky had only six.[75]

Their names included a delightful collection of rustic noms-de-guerre – Septimus Ands, James Biggerstaff, James Careless, John Colbreath, Francis Diguinan, Samuel Dring, William Eggs, Darby English, Michael Kettleband, Jeremiah Looney, Felix McHuskane, Jonas Neep, Thady Peterson, Darby Starr, Hiram Toy, Jepson Vickars.

The men had their own language and customs that would have been incomprehensible to strangers. The English, being largely Nottingham and Derby men, would have greeted each other with 'eyoopmedoock'[76] or 'ayergorrawiya',[77] while men from the villages often used different words and phrases from town-dwellers. Nearly all smoked, but pipes, not cigarettes. Many also chewed tobacco plugs, a habit more commonly associated with soldiers in the American Civil War, but it was widely practised by British rank-and-file of this earlier era. Few read books or papers, since a large proportion of men were illiterate.

The military salute was we know it today was embryonic in 1808, really just fingers touched to the peak of a shako, a memory of lifting a hat in salute, and thus only ever delivered when officer and other rank were both wearing headgear. When bare-headed, other ranks merely stood to attention and stared into the middle-distance, but without the exaggerated knee-lifting and boot-stomping of British troops in later eras. All save the very youngest had shaggy collar-length hair and industrial-strength sideburns, yet only a few officers had moustaches; and only the pioneers had beards. The French wore their hair short and un-powdered after the style of their Emperor, and considered the British quaintly old-fashioned.

The men were, statistically, mainly between five-foot-three and five-foot-eight tall, the average being perhaps five foot-six or -seven. Men five-foot-nine and over were typically selected for the Grenadier Company. Men six feet and over were few and far between; Private Michael Kelly of the grenadiers at six foot and one half-inch tall was considered a giant. Having survived on an army diet, they were nearly all lean, there being no scope for weight gain on army bread and minuscule salted beef rations. They bathed once a week in barracks and when camped next to a river on campaign, and so soon got used to the collective smell, which revolted the more gentile elements of the population whenever they marched through a town.

The years 1806 and 1807 had been boom years for army ordinary recruitment[78] (close to 20,000 men in 1807 alone) and many in the ranks were from this class. The largest former occupational group listed on attestation papers is 'labourer' which was an army catch-all term for anyone without a formal trade. Detractors have used this singular fact to underline the ne'er-do-well nature of the army's rankers, but to do so is to misunderstand the application of the term; after all, how was a 16- or 17-year-old recruit to have a trade behind him? In descending order of frequency came framework-knitters, weavers and hosiers, tailors, cutlers, potters, servants – this last-named being a common profession for Irish recruits – masons, shoemakers, butchers and carpenters.

Amongst the Nottinghamshire men, a disproportionate number were former framework knitters. Long one of the commercial pillars of the county (no thanks to the Corsican Ogre) the hosiery industry had suffered the loss of most of the continental markets. Preferring the army to starvation, the unemployed of Mansfield, Newark, Worksop and Arnold had boosted the ranks of the 45th. A framework-knitter, if he could find a job, earned typically fourteen shillings a week against twenty shillings for a printer, twenty-five shillings for a hand-weaver in Lancashire, or twenty-eight shillings for a dockyard worker.[79] It was an improvement upon an agricultural labourer's ten shillings a week, but only just. The only reason to be attracted to a private's wage of seven shillings a week was a recruitment bounty (ranging anywhere from twelve to twenty-three pounds) and the prospect of job security, a roof overhead and a regular meal. Unemployment and job uncertainty together made the price of a recruit's loyalty, not drink as Wellington famously (or infamously) later quoted. Once a recruit donned the red coat (or the 'red rag' as the men called it) he became the most identifiable article in the kingdom, and one of the least-respected.

The men wore the same uniform design they had worn since about 1800 – dull red jacket, tight-waisted and indifferently made with dark green collars and cuffs, edged in white; eight pointed loops with a green inwoven leaf pattern in four pairs down the front and silver pewter buttons; white tight-fitting breeches and black knee-length gaiters. The cap – or shako – was a cylinder of black felt with large brass badge emblazoned 'GR' on the front, and a small tufted feather at top centre. The King's Regulations for the Clothing and Appointments of the Army dated 22 April 1803 outlined a man's clothing entitlements – in a regiment of infantry of the line serving in Europe, North America, or New South Wales, (Highland corps excepted) each serjeant was allowed annually, a coat, the sleeves unlined; a pair of breeches, made of materials of the same quality as the coat; a cloth waistcoat, lined, with sleeves of milled serge; and a pair of military shoes; and once in every two years, a 'lackered' felt cap, with a cockade, and feather or tuft. Each corporal, drummer, and private man was allowed a coat and breeches as above; a kersey waistcoat, with serge sleeves; and a pair or military shoes: and once in every two years, a cap. If a serjeant was reduced to the ranks, his clothing was to be given in for the use of his successor; and he himself was to receive private's clothing equally worn (or as nearly may be) with the clothing he had given in. One coat a year, and that to be worn every day for 365 days. The only inter-company distinctions were frilled shoulder pads or 'wings' for the grenadier and light company men, and distinguishing feathers on their shakos – white for the grenadiers and green for the lights. Drummers wore dark green coats with red collars and cuffs, all other details being identical. Serjeants wore crimson sashes and carried pikes rather than muskets. The officers had scarlet coats with wide dark-green lapels down the centre, crimson sashes and sword-belts. It was not a practical uniform; the most hated item being a thick black leather stock worn under the collar, the aim being to keep a man's head erect. The trousers were too tight for summer service and the gaiters wore out and disappeared quickly once on the march. The boots were really ankle shoes, made without differentiation for left of right, and designed to be worn on the other foot every second day to even out the wear; the only result was footwear that was uncomfortable no matter which foot it was on. The felt shakos lost their shape very quickly on campaign and when wet it was like wearing – well, a bag of wet felt on your head.

The 45th were not considered a 'smart' regiment. The Guards, the light infantry, the Rifles were smart regiments, as were some of the 'Royal' regiments, such as the Fusiliers, who like the Guards, wore bearskins when on home ceremonial duty (but never on campaign, pace the tendency of jingoistic Victorian artists to show them in Wellingtonian battle scenes). You had to be five foot nine to gain entry to the Guards, whilst their NCOs, resplendent in scarlet coats with gold lace like the officers, were considered unholy terrors. The light infantry and Rifles recruited men who were nimble, independent and crack shots; the perfect home for hunters and poachers, rather than townsmen and textile-workers. Rather, the 45th were the epitome of a solid English county regiment, slow-moving but reliable, more tight-knit than most since more than half the men came from a catchment area around the regiment's home county of Nottinghamshire. Only the Highland regiments could boast such regional integrity, or perhaps their old friends the 88th, the Connaught Rangers, very nearly Irishmen all.

The other ranks had one friend and one enemy. The friend was army rum, black, strong and treacly, carried in wooden casks and doled out as a reward or held back as an incentive, or occasionally, used as a brave-maker. The enemy was the Three Sisters, the triangle created by lashing together three serjeant's pikes, upon which men were flogged for breaches of discipline. On average, one man in fifty was flogged each year; the maximum dose that a court-martial could inflict was 1,000 lashes, administered by drummers in rotation as their arms tired. The fainting of any recipient caused the cessation of proceedings until he revived, or until resumption at some other time. Punishments ranged from fifty lashes for being slovenly to 1,000 lashes for desertion. Although written by a serjeant in a different regiment, the following description of a punishment parade on campaign in 1805 is fairly typical for the period:

'During our stay in Bremen, which was about six weeks, we had a parade to attend morning and afternoon. The officers commanding companies received orders from Major B. to inspect their men closely, and turn out such as they found dirty to the front; a square was then formed for punishment, and the men who had been found fault with, were marched in, tried by a drum-head court-martial, and flogged, to a man, without reference to character ... I say, at one of these parades, a brave old soldier, whose character was unimpeachable, happened to cough in the rank. He turned his head a little on one side to discharge the phlegm, and was instantly ordered into the centre of the square, stripped of his accoutrements, and placed in front of the halberts [sic]. He went through the mock form of trial, by a drumhead court-martial. Major B. swore he was unsteady in the ranks; and on the ipse dixit of that tyrant, he was sentenced to receive fifty lashes. After the brave veteran was tied up he implored hard for mercy, adding, that he had been twenty years in the service, and was never till then brought to the halberts ... his appeal was useless, he had every lash of his sentence, weeping and crying bitterly during the infliction; and although he only received fifty lashes, he never looked up afterwards. It had wounded his best feelings; he was constantly in hospital, and but a little time elapsed before he was discharged.'[80]

The regimental surgeon responsible for dealing with the aftermath of the above was John Boggie, later of the 45th. The alleged tyrant – Major John Frederick Browne – later went on to earn hero status on the Peninsula battlefield of Barossa. One wonders how one becomes sufficiently drilled to flogging? Trial and error perhaps. The flogging was no less traumatic for the poor drummers (more often than not mere boys) inflicting the lash:

'From the very first day I entered the service as drum-boy, and for eight years after, I can venture to assert, that, at the lowest calculation, it was my disgusting duty to flog men at least three times a week ... After a poor fellow had received about a hundred lashes, the blood would pour down his back in streams, and fly about in all directions with every additional blow of the cat, so that by the time he had received 300, I have found my clothes all over blood from the knees to the crown of the head. Horrified at my disgusting appearance, I have, immediately after parade, run into the barrack-room, to escape from the observations of the soldiers, and to rid my clothes and person of my comrade's blood.'[81]

---

[72] The 45th muster rolls in WO12 are full of examples of this policy.

[73] An army term that meant born to a serving soldier on campaign or in barracks.

[74] Soldier details in this section are based upon biographical details taken from various sources in WO25, WO79, WO116 and WO119.

[75] Based upon muster rolls in WO12/5727.

[76] Evidently still used today. Means 'what's up?'

[77] 'How goes it with you?'

[78] As distinct from transferment from the militia.

[79] This comparison is relevant only for 1808, for unemployment soared and wages plummeted as the war dragged on.

[80] The flogging story extract is from the *United Service Journal* for 1843, Volume 42.

[81] ibid, p.255.

Chapter 5

Roliça and Vimeiro

It was boiling hot by nine o'clock in the morning of 10 August 1808; the men mopped brows and gasped as they struggled through the ankle-deep sand that rose in clouds to coat their sticky faces and hands. The landscape was all undulating heath-land on white sand, with occasional clumps of pine trees. Every so often they saw a cultivated field or vineyards, but this was not a densely populated part of Portugal. The sea-breeze was refreshing, when not blowing sand in their faces; but when they were on the road, they were shielded from the breeze by hedge-rows and voluminous prickly pears, and so got hotter in the shade.

The second day was another thirteen miles in the enervating heat to Leiria, where they camped for twenty-four hours to allow the mostly inexperienced troops a breather. The following day they were at Calvario where they were joined by a force of Portuguese infantry and cavalry dressed in brown and blue, at least those who had uniforms. The men envied the wide-brimmed straw hats of the locals. There were no tents for the men; they slept under the stars. The weather was still hot by day, but dewy by night, and the men snoozed huddled around their camp-fires. On the 14th they advanced through the ancient town of Batalha with its medieval abbey. The French had departed the day before and left clear signs of their occupation – looted shops and houses, limp bodies being cut down from gallows and wailing women. A little later they arrived at Alcobaza, and on the 15th forced-marched in two columns across the hills down onto a coastal plain; something was up. They camped at Caldas, and on the next day, near the picturesque walled town of Obidos, they saw their first Frenchmen, albeit from a distance.

Blue-coated *tirailleurs* (skirmishers) occupied the Moorish castle perched on a hill. Eight companies of Rifles skirmished forward, green-coated specks on a yellow plain. The French did not make an event of the defence and rapidly retired, south-west, shielded by a handful of light cavalry. The Rifles, four companies from each of the 60th and 95th, followed; the rifle-pops receded into the distance, and the troops, from a distance looking like grasshoppers on a field, disappeared from view, shielded by a spur of hills. There followed several hours of boredom under the hot sun, and a warm night. The topic for discussion in the camp that night: what had become of the green-jackets?

The green-coated survivors re-appeared shortly after dawn, double-timing it back to the main force. Their tale eventually percolated through the camp. Having pursued the French for upwards of three miles, they then spent the entire night in formation upon a knoll after being ambushed by concealed French reinforcements. One officer was killed and one wounded, and a small number of men wounded, but twenty-one were missing, presumably taken by the French. Wellesley later privately wrote, 'The affair of the advanced posts yesterday evening was unpleasant, because it was quite useless.'[82]

The Riflemen were exhausted, but there would be no sleep for them this day. The French were close and a general action seemed imminent. The camp was still in the village of Caldas but oddly there was no advance ordered – perhaps the commissary had not yet caught up with the Army. So the 45th sat in the sun and waited; the hurry-up would come soon enough.

It came at four in the morning on the 17th, as the battalions were ordered into their start positions for the advance on a distant village besides a hill, which the men now knew was called Roliça. On the far right, skirting some low hills, were three scratch battalions of Portuguese, many of them dressed in their civilian clothes and wide-brimmed hats. Next came the 1st Brigade of Major-General Rowland Hill. The 45th were in the centre. On the left, up in the hills, were the brigades of Ferguson and Bowes, shaded by Fane's riflemen. The central column, immediately south of the castle at Obidos, had Nightingall's 3rd Brigade in front (the 29th and 82nd Foot), whilst Catlin Craufurd's 5th Brigade formed the reserve immediately behind, right-in-front – which is to say, the 45th (as the senior regiment) leading. The three large columns snaked forward under a searing sun, presumably in parallel but it was hard to tell since the left-hand column was on the high ground. The advance was anything but secret, since the central column alone had five bands playing. The 45th had a small band, only five men, and unfortunately we do not know what mix of instruments they had, but without question they were playing the regimental march, the song *The Dandy-O* from the comic opera *Robin Hood* (fittingly) which would in 1813 received fresh lyrics and become be re-titled *The Young May Moon*.

French *voltigeurs* skirmished very briefly with British light infantry from the hill above Roliça before withdrawing to the base of a line of hills about half-a-mile behind the village. The three columns – Ferguson's debauching from the hills – converged just south of the village as Wellesley ordered the formation of a battle array to face the brigade of Frenchmen; Hill on the right, Nightingall in the centre, and the 45th alone of Craufurd's brigade forming the left flank of the assault. Behind the 45th sat the 50th and 91st in reserve; farther behind, Ferguson's command of two brigades – five battalions – had not quite caught up with the other two columns. But the French were outnumbered and of no mind to fight on the plain. With a rapidity that startled the British and shielded by a few *voltigeurs* and *chasseurs a chèval* they retired up the hillsides, and formed a new line on the pine-covered crest to the rear, masked by a line of grey rocks that described the ridge-line.

The five beautifully aligned British battalions in the first line now found themselves all dressed up and with nowhere to go; French artillery balls rained down from the heights as the first Royal Artillery brigade commenced a bombardment from a position near a windmill to the rear. The line was ordered to wheel by the left and halt at the foot of the ridge, whilst waiting for Fane's riflemen to turn the French flanks. But the 29th, or rather part of it, disrupted by an advance through a village, found itself at the base of one of two large ravines cut into the hillside, and its commander, Lieutenant-Colonel George Augustus Frederick Lake, the 38-year-old eldest son of General Lake of Irish Rebellion fame, allowed his fox-hunting instincts to take over. He only had five companies with him – perhaps 400 men – but hared off up the ravine nonetheless, towards the 4,000 Frenchmen lining the crest. Up, up the gully they clambered; Lieutenant-Colonel Lake first on his enormous charger, then the Grenadier Company of the 29th, then the remaining companies.

For the French on the crest, it was like shooting fish in a barrel. At last the 29th got enough men forward to form a much-reduced battle line, but when called upon to surrender, Lake refused, and was shot out of his saddle, resplendent in a new uniform donned especially for his first battle.[83] The 29th lost nearly 200 men this day out of the 400 or so who climbed the gully. The 9th Foot close behind them – presumably sucked up the ravine in the wake of the advance – lost 72 men also, but arrived in time to secure a foothold on the ridge, despite several French counter-attacks.

Seeing the plight of the 29th, a general advance was ordered, and soon the 45th was ordered to climb. No gully for them, but a precipice, three hundred yards east of the 29th. So they clambered up like mountain goats, losing all formation as they did so, hauling themselves up by grabbing rocks and the trunks of scrubby bushes. The toughest job of all went to the young ensigns carrying the colours, Ensign Dawson carrying the King's Colour, and Ensign Phillips carrying the Regimental Colour, for they had to clamber whilst maintaining a hold on thirty-nine square feet of flapping silk on a nine-foot pole. Notwithstanding this difficulty there is reason to believe the Colour Party and the centre of the battalion reached the crest first, since nearly all the casualties on this day were in the companies flanking the colours – those of Captains Smith and Milne. As they crested the ridge, they came within sight of the French artillery. Ensign Robert Dawson, the son of an innkeeper from Ashbourne in Derbyshire was riddled by canister-shot, and down went the King's Colour; serjeants from the colour party leaped forward to take the flag. The timber staff of the Regimental Colour was broken in two by the same discharge, leaving its holder Ensign Phillips miraculously untouched. The 45th formed a line of panting jelly-legged men on the crest in support of the 29th. Lieutenant Richard Burke of Captain Milne's company was wounded as they tried to assume proper formation, and nine other ranks also, but the men were too winded to advance further.

Adjutant James Campbell wrote anonymously to *The Star* newspaper from Torres Vedras on 20 September, and it was published on 1 November 1808: 'In the action of 17 August we attacked the strongest part of the enemy, headed by the gallant General Spence, but, from the 29th Regiment having advanced too quick, they having the road on our right, and we being obliged to climb a precipice, they suffered, as you have seen by the Gazette, very severely ... scarcely a man could stand when we got to the top of the precipice, some places of which only two men could get up at a time. You may recollect the rocks called Boor Hill near Ayr; the place we had to go up was something like it.' The fact that Wellesley's after-battle dispatch did not mention the 45th obviously irked him. 'The French, since the business is over, have frequently inquired the name of the mad Regiment that climbed the rocks, and the still madder Officer that led them ... They retired in astonishment when they saw the 29th and us formed in perfect order on the hill. We never fired a shot, and in consequence were not mentioned in orders; but all the army agree that we deserve to have been noticed in the strongest terms.'[84]

Coupled with the efforts of the 9th, there were by now twenty-three British companies on the crest, about 1,800 redcoats to face the 4,300 Frenchmen. But the 5th, 38th and 82nd were still clambering, and the French commander faced a real threat from Fane's greencoats who threatened to get behind his right flank, having clambered extra-hard themselves. So Général de Division Delaborde decided it was time to withdraw. It was perhaps four on a hot afternoon, and his defence was intended as a delaying action, nothing more, whilst Junot and Loison marched to reinforce him. Light cavalry and *voltigeurs* acted as a screen as the French retired through a village and along a spur. His delaying tactics had been masterful, his sense of timing superb, his movements done at a speed that astonished Wellesley's men. The British had achieved their aim of driving the French from the ridge, but that was all they had to show. The French aim had been to distract Wellesley and buy time for Junot's other brigades to come up, and Delaborde had succeeded royally on both counts.[85]

The 45th camped on the spur near the village – which they learnt was called Zambugeira, or for the common soldier, Zambuggery – and although the 45th had not fired a shot in anger, those who were not at Buenos Aires could no longer be considered Johnny Raws.

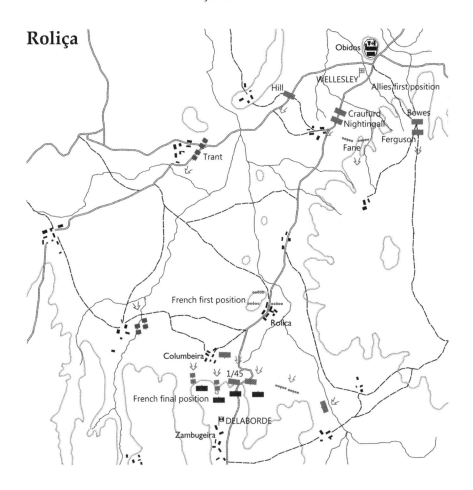

The officers' baggage did not arrive until late in the evening, and with it Surgeon Boggie's main kit. He inspected the wounded, and consigned six of the men to hospital. For the unfortunate Captain John Payne, in agony at the re-opening of his Buenos Aires wound, there was nothing to be done but to send him to the Field Hospital. Somewhere in another corner of the field, privates would have been digging a solitary grave for Ensign Dawson, attended by the funeral party – three fellow ensigns and 27 men, as laid down by the regulations. The men would have fired three rounds into the air as the chaplain (an army chaplain, there being no regimental ones) closed the service. At best there might have been a wooden cross, or maybe a timber headstone cut by the pioneers.

After sunset, men wanted to sleep, but too many were still high from the day's action to rest. Then there was the terrible distraction from the camp of the 29th; the surgeons were at work on the wounded, and the balmy evening was ruined by shrieks and screams from a hovel on the edge of the village.

In the morning they were on the road early, marching south-west, a different direction to that the retiring French had taken yesterday evening. Was it a flanking manoeuvre? Were there French on two sides? They marched down from the ridge-line, across a large plain with many cultivated fields to a dirty village called Lourinha, where they could hear the ocean and feel the sea breeze once again. Then skirting a range of low hills to their right, they marched five miles south to a village set amidst rolling farmland where a small river runs to an ocean inlet – Vimeiro.

There was a handsome white church in the oddly asymmetric Portuguese style on the edge of town, but beyond that, little else of interest, at least to the other ranks. But several officers went down to the inlet, and saw much of interest – several Royal Navy frigates and a host of transports lying off shore. Reinforcements were arriving, and Wellesley obviously needed a fortified landing spot to land two brigades. There, at the tiny fishing village of Porto Novo with its small beach and rocky cliffs, over 4,000 men would soon land in longboats, coming out of the choppy surf.

It looked a risky proposition. In a villa at Lourinha, Lieutenant-General Wellesley wrote enclosing a set of recommended promotions to the Commander-in-Chief, the Duke of York. Most were concerned with the vacancies created in the 29th Foot, but he also recommended a young volunteer[86] then serving with the 32nd Foot, Hans Stevenson Marsh, to the vacant ensigncy in the 45th created by Dawson's death.

Another piece of good news arrived that day in the form of reinforcements for the 45th. Captain Edward Scott, Lieutenants Theophilus Byers Costley, William Persse and Robert McCally, four serjeants, four corporals and 199 privates from the second battalion had left Nottingham on 11 July, marched down to Hilsea near Portsmouth (where they had arrived on 26 July) and then transported to Figuera de Foz, where they had landed too late to join the main column. From there they had marched briskly south to join the Army at Vimeiro.[87] The new arrivals were distributed to the ten companies and for the first time in several years the battalion was close to establishment strength – over 900 men. 'What have we missed?' the new men asked. 'Nowt burra lorra hill clahmin!' undoubtedly came the response.

The four new officers were put on the strength as supernumeraries, not attached to any company but available to plug any gaps in the officer corps as they arose. The reinforcements landed in the bay allowed Wellesley the opportunity to re-structure his army, so the 50th were removed to a new brigade under Brigadier-General Henry Fane, leaving the 45th with only the 91st Highlanders and one company of the 60th Rifles for company in Craufurd's brigade. The Army now comprised nine infantry brigades[88] and a small cavalry brigade supported by eighteen artillery pieces. The 45th camped on a ridge on the south-western side of the Maceira River, about a mile west of the village of Vimeiro. Craufurd's men were wedged between Hill's and Nightingall's brigades.

Rumour in camp that evening was rife. Some said that Wellesley had been replaced by a superior officer, others that he had been sacked and replaced by Sir John Moore. The officers eventually confirmed that Wellesley had indeed been superseded, by Sir Harry Burrard, a 53-year-old Guardsman lately arrived from England. Moore was confirmed as being on his way with another division; and God forbid, an Army of such size could not possibly be commanded by so junior a lieutenant-general as Wellesley.

Orders came down that the men were to sleep accoutred in readiness to move out, and to be under arms by three o'clock in the morning. They dozed around their stands of muskets whilst picquets kept a nervous watch. The 45th stood to at the appointed time but on seeing no French present, were allowed to disperse for breakfast. Perhaps there was to be no battle today. But that all changed before seven o'clock; dust-clouds could be seen well to the west; the French were on the march. The dust-clouds crawled forward at a snail's pace, and eventually seemed to split into two parts. The larger cloud moved towards the village of Vimeiro, the centre of the British line, whilst a smaller cloud advanced north toward Lourinha. The attack in the centre was too far away to be seen by the 45th, but the timing of a French assault was audible by the rolling volleys that crackled between the bangs of artillery discharges.

To the nervous 45th, high up on their ridge, it seemed only a matter of time before they were fed into the defence of the village and its surrounding hills. The order came just after nine o'clock, and the 45th followed three other brigades down off the ridge, but not towards Vimeiro, but rather to the north of the village, across the stream and up onto a ridge that ran north-east of town. The artillery fire and volleys continued from the hills where the brigades defending the main French assault were positioned; it sounded like hot work. But it was now clear that the 45th were aimed at the flank, towards the second French dust-cloud far out to the north-east. Craufurd's brigade was ordered to halt about a mile from the village and face south-east, at which they could see the hills in front of Vimeiro littered with white-coated casualties.[89] To their left, the brigades of Nightingall, Ferguson and Bowes continued their advance and waited in the lee of a hill for nearly an hour for the obvious clash. Against the rub-a-dub of French drums and the hoarse Gallic chanting came the ripple of platoon volleys, delivered almost continuously for what seemed like two minutes, and then the rumble of six thousand pairs of feet; three thousand British charging with bayonets and three thousand French retiring. They captured some French cannon, and were momentarily discomfited when a supporting French brigade arrived on the scene to take them back, only to be sent packing by the 71st Light Infantry. It was 11:30 in the morning, and the battle was as good as over. The French had ceased their attacks in the centre – four separate attacks, all of which had been repulsed – and their right wing was in retreat. Thus Wellesley's first signal victory in the Peninsula was won, at a cost of 135 killed, 534 wounded, and 51 missing. The 45th had played no part, being mostly spectators – although the neighbouring 91st suffered one casualty, so they perhaps the brigade came under a distant fire at one point.

They camped on the battlefield for a few days whilst the dead were buried and the wounded patched, all the while wondering why there had been no pursuit of the defeated French. Captain James Dawes Douglas did not have to wonder. He had seen full well why there would be no pursuit; it is one of the great vignettes of the war, and worth repeating verbatim.

'Sir Harry Burrard, a Senior Officer to Sir A. Wellesley, had landed that morning, but, finding the battle actually begun, and ignorant of the nature

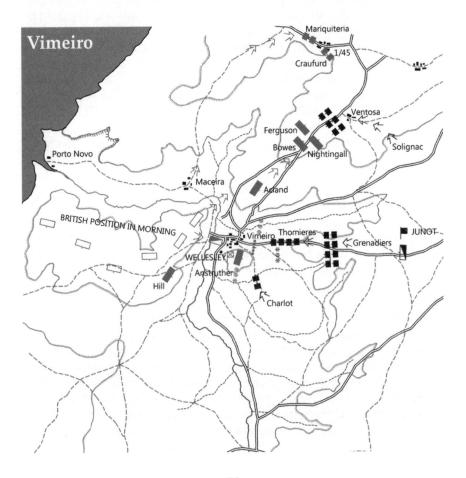

of the ground, he very handsomely placed himself under the orders of his junior. At the close of the action I was witness to the following scene, being on horseback by the side of Sir A. Wellesley. He rode up saying, "Sir Harry, the enemy is beaten at all points, our men are fresh, having been attacked on their own ground; not half of them have been engaged; we can be in Lisbon before the enemy."

'A pause of about ten seconds ensued. Burrard had his Adjutant-General on one side, and his Quartermaster-General on the other. The Adjutant-General first said, "A great deal has been done, Sir Arthur"; the Quartermaster-General then said, "A great deal has been done, Sir Arthur"; and Burrard then said, "A great deal has been done, Sir Arthur." It was decided that nothing more should be done, and the most glorious of triumphs was wrested out of the hand of the conqueror. There can be no doubt that we could have been in Lisbon before the French Army, and what would have become of them it is not easy to say. They would not probably have surrendered, but, having left their baggage in Lisbon and lost most of their cannon on the field of battle, not half of them would have escaped over the frontier of Portugal.'[90]

And so the British Army camped on the field of battle. Looking back at the event later in life, Douglas rued the British inability to pursue a beaten foe compared to the French. 'We know that the Englishman is a stronger, more manly, better-fed animal than the Frenchman,' he wrote ruefully, 'and he has proved these advantages from the days of Crecy to those of Waterloo! Why is it that in pursuing his enemy he cannot accomplish what the Frenchman does? Why is it that a delicate girl who can scarcely walk two miles, can dance for six hours and tire a strong man? She is a creature of excitement. In like manner the Frenchman in pursuing.'[91]

---

[82] Wellington's Dispatches, Vol. 3, p.80.

[83] Edwards, p.50.

[84] 1935 Regimental Annual, p.190.

[85] The account of Roliça is based upon accounts of the battle in Weller and Edwards.

[86] A volunteer was a young gentleman short of the price of a commission serving in a regiment as a private (but messing with the officers) without rank or pay until a vacancy arose due to death.

[87] WO12/5727.

[88] One of which was Portuguese.

[89] The French wore white linen coats against the Portuguese summer and their blue uniforms rolled atop their packs.

[90] 1938 Regimental Annual, pp.218-9.

[91] ibid, p.220.

Chapter 6

A Piece of Plate

The morning after the battle, the disillusioned Captain Douglas was given another assignment, one which caused him some embarrassment. He was ordered to go on board of a line-of-battle ship off the coast and enquire whether any tidings had been received of Sir John Moore, who was expected with 10,000 reinforcements to form the backbone of the army for the conquest of Spain. He was informed by the captain of the ship that Sir John Moore's force had not been seen anywhere off the coast. Returning on shore to make his report, he found Sir Harry Burrard and Sir Hew Dalrymple (who had lately arrived to supersede Burrard) dining with Sir Arthur Wellesley, and, being ushered into the room, delivered the message he had received from the Captain of the ship. 'I was struck with the remarkable sensation this message appeared to cause,' Douglas later said, 'and was followed by a couple of A.D.C.s out of the room, who exclaimed, "How could you give such a message before the French General Kellerman?" [sic] to which I replied "How could you allow me to go into the room to make a report without informing me there was a French General there?" The English Generals took this view of the case but nothing could be more unlucky than my report, for Kellerman had been sent in by Junot to make what afterwards became the Convention of Cintra, and the speedy arrival of Sir John Moore with a reinforcement of 10,000 men had been strongly urged upon him.' To further defend his position, Douglas added: 'Kellerman was a little man with a broad Alsatian face, and in a blue great-coat, whom one might see fifty times without suspecting him to be a General.'[92]

Notwithstanding this faux pas, a 'Definitive Convention for the Evacuation of Portugal by the French Army' was signed by Quartermaster-General George Murray for Britain, and Général de Division Kellermann for France on 30 August, by which time Sir John Moore's force had landed. But Murray was acting under the orders of the timid Lieutenant-Generals Burrard and Dalrymple; Sir Arthur Wellesley was largely a bystander. All the places and forts in the kingdom of Portugal, occupied by the French troops, were to be be delivered up to the British Army in the state in which they were at the period of the signature of the Convention. All French troops were to evacuate Portugal with their arms and baggage; they would not be considered as prisoners of war; and, on their arrival in France, they were to be at liberty to serve again.[93]

The British public was outraged when news of the Convention of Cintra reached home. Wellesley had twice defeated the French, only to have 25,747 of them repatriated home with all honours of war at the British taxpayer's expense. Burrard and Dalrymple were eventually recalled and never again held active commands. Some of the mud stuck to Wellesley also, who sailed home in disappointment on 20 September, later to be castigated in the street and in the grounds of Chelsea Hospital.

The Army probably did not expect to see Wellesley again. After all, Lieutenant-General Sir John Moore had arrived, a popular 46-year-old Glaswegian who stood fifty places higher than Wellesley on the seniority list, and most probably expected him to assume overall command once the disgraced Burrard and Dalrymple were shipped home.

The 45th marched north on 27 August to Sobral de Montegrace (modern Sobral de Monte Agraco) in rolling farmland about 20 miles north of Lisbon in the Torres Vedras mountains, leaving two companies left behind at Vimeiro, probably to guard the lines of communication to the landing-place at Porto Novo. On 1 September the number of men sick in hospital had risen to 120, and four serjeants, five drummers and 171 men were detached 'on command',[94] most of these being in two companies at Vimeiro. The second battalion men who had arrived just before Vimeiro had arrived poorly equipped for campaigning, being deficient in equipment, camp kettles, and arms; therefore headquarters no doubt felt it best to put the battalion 'out to pasture' for a period to allow it to re-equip and train the new men.

In a General Order of 5 September, temporary commander-in-chief Lieutenant-General Sir Hew Dalrymple re-brigaded his army, the 45th being moved to Major-General William Carr Beresford's brigade in Lieutenant-General Wellesley's 4th Division. Dalrymple was recalled to England on 17 September and resigned the command to Burrard. On 25 September Lieutenant-General Sir John Moore received the overall command, and Burrard was made commander of the garrison in Portugal. He in turn was recalled to England on 1 November and replaced by Lieutenant-General Sir John Francis Cradock. Taking the offensive to the French, and with the promise of aid from his Spanish allies, Moore advanced into Spain on 27 October at the head of 21,000 men, leaving part of the force – including the 45th – behind in Portugal.

Captain James Douglas went along as an aide-de-camp. 'He was the beau-ideal of a Commanding Officer,' he later wrote. This was from an intelligent young officer who also counted Wellesley as a friend, so his comparison is interesting: '[Moore was] a more imposing man than Lord Wellington, [but] he had not his genius, nor the same habit of seeing the right thing to do, without apparently giving himself much trouble to find it out. 'Describing the two men to a French officer, [I] said, "*Monsieur veut dire que l'un avait plus d'inspiration, l'autre plus d' instruction*". [With one we had more inspiration, the other more instruction.]'[95]

Not that any of this command comparison meant much to the men in the ranks of the battalion. They were to stay behind in Portugal, there was a job for them to do, and the Light Company under Captain Greenwell was the one to do it.

Fishing for Pilchards

The Light Company was selected to receive the surrender of the French garrison at Peniche, some twenty-six miles north-west of Sobral. The garrison turned out to be Swiss rather than French, six companies of disaffected red-coated mercenaries who had love for neither the French nor Portuguese. Captain Greenwell received the sword of the battalion commander within an ancient circular fort perched atop a rocky headland with all the dignity required of such things, after which his company escorted the Swiss south to Lisbon.[96]

The rest of the 45th moved into Peniche in late September, which they found a pleasant, if windy spot. It was a town of about 5,000 inhabitants connected to the mainland by a sandbar, completely surrounded by heathland. The principal industry was pilchard fishing. By 1 October the whole battalion was there, less one company (probably Greenwell's) 'on command' in places such as Torres Vedras, Lisbon and Caldas and strangest of all, on the tiny island of Berlenga Grande about ten miles offshore. But the number of sick had increased again, to 174 men; perhaps spiced pilchards did not suit the Anglo-Irish constitution. Whilst at Peniche the battalion suffered the loss of a further ten men due to sickness (the majority being recently arrived second battalion men, rather than Buenos Aires veterans); and lost its first deserter on campaign – Private Michael Reilly from Captain Lightfoot's company.

Sometime in early November, new Ensign Hans Stevenson Marsh arrived to join the 45th. He was the middle son of the Reverend Jeremy Marsh, Rector of Mountmellick, Queens County in Ireland, and had attached himself to the 32nd Foot as a volunteer hoping for a leg-up to ensign once the casualties started. Another new arrival from the second battalion on 23 December was Ensign James MacPherson, a determined and fiercely independent 18-year-old from Laggan, the youngest son of Lachlan MacPherson of Ralia, Deputy Lieutenant of Inverness-shire. He was sent to fill the late Ensign Dawson's position in Captain Gregory's No.10 Company. On 29 December the senior Lieutenant James Campbell was officially gazetted captain, which would effectively put an end to his role as adjutant (since captains were needed to command companies), but not for a little while yet.

With the departure of Sir John Moore's column and Sir Harry Burrard, there was a command vacuum for a few weeks until the arrival of Sir John Francis Cradock on 14 December. Cradock, a 49-year-old scholarly and warm-hearted Irishman, known to the Army as 'Beau', was a better administrator than front-line commander, and his brigadiers found him pessimistic and slow. He was left to his own devices in Portugal with less than 9,000 British troops. Just across the frontier, Napoleon commanded 127,000 veteran Frenchmen marching on Madrid; Soult had 25,000 men in the Asturias; Victor was at Madrid with maybe 20,000 more. Cradock kept eight battalions at Lisbon (2/9th, 29th, 3/27th, 2/31st and four King's German Legion battalions) together with some cavalry; three battalions, including the 45th, were ordered northwards to Oporto; the 1/40th Foot went to Elvas. He spread his troops as thinly as he dared and relied upon his cavalry screen to be the trip-wire in the event of a French advance.[97]

The left wing of the 45th under Major Patton marched into Oporto on 19 November, followed by the right wing under Major Gwyn two days later. They were placed in a new brigade under Brigadier-General Alan Cameron alongside the 1/82nd Foot and the 97th Foot. Cameron was another Scotsman, a 55-year-old laird and outspoken eccentric who had raised the Cameron Highlanders at his own expense; and a man who strongly believed in the merits of Highlanders over Sassenachs. The sick had reduced to a mere 38 men but 328 men were on command – 157 at Lamego, 81 still at Peniche and 74 at the battalion depot in Ireland.

Six companies moved to the ancient fortress town of Almeida sometime around mid-December, about the time that Moore wrote to Cradock and asked if he might take the 45th and 82nd with him into Spain. Lieutenant-General Cradock agreed and intended to send Cameron's brigade across the border. However the 45th was still too widely dispersed and only the 82nd Foot were available to send; they managed to break through to Moore's forces at Salamanca,[98] and so the 45th missed the Corunna campaign – luckily for them, or their war might have looked very different.

The 45th celebrated their first Christmas on campaign at the Misericórdia church across the square from the barracks in Almeida. They had seen two battles, but only lost a handful of men, were yet to fire a shot in anger and were comparatively safe and warm against the Portuguese winter behind the walls of a fortress city and dispersed villages. Little did they know there were five more Iberian Christmases to come.

---

[92] ibid, p.219. Kellerman spoke fair English, hence the consternation.

[93] The wording of the convention is from *Wellington's Dispatches*, Volume 4.

[94] 'On Command' was a catch-all term for men detached on anything from manservant duty to baggage guard.

[95] 1938 Regimental Annual, pp.219-0.

[96] Not that the Swiss would have enjoyed this liberty. They were mercenaries and therefore out of work.

[97] Cradock details from Burnham and McGuigan, pp.61-4.

[98] Although as we shall see in the next chapter, they may have taken a company of the 45th with them.

Part III

1809

Chapter 7

Sleeping Under the Stars

William Brown, a 19-year-old former weaver from Kilmarnock in Ayrshire, volunteered to join the 45th from the Argyle Militia on 7 April 1809 for limited service (which in his case was seven years). Volunteers cited various reasons for moving from the relative safety of the militia to the uncertainties of life in the regulars. In Brown's case, an order was read one morning on parade, intimating that 'all those who wished to extend their service, had now an opportunity of gratifying their honourable intentions, as a number of volunteers were wanted for the regular army; that now the road to preferment was open to all young men, ambitious of serving their king and country in a just and necessary war.' Brown had found twenty months of static outskirts garrison life in the militia tedious in the extreme and so stepped forward. 'Although I had no thought of, or even a wish for preferment, I had, as already hinted, been long resolved upon leaving the militia. I therefore volunteered into the 45th regiment, then serving in Spain, but which had a second battalion recruiting in England.'[99]

After surviving a rugged boat ride from Aberdeen to Newcastle-upon-Tyne he joined the second battalion at Nottingham in May 1809 and observed that 'the regiment I had now joined was composed of a heterogeneous mass of old men and boys, all either English or Irish, with the exception of one man, who was a countryman of my own. Being generally illiterate, and consequently ignorant, I found little pleasure in their company. Their whole conversation was on eating and drinking, and their amours, which were mostly carried on with profligate and abandoned women. I therefore associated little with them.'[100]

Brown also found little positive to say about the officers. 'The Colonel, being a member of the legislative assembly of the empire, was often absent; and, no doubt, in his senatorial capacity, deeply engaged in business of vastly more importance than drilling a few boys.' The command devolved upon Major George Purdon Drew, 'under whose fostering care, and, I am sorry to say, the battalion did not seem to make much improvement. The

61

major, I believe, had seen a deal of service, but, strange to tell, had yet much to learn ... he seldom or never knew when any manoeuvre was done right; but by instinct, for I hardly think it was by acquired knowledge, always found out when it was wrong.' As to the good major's physical bearing and appearance, 'The major was a man pretty far advanced in years. He might have been an efficient officer in his day, but was at the period I am speaking of, in no way calculated to command a regiment. In his person, he was long and lank, and had such a portion of anxiety depicted in his face, but I never beheld him without remembering the Knight of the Rueful Countenance.'[101] In fact Major George Purdon Drew was, at the time, only about 36 years old and recently married, having served in the regiment for sixteen years, including the assault on Buenos Aires. No doubt he only appeared old to the teenaged and inexperienced Brown. His bumbling drill technique was perhaps preferable to the alternative – a certain something offered by the arrival back from his 'senatorial' duties by the commander of the second battalion, Lieutenant-Colonel the Honourable John Meade.

'I had been a short time in the Regiment when the Colonel, the Honourable J(ohn) M(eade), assumed the command, and under his administration I found things no better; indeed, it was like getting out of the frying pan into the fire: for, while the same course of discipline was carried on as before, the disposition of the commander seemed to be tinged with a sanguinary hue, being nowise loathe to distribute a few hundred lashes among the boys, in the morning, by the way of letting them know that they were free-born Britons, and in the service of Old England.'[102]

The Honourable John Meade was the son of the first Earl of Clanwilliam, the younger brother of General Robert Meade, and a Member of Parliament for County Down from 1805 onwards.[103] He had nothing in common whatsoever with the junior officers and men of the 45th and gives the impression of having endured his military career as a necessary evil on the road to a high government appointment, or perhaps as a way of keeping up with his older brother.

William Brown was typical of the many recruits received by the Army in 1809; physically he was five-foot-six tall, with a dark complexion, long face, blue eyes and brown hair, almost generic in most respects for someone of an English or lowlands Scots background. He had volunteered from the militia, as had 23,884[104] other militia-men that year, spurred on by the successes at Roliça and Vimeiro. Some 328 men from the Derbyshire Militia volunteered for the regular army in April 1809 alone, with the 45th being one of the most popular destinations. Militiamen were considered a superior class of recruit, being men who had experienced the military life for a time and were committing to make it a long-term career; they also came partly-trained. The second battalion of the 45th had, on 1 April 1809, an effective strength[105] of 592 men, of whom 351 had volunteered from the English militia, and 241 from the Irish militia. It was probably less of the 'heterogeneous mass of old men and boys' that Brown described, although a number of them were certainly present. In the years to come the second battalion would produce many fine front-line soldiers for the first battalion, hence their destiny is entwined with this story.

Private William Brown volunteered from the second battalion into the first for active service on 27 August 1809, thus joining two serjeants and ninety-four other privates from the second battalion volunteering for service abroad,[106] and commenced the long journey south. It would take them about six weeks to reach the first battalion in Portugal.

The headquarters of the first battalion 45th was still safely holed up in Almeida on New Year's Day 1809. This being the frontier, companies were widely dispersed to act as outposts. Captain Coghlan's company was at Lisbon, the companies of Captains Smith and Lightfoot at Oporto, whilst a detachment under Major Patton was still at up-river from Oporto at Lamego.[107] Interestingly, two officers, Captain Francis Drew and Lieutenant Bob Hardiman, together with two serjeants, two corporals and 55 privates, are shown in the returns as 'detached with Sir John Moore's army'. Captain James Douglas was also so engaged, being on the staff. It is unclear how Drew's men came to be separated from the rest of the battalion. One possible explanation is that Captain Drew's No.8 Company was detailed to accompany a baggage-train of stores and medical supplies sent into Spain bound for Moore – the Grenadier Company of the 3rd Foot is also known to have accompanied this train – and somehow become separated, thus involuntarily joining the column bound for Corunna. Proof of Drew's company's presence at Corunna is explained by the award of the clasp 'Corunna' to the General Service Medal awarded to Private James Talbot of Captain Drew's company in 1847, the only man among the sixty-three-man detachment to gain the honour.[108] In fact Captain Drew experienced some trying times on the road to Corunna, if the charges that were later laid against him at his court-martial are to be believed:

'1st. That Captain Drew did, on the 4th January, 1809, at, or near Los Benos, in Spain, behave in a manner highly disorderly and unofficerlike, in addressing Lieutenant-Colonel Peacocke (then commanding a detachment of the British Army employed on a particular service, to which he, Captain Drew, belonged,) in a peremptory and disrespectful tone … 2nd. That Captain Drew did, on the 4th day of January, 1809, at, or near, Los Benos, in Spain, begin and excite a mutiny in the detachment of the British Army, under the command of Lieutenant-Colonel Peacocke, consisting amongst others of part of the 45th Regiment of Foot, to which Captain Drew belonged.'[109]

Lieutenant-Colonel Nathaniel Levett Peacocke of the 71st Foot was, at this time, merely a prickly Irish minor aristocrat who had great difficulty getting along with his peers, or in fact people in general. It would not be until December 1813 that he would create history by being the only British officer in the entire Peninsular War to be dismissed for cowardice. Los Benos is, in all probability, modern La Bañeza on the road between Astorga and Benavente, and further confirms that Drew and his 62 men were indeed caught up in the retreat with Sir John Moore's forces, although the date of 4 January is almost certainly in error, since the French were well and truly in possession of that town at that time, Moore's army being much farther to the north-west.

Sometime before 6 January, Lieutenant-Colonel Guard called all the outlying detachments of the battalion back to Almeida. On that day Brigadier-General Cameron once again led the 45th and 97th into Spain, but meeting a large party of convalescents from Moore's force on the road, he was advised that further advance was fruitless, since the French had possession of the road. Cameron sent the 45th on ahead to reconnoitre but the hopelessness of the situation soon became apparent; Lieutenant-Colonel Guard wrote from Torre de Mincorvo on 9 January passing on Cameron's instruction that the garrison of Almeida should destroy the store of shrapnel shells there and retire to Oporto and Lamego.[110] The 45th retired back into southern Portugal accompanying the band of stragglers 'committing every kind of excess' and lost two more deserters during this vain adventure. The weather was foul, the roads execrable and the men's shoes reached their effective use-by date. Once back safely inside Portugal Cameron organised two battalions of detachments from the sick and stragglers. The awful news of Moore's death and the evacuation from Corunna hit the British garrison of Portugal hard. Moore had been one of the idols of the Army and respected for his humanity.

But worse was the fact that the few battalions now remaining in Portugal were at the mercy of 350,000 Frenchmen. The coming of spring would no doubt see renewed action on the frontier and with less than 20,000 British and Portuguese troops as defence against potential invaders. Cradock drew the available forces into a tight arc around Lisbon and waited, wondering what the French would do next.

The Exploring Officer

To his credit, Cradock did not just sit back and wait. He enlisted officers who were fine horsemen, had some linguistic skill, and were able to express write or sketch clearly, as 'exploring officers'. Captain William Smith of the 45th seems to have been one of the first four officers so enlisted. Smith, a fifteen-year veteran of the regiment, was at the beginning of 1809 second-in-line for promotion to major. Like Gwyn he was a survivor of seven years' service in the West Indies, fluent in French and 'capable in the Spanish tongue'.[111] In his early thirties, he hailed from the border regions of Northumberland and Roxburghshire. He had purchased an ensigncy in the 45th on 26 February 1793, the month war was declared with France; and had risen steadily through the ranks; lieutenant in October 1794, adjutant in June 1798, captain in June 1803. He was a man who did things strictly by the book, but always with consideration of his men's welfare uppermost. It was Smith who had been sent out from the Residencia on 7 July 1807 to negotiate for provisions; his facility with Spanish, natural intelligence and military bearing suited him for such tasks. These qualities would not go unnoticed in 1809.

Given an officer caught behind enemy lines out of uniform could be shot as a spy, most wore their uniforms while they went about their tasks. Smith appears to have undertaken his first 'mission' between 20 and 31 January for which we have details from his diary: '21st January 1809. An officer who had been at Corsa five days ago reports that no French were in the southern parts of Spain ... 23rd January – An officer arrived from Carsen yesterday at 2 p.m., and reports there had arrived in that place two couriers from Truxillo, bringing intelligence that a division of the French, consisting of 4,000 cavalry and 2,000 infantry with 30 pieces of cannon, passed on the 20th the bridge of Almaraz ... 24 January – they likewise remark that the French were briskly opposed by the Spanish troops, which prevented the French entering the town ... 31 January – arrived at Lisbon – called immediately on General Cradock and made him acquainted with the purport of my journey. The information I gave him respecting the enemy he had never heard of, and expressed himself pleased with my conduct.'[112]

Down in Lisbon, news arrived from Oporto on 1 February that Sir John Moore had been killed and Sir David Baird and Lord Paget badly wounded, and that part of his army had been embarked, after which the enemy forced his entrenchments and killed and took prisoner a very great number. Some in Lisbon gave little credit to the news. The news feed was bolstered on 5 February by an account 'setting forth that they fought on the 15th, 16th and 17th, were successful for some time but ultimately forced to retreat with the loss of a great many men, all the dragoon horses and artillery, and that Sir J. Moore was killed, also Brigadier-General Crawford and many general officers badly wounded – this news is believed by General Cradock.' Further, but still not quite accurate news arrived on 11 February. 'The news by the packet last night confirmed the death of Sir J. Moore and the fall of that army; but our loss appears not to be so great as first reported. Altogether on the three days they did not lose more than 5,000. The artillery and the greater number of dragoon horses were embarked. It is said Sir John Moore was killed on the beach on the 17th by a cannon shot. Sir D. Baird mortally wounded and Genl. Crawford killed.' After the above, Captain Smith observed that 'Sir John Cradock is in good spirits, from which it is supposed he has had good news from England, probably being allowed to act with his troops in point of quitting this country as he may judge best.'[113] But Cradock did not quit Portugal. Smith received some fresh set of secret instructions from Colonel Rufane Shaw Donkin, Deputy Quartermaster-General dated 16 February 1809, of which the following bear repeating:

'Your object will be to obtain every possible information of the position, force and intention of the enemy in that neighbourhood ... You will avoid all political conversations or discussions – much mischief has been done by an indiscreet introduction and handling of these matters, but if anything is said on the re-embarkation of the English army at Corunna you may simply say that it was done with little loss, and with a view to carry the war into the south of Spain, where things wear a more favourable aspect.'[114]

This mission seems to have lasted from 18 February until early March, and covered much ground. Smith received to undertake a third mission in a letter from Colonel Donkin dated 1 April: 'Captn. Smith will of course use his utmost endeavour to obtain correct information as to the number and object of any corps of the enemy he may meet with, and will remain near Alcantara as long as he may judge it expedient to do so for the above purpose. As soon as Captn. S. has ascertained that the enemy's column has actually entered Portugal with a view really to penetrate, he will immediately return to headquarters and make his report.'[115]

So it was that Smith and three other officers operated as Cradock's eyes and ears on the frontier for the first half of 1809. Despite the later fame of Wellesley's 'Exploring Officers', it appears that Cradock started the system four months before Wellesley's return to Portugal, with Captain William Smith of the 45th as one of the early pioneers of the craft.

The Nursery
At the start of February the battalion was enjoying the fruits of the capital, Lisbon. It was situated on the right bank of the Tagus, near its mouth, which formed a fine harbour; and stood chiefly on precipitous hills, the highest of which was occupied by the castle of Saint George. The ancient city still exhibited marks of the terrible earthquake which had almost completely destroyed it in 1755. The great squares contained some magnificent edifices, 'noteworthy for the fineness of their pillars'. The streets were narrow and winding and dirty, worse since the French had left the city in a desolate state; notwithstanding 'the general view of the city and its environs from the harbour at a distance was very beautiful, the sides of the hills being clothed with plantations and numberless vineyards, and the buildings extending for a mile and a half or two miles along the coast'.[116]

The number of sick in the 45th had fallen away to a small number again and 246 men were detached as garrisons of nearby towns. By March the battalion was up-country again, cantoned between Lamego and Almeida, less the sixty-three men gone to England or who-knows-where with Moore's force, and less one company at Oporto.

There were some changes in the 45th at this time: Captain James Dawes Douglas, back in England having survived the retreat to Corunna, took his leave of the 45th and officially transferred to Portuguese service in February. Fellow Scotsman Lieutenant Alexander Martin got his vacant captaincy, and Captain Edward Scott command of his No.2 Company. Ensign Ralph Ousely joined No.8 Company from the second battalion, having finished his year at the Royal Military Academy; he was the son of a distinguished family from Dunmore, County Galway. Recent arrival Lieutenant William Persse's start was inauspicious; he got involved in an affray in Lisbon during the night of 3 March, which somehow resulted in the death of a local. Persse was twenty-four, a rector's son from Tynagh in County Galway, and a charge of murder of manslaughter would result in a difficult letter home. Luckily a regimental court-martial on 15 March found him blameless.

It was an eventful twenty-four hours on the 15th, for that night something else untoward happened in the 45th. Lieutenant Edward Keating, when subaltern of the picquet, allegedly used abusive language towards his superior officer, Captain Lightfoot of the 45th, at that time commanding the said picquet. He was court-martialled at Camarata on 21 and 22 March, found guilty and sentenced to be cashiered.[117] A private would have felt at least 300 lashes whilst tied to the Three Sisters for such behaviour. But Lieutenant Keating got a tongue-lashing instead, and the ignominy of being sent home in civilian clothes and at his own expense, the purchase cost of his commission forfeit; Ensign Francis Andrews was duly promoted to the vacant lieutenancy in No.1 Company.

Was Lieutenant-Colonel Guard losing control of his junior officer corps? Certainly six months of garrison duty seems to have made them bored and cranky. Guard's cause was not helped by the loss of Major Andrew Patton, who went home in poor health at the end of March (shortly to retire from the Army), leaving William Gwyn as the only major – and of the senior captains, the battalion had already lost James Douglas, John Payne, Francis Drew and Aeneas Anderson. The number of sick was on the increase again also. The battalion needed something to do.

The French under Maréchal Nicolas Jean-de-Dieu Soult duly obliged by invading Portugal again in March and swiftly capturing Oporto, although the Spanish managed to delay them at the border-posts of Ciudad Rodrigo and Badajoz. The 45th marched out of Lisbon on 22 April, headed north. If the battalion needed a further fillip, it came the following day with the news of Lieutenant-General Wellesley's arrival at Lisbon with 7,000 reinforcements. Cleared of any stain from the Cintra Affair, he was now back in Portugal as commander-in-chief and wasted no time in re-organising the troops at his disposal. By a general order issued from Coimbra on 4 May the 45th found itself officially joined with the 3/27th and 2/31st in a brigade under Major-General John Randoll Mackenzie, yet another Highlander known simply as Randoll to his friends, aged about forty-five, mild-mannered and friendly in contrast to the loud and opinionated Cameron.

The other battalions were all new arrivals symptomatic of the new regiments being sent to Portugal in the wake of Corunna – second and third battalions originally intended as training units suddenly thrust into the front line, filled with callow youths and men previously thought 'worn out'. The same general order also directed that light infantry companies belonging to, and the riflemen attached to, each brigade of infantry were to be formed together on the left of each brigade, under the command of a field officer or captain of light infantry.[118] The 45th being the only tried battalion in the brigade, it was only natural that it provided the commander for this light infantry detachment, and so Captain Leonard Greenwell assumed a role he would fulfil with distinction for much of the war.

Major-General Mackenzie had a few days previously earlier received various orders from Wellesley: 'The corps of troops placed under your command is destined to watch the movements of [Maréchal Victor] the enemy on the Eastern frontier of Portugal, and to guard the passes into this country on the right of the Tagus, during the period that the main body of the British army under, my command will be employed on the Douro.'[119] In addition, Wellesley attached eleven battalions of Portuguese infantry, five squadrons of Portuguese cavalry and some militia to Mackenzie's 'corps'. Thus the brigade went on outpost duty on the frontier, guarding the bridges of the Upper Tagus against invasion by the French whilst the other seven brigades in Wellesley's army tangled with Maréchal Soult at Oporto; the 45th spent the month in cantonments at Vila Velha, about a hundred miles north-west of Lisbon, less than ten miles from the Spanish frontier.

On 24 May the lives of the officers was suddenly made more bearable. The Commander of the Forces felt disposed to supply the army with tents from the public stores, in the proportion of one tent for each field officer, and one tent for the officers of each company, and one for the staff.[120] There was no such luck for the other ranks, however, who continued to sleep under the stars, and would do so until very late in the war. Life was indeed tough for a ranker, and the discipline of the army was under question, as demonstrated in this order from the Adjutant-general dated 29 May:

'The Commander of the Forces is much concerned to be obliged again to complain of the conduct of the troops; not only have outrages been committed by whole corps, but there is no description of property of which the unfortunate inhabitants of Portugal have not been plundered by the British soldiers … The Commander of the Forces … therefore desires that the soldiers of every company, in each of the regiments, may be formed into as many squads as there are Non-commissioned Officers, each squad having in it one Non-commissioned Officer, who must be responsible for the conduct of the soldiers in his squad. The Non-Commissioned Officers must always be quartered with the men of their squads.'[121]

Companies already had platoons (half-companies)[122] and sections (half-platoons) which were vital to British Army formation, drill and manoeuvres. However, what Wellesley was authorising was a more informal internal structure - a company might have four sections but six or seven NCOs - that placed responsibility for the squad (maybe ten men) upon the NCO at all times, not merely at drill. It was a change in military thinking that sounded good in principle – but would it work?

[99] Brown, pp.35-6.

[100] ibid, p.43.

[101] ibid, pp.43-5.

[102] ibid, p.46.

[103] Evidently he never spoke in Parliament, despite serving for eleven years.

[104] This in fact was more than was raised by ordinary recruiting.

[105] Effective strength was rank-and-file only. Typically another thirty or so officers and about seventy NCOs would need to be added to the total.

[106] ibid.

[107] WO17-57; 1923 Regimental Annual, pp.108-9.

[108] 1923 Regimental Annual, p.110.

[109] Collection of the Charges, Opinions, and Sentences of General Courts Martial, pp.312-4.

[110] Wylly, p.145.

[111] From Smith's service record in WO25/748.

[112] 1929 Regimental Annual, pp.177-9.

[113] ibid, pp.179-80.

[114] 1930 Regimental Annual, pp.189-90.

[115] 1930 Regimental Annual, pp.190-1.

[116] The Autobiography of Sergeant William Lawrence, Chapter VI.

[117] Collection of the Charges, Opinions, and Sentences of General Courts Martial, p.309.

[118] General Regulations and Orders, p.205.

[119] *Wellington's Dispatches*, Vol. 4, p.265.

[120] General Regulations and Orders, p.289.

[121] *Wellington's Dispatches*, Vol. 3, p.258.

[122] Although companies at low strength usually reduced themselves to a single platoon, otherwise the sections became impracticably small.

Chapter 8

Into Spain

Captain Francis Drew, back in England after the retreat from Corunna, finally faced the general court-martial that had been looming since January. It started on 3 June at Chelsea and continued intermittently until 15 June. He was found guilty of the first part of the first charge, that of insubordination, but not guilty of inciting mutiny. Nevertheless, Drew was dismissed from His Majesty's service.[123] Francis Drew was not a novice officer, and had not fallen out with Lieutenant-Colonel Peacocke on a whim. True, they had probably both been tired and emotional on or about 4 January 1809, and by his record Peacocke seems to have been a man undeserving of respect; nonetheless, Drew was dismissed, and the 45th, and the army, lost a good company commander. Or did it? One Francis Drew was gazetted 2nd lieutenant in the 3rd Ceylon Regiment in March 1810, then promoted to lieutenant without purchase in the 2/48th Foot on 22 June 1810. This Francis was killed in action at Albuera on 16 May 1811, and we are left wondering whether the youngest of the four Drew brothers died on a battlefield, rather than in disgrace.

Speaking of which, Andrew Patton's resignation from the Army about this time meant that Francis's elder brother George Purdon Drew from the second battalion was now the second-most senior major in the regiment and therefore due to transfer to the first battalion, leaving Thomas Forbes and whoever filled Patton's vacancy to serve with the second battalion.[124] According to the rules, Captain Andrew Coghlan, as the senior captain, was to be offered the vacant majority but he obviously refused (or more likely could not afford the price of purchase) since William Smith, second on the list of captains, purchased the majority on 13 July. Thus Coghlan was leap-frogged, just as Gwyn had been by Guard. And so the best trainer of men in the regiment started to cast around for a vacant majority without purchase and found one in October, in the 2nd Garrison Battalion, a strictly no-frills no-glory unit of semi-retirees. It was a great loss to the 45th, for they lost two good company commanders in the process, making six in total since the landing in August. As for Smith moving to the second battalion as his junior place on the list of majors required – well, Wellesley knew a good officer when he saw one, and so some time later he ordered Smith to serve with the 1/45th in Spain even though officially rostered to the 2/45th. That 'Knight of the Rueful Countenance' Major George Drew would have to stay at home.

For Want of Money

New company commanders were needed and consequently found. With Captain Scott and Lieutenant Persse delayed at Lisbon (effectively under house-arrest), Scott's No.2 Company went to a newly-arrived officer from home, Captain Charles Huson, a 26-year-old from Castlebridge in County Wexford, the son of a former commanding officer of the Wexford Militia. Alexander Martin got James Douglas' vacant captaincy without purchase in March and took over No.4 Company from David Lecky, who moved across to command the Grenadier Company. Lieutenant Brinsley Purefoy was also elevated to captain on 20 July, and took over Captain Drew's No.8 Company. At the start of June the 45th was in the mountains behind Castello Branco and en route to occupy Alcantara, a town recently occupied by a French patrol until the retreat of Maréchal Soult had hurried their retirement. The brigade had not received pay for some weeks, and Mackenzie wrote to Wellesley in early June stating a 'general distress for want of money'. Wellesley reassured him with the comment that 'all that comes shall be given to your corps'. The army as a whole was two months in arrears and in debt to the tune of £200,000.

On 15 June a fourth battalion was officially added to the brigade, the 2/24th, although in reality this green unit had been serving with Mackenzie's brigade since the end of April. Three days later a famous order came down from the adjutant-general's office at Abrantes, ordering the formation of four divisions, with Mackenzie's brigade being the senior (or right) [125] brigade in the 3rd Division. On 21 June another order came down that all officers currently on leave in Lisbon were to return to their units forthwith, and even Blind Freddy could see that a campaign was imminent; a theory supported when on 26 June the troops received four day's supply of bread. On 25 June the battalion received a draft of one captain, one ensign, two serjeants and 131 privates from the second battalion,[126] the first sizable batch of fresh faces since leaving Cork eleven months before, which increased the battalion strength to over 900 men. New arrival Captain Archibald McDonald had left a young Irish wife behind in England, the daughter of the rector of Mellow in County Cork, and was an organised young man with a particular talent for staff work. Ensign James Miles Milnes was Captain George Milne's younger brother, a smart teenager from Stirlingshire with anxious parents at home. Back at full strength, the battalion was primed for the coming campaign.

The advance started at dawn on 27 June. The columns marched at two-and-a-half miles per hour, stopping for ten minutes every hour and a half.

The advanced guard crossed the Spanish frontier at Zarza La Mayor on 2 July. The 45th were in the advanced guard, together with the 2/24th, 2/31st and 2/87th and the 88th regiment under the command of Major-General Mackenzie, with five companies of the 60th Rifles. The commander of No.9 Company, Captain Thomas Lightfoot described the advance in a letter home dated 9 July and written from near Plasencia: 'You will see by the address of this that we have entered Spain once more. I hope we may meet with a more honest reception than the unfortunate Sir John Moore's army met with; at least, let us not again be sacrificed by traitors, nor led into the snare or imbecility of our agents of the Junta; at present we have had no reason to complain. It is true we have found none of that enthusiasm for the cause so sung in our ears by the English news-writers. We have heard no bells nor shouts of Viva! But I believe at bottom the people are not sorry to see us. We have found a sensible improvement in the country and people since we left Portugal.'[127]

The British and Spanish armies united near Oropesa (about eighteen miles east of Talavera) on 20 July. The forces of Maréchal Victor were unsupported and so the French fell back behind to a position east of the Alberche stream, where General Cuesta suddenly refused to co-operate with Wellesley. The Spanish eventually followed Victor but got a bloody nose for their troubles; for Victor was a bold general, quick to see and strike a weak point. He would put that talent to good use in the next few days.

Crisis at the Casa de Salinas

As part of the advance guard of the army, the 45th was amongst the first troops to pass through Talavera. Captain Lightfoot wrote that 'we arrived at Talavera, a large old town, which the French had nearly destroyed by converting every house into a barrack … here we learnt that the enemy occupied a position behind the River Alberche, where he had long lain encamped, and meant to give us battle. Their force was estimated at about twenty thousand. It was Sir Arthur's intention to have attacked him here early in the morning of the 23rd, but our want of bread delayed our advance from Talavera about six hours.'[128]

The battalion was mustered the following day and found to be weak in officers, only twenty-five being present for duty. Of those absent, Captains George Miles Milnes and Edward Scott were at Lisbon, as were Lieutenants William Persse, Bob Hardiman and Theo Costley, the second having just arrived back from England; whilst Captains Francis Drew and John Payne were in England, the former in the process of being dismissed from the service and the latter still unable to join due to his wound.[129] A whole clutch of officers from the second battalion were either on their way or still serving in England. The other ranks mustered 756 effectives and 116 men were on the sick list; the battalion strength was therefore 183 men more than on 25 August, due to the addition of the second battalion men in June.[130]

The brigade then marched on eastwards, crossing the Alberche stream on the Madrid Road about four miles east of Talavera, and bivouacked for the night, not having sighted a Frenchman all day. The Spanish Army was separated from the British and was left to pursue the enemy to Toledo alone. On the morning of 26 July a cannonade was distinctly heard in their camp; consequently about midday they were ordered to fall back on a small village on the road to Toledo, where the French had had part of their late camp, in order to cover the retreat of the Spaniards, who were in full retreat, not without considerable disorder.[131] That the French liked to live comfortably when on campaign was becoming obvious to the British, especially Lightfoot; 'There we remained on the night of the 26th, occupying the huts built by the French, and excellently thatched with the finest ripe wheat I almost ever saw, and accommodating four thousand troops, the thatch being nine inches thick.' Such admiration could not last. 'The following morning, 27th July, the enemy, strongly reinforced, came down on our outposts, and the whole advanced corps immediately got under arms.'[132]

What happened was this – before daybreak on 27 July, the Spanish corps under Capitano-General Gregorio Cuesta crossed the Alberche with its tail between its legs, having been routed by Maréchal Victor's advancing French corps at Torrijos the day before. The British division of Lieutenant-General John Coape Sherbrooke followed them across, leaving Mackenzie's two brigades and the light cavalry brigade of Brigadier-General Anson as the rearguard. The 45th joined the other battalions of the brigades (2/24th, 2/31st, 2/87th and 1/88th) in setting fire to the line of low huts built by the French on the eastern side of the stream, before crossing the fords at Cazalegas in the bright summer sun whilst the smoke from the torched huts blew in their direction. They fell back about a mile to a ruined villa known as Casa de Salinas (House of Salt) deep in wooded countryside, surrounded by scrubby olive and cork trees.

In the afternoon the men sought shelter from the fierce summer sun in the shade of the olives and corks whilst the French crossed the stream, muskets held aloft due to the water up their armpits, under the cover of the smokescreen, watched by – or rather not be seen by – a token picquet on the British side. Général de Division Lapisse had twelve battalions in the woods between the Casa and the stream before the alarm was even raised. Lieutenant-General Wellesley and his staff were unfortunately in the tower of the ruined Casa ostensibly to observe the movements of the French when a sudden burst of shouting, hoof-falls and popping of musketry caused him to train his telescope quite close and to his left, where the all blue-clad 16e Léger burst out of the woods and pushed Mackenzie's picquets back, bayoneting drowsy prone redcoats as they went.

Wellesley and his staff tumbled down the turret stairs and bounded to their horses to beat a hasty retreat, as French light troops appeared in almost every direction. Mackenzie's four battalions posted farthest forward, the

2/24th, 2/31st, 2/87th and 1/88th were (in the case of all but the 1/88th) untried units, lying in bivouac with arms piled and camp-fire burning. They melted away in the face of the large crowd of French skirmishers. In a few minutes ninety-three men were captured, and Wellesley only just made his escape, stopping to rally the 2/31st as he rode westwards.

Disaster was averted by the steady behaviour of the 45th, which stood firm on the right flank; a fortuitous position that placed them farthest from the initial French attack, and therefore with the most time to prepare some sort of defence. With the help of several companies of the 5/60th on their left they provided a solid mass of formed infantry on which the fleeing troops could rally. Anson's light cavalry (23rd Light Dragoons and 1st Hussars of the King's German Legion) arrived in support as the brigade started to withdraw westwards; the French responded by bringing forward two batteries of horse artillery to harass them.

Lieutenant-Colonel Guard was hit in the thigh by a marksman's shot and was badly wounded; command of the 45th passed to the ill Major Gwyn,[133] who split the battalion into two parts to facilitate a rapid retreat, six companies under his command retiring due westwards to the centre of the British line, whilst the remaining four companies under Major William Smith fell back somewhat south-westward, towards the town of Talavera itself. The adjutant of the 45th, James Campbell later wrote about events that day: 'Some young corps were surprised, and consequently did not behave well. Lord Wellesley himself, if I mistake not, and some of his staff were placed in a very perilous position in an old house.'[134]

The rearguard action at the Casa de Salinas on the 27 July cost the 45th Lieutenant-Colonel Guard and another four wounded, two men killed and seven captured. The battalion got off fairly lightly compared with other units in the brigade; the 2/87th lost 198 men and the 2/31st 119 men, out of a division total of 442 men. Gwyn's six companies retired with the rest of Mackenzie's brigade to a position on the plain about a mile-and-a-half north of Talavera, about a mile too far south to be involved in the confused events of sunset when a French division surprised four British brigades enjoying their evening meal high up on the Cerro de Medellin – Maréchal Victor's audacity yet again – and Major Smith's four companies found themselves jumbled in the pell-mell retreat of the Spanish towards their position in front of Talavera, and so could not re-join the rest of the battalion until daylight on the 28th.

It had been a bad day for Wellesley's army. Two-thirds of Mackenzie's advanced guard was sent helter-skelter in their first encounter with the French; French casualties had been inconsequential; and as at Roliça nearly twelve months before, British obstinacy had been bested by French dash and manoeuvrability.

With Lieutenant-Colonel Guard out of action, command devolved upon Major William Gwyn. Gwyn had started his military career as an ensign in

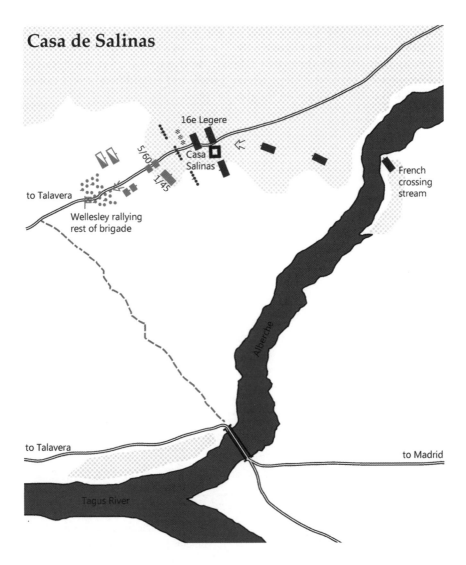

Casa de Salinas

16e Legere

5/60th

1/45

Casa
Salinas

to Talavera

Wellesley rallying
rest of brigade

French
crossing
stream

Alberche

to Talavera

to Madrid

Tagus River

the 45th foot in August 1788, making lieutenant two years later. He served in the West Indies, in 1794 volunteering to command a company under Sir Charles Grey at the reduction of the Islands of Martinique, St. Lucia, and Guadaloupe, somehow survived the fever, and returned to England in May 1794. He obtained a company in September 1795, and again served in the West Indies, being employed as an assistant engineer on Dominica. After his escapades aboard ship returning to England (see Chapter One) he rejoined the 45th in January 1802. In February 1804 he embarked for the West Indies for a third time employed as brigade-major with Brigadier-General Montgomerie. He returned to England a major in May 1805, bearing dispatches from the Commander of the Forces. He joined the 1/45th battalion in Ireland in October 1805, and served in the Buenos Aires expedition in 1807. By the eve of Talavera he was a twenty-year veteran of the regiment, a man who knew his craft well, and would need every ounce of skill and determination on the day to come.

---

[123] Two other officers, Captain John Balderson of the 4th Foot and Captain James Payler of the 52nd Foot, were slapped over the wrists for the same incident.

[124] This is how the seniority system worked; the most senior of each rank for the first battalion, the most junior for the second.

[125] The senior brigadier in any division commanded the right-hand brigade, that being the position of honour. More of the seniority system at work.

[126] Derived from WO25/1275.

[127] In fact the 60th were officially the Royal American Regiment of Foot, but contained a high proportion of Germans.

[128] Wylly, p.160.

[129] Payne died from his wound at Land's End in June 1810.

[130] Based upon WO12/5728.

[131] Wylly, p.161.

[132] ibid.

[133] Major Gwyn had left his sick-bed to be present at the action.

[134] Campbell, p.133.

Chapter 9

Talavera

Talavera (or Talavera de la Reina to give the town its correct title) was built on a low plain, extending about three miles in breadth, having a range of hills on the right and left. The plain was covered with a plantation of olives, stretching lengthwise for a great distance. Wellesley's right rested at Talavera and the hills overlooking it, his left on a height commanding the greater part of the field of battle, and the centre was covered by the plantation of olives on the plain. The front line was an open space which had been a cornfield of near two hundred yards in breadth, and stretching nearly to the hills on both sides, beyond which was another wood of small oaks, which covered the centre of the French line. The French force consisted of between forty and fifty thousand men commanded by King Joseph in person. The British had not more than twenty thousand, together with a force of Spaniards, principally cavalry.[135] Talavera, the ancient capital of ceramics, had much suffered from the passage of the French. Most houses were deserted, their contents souvenired or broken up for heating fuel. The magnificent Plaza de Toros was desolated. The cathedral was intact, but the French had taken all objects of worship; the church of San Antonio had been converted into an infantry barracks.

Dawn rose on 28 July and it looked like another hot day. It revealed more than 46,000 Frenchmen on the olive-covered plain opposite. At 5 a.m. a lone French cannon shot signalled their attention to attack that day, and the solo round was followed by an immense cannonade from eighty large calibre pieces, eight- and twelve-pounders, whereas Wellesley had only perhaps two dozen guns able to return fire, mostly of small calibre.

Mackenzie's brigade, with the 45th in the centre, was positioned in the second line behind the brigade of Guards, just to the south of the Cerro de Medellin. Cannonballs occasionally passed through the line of the brigade, and the battalions were ordered to lie down. The artillery fire subsided at about 7 a.m. and the day descended into a lull at the southern end of the line, whilst both sides removed their casualties and made their breakfasts as best they could. The French were renowned for not being a morning

77

army and could not seriously contemplate an assault without a full repast. However things had been hot at the northern end of the line, up on top of the Medellin, where General Hill's division had put Général de Division Ruffin's French division to flight. Sometime in the morning a Spanish division under General Bassecourt was sent from behind Talavera to a position behind the British northern flank, and Captain Smith's wing of the 45th seems to have gone with them; for Hill called on the 45th's support at some point in the action, although there is no indication that they were engaged in combat. This northern action was invisible to the rest of the 45th, but quite audible. Forty minutes of action were followed by two hours of armistice as both sides retrieved their wounded, and Captain Smith's four companies re-joined the rest of the battalion in the centre of the line.

At about 2 p.m. the cannonade recommenced, the heaviest the British troops present had ever experienced. For thirty minutes they hugged the earth (although some brigades, such as the Guards, refused to stoop so low) and were grateful when the sound of artillery subsided and was replaced by the sound of rattling drums and distant cries of 'Vive l'Empereur!' An attack was brewing to the right of Mackenzie's men, against the brigades of Campbell and Kemmis, and Mackenzie sent the 2/24th down on their left in support. Two assaults by the French (actually German and Dutch troops allied to the French) were driven off by these brigades and an emplacement of artillery on their right, the 2/7th and 2/53rd being especially conspicuous in the action.

Both French flanks had advanced and failed; but at 3 p.m. the attack came in the centre, by 15,000 troops of Général Lapisse's and Sebastiani's divisions. To hold it back was a thin red line of brigades on the west bank of the Portina Brook, and Mackenzie's brigade of two battalions (less the 2/24th, lent to Campbell) plus two dragoon regiments in the second line. It was twenty-four French battalions in dense columns against eight British and King's German Legion battalions in line.

However, the French formation allowed no room for deployment into line, whilst the temperament of the Guards facing them allowed no room for preliminaries such as musket volleys. The Guards advanced to within a hundred yards of the French column and then broke into a bayonet charge. The French were mainly veterans, but no troops in the world at that time could withstand a bayonet charge delivered at speed and in a disciplined line, and the French clambered over each other in the desire to retire. Sebastiani's column evaporated. The Guards pushed on wildly, supported by the King's German Legion troops on their left, who at least had bothered to fire at the French first before charging. But both brigades lost all formation in their charge across the brook, and then ran up against a second column advancing behind the first. Strung out and disordered across the plain, the two British brigades made a wonderful target for all the French artillery in the vicinity, and especially the prowling French cavalry half-a-mile to the east. French dragoons harried the Guards and fresh French troops cut off the KGL, who lost nearly fifty percent casualties in twenty minutes. The Guards retired as a milling crowd, pursued by French officers waving their men on shouting, 'Come, my children, they are our prisoners!'.

Suddenly there was a large hole in the middle of Wellesley's line. The 2/24th had occupied the ground where the Guards had started, but they were now the only formed troops between the French and Mackenzie's brigade farther back. The retreating Guardsmen ran through and around the 2/24th and the 45th in turn, and re-formed in the rear 'with great alacrity'. The 2/24th fell back to form a line with the 2/31st and the 45th, who now had the grand spectacle of over 10,000 French troops from the reformed French columns advancing head-on towards them. In support, they had only the 14th and 16th Light Dragoons to guard their flanks, and the 1/48th Foot (one of Wellesley's favourite units) double-timing down from the Cerro de Medellin on the left as a backstop.

Mackenzie formed his three battalions as a solid line, the 2/24th on the right, the 45th in the centre, and the 2/31st on the left. Captain Lecky's grenadiers were on the right of the 45th, in contact with the 2/24th, whilst Captain Greenwell pulled his light company back to join the main line of the 45th on the left flank. A French brigade was marching directly towards them, six battalions of noisy blue-coated infantry, the 32e and 75e Ligne in front, drums rattling out a beat the British already called 'Old Trowsers'. Each battalion was a block of men fifty files wide by nine ranks deep, three battalions in the first line and another three in the second.

Behind the 45th, serjeants marched up and down behind the second rank, exhorting the men to keep eyes front, and to wait for the command. The men stood silent, their muskets loaded and ported (held upright, thumbs ready to pull the flint back) and sweated in the hundred degree heat. A few fumbled for canteens. The French were two hundred yards away. Majors Gwyn and Smith rode up and down behind the line. 'Steady, men,' they said. Fire on the command. Not much longer now. The French were a hundred and fifty yards away. A few premature shots rang out from the French line, but did no damage, aimed much too high. The French were a hundred yards away. Major Gwyn rose up in his stirrups, roared, 'Volley fire by the right. On the command!' and raised his sword. Up and down the line serjeants barked orders and the ported muskets dropped into the fire position. 'Aim low, lads!' the corporals yelled, and the line of muskets dipped slightly. The French were at eighty yards. Every company commander, eyes focused on Major Gwyn, waited for the signal. The major's sword arm dropped, and the battalion commenced a rolling volley from the right, the grenadiers firing first, then by each company sequentially down to the light company on the left. The French instantly disappeared behind a pall of grey smoke and a torrent of shrieks and yelling. The men of the 45th reloaded as fast as they could, biting and spitting the paper away from the foul powder and ball cartridge, ramming the ball and charge down the barrels of their Brown Bess muskets. Every man knew that the French response would follow, so they all stood as side-on as possible to minimise their size. Then it came; a blast of musketry, hundreds of orange muzzle-flashes through the smoke, and twenty men in the front rank went down. Drummers pushed through the rear rank to grab wounded men and pull them to the rear, but the men were reloaded, and the order came again; firing by the right.

And so the process was repeated, another rolling volley, and many more shrieks from the French, invisible other than by their muzzle flashes. Then came the order: Fire at will. So the 45th continued the process like automatons: fire, ground musket, retrieve cartridge, bite, spit, load, ram, cock, present, fire. After twenty rounds their shoulders were bruised black, their faces sweaty and grimed like trolls, their mouths parched, coughing in the clouds of acrid smoke. Behind the line, serjeants paraded up and down, pushing men from the second rank into gaps created in the first. There was no wind, so the powder-smoke hung low and did not disperse. At some point a French battalion worked its way into the gap between the left wing of the 45th and the right of the 2/31st (perhaps unseen in the smoke) but Captain Greenwell, as alert as ever, wheeled the three left-hand companies left-about to pour a volley directly into their flanks, at which point they retreated.[136] On the right, Captain Lecky seems to have led a party of grenadiers to see off some Frenchmen who had worked their way into the gap on the right of the battalion, was cut off and was captured.

Major-General Mackenzie was killed early on, being close enough to the action for heroism but not far enough away for tactical overview, or continued existence. Major Gwyn was hit three times (officers on horses being easier targets), twice in the torso and once in the upper arm;[137] this put Major Smith in command, the battalion's third commander in two days. Serjeant-Major Pilling also went down, hit in the back whilst talking to Major Smith, but not seriously.[138] Through the smoke the French columns were seen inching back, then shuffling, then running, leaving the ground dense with blue-coated bodies. 'Cease fire!' came the command, and oddly there is no record of a bayonet charge having taken place. Almost immediately every man of the 45th would have reached for his canteen, taken a long swig, and many would have poured the contents over their heads. Each man had fired more than fifty rounds. The ground behind the battalion was littered with groaning wounded men, as Surgeon Boggie and his assistants started to inspect them to choose the most critically injured for immediate attention. It had been Peninsula warfare at its ugliest, a taste of things to come at Albuera (and Waterloo), a clear signal of the superiority of two-rank line over dense column when the line refused to budge. Some seventy-four of Mackenzie's heroic brigade were killed, 519 were wounded

Talavera

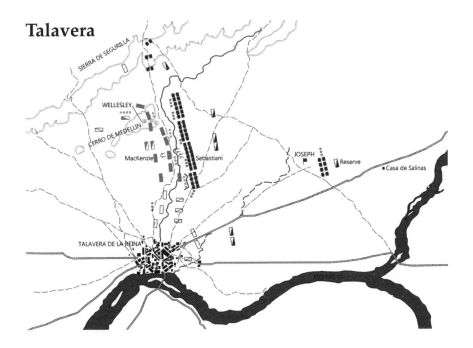

and thirty-nine missing; the 2/24th on the right of the brigade were particularly hard-hit. The 45th's losses for the day were nine men killed and Major William Gwyn, Lieutenant John Robinson, Lieutenant John Cole, Ensign James Miles Milnes and 133 men wounded, while Captain David Lecky and thirteen men were missing[139] – and all within a twenty minute period. Sebastiani's division had lost four Colonels, seven out of twelve battalion commanders, seventy officers and 2,100 other ranks; they had suffered three times the casualties as the brigades opposed to them.

The 1/48th filled the gap previously held by the King's German Legion and repulsed another assault by Gènèral Lapisse's division and the battle died down to a fitful skirmish, leaving all to retrieve their wounded and dispose of the dead. The French retreated that night, their losses being seventeen guns and more than 7,200 men. British losses were 5,363 killed and wounded, more than at any other battle since Malplaquet, almost exactly a hundred years earlier. Amongst the slightly wounded was Lieutenant-general Wellesley, hit and bruised in the collar bone by a spent musket-ball. Another few feet per second and a slightly higher trajectory, and the rest of the war might have looked quite different.

The morning after the battle bugle blasts announced the arrival of Brigadier-General Robert Craufurd's Light Brigade, marching into camp having marched forty-two miles in twenty-six hours in a vain attempt to reach the army in time for the battle. The same day, Lieutenant-General Wellesley composed his dispatches to send home.

'The Commander of the Forces returns his thanks to the Officers and Troops, for their gallant conduct in the two trying days of yesterday and the day before, in which they have been engaged with, and beaten off the repeated attacks of, an army infinitely superior in number...

'He had opportunities of noticing the gallantry and discipline of the ... 45th on the 27th ... and he requests their Commanding Officer(s) ... Colonel Guard ... to accept his particular thanks.'[140]

Unfortunately the 3rd Division was leaderless,[141] and so could not submit an after-battle report; therefore the 45th, 2/31st and 2/24th did not rate a mention for their valiant actions on 28 July, actions which were not witnessed by Wellesley himself. The actions of the previous two days were far less invisible to Surgeon John Boggie and his two assistants, John Mousdale and Robert Chambers. The 45th had just fought its first big battle and the medical staff was swamped by the 146 wounded. Wounds ranged from the very slight to amputations.

Private James Clifford, a 19-year-old tailor from Tipperary had to be held down as his right leg was amputated at the thigh; the whole process was then repeated on the left leg of another 19-year-old, Private Thomas Clifton from Doddington in Lincolnshire, usually without washing the instruments in between. Both had just fought in their first and last battle. Try imagining you are the patient, fully conscious and without the aid of anaesthetic whilst the operation is performed. Imagine as well that you are nineteen years old, away from home for the first time – in a foreign country for only a few weeks – and lying in a dirty cottage in one hundred degree heat. Also imagine that the whole procedure is rushed, since there are many, many, more awaiting attention. Those waiting must have included 21-year-old Private Zachariah Smith from Belper in Derbyshire, almost blinded in both eyes, probably from a shell-blast; and Serjeant-Major Pilling, hit between the shoulder blades – but obviously not seriously, since he was back in the ranks in August. Most of the wounds were in the extremities, the result of un-aimed musket-fire through dense smoke, and many had to wait twenty-four hours or more for treatment. Many of the lightly-wounded dressed each other using their spare shirts as bandages.

Ten Days' Bread
In the aftermath of the great battle the supply system collapsed completely. Wellesley, close to the end of his tether with his Spanish allies, wrote on 31 July: 'It is positively a fact, that during the last seven days the British Army have not received one third of their provisions, and that at this moment there are nearly four thousand wounded soldiers dying in hospital from want of common assistance and necessaries, which any other country in the world would have given, even to its enemies.'[142] With a major victory in the bag, the troops were buoyant, even if their commander was not. But there had been no pursuit of the defeated French; nearly two-thirds of the

British troops were engaged caring for the sick and wounded, whilst the supporting Spanish appeared indolent and disorganised. On 2 August Wellesley received news that the French had taken Plasencia, cutting his shortest east-west communications route with Portugal. Whilst the Spanish General Cuesta made all sorts of madcap plans for the ongoing campaign, Wellesley drew plans for a retreat to the west, since the defence of Portugal was always his main priority. Otherwise his army was 25,000 men adrift in Spain surrounded by ten times his number of Frenchmen.

The British marched before dawn on 3 August, leaving the wounded behind in Talavera in the care of the Spanish. Perceiving the threat to be to the north, they crossed the Tagus and passed through Almaraz on 6 August. The road taken was across country, and so bad that they were 'obliged to employ pioneers and strong working parties to enable us to get on. From these unavoidable causes and delays, our marches on many days did not exceed ten miles, and our provisions became very limited.' The weather turned nasty. 'We had much rain, and our men suffered much from sickness, fevers, agues, and dysentery; the latter was much increased by the quantity of raw Indian corn and wild honey which the country produced, and which the soldiers consumed in spite of every threat and order to the contrary.'

With Lieutenant-Colonel Guard left wounded at Talavera, command of the battalion officially passed to the wounded Major Gwyn, who delegated command to the less experienced Major Smith. On 3 August 1809 the 3rd Division marched to Almaraz via a mountain road, and Paymaster Dalhunty was ordered (presumably by Major Smith) to leave the camp in charge of a large sum of money received the night before from the Paymaster-General. However he soon disappeared and did not re-appear until 24 August, at which time he was placed under house arrest. He found himself in front of a general court-martial at Badajoz a month later, and found not guilty of of the first part of the charge preferred against him, for absenting himself from his regiment without leave, on the grounds that that he was sanctioned in so doing by his Commanding Officer. However he was found guilty of the latter part of the charge preferred against him, of proceeding to the rear without leave.

The 3rd Division reached Puerto de las Casas near Almaraz on 5 August, and stayed there until 21 August, suffering terribly from starvation and sickness. Most regiments had barely received ten days' supply of bread in the past month. Part of the problem seems to have been camp-followers. On 23 August orders came down that officers commanding divisions and brigades should prevent the women, and followers of the army, from buying up the bread which was prepared for the soldiers' rations; and also that the women of the army should be prevented from purchasing bread in the villages, within two leagues of the station of any division of the army. Any woman found with bread in her possession, purchased at any place nearer than two leagues, was to be deprived of the bread by the provost or his assistants. Women disobeying the order would not be allowed to receive rations.[143] The fact that the women may have been buying the bread for their soldier husbands was obviously beyond the grasp of army logic!

The brigade then marched as far westwards as Portalegre before a staff blunder was noticed and the troops recalled to Campo Mayor, a fifty mile run-around that cost the starving division many additional sick and exhausted men. On 25 August at Arroyo the 45th mustered 505 effectives with 340 men on the sick list, an increase of 224 men in the past month, a high-water mark for the entire war. Some 140 of the sick were men wounded at Casa de Salinas and Talavera, the rest those ailing from the harsh conditions of the campaign and an enemy far worse than the French – Guadiana Fever.

Something Extraordinary Had Happened

The wounded of Talavera – from both sides – had been herded into the town of Talavera on 29 July to find shelter from the harsh summer sun. The 45th's future brigadier, Captain and Lieutenant-Colonel Henry MacKinnon of the Coldstream Guards, was ordered to take charge of the wounded on 1 August. He noted that the sick were principally placed in the large convents of the town, and some in deserted houses. As far as he could calculate, the number of men, attached, and forming part of this hospital, could not have been far short of 5,000. On 2 August the departing Wellesley gave MacKinnon command at Talavera, 'and that he had desired Gen. Cuesta[144] to communicate confidentially with me'. At eleven o'clock on 2 August General Cuesta told him that Soult, with 85,000 men, was at Plasencia, and Victor only six leagues in Cuesta's front: he would retire at dusk with his army, and MacKinnon 'had better get off with the hospital before that time'. MacKinnon had to move quickly. 'I assembled the officers and surgeons doing duty with the Hospital, and informed them, that all the men who could march were to assemble at three o'clock, and were to march to Calera that night: With difficulty I procured seven waggons from Gen. Cuesta, to carry off a few wounded men and officers and at five o'clock the rearguard left the town. I left it myself at eight, passing through some thousand Spaniards who were making off.'[145]

Those too wounded to move – 1,500 or more men, a number which included Lieutenant-Colonel Guard, Lieutenant John Cole and fifty-four men of the 45th – were left behind at Talavera. The precipitate evacuation of the town was followed by two days of eerie quiet, then a more leisurely occupation on 6 August by Maréchal Victor's French corps and their vastly superior medical services; thus were a good many lives saved, but at the cost of five years in captivity. The before-mentioned amputees Clifford and Clifton were amongst the prisoners.

MacKinnon's miserable column continued its agonising retreat to the south-west. The first night they got to Calera, a town which been completely destroyed by the French. MacKinnon had been furnished with forty bullock-cars to transport the sick, but such a state were the roads in that only eleven of them arrived at Deleitosa.[146] The view from the ranks was more directly painful; The road to Oropesa was covered with our poor, limping, bloodless soldiers. On crutches or sticks, with blankets thrown over them, they hobbled woefully along. For the moment panic [and] terror lent them a force inconsistent with their debility and their fresh wounds. Some died by the way, others, unable to get further than Oropesa, afterwards fell into the hands of the enemy.'[147] Doctor Boggie and his surgical staff of the 45th were detached from the regiment and active with this column. Corporal Thomas Barker from the Grenadier Company was one of the poor, limping bloodless soldiers who died during the retreat on 8 August. MacKinnon's column of 2,000 convalescents eventually arrived at Elvas on 18 August, having covered 184 painful miles and lost 500 men in fourteen days. They often say that the victors are often more disorganised by a victory than the vanquished are by defeat, and this was certainly true of Wellesley's army after Talavera.

[135] Wylly, p.162.

[136] ibid, p.158.

[137] From Gwyn's service record in WO25/745.

[138] From Pilling's service record in WO25/805.

[139] Wylly, p.160.

[140] *Wellington's Dispatches*, Vol. 3, p.376.

[141] So heavy were the senior officer casualties in Mackenzie's brigade that it was commanded at the end of the battle by a major – Thomas Chamberlain of the 2/24th Foot.

[142] Wylly, p.163.

[143] General Orders and Regulations, pp.321-2.

[144] General Cuesta was commander of the Spanish corps at Talavera.

[145] MacKinnon, pp.36.-7.

[146] ibid, p.37.

[147] Wylly, p.163.

Chapter 10

Let Loose From a Cage

The French entered Talavera on 6 August and commenced plundering the town – Maréchal Victor usually turned a blind eye to any such excesses. However they showed considerable sympathy to the British wounded in the town, even handing out ransacked mattresses and blankets to the convalescents. The greater majority of the wounded were in the convent. Victor gave strict orders to his troops to treat the prisoners of war (PoW) civilly, and not to steal, but to pay for anything bought from the captives. The convent was constantly crowded with French soldiers come to get a sight of the British wounded, and to purchase any shoes which might be surplus to requirement after men died. Rations came the next day, three pounds of coarse bread for every eight men, and a very small quantity of beef to make bouillon – without salt or vegetables. Local villagers – who had pleaded complete scarcity of any provision when the Allies were around – miraculously produced white bread, fruit and wines for the town market once money was circulating. On 15 August the French artillery fired a *feur de joie* to celebrate the birthday of Napoleon. A few days later fever decimated the wounded prisoners and carried off great numbers. The 1,500 captives were getting thinned rapidly by death and desertions; some had been able to escape, but many were caught.

In order to stop the leakage, all who could walk (about 500) were mustered and forty cartloads of wounded were sent off to Madrid. The arrival of the prisoners in the capital excited much interest and more than a few instances of kindness from the local population, most of whom had never seen a British soldier; the prisoners were sent to the Puerta del Sol, a spacious square with many streets leading from it. Crowds of people gathered round, asking questions and giving out bread and money, until the French drove them off with the butts of their muskets.

Once in Madrid the wounded were placed in a convent, to be treated by Spanish surgeons and nurses; other ranks went into a French prison to be fed brown bread and water; the officers were granted parole and therefore free to move about the city. The allied victory at Talavera had caused a sensation in Madrid and the locals made every effort, usually clandestine, to shower the prisoners with comforts and money. After ten days the PoWs were joined by 500 Spanish PoWs and marched to Segovia. The British prisoners were sickened by the random executions of Spanish PoWs who could not keep up with the pace of the march; some thirteen were shot by the French in the fifty-seven-mile march between Madrid and Segovia, whereas British stragglers were usually just given some encouragement by musket-butt. In the latter place the prisoners received even greater kindnesses from the local population that at Madrid, if that were possible.

On their second day in the town, King Joseph of Spain (the 40-year-old elder brother of Napoleon) arrived with his retinue. The church bells rang out, but the local population stayed stolidly indoors and silent. After three weeks in that place, and being joined by another party of PoWs from Madrid, the contingent was marched north to Valladolid, where the prisoners received a muted welcome from the local population; apparently the populace had already been severely punished for assisting in the escape of thirteen stragglers from Sir John Moore's army a few months prior. It seems that Colonel Guard was with this contingent, for Sir Robert Wilson (a British officer commanding Portuguese regiments on the frontier) unexpectedly received a letter from Guard, escorted through the French lines, dated 17 September, wherein Guard informed Wilson that most of the British officers left behind at Talavera had recovered from their wounds. He also mentioned that local commander Général de Division Francois Étienne de Kellermann (the man James Dawes Douglas had described as 'un-general-like' at Vimeiro) had received those passing through Valladolid 'with the greatest kindness and attention'.[148]

On 18 September the PoW contingent marched out of Valladolid bound for Bayonne. That night they camped at Seveco (modern Cevico de la Torre) where Private Hugh Martin of the 45th and three companions made their escape.[149] Martin, a sandy-haired 26-year-old Buenos Aires veteran from Enniskillen, followed a serjeant of the 3rd Foot Guards and two privates, struck out westwards, and received exceptional kindness and guidance from Spanish locals. Fearing that the French had moved into northern Portugal, the locals guided the escapees towards the remnants of La Romana's Spanish Army at Astorga, where they had dinner with the Governor on 1 October and received a military escort to Corunna. From that port they were able to escape to Britain aboard the frigate HMS *Arethusa*. The four men later attributed their success to the fact that the guerrillas so completely controlled the countryside the French would not venture far out of their camps and barracks; the quartet had walked nearly 300 miles across open countryside without seeing a Frenchman. Hugh Martin later re-joined the 45th in Portugal during 1810, and served on until 1813.

Maréchal Edouard Mortier, at six-foot-six the tallest and probably most decent of Napoleon's marshals, and the only one who could speak English (fluently but slowly; he was from Calais and his mother had English friends and relatives who visited often) attended the hospital at Talavera on 4 November. He told the remaining prisoners he was sorry it was not in his power to supply them with many things they needed, but while bread was to be available for his own troops they should be first served; that the French had served them better than their own army had done, in leaving them in the state they found them; for the Spaniards, being their friends, could have provided the means of transporting the wounded if their commanders chose; but instead of this they had been left a burden to the French. However he also warned that many British prisoners had made their escape, and some had been shot – and if any were caught in future a mile from the town they might expect to be served in the same manner.[150] On leaving he gave the guards 160 doubloons to purchase wine and food for the use of the hospital, although how much of it went to that purpose is doubtful. The French veterans who had fought in the field were always noted as kinder and readier to assist the prisoners than young conscripts who had pulled guard duty.

On 9 November, with a Spanish siege force close, the French made to march out of Talavera at night; many of the prisoners, seeing the Spaniards so close, resolved to escape. However more French troops arrived from Madrid, and to close the flood-gates for once and for all, all British officers, doctors, and every man that was expected to live were turned out to the main square on the morning of 12 November, and were put on bullock-carts, and driven out of the town on the road to Madrid. They crossed the skeleton-strewn battlefield and the river Alberche, and reached the outskirts of Madrid on 15 November. Those who could were later marched or carted in stages to France, and moved about between various towns. Internment camps also existed, and common soldiers were usually pressed into service on French public or military works. The wounded were well cared for. Officers could be paroled or exchanged, however an obligation would be placed on the officer not to serve in a theatre of war for an agreed period of time. Usually captured British officers stayed in and around small French towns far from the front 'on their honour' until exchanged; captured French officers did the same in villages far removed from the south coast of England. Colonel Guard's column (less Private Hugh Martin and his three companions) marched from Valladolid on 18 September, and probably marched via Burgos, Vitoria, Villareal, Hernani and Irun to Bayonne. At night they would have been locked within barns to prevent escape; at the larger towns, the officers would have been allowed to move about after giving their parole. From there they would have marched across France to various towns in the north of France. The Napoleonic equivalent of Colditz was Verdun, the impressive fortress town about 140 miles east of Paris, far away from the English Channel and any hope of easy escape. The officers' quarters were quite comfortable and they were occasionally allowed to wander the streets of the town; evenings were spent in a Club Room with backgammon, chess and even English papers for entertainment. William Guard and a fellow captive, Thomas Gordon, a captain in the 3rd Foot Guards, arrived there on 3 November 1809.[151]

Most Un-Officerlike

The still-wounded Serjeant-Major Oswald Pilling was awarded a commission on 30 August, an ensigncy in the Royal Africa Corps,[152] and officially left the regiment on 4 September. It was the generally accepted practice that an NCO awarded a commission moved to another regiment, the view being that as a new officer he would find acceptance difficult amongst his former superiors, and so Pilling left the Peninsula to join his new regiment in England in November. His replacement was Nathaniel Carter from Captain Lightfoot's Company. Other changes around this time included the promotion of the former drummer-boy Campbell Kelly to paymaster-serjeant, after seventeen years' service with the regiment. Serjeants William Donovan, Richard McElligott, Thomas McInherney, Thomas Taylor, Joseph Wellon and James Yates were officially listed as prisoners of war on 8 August, although strangely no immediate action was taken to replace them. Lieutenant-Colonel Guard, Captain Lecky and Lieutenant Cole were also listed as prisoners of the French in the September return.

The battalion stayed at Campo Mayor during September and October, as the sick-list stayed unacceptably high – on 9 November the army had 9,100 sick (including wounded) out of 33,000 effectives. Sometime during the month quite a few prisoners somehow returned to the regiment (probably escaped from the convent), since on 25 November the number of prisoners was given as one officer (Guard), four serjeants, one drummer, one corporal and 55 privates. Miraculously, Serjeants Tom McInherney and Jim Yates escaped from the French and rejoined the battalion on Christmas Day, bringing the Light Company NCO numbers up to full strength.[153] They brought the news that Corporal Joe Swain from the Grenadier Company had died of wounds whilst in captivity.

Lieutenant Persse, exonerated at a regimental court-martial on 15 March, frustratingly found himself hauled up again, this time in front of a general court-martial[154] regarding his 'affray'. They found that 'no guilt attached to him, in as much as it appears he was extremely active, and did all in his power to quell the disturbance, and do therefore acquit him; which sentence has been confirmed by the Commander of the Forces'.[155] So, after six months of anxiety and isolation in Lisbon, William Persse was free to join his regiment again.

For victory at Talavera, Sir Arthur Wellesley was made a peer and voted the thanks of both Houses of Parliament. From now on he was Viscount

Wellington, or simply Wellington. But to the rankers he was still 'Old Nosey' or 'Our Attie'. If he had learnt one thing at Talavera, it was that the Peninsula would never be freed by the Spanish Army. It would require a much larger British Army, boosted by the emerging Portuguese regiments, and that would take much time and energy. The war would not be over by 1810, perhaps not even in 1811. More troops would be needed.

The Draft

Let us return to the 2/45th in Nottinghamshire. The number of serving officers at the time suggests that the second battalion did not have the full complement of ten companies – perhaps only eight – and with five captains absent on recruiting duty, much of the day-to-day supervision of the recruits was left to the lieutenants and ensigns. For a young officer, it meant considerable trial and error, with Serjeant-major Will Buxton on hand to offer them practical advice. But there was still Meade's unyielding discipline and Drew's shuffling; perhaps sick of this routine, 109 volunteers stepped forward whilst on parade in Mansfield on 27 August to join the first battalion in Portugal.[156] Amongst them was Private William Brown, the chronicler quoted previously. The volunteers were marched south to Portsmouth, taking ten days to get there; once at the harbour they were immediately put aboard boats and rowed out to the transport *Peace*. Once aboard the crowded stinking troop-ship, they were held in port for six weeks whilst numerous other reinforcements were loaded.

The hurry-up-and-wait of the process was part army muddle, part reluctance to have troops at a loose end about the town whilst they waited to go aboard ship. The day before sailing none other than Major George Purdon Drew joined them, bound for active duty. Hundreds of ships left Spithead on a sunny afternoon in early October, some bound for Lisbon, others the Mediterranean. Also aboard were Captain Oliver Mills and Captain Henry Dabsac, two very experienced second battalion men, Mills a 31-year-old married man from Coventry with a love of (but no especial talent for) landscape sketching; and Dabsac the son of a Dublin rector; also Lieutenant Francis Powell, a 27-year-old from the Home Counties who had enticed ninety-nine men to join the 40th Foot from the Bedford Militia in 1805, earning himself an ensigncy in that regiment as a reward. Having established a reputation for persuasion, he had spent the previous six months on recruiting duty with the 2/45th in England. Amongst the detachment were Volunteer Alexander Bell and Volunteer James Coghlan, serving as private soldiers, hoping for a vacancy in which to earn their ensigncies. Alex Bell was eighteen years old, without the money to pay for a commission, serving with the other ranks but messing with the officers, hoping for a vacancy to acquire and ensigncy. He did not have to wait for long; the exodus of so many officers in August and September created more than enough vacancies.

The reinforcements disembarked at Lisbon on 21 October 1809, and after eight days at Belem, crossed the Tagus and marched eastwards in the full blaze of a Portuguese summer, men dropping on the road as they marched. Two days later the draft passed a roadside bread-baking oven, at which a notorious thief, Thomas Horsley, encouraged some other men to tear down the oven and steal the bread. Major Drew rode up and had Horsley given to a provost-serjeant, after which he recompensed the Portuguese baker from his own pocket. Horsley was a known rogue, having received a hundred lashes for theft shortly before leaving Nottingham.

The draft arrived at Badajoz on 3 November, and marched to the 45th at Villa del Rey near Campo Mayor in mid-November, just in time to be part of the worst period of sickness experienced by the army during the entire war. Wellesley had congregated his forces within a bulge of the Portuguese frontier west of Badajoz, guarded by the Guadiana River.

Already weakened by the Talavera campaign – where poor rations and fatiguing marches had caused more damage than the French – the troops now fell prey to the Guadiana mosquito, which thrived in the damp and swamp river hinterland, spreading a disease which started as a cold shiver and grew to a raging malarial fever followed by almost complete debility for weeks. The fever had started to bite in the ranks of the 45th from about 11 September onwards, and continued unabated until Christmas. The army lost more than 1,200 men in November 1809 alone, and in excess of over 600 men per month for several months preceding and following. The 45th had 116 sick in July, peaked at 340 in August[157] and did not drop below 245 men until February 1810; twenty-nine died in October, forty-nine in November (fifteen alone dying in the second week of the month), and seventeen in December.

The situation was exacerbated by the fact that the army had detached a large percentage of its medical staff to treat the wounded after Talavera. New arrivals were especially susceptible. Private William Brown came down with the fever on his first day at Pinhel. It had been a long and fatiguing march, and being very hot when he got to his quarters, he stripped to his shirt and trousers, drank some water and sat down to rest himself. 'I was instantly seized with a fit of the ague, and after the cold shivering had left me, a fever ensued, under which I became delirious, and was carried to the hospital,' he later wrote. 'After being a few days there, I was sent, in company with nearly three hundred more sick belonging to the division, to the general hospital at Coimbra which march I will never forget … Having arrived at Coimbra, we were put into a convent, of the order of St. Augustine, where a staff-surgeon attended once a day. His visits, however, could have little influence on his patients, for in walking down the passage, on one side of which the sick were arranged like so many spectres, he seldom or never spoke, or even deigned to look at any of us, but passed on with as great majesty as if he had been a Turkish Bashaw. The general doctor, who appeared to be a humane and feeling man, and seemed to have our welfare at heart, sometimes visited the hospital. On such occasions, our friend, the stucco-man, as the patients called the staff-surgeon, was servile, even to meanness, making good the old adage, that he who is haughty and supercilious to inferiors, will, in the same ratio, be fawning sycophants to superiors.'[158]

The epidemic cost the army, between October 1809 and January 1810, nearly 3,800 dead soldiers, of which the 45th's share was 121 men listed as 'died in Portugal' on the muster-rolls. It was more than the total of British war dead since 1 August 1808, by a considerable margin.

Uniform Good Conduct

The men wore the same uniforms they had served in since (probably) the beginning of 1808, and were well overdue for the annual issue of new jacket and 'trowsers'. An order issued from Badajoz on 1 October 1809 confirmed that a new issue had arrived from England, although the means of conveyance required careful management; the staff had noted that the women of the regiments had come up from Lisbon along with the clothing, 'to the great inconvenience of the army and to their own detriment: and as they travel on the cars, they delay and render uncertain the arrival of the regimental clothing for the troops, and defeat all arrangements for bringing it up to the army.' the officers and non-commissioned officers coming up from Lisbon in charge of clothing were ordered to prevent the women from travelling on the carts.[159] Once again, the life of the army wives was made more difficult. This order was issued by a Colonel Peacocke – yes, the same Nathaniel Levett Peacocke who had caused Captain Drew to be court-martialled at the start of the year; he was now commandant at Lisbon. This order also confirms that the army wives were not present during the Talavera campaign, and seem to have spent the time at Lisbon – but were on their way back.

The good conduct of the 45th on campaign had not gone unnoticed by Wellesley. On 6 October, he generously wrote to the commander-in-chief: 'In consequence of the uniform good conduct of the 45th regiment since they have been under my command, I beg to recommend Lieut. Urquhart, the senior Lieut. of that regiment with this army, to the company in the 45th regiment, which the Commander in Chief has been pleased to appropriate for such Lieut. of this army as I should recommend. I beg also to recommend Ensign Ousely, the senior Ensign, to be Lieut. vice Urquhart.'[160] Outright recommendations like this were few and far-between; and so Urquhart and Ousely prospered by Wellington's hand. The Iron Duke has long been characterised as Spartan in his praise, but he knew and valued good men when he saw them, and he probably lifted more deserving officers and men to higher rank than he is given credit. Thus Urquhart was gazetted captain and Ousely – the Royal Military College graduate – lieutenant on 26 October.

On 29 November Captain and Lieutenant-Colonel (brevet colonel) Henry MacKinnon of the Coldstream Guards – whom we last met transporting the wounded after Talavera – was ordered to Wellesley's headquarters and there informed that he was now a colonel on the staff, and was to take command of Mackenzie's former brigade at Campo Mayor.

MacKinnon had been born in Longwood in Hampshire in 1773, studied mathematics and fortifications at the School of Artillery at Valence in France where he actually met Napoleon, then a young artillery officer serving with the La Fère Artillery Regiment, who sometimes visited his father William residing (at the time) in the Dauphiné.

He entered the army in May 1790 as an ensign in the 43rd Foot. He purchased a lieutenancy in April 1793, and after another six months at the hustings transferred to an Independent Company and then the Coldstream Guards as lieutenant and captain in October 1793, Some recruiting duty followed, but then he landed a role as brigade-major to Sir George Nugent in Ireland from 1795 to 1799, at which he saw service at during the '98 Rebellion. He accompanied the Guards to Holland in late 1799 to see his first real actions, at Bergen and Alkmaar on the Helder peninsula. On 18 October 1799 he purchased the rank of captain and lieutenant-colonel (a uniquely Guards rank that rated as a captain in the Guards but as a lieutenant-colonel in the line) and after a year of duty in London, sailed with the expedition to Egypt and fought with Abercromby. Four years later he served in the abortive expedition to Hanover and in Lord Cathcart's more successful expedition to Copenhagen.

The 45th got its first view of MacKinnon when he reviewed them at Salvaterra on 4 December; he was an immensely tall man for the time, six-foot-three tall with blue-green eyes, dimpled chin and a mane of dark brown curly hair that hung down over his forehead. Fluent in French, well-versed in history, mathematics, antiquities and fortification works, he was as much a scholar as a soldier. Being a Guardsman, MacKinnon was not familiar to the battalion's officers, but he seemed a decent enough chap; mild-tempered and amiable, a father to two small boys at home, with a particular love of antiquities and a fondness for riding off alone to explore historic sites. But like all Guardsmen, he was a firm believer in order and discipline.

In December three freshly-minted triple-barrelled ensigns, Edmund French Boys, John Evans Trevor and Robert George Sparrow joined the first battalion. Boys was a Dublin teenager at the start of a long military career, and Trevor a 19-year-old former subaltern in the Nottinghamshire Militia from Gainsborough in Lincolnshire. Sparrow was a Londoner with a daredevil spy-courier for a father; George Sparrow, who left Whitehall on 16 May 1807 with dispatches for Lord Pembroke at Vienna. Four months later he was attacked and stabbed at Cefalu in Sicily; his portmanteaus had gone and so had his dispatches. His sacrifice in the service led to a commission in the Army being given to his son by H.R.H. the Duke of York.

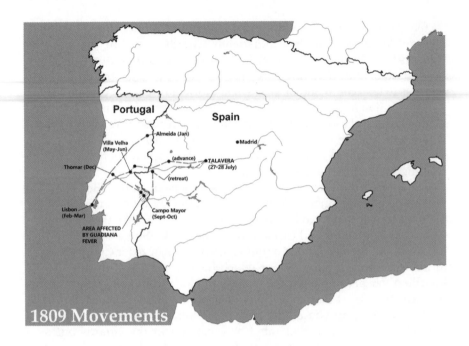

Portugal

Spain

Almeida (Jan)

Villa Velha
(May-Jun)

Madrid

(advance)

Thomar (Dec)

TALAVERA
(27-28 July)

(retreat)

Lisbon
(Feb-Mar)

Campo Mayor
(Sept-Oct)

AREA AFFECTED
BY GUADIANA
FEVER

1809 Movements

The 45th certainly needed as many officers as it could get as a trickle of men going home from August onward had now turned into a flood. Captains McDonald, Martin, Campbell, Coghlan, Drew, Purefoy, Gregory, Huson and Scott, and Lieutenants Phillips, Parr and Andrews had all departed since July. Lieutenant Richard Jones Colley was officially appointed adjutant on 28 December in lieu of James Campbell, the delay in appointment suggesting he had been actually undertaking the role for some time without official Army List approval. More and more the battalion was looking distinctly different to the one which stepped ashore on 1 August 1808.

On 18 December MacKinnon put his new brigade on the road for a lengthy march to Pinhel, some two hundred miles to the north. Marching was something every new recruit had to become inured to, but the 45th seemingly acquired a good reputation in this regard, for in the opinion of Ensign William Grattan of their brigade-mates, the 88th Connaught Rangers, 'there was that first-rate battle regiment, the 45th, a parcel of Nottingham weavers, whose sedentary habits would lead you to suppose they could not be prime marchers, but the contrary was the fact, and they marched to the full as well as my own corps, which were all Irish save three or four.'[161] To put this high regard to the test, the 45th joined the rest of the brigade at Portalegre and marched westwards through Abrantes to Pombal, then to Coimbra, where they spent New Year. One private, Michael Fahie, a 31-year-old former gardener from County Galway, took the opportunity

94

to slip away from the ranks. But even more controversially, so did Assistant-Surgeon Robert Chambers. Chambers, in trouble in May for striking a hospital orderly, had been absent in Lisbon since September and simply failed to return. Perhaps he did not wish to live through another Talavera. He was subsequently dismissed from the service (assistant-surgeons ranked as lieutenants, so as an officer in all but name he was spared the lash) and went home to Ireland, where he ended his days as assistant-surgeon to the Kilkenny Militia.

The battalion celebrated Christmas Day at Thomar, about seventy-five miles north-east of Lisbon. The number of sick was still high at 245 men, and the battalion had lost a further seventeen men dead from disease during the month – bringing the total to 121 in the last four months. The battalion's death toll from disease far outstripped the number of battle casualties from the three actions it had fought,[162] and would surely destroy the brigade – no, the division – unless the effects of Guadiana Fever began to subside.

---

[148] *The European Magazine and London Review*, Vol. 56, p.303.

[149] National Library of Australia, 20th Century British Newspapers Online.

[150] From Daniel Nicol's diary in *Napoleon at Waterloo and Other Unpublished Documents of the Waterloo and Peninsular Campaigns*, 1911.

[151] Register of British Officer Prisoners Held at Verdun 1804-1813, Napoleon Series.

[152] A regiment of mostly West Indian and African rank and file serving under British officers, designed for service on the west coast of Africa.

[153] WO25/1275.

[154] A general court-martial involved an officer being judged by higher-ranking officers not of his own regiment.

[155] General Orders, Vol. 1, pp.204-5.

[156] From WO25/1275.

[157] Which represented 37% of the battalion strength at the time.

[158] Brown, pp.57-9.

[159] General Orders, p.322.

[160] *Wellington's Dispatches*, Vol. 5, p.211.

[161] Grattan, Vol. 1. p.85.

[162] The battalion lost 163 men dead during the year, of which thirteen were killed in action.

Part IV

1810

Chapter 11

Bifes

The 45th found Coimbra a large and populous city, with a very fine ancient university, which appealed to the inquisitive and bookish Colonel MacKinnon. Then they marched on to Viseu, where the battalion was split in two due to the terrible state of the roads; half to go via Celerico, the rest via Trancoso. En route they lost the five companies of riflemen from the 5/60th, which were transferred to other divisions. The reduced brigade (45th and 88th) arrived at Pinhel on 11 January and the 45th was put into cantonment in a variety of local towns to the south of Pinhel, including Vascoveira, Manigoto, Pova de Concilia and Lameiras.

The men adjudged the villages labyrinthine and filthy, the peasants friendly but odd in their manners. Some men learned a rudimentary pidgin-Portuguese for transactions, whilst the locals called the men 'bifes'.[163] The troops relieved the boredom by swimming in the nearby River Pega; Sundays were enlivened by a divine service held by Major Smith on a green beside the village church in Manigoto, which the three companies stationed in the village attended in full marching order, after which they drilled and later stripped off and went swimming. Upon the bugle call the naked men were lined up on the riverbank and given an inspection by Major Smith; it is unclear whether this was of the short-arm variety or more likely just a general check on the men's condition, since February brought the first significant drop in fever cases in the battalion, down by a hundred in a month. For in this peaceful place, the 45th recovered its health. Sickness cases dropped to 139 in March and 104 in June. Those on the sick-list were sent to Trancoso or Celorico every week for inspection.[164]

It was easy to forget there was a war on. The army celebrated the queen of Portugal's birthday by receiving a double ration of wine on the 18th, 21st and 28th of January. Mail for home had to be delivered to the adjutant-general's office in Vizeu before two o'clock each Wednesday afternoon. Major Gwyn and Captain Milne found themselves assigned to court-martial duty and had to make the long trek down to Lisbon (well over two hundred miles and much of it over poor roads) in early February. On one occasion Quartermaster-Serjeant Tinkler joined a group of privates at lunch and challenged one of them, a well-known 'bolter' (glutton) to eat four freshly baked rye loaves, each to be washed down with a quart of wine. The bolter, Private David Evans, eagerly accepted the challenge and in an hour 'yammed' (ate) the four big loaves and drank the four quarts of local red; and all this less than an hour after breakfast. But there the fun ended. The rye swelled inside him and bloated him to such a degree that he had to be rolled out of the barn squealing in agony. Grease and oil was rubbed on his belly (to no effect) after which he was taken to the hospital to recover.[165] The quartermaster-serjeant got a dressing-down from Major Gwyn for his shenanigans. But even eating local produce could be hazardous, as general order from the adjutant-general on 23 March made plain – 'the soldiers of the army are desired not to eat roots, particularly the onions which they find growing wild in the fields, and even in the gardens. Many of them are poisonous, and a Serjeant of the 57th Regiment has died of the consequences of eating some of them.'[166]

Life within the battalion headquarters went on. In January the 45th received a new officer from home, Lieutenant James Henry Reynett, a 23-year-old Irishman from Waterford descended from French Huguenot refugees. In April the battalion received the services of Assistant-Surgeon Henry Wyat Radford, a 19-year-old from Attercliffe in Yorkshire. He had been in Portugal since November 1808 and had served at Oporto as a hospital mate on the staff before gaining a step-up in rank on joining the 45th, ostensibly to fill the gap caused by the dismissal of Robert Chambers, dismissed for going absent without leave in December.

Another who was facing dismissal was Lieutenant Mathew Handcock. He had allegedly absented himself from his duty without leave whilst attached to the sick and wounded on the retreat of the General Hospital from Talavera, between 3 August and 14 October, and proceeded to Lisbon without authority. Secondly, he was accused of grossly insulting and threatening Captain Charles Carthew of the 39th Foot in a letter addressed to him, dated Campo Mayor, 14 October 1809, whilst under an arrest for the preceding charge; and thirdly, for breaking his arrest by absenting himself from the headquarters of the 45th between the 18 and 20 November, whilst under arrest. He was court-martialled and acquitted of the first charge, but found guilty of the second and third (although they stemmed from the first charge); he was duly cashiered and sent home.[167] The one good thing to occur on account of the unhappy incident was the elevation of Ensign James MacPherson to Handcock's vacant lieutenancy.

Picton

On 22 February the brigade and the 3rd Division received a new commander – Lieutenant-General Thomas Picton, a 51-year-old hard-nosed Welshman who had joined the Army at the age of thirteen and had lately served in the West Indies for twelve years. Abrupt, blasphemous, plain-spoken, often informally dressed, yet capable of invigorating speeches and fluent in French and Spanish, Picton seems from this distance like a nineteenth-century Patton; one could easily imagine him slapping a shirking private in the field hospital.

His reputation certainly preceded him. Ensign William Grattan of the 88th Foot recorded his first impressions: 'I never saw a more perfect specimen of a splendid looking soldier. In vain did those who had set him down in their own minds as a cruel tyrant, seek to find out such a delineation in his countenance. No such marks were distinguishable ... But if his countenance did not depict him as cruel, there was a caustic severity about it, and a certain curl of the lip that marked him as one who rather despised than courted applause ... his appearance denoted him as a man of strong mind and strong frame.'[168]

Picton had been placed on civil trial in 1806 for alleged cruelty charges against a mulatto woman on Trinidad, a case that had caused a sensation with the Army. He had been found guilty and later acquitted at a re-trial, but the case 'cost him his health and his fortune'.

Public and Army opinion was still equally divided, but Picton found his true destiny that day at Trancosa when he met the 3rd Division for the first time. Henry MacKinnon was appointed a colonel on staff to the brigade, a piece of bureaucratic shuffling that effectively allowed MacKinnon to keep command of the brigade in Picton's name whilst the latter was commanding the division. So in reality nothing changed; Mack was still the brigadier. A few weeks earlier a third regiment had been added to MacKinnon's brigade, the Scottish 74th Foot commanded by Lieutenant-Colonel the Honourable Robert Le Poer Trench. The 74th were a highly-respected regiment who had served with Wellesley in India, covering themselves with glory at Assaye. The brigade was now truly a 'Union' brigade of three battalions – one English, one Irish, and one Scots. Although the five companies of the 5/60th Rifles had been removed from the division, one company was officially attached to the brigade, adding some Germans and Dutchmen into the mix also. A Portuguese brigade from Coimbra comprising the 9th and 21st Line was also added to the division.

A Day In The Life

What was a typical day in Manigoto like? We have no way of knowing for sure, but it is possible to reconstruct a typical day in late May 1810 from diaries and an understanding of barracks life.

There were no tents for the other ranks in 1810, so the men in Manigoto slept in barns, sheds and at occasionally in commandeered cottages. All the good houses were taken by officers. Before going to bed, a serjeant read the list of names on a paper attached to the door of the quarters to check that all were present and accounted for. Anyone not present was reported to the company commander. The officer of the watch – doing his rounds on the two o'clock to four o'clock shift – looked at his pocket watch during the early morning shift, keeping an eye out for the waking hour, half-past three. At twenty-five past he woke the drummers, who dressed quickly, strapped on their drums, and positioned themselves throughout the village to be heard by all men. Manigoto was a poor village, with filthy streets, and, naturally enough, it was pitch-black at that time in the morning. Once in position, each drummer beat 'Reveille' on his drum, and the men in the houses and barns stirred.

Invariably first to his feet was the NCO, shouting at his squad something along the lines of getting their lazy arses out of bed and to their bloody feet or else. One private lit the sole candle in the room using an ember from the nearly-dead fire whilst another was detailed to go to the well and draw water for the squad. This was not a popular task, since the large oak bucket full of water was heavy. Each man rolled and stored his bedding, then wandered over to the water bucket and washed his face, hands, and splashed some cold water on his neck and over his head. Whilst waiting, each man lit his clay pipe using the candle as a source of flame. Several used the time to urinate behind trees or in corners of yards. Scratching was epidemic, since as a rule the villages were filthy and most men slept on the ground or the floor. The mess orderlies brushed out the rooms using primitive brooms, put the fire out, and dumped the embers in a safe place.

Morning parade was at sunrise – a quarter past six. The drummers and buglers played 'Troop' and all men fell in except those still on guard duty, wearing their fatigue uniform, consisting of a short white wool jacket, forage cap and 'trowsers'. Men were inspected for cleanliness and any missing men were reported to the company commander. Whilst on parade, the officer of the day went around and inspected the quarters, ensuring that all was clean and tidy and in accordance with the regulations. After morning parade, men were dismissed and went to work on assigned tasks. These tasks varied depending upon the whim of the officers and NCOs, and probably varied with the talents of the individuals or the needs of the battalion. At Manigoto there would have been no requirement for road-building or heavy labour, so many men were probably put to good use attending to market gardens and helping farmers harvest foodstuffs. New recruits, anyone deemed requiring extra drill, and prisoners awaiting regimental court-martial were paraded in full uniform and arms and marched off for drill with the adjutant and serjeant-major for two hours.

Breakfast was at nine o'clock, and was generally fairly informal. Those assigned to mess duties did the cooking and serving. In Manigoto breakfast might have been a lump of bread, a slice of cooked ham, a mug of tea and just maybe, a tot of rum.

At twenty minutes to ten the drummers sounded the 'Pioneer's March' and breakfast was over – the men were free to pursue their own ends but given that full dress parade was at eleven o'clock, the more conscientious chose to clean, shine and blanch their uniform and kit. This laborious process involved applying pipe-clay to all white belts and straps, polishing the steelwork on muskets with oil and emery, and applying blacking from a blacking-ball to ammunition pouch, stock, shako and shoes. One non-commissioned officer was appointed master tailor, responsible for the conduct of the soldier-tailors employed under him. The tailors were required to assemble each morning at half-past six in the summer and half-past seven in the winter, in their fatigue dress, and were to work until six o'clock at night, allowing necessary intervals for their meals – three-quarters of an hour for breakfast, and an hour for dinner. During the period for altering the regimental clothing, no other work was to be done by the tailors of the regiment without the sanction of the commanding officer.

Full-dress parade was at eleven o'clock in the morning. The drummers played 'Troop' again and all men not on guard duty fell in with full kit (except knapsack) and musket. Officers and NCOs inspected the men and their arms and accoutrements in great detail, noting any infractions. On the approach of the officer, the serjeants barked: 'Attention! Shoulder Arms!' The senior NCO then presented his report. If the lieutenant and ensign were present, the captain usually directed the youngest in rank to go through the inspection.[169] The inspection comprised a number of drill movements, after which the companies were dismissed.

The guard was changed at noon. Sentries did twenty-four hour shifts, with two hours on duty and two hours off. They slept fully clothed in the guardhouse whilst off-duty. 'A sentry is not to quit his post on any account whatsoever. Should he be taken ill, he must pass the word to the guard; but he must not permit himself to be relieved by any person except the corporal of his own guard,' general orders required. 'Every instance of remissness and intoxication will be severely punished.' The responsibilities of the officers were just as exacting. 'Young officers should, above all others, be scrupulously exact in the unequivocal discharge of' this important duty,' general orders warned.

A captain and subaltern of the day[170] came on duty at guard mounting, and were responsible that good order and regularity was maintained throughout the billet, which they could not quit except on duty, until relieved at guard mounting the following morning. The orderly captain was charged with the general superintendence of the daily duties in barracks; he had to examine the report of the subaltern, and enclose it with his own to the commanding officer by 10 o'clock in the morning. The orderly subaltern had to report to the captain of the day at guard mounting, and to receive any particular orders he may have to give. The captain and subaltern of the day had to attend all parades, but if the regiment marched out, they had to remain in quarters unless specially required. Tuesday and Saturday were drill days, often involving four hours of square-bashing.

Quarters were subjected to detailed inspections on these days also. Sunday involved a church service given by Major Smith between breakfast and full-dress parade, and two hours of compulsory drill. Plus, of course, a dip in the river followed by Major Smith's regular inspection. Each soldier having two shirts and two pairs of socks, these were changed every Thursday and Sunday.

Lunch was at two o'clock and was a much more formal affair than breakfast. It was the largest and heaviest meal of the day and required all men to be seated. Wine was frequently served. The men were off-duty again by three. Many frequented the canteen, which sold liquor; there was no rule against soldiers imbibing alcohol, they just weren't allowed to get drunk.

When the entire battalion was paraded together, which at Manigoto happened at least once per month – the 25th, pay-day – the colours were placed in the centre of the battalion, and of the officers appointed to carry the colours, the eldest (in rank) was to carry the King's, the youngest the regimental colour.

The senior officer present on parade, at the officers' mess, and all other times and places, was held responsible for ensuring that 'no irregularity or impropriety passes unnoticed by him; on the contrary, he must immediately take proper steps to check or correct any such conduct.' Wet-behind-the-ears ensigns were occasionally drilled privately by more senior officers and the serjeant-major. All officers paid a set equivalent amount (regardless of rank) towards the cost of the officers' mess, which covered the cost of food, drink, and a little something for the cooks and the mess-servants.

Majors Gwyn and Smith had quite specific duties; when both were present, each had the superintendence of a wing of the regiment, the senior of the right, and the junior of the left wing; when there was only one major present, the charge of both wings devolved upon him. The majors were responsible for seeing that the private parades of the companies were properly conducted, that the officers attended parades punctually, and that they did not collect in groups, or leave their companies until dismissed. Occasionally they were required, whilst on parade, to examine the companies' field states. Part of their duty was to visit the billets and the messes of their respective wings and the hospital, at least once a week; and they were to examine the books, bills, and receipts of the companies under their superintendence, once every month. Last but not least, the instruction of the other officers in sword exercises and salute, and of the subaltern officers in drill, was under the especial superintendence of the majors.

Each captain was responsible for the internal arrangements and good order of his company, as well as for the arms, accoutrements, clothing, and ammunition in possession of his men. It was his duty to pay particular attention to the messing of his company, to see that the men had sufficient good and wholesome food; and also to take care that every man (unless considerably in debt) was at all times kept complete in regimental necessaries. Officers commanding companies took charge of all sums of money received on account of their men; large sums were never placed in the hands of the pay serjeants. The payments to the men had to be made in the presence of an officer. Needless to say all applications for promotion, furloughs, passes and all complaints, crimes, and reports had to pass through the captains of companies. Each subaltern was to have charge of a subdivision, or two squads of the company to which he belonged, for the appearance and regularity of which he was responsible to his captain. He had to take care that the non-commissioned officers of his squads paid proper attention to their duties.

Each regimental officer was allowed one manservant; field officers, the surgeon, and adjutant were permitted to have two. No soldier could be taken as a servant without the sanction of the commanding officer. No soldier could be employed as servant until he had done least three years duty in the ranks; all servants had to be rear rank men of the same company as the officers whom they attended.

Serjeant-Major Nathaniel Carter was expected to display 'a deportment ... in conformity with the high situation he holds in the corps; his regular and soldier-like conduct and unremitting attention to his duties, must afford an example to all the non-commissioned officers and privates in the regiment'.[171] He was the assistant to the adjutant, under whose immediate orders he acted. He was expected not to be too familiar with the non-commissioned officers, but to preserve a proper distance and authority over them. He was required to keep rosters of the non-commissioned officers with great accuracy, and to detail the number of men which each company was to furnish daily for duty. Most of all, he was to 'pay strict attention to the conduct, dress, and carriage of the non-commissioned officers and privates; and never to allow either the one or the other to pass him in a slovenly or un-soldier-like manner without noticing it'. Soldiers, when addressing the serjeant-major, were required to stand at attention, but never to say 'sir'. Serjeants and corporals were, of course, the men who made the battalion tick. 'So much depends upon the attention, intelligence, and integrity of the non-commissioned officers of the regiment,' a set of general orders ran, 'that too much care cannot be employed in selecting for the situation men of sufficient capacity and zeal; soldiers possessing those qualities may feel assured of receiving every support and encouragement from the commanding officer'.[172] The minute a man sewed on the stripes, a gulf existed between him and the privates of his company. This is the main reason that a man so promoted was usually moved to another company, away from his too-familiar friends and former mess-partners. No serjeant was ever to associate or drink with a private soldier; nor could he ever come into personal contact with a drunken soldier (whenever it was necessary to use coercion to confine a drunk, private soldiers were to be employed for the purpose). When warning a soldier for duty, a serjeant was never to do it in a familiar manner, nor was he allowed any freedom either in casual conversation or behaviour with the soldier. A new corporal was likewise advised to 'withdraw himself from the society of the privates, and live with those of his own rank in the regiment'.

Whenever a recruit joined a company he was appointed to a squad, and placed as a comrade to a steady old soldier, who was directed to instruct him in cleaning his appointments and suchlike – at least in theory.

When a soldier died, the officer commanding the company took charge of his effects, made an inventory thereof, and furnished the paymaster with a statement of his accounts. An officer was required to attend the funeral.

When a soldier wished to speak to an officer on any subject connected with duty, he had to be accompanied by a non-commissioned officer of his squad; if entering a room he kept his shako on, and had to salute with his right hand,[173] stand at attention whilst addressing him, and salute him again before quitting the room. When spoken to in the ranks by an officer or non-commissioned officer a private soldier was never to reply unless a question was put to him directly. And very importantly, every soldier was positively forbidden to disobey any lawful order he may receive from his officers or non-commissioned officers.

Any soldier standing court-martial (which was arranged by the adjutant) had to be duly warned and furnished with a copy of the charges preferred against him, including any former convictions to be produced against him. The adjutant was responsible for forewarning all witnesses, both for the prosecution and defence, to attend. Any man absent for more than forty-eight hours was considered a deserter until such time as he might re-appear and prove otherwise. The effects of a deserter were not required to be sold until his name appeared in orders to be struck off the strength of the regiment. If a deserter re-joined prior to the sale of his effects, the captain of his company had to apply to the commanding officer for permission to restore his effects.

Adjutant Richard Jones Colley was required to possess 'a perfect knowledge of all general and regimental orders, and of the various duties appertaining to his situation'. He was required to regulate the roster of officers with the greatest exactness, and upon no account to alter an officer's tour of duty without the sanction of the commanding officer. Under the directions of the majors, he had to superintend the drill of the young officers of the regiment; he was also responsible for making sure that all guards, detachments, and armed parties were commanded by officers. But his most arduous task was the regimental books, eighty-three of which recorded the life of the battalion. Fourteen were under the direct care of the adjutant, and it was just as well that he was free from company duties, for upkeep of the records must have consumed nearly every spare waking hour.

Army mythology has it that the court-martial book had a black cover (hence, 'to be in the black books') – however in the days before mass-production the actual books themselves may have been whatever could be procured locally. Each company had six books, nominally kept by the captain commanding but more usually delegated to a reliable clerk from the ranks. They were: a Day Book; a Ledger; an Order Book; a Description Book (containing the vital statistics of each man in the company); a Clothing Book; and a Weekly Mess Book. Quartermaster Edmund Thresher was responsible for six books, the first five being detailed accounts of goods received and how distributed – separate books for clothing, accoutrements, arms, ammunition, fuel and forage – and the sixth book was a letter register containing all correspondence written by the C.O. concerning the foregoing.

Surgeon John Boggie looked after three books – a medical diary containing the names of all men admitted into hospital; a medical registry outlining the treatment and cure (or not) of each man; and a hospital accounts book, showing how money owing to men in hospital was paid. The surgeon was mainly responsible for the regimental hospital and everything connected with it, being accountable for its interior management and cleanliness. Whenever an officer was taken ill, a report had to be sent by the surgeon to the adjutant, for the commanding officer's information, and the officer's name was to be inserted in the daily report of sick. Whenever a soldier was taken ill he was to be removed to the hospital, and the surgeon was to be made acquainted with the circumstance (by the orderly serjeant of the company to which the man belongs), and either the surgeon or the assistant surgeon was to see the man as soon as possible. One or more hospital serjeants were usually appointed, under the immediate orders of the medical officers. When a soldier was taken into hospital his arms and accoutrements were placed in the company arms chest, and the serjeant of his squad gave his knapsack to the hospital serjeant, until they were delivered over by him to the pay-serjeant of the company on the discharge or death of the soldier.

On the receipt of the route for the march of the regiment or a detachment, Quartermaster Edmund Thresher had to take the proper means of procuring waggons or carts for the conveyance of the baggage. He was required to precede the regiment by a day's march before arriving at its destination, in order to identify and take over the billets sufficiently early to prevent the men being kept under arms after marching in. The quartermaster then had the general charge of the barracks and billets occupied by the regiment, so far as regards damages and repairs, so he therefore frequently visited them, in order to ascertain their exact state. In his primary duty the quartermaster had charge of, and was accountable for, all the regimental stores, the clothing, appointments, arms, and ammunition, not in possession of companies, the receipt of which he had to carefully book, as well as all invoices and letters connected with his department. He was accountable for all provisions, fuel, and other allowances received for the service of the regiment; and had the general superintendence of the regimental armourers, tailors, shoemakers, and workmen of every description, as well as of the pioneers.

Quartermaster-Serjeant Francis Tinkler was an assistant to Quartermaster Thresher in all the details of his department. He was required to be present at the issue of provisions, fuel, straw, ammunition, and suchlike, and to superintend all fatigue parties in the removal of regimental stores and cleaning barracks, and to attend all barrack inspections.

Serjeant-Armourer Joe Baker's main duty was to repair arms – but never without an order in writing, signed by the pay-serjeant of the company to which the arms belonged, which had to accompany his bill as a voucher. He sent in his charges against the different companies to the pay-serjeant on or before the last day of each month. The armourer-serjeant was required when practicable, to examine all arms monthly, and to make a nominal charge for each firelock taken to pieces.

Dinner was an hour before sunset (which is to say, about half-past seven at this time of year) and like breakfast, was an informal meal, usually men standing around and chatting whilst they ate, then puffing away on their pipes. Nicotine was every soldier's addiction – a hundred years later it was no different. Serjeants were required to wear their uniform coats at every meal, but it was optional for the other ranks. At sunset the drummers beat 'Retreat' and the men assembled yet again, without arms, while the officers made the roll call, and read out any specific orders for the company on the morrow. The drummers beat 'Taps' at ten o'clock (eight o'clock in winter) at which point the NCOs went around and checked that all their men were safely indoors; and so the day ended.

One of the King's Hard Bargains

A Portuguese peasant and his wife on their way home from a country fair were attacked by four privates and one drummer of the Grenadier Company of the 45th near the bridge of San Euphemia on 12 March; they were robbed of all that they had. Wellesley had adopted a zero-tolerance policy towards acts against the Portuguese population.

The culprits – all recently-arrived second battalion men – were swiftly found and brought before a court-martial. It was that rogue Tom Horsley again, and some friends: Joseph Norman, Edward Perrot, and drummer Joseph Freeman. They were found guilty and sentenced to be hung by the neck till dead, 'at such time and place as His Excellency the Commander of the Forces may deem fit'.[174]

Private Thomas Horsley was one of the King's Hard Bargains to be sure, although his previous record did not necessarily suggest it. Born in Carlton on the edge of Nottingham in 1788, he had served several years in the Derbyshire Militia before volunteering into the 2/45th on 4 April 1809. Generally militiamen made good soldiers, but not this one. Whilst in prison for the above charge, he had robbed a French officer of his watch and money. To make matters worse, two more privates of the 45th, Thomas Stevenson and James Connolly, were placed in prison on 24 March for petty theft, although they ultimately escaped with a few hundred lashes rather than the death penalty. Another hard bargain was Private Michael Fahie, who hadn't got far after deserting just before Christmas; he was sentenced 'to be transported as a felon for the term of seven years, and at the expiration of the said term of seven years, to be at the disposal of His Majesty, to serve as a soldier in any of His Majesty's forces, at home or abroad, for life'.[175] What this meant in reality was aboard a ship bound for Portsmouth in chains, then a six-month transit to distant New South Wales, Van Diemen's Land[176] or Norfolk Island, seven years of breaking rocks on roads or clearing bush-land, then probable enlistment in the New South Wales Corps for life. His chances of surviving long enough to even make enlistment were probably minuscule.

General courts-martial had to be composed of more than thirteen officers; imposition of the death penalty required the vote of at least nine members, so more than two-thirds majority. The menu of punishments ranged from flogging almost to death, all the way up to and including death. Desertion to the enemy required the culprit to be shot by firing-squad; mere desertion (running away without joining the enemy) attracted anything up to 1,200 lashes. Violence against civilians, murder and sodomy caused a guilty man to be hanged. Theft and plundering required an offender to be transported to a colony, or given up to 1,200 lashes. Transportation was in fact a fairly common punishment for crimes up to and including the death sentence, as many such executions were invariably commuted to service abroad for life. Twenty-two men in the two battalions of the 45th received the punishment of penal transportation between 1806 and 1815,[177] and, interestingly, only three of these men were serving soldiers in the first battalion; the rest were all from the second battalion, strongly suggesting a tighter rein on discipline by officers and NCOs at the front, plus the lack of opportunities to desert (or places to desert to) on campaign. Only one man of the 45th appears to have been executed as a result of a general court-martial, Private James Kelly in December 1813.

Holiday in Pinhel

The Light Company practised skirmish tactics in the woods and plains around the villages south of Pinhel. Captain Greenwell was a fastidious company officer who demanded discipline and absolute obedience to orders. The fact he could not tolerate inferior non-commissioned officers is shown by the Light Company's record of having thirty-one NCOs serving within the ranks during the war, more than any other company by a fair margin. Some men simply weren't good enough for Greenwell; but when he found good NCOs, he hung onto them dearly. In his spare time, he painted water-colours (a common past-time amongst British Peninsula officers) but does not seem to have been a prolific letter-writer.

Around this time Major-General Picton instituted a 3rd Division composite light battalion as a tactical innovation for deployment on the battlefield, a step beyond the brigade light battalion ordered by Wellesley the year prior. The light companies from all ten units in his three brigades – 1/45th, 1/74th and 1/88th from MacKinnon's brigade, 2/5th, 2/58th and three companies of the 5/60th Rifles from Stafford Lightburne's brigade, and one light company from each of the 9th and 21st Portuguese Line – were trained to fight together as an ad-hoc single formation under the overall command of Lieutenant-colonel William Williams of the 60th. It would be some months before they were able to test their skirmishing tactics in battle.

In early June the battalion was ordered to place all greatcoats and blankets into winter storage at Celorico. The following month none other than Lieutenant-Colonel the Honourable John Meade joined from the second battalion, taking over command from Major Gwyn (who had held command for nearly a year) at Val de Madeira. He had spent the prior five years with the second battalion in Mansfield, or more commonly, listening to the hot air of the day from the rear of the House of Lords.

Major William Smith, ever alert to the situation around him, could sense something was afoot, and perhaps even had a premonition of things to come. He drafted his last will and testament at Val de Madeira on 2 June, leaving £400 to Major Potter[178] ('late of the 45th Regiment') and everything else to his sister, Isabella Lilley of Berwick-upon-Tweed. A few weeks later he commanded a detachment of the 45th on outpost duty on the line of the River Coa, where he acquired the friendship of Major Hew Ross, commanding A Troop of the Royal Horse Artillery attached to the Light Division.[179] Major Ross wrote to him after his return to Pinhel on 11 July: 'We are all plunged into the deepest distress by the unfortunate and ill-managed affair which took place this morning. Our General endeavoured to cut off a French patrol of cavalry and infantry … you may be assured if there existed a doubt in anyone's mind before there is none remaining as to our great good fortune in being so commanded … No blame attaches to the cavalry for making their charge, for after they were led to attack one of our own squadrons supposing it the enemy, no one but the General I understand knew of friends in that direction.'[180]

'Our General' was Brigadier-General Robert 'Black Bob' Craufurd, commander of the Light Division. His sarcastic comments on Craufurd (coming as they do from the senior artillery officer in the Light Division) are an illuminating antidote to the hero-worship often attached to Craufurd. Ross finished his letter with some disconcerting news. 'We learn from the prisoners that [Ciudad] Rodrigo surrendered yesterday evening at 6 o'clock. We shall soon be enquired for by our neighbour Masséna, who entered the place himself.'[181] Ciudad Rodrigo had held out for eleven weeks against a French army of some 42,000 men; the small Spanish garrison had surrendered after the walls were breached, after which the French sacked the city. It was becoming clear that the phony war on the frontier could not last much longer. The holiday in Pinhel was about to end.

Our Neighbour Masséna

The enquiry came soon enough. On 24 July Brigadier-General Craufurd's Light Division retired across the River Coa under fire at a bridge near Almeida in the face of an overwhelming French force commanded by Maréchal Andre Masséna. The bridge was barely eight miles south-east of Pinhel, and little did the 45th know of the 65,000 French troops massed to cross it and invade Portugal down the Mondego Valley.

The Light Division, who had been placed outside Almeida as a trip-wire, retired to Carvahal the next day. On the 26th, after six bucolic months around Pinhel, MacKinnon's brigade shouldered arms and marched west. The locals panicked and evacuated Pinhel; within a few hours there was barely a stray dog on the street. At three o'clock in the morning on 29 July, the brigade marched through Celerico en route to Linhares, on the south bank of the Mondego River. They had marched some seventy miles in three days without so much as seeing a Frenchman. They camped in Linhares for two weeks, during which time the French had commenced a siege of the allied garrison of Almeida. On 19 August they were ordered back up the road to Celerico, where high on the end of the Serra da Estrela they could see the discharges of the French artillery against the walls of Almeida in the clear air, but were at too great a distance to hear it. By 20 August they were camped under the stars in pouring rain at Villa Franca das Naves, about twelve miles west of their long-time cantonment at Manigoto, as part of a line defending the pass at Celerico. An enormous explosion at daybreak on 26 August signalled the accidental detonation of the main powder magazine at Almeida, and the end of its resistance. In the dusk on 27 August the brigade marched south-west again, past Minhocal in a raging lightning-storm, finding nearly all villages deserted as they went.

Attached to the 3rd Division was a brigade of Portuguese troops, including a regiment commanded by brevet Lieutenant-Colonel James Dawes Douglas, previously only one step above Major William Smith on the Army List. This must have exercised Smith's mind on the matter of seniority, for on 8 September he penned a letter to the Deputy Adjutant-General, Colonel Edward Pakenham. 'As I am the junior Field Officer of the 2 battalions and voluntarily serving with the 1st, with which Lt. Col. Meade and Major Gwyn are present, and as apparently I might be spared from it without inconvenience … should his Lordship deem me equal to the command of a Portuguese battalion, and my promotion in the British service be not thereby injured or retarded, I would heartily and willingly undertake that charge during the junction of the British and Portuguese forces on the continent, or while my duty with the 45th can be dispensed with.'[182] Although his entire career had been with the 45th, Smith was plainly an ambitious man, and perhaps even bored by his present circumstances.

Pakenham replied from Gourica on 11 September. 'His Lordship ... proposes to mention your name to Marshal Beresford as an eligible officer to appoint in charge of one of the Portuguese regiments of the line.'[183] Smith's cautious excitement was evident in his final reply: 'I obtained my first and present commissions in the 45th regiment by purchase, and would be exceedingly happy to have an opportunity to succeed to a Lt. Colonelcy by the same means.'[184] But events were overtaking them, and Pakenham was not able to provide a confirmation in short order. In any event, Wellington had much bigger issues at hand – such as where to stop and fight Masséna.

From Galizes the brigade marched via Friumes at Penacova, which they reached on 20 September. Opinion in the battalion was that they were headed for Coimbra. However they were turned northwards, buoyed by the news that the 2nd and 5th Division were coming up from the south and close to joining with the main army. They reached Contenças on the 21st and finally came in sight of a long north-south ridge in heavily wooded country, which they ascended on the evening of 25 September. At the northern end of the ridge sat a disused convent – named Busaco.

---

[163] Meaning steak. Similar to the French 'rosbifs'.

[164] Sickness figures from WO17/157.

[165] Luckily Evans survived the war and was discharged in 1815.

[166] General Orders, Vol. 2, p.46.

[167] General Orders, Vol. 2, pp.26-8.

[168] Grattan, Vol. 1. p.16.

[169] James, *Regimental Companion*, p.172.

[170] Officers of the day were identified by the wearing of a crescent-shaped silver gorget below the neck-line.

[171] Standing Orders, 95th or the Derbyshire Regiment, 1856. It is unlikely that the definition in 1810 was any different.

[172] ibid.

[173] Although as indicated in an earlier chapter, the salute was less formal than the modern salute. More of a touching of the hat brim.

[174] The Principles of War, Exhibited in the Practice of the Camp... in the late Campaigns on the Peninsula; pp.308-9.

[175] General Orders, Vol. 2, p.94.

[176] Not called Tasmania until 1856.

[177] With 1809 being the worst year, with five offenders.

[178] Possibly Captain Leonard Busteed Potter of the 28th Foot, a brigade-major in the 4th Division, although there is no evidence he ever served in the 45th Foot.

[179] The famous 'A' Troop, later called the Chestnut Troop, the artillery battery *par eminence* of the allied army in the Peninsula.

[180] 1930 Regimental Annual, pp.193-4.

[181] ibid, p.194.

[182] ibid, pp.194-5.

[183] ibid, p.195.

[184] ibid, p.196.

Chapter 12

Busaco

The 1/45th battalion roster on 25 September 1810 included 227 men listed as sick; the 45th had added more than 120 men to the sick list in the past two months due to the marching and counter-marching in the summer heat.[185] As at Talavera, the battalion was deficient in officers, there being only twenty-two available for company duty, including a handful of captains – Greenwell, Lightfoot, Dabsac and Urquhart – and a solitary ensign. With only four captains present, most of the companies would enter the coming battle commanded by lieutenants. They camped that night along the ridge-line and ate cold vittles; Wellington had ordered that no camp-fires be lit. The French, some three or four hundred yards below on the plain, made no such efforts at secrecy, and the valley floor was a star-field of camp-fires.

Lieutenant-General Picton's aides positioned MacKinnon's brigade across a road that ran east-west up and over the sierra, on one of the few routes that connected to a road that ran along the ridge-line. Picton was concerned by a large gap in his line, between MacKinnon's brigade and the right-hand battalions of his northernmost brigade belonging to Major-General Stafford Lightburne. Waiting until dark, he detached the 88th and sent them north to occupy a spur on the northern side of the pass of San Antonio de Cantara, thus reducing the unoccupied space – nonetheless, a gap of perhaps a thousand yards still existed. Immediately to the south of their position was a Portuguese brigade; three battalions of blue-coated locals in two-tiered shakos, officered by British volunteers who had gained a step in rank by offering their services to the nascent Portuguese Army, just as William Smith considered doing.

The night of the 26 September was cold and windy on the ridge-line. A small party of officers – Captain Charlie Urquhart, Lieutenants John Tyler, James MacPherson and Ralph Ousely – was either posted or went of their own volition towards the bottom of the valley, which is to say, the French lines. Here they found some straw, which they found too tempting as a way of catching a few minutes' sleep. Unfortunately the cacophony of French voices nearby was their alarm-clock. They awoke on the 26th to thick fog, and the sounds of imminent action. Realising they were probably in trouble they tried to conceal their attempts to re-join the formed 45th, attempts which did not escape the attention of Lieutenant-Colonel the Honourable John Meade. The CO made a fuss of their absence and promised to report the matter to Lieutenant-General Picton, and might have made more of it had not the French stolen his thunder.[186] For the fog now produced an unusual sound that the Johnny Raws couldn't identify, but the Old Sweats could; it was the sound of French gun teams being wheeled into position below and directly in front of them. After a nervous breakfast the serjeants called the roll; there were twenty-two officers, thirty-six serjeants, fifteen drummers and 512 rank-and-file present and under arms, out of a battalion total of 870.[187]

Two batteries of Portuguese artillery under Captain Victor von Arentschildt (on loan from the King's German Legion) spanned the road up the pass, with the 74th Foot and the 21st Portuguese Line protecting their flanks. The 45th Foot and the 9th Portuguese Line were placed in reserve behind the artillery. The light companies of the brigade under the command of Lieutenant-Colonel William Williams of the 60th Rifles, placed across the Palheiros road near the bottom of the hill, soon gave advance warning of the approach of large numbers of a French column a little after 6 a.m.

Captain Greenwell's light company was hard-pressed by the sheer numbers of French *tirailleurs* and backed up the hill as slowly as they dared. Eleven battalions in three immense columns were climbing the hill towards the gap to the south of the 88th. MacKinnon, posted with the 88th, saw the French coming out of the mist and collecting in a ravine below the spur occupied by the 88th and calculated the odds; eleven battalions against one. Not good. He galloped across to Picton to warn him of the danger. Picton turned to Lieutenant-Colonel the Honourable John Meade and ordered him to send half the 45th across to aid the Rangers, promising to send a further Portuguese regiment in support. Meade ordered Major Gwyn to take the left wing of the battalion across at the double; not an easy task on rocky, brambled terrain. The left wing hustled northwards only four companies strong, those of Captain Lightfoot, Captain Dabsac, Lieutenant Costley and Lieutenant Anderson,[188] given the Light Company was detached somewhere off to the right in the valley below. They arrived just in time. The French columns were closing on the 88th, but were slowed and exhausted from the climb. Major Gwyn formed his four companies into line as the mass of French infantry, wearing greatcoats against the cold of the morning, massed on the slope below them.

Captain Thomas Lightfoot of No.9 Company was second-in-command to Gwyn. 'The enemy, under favour of the fog, had already arrived to near the top of the hill,' he later wrote, 'that the instant the leading section of the detachment appeared on the brow of it, a fire was poured into them from a body of *tirailleurs*, so close, that it resembled rather the fire of a close battalion'.[189]

The odds were now reduced to eleven battalions against one and a half. The French were in three immense columns, each about 240 files wide by nine ranks deep, shielded by the mass of *tirailleurs*. The 45th had perhaps 180 muskets to fire against the 6,000 Frenchmen, and it seemed that the only possibility was a holding action until reinforcements came up. Riding up and down behind the ranks of the 45th, Major Gwyn ordered them to present, and then fire by rank – platoon volleys being impractical for such a small formation. The serjeants screamed at the men to fire low, given that the French were downhill of them.

Sometime early during the fire-fight Major Gwyn was hit in the groin by a musket-ball and had to be sent to the rear. The senior captain (Greenwell) being absent with the Light Company, Captain Thomas Lightfoot took command of the left wing. He brought the remainder of the companies into position. 'Upon this point the whole fire of the enemy seemed to be concentrated, and which we endeavoured to return with all the energy we were masters of, but our fire was too insignificant to contend with the mass opposed to us.' he recorded. 'The companies, exposed from their feet upwards on the brow of the hill, received every shot into them and fell so fast it seemed a perfect massacre, [and] their fire was quite insufficient to check their opponents. Their line steadily advanced, and we found ourselves at length involved in the smoke of each other's muskets at the distance of a few paces only, unable to see beyond the muzzles of them.'[190]

A large group of French skirmishers took cover in a rocky outcrop and commenced a galling fire into the nearby 88th. Lieutenant-Colonel Alexander Wallace of the 88th saw that only a bayonet charge would clear the ridge and sent three companies forward with a yell to clear the snipers away, which soon degenerated into bitter hand-to-hand fighting. The 8th Portuguese Line (under the command of Lieutenant-Colonel James Dawes Douglas, the ex-45th man) arrived on the right flank of the 45th and joined the musketry-fray, even engaging in some hand-to-hand combat. 'My eye now caught the view of the enemy on the top of the projecting rocks upon which my left rested, and in the act of firing down on my party [now greatly reduced] from thence, [the French fire] compelled me to fall back a few paces,' said Lightfoot. 'When now I perceived the 8th Portuguese, or a wing of them, marching into position on my right, in sections; and some *tirailleurs* having at the same moment gained possession of the rocks in front of them, the first section of the Portuguese Grenadiers and they came suddenly and unexpectedly into collision, bayonet to bayonet.'[191]

The 8th Portuguese comprised mainly teenagers who had been with the colours for less than six months, but they blazed away with youthful vigour. The fire of the raw Portuguese was doubly disadvantageous, since they were firing across the route the 88th needed to advance down to meet the French column. An officer of the 88th sent to halt their fire received two musket-balls in his body,[192] and they fired away regardless until Lieutenant-Colonel Wallace, on foot, placed himself in front of the combined companies of the 88th and 45th, and yelled, 'Press forward!' Captain Lightfoot was still on the scene: 'The enemy came no further; for now the 88th charged round the rocks on their right into the flank of the enemy column on the slope of the hill, and drove them precipitately down it. The four companies of the 45th, and I believe, the 8th Portuguese joined in the pursuit as far as midway down the hill and thus terminated the attack.'[193]

The wild Irishmen of the Rangers needed no further encouragement and charged obliquely into the flank of the French column; the line swept down the hill with the 45th and 8th Portuguese in support, sending the winded French into headlong flight. The right-hand French regiment was almost completely destroyed, losing 300 prisoners as the howling redcoats and their Portuguese allies chased them to the valley floor.

Another French column emerged from the mist on the main road barely 300 yards in front of Arentschildt's artillery batteries. The veteran Hanoverian's eyes no doubt lit up as he commanded his Portuguese gunners to fire using a mix of German and beginner-level Portuguese. Arentschildt's twelve three-pounders did great execution in the French ranks, causing the first two battalions to halt and try to change formation from column to line. The Portuguese guns may have been small calibre by the standards of the day, and served by inexperienced gunners, but at that range they could not miss.

Five companies of the division under Lieutenant-Colonel William Williams gave the column a hot reception as it puffed up the incline – three of his own companies of the 60th Rifles, the Light Company of the 45th under Captain Greenwell and Captain Urquhart's No.1 Company of the 45th sniped from amongst the rocks as the French advanced. Three companies of the ever-steady 74th Foot and the 21st Portuguese Line under the personal supervision of Colonel MacKinnon advanced, presented arms and fired volleys into the head of the French column at a hundred yards range, whilst the detached light companies attacked the left of the column; for some time the two lines stood and traded musketry (during which Captain Urquhart was killed), until the French broke and retired to the village of San Antonio de Cantara in their rear, leaving it to their own cannons to give the British and Portuguese on the ridge a taste of the same medicine. The artillery and sharpshooters nonetheless continued barraging and sniping for some time.

There was more action to come. A third French column of seven battalions loomed out of the fog, midway between the first two attacks and twenty minutes later. This one came on much faster, its confidence boosted by the French artillery at its back, led on by a double-timing light infantry regiment in all-blue. To see it off, Picton had only the right wing of the green

8th Portuguese Line, the more experienced 9th Portuguese Line and the five remaining companies of the 45th on hand – three-and-a-half battalion against seven.

Somewhere in the area were the three depleted light companies under Major Smith, still re-forming after their vigorous skirmish with the first French column. Leaving MacKinnon to look after things on the man road, Picton and Assistant Adjutant-General Edward Pakenham rode across to a rocky hillock that looked to be the focus of the third French column, having ordered his aide-de-camp Captain Robert Cuthbert and his Deputy Assistant Quartermaster-General Captain Thomas Anderson to bring up a battalion of the 8th Portuguese Line and the rest of the 45th on the double. Picton and Pakenham arrived at the rocky hillock to find the light companies of the 74th and 88th falling back in disorder. Major William Smith rode up and on a nod from Picton, rode boldly forward to rally the light companies and lead them in a charge on the French *tirailleurs* barely sixty yards away, waving his hat over his head as he did so, presumably to stall the head of the French column until the reinforcing battalions arrived.

Smith, who a fortnight before had expressed himself 'being actuated by a strong desire to be somewhat more actively employed in the existing contest', paid for his reckless courage in the full amount. A musket-ball plucked him from his horse, as French skirmishers closed around him and bayoneted him to death. It was a cruel end for a valiant soldier, a fighting man who had once admonished a less bold fellow officer thus: 'I don't like your prudent officers, Sir, who deal in long shots, and who talk so much of sparing the effusion of human blood – their prudence, sir, always increases it in the end, sir.'[194] He ended his career as he had started it, an officer in the 45th, and Wellington would have to look elsewhere for a lieutenant-colonel for one of his new Portuguese regiments.

At that moment, Captain Anderson arrived with Major Walter Birmingham and his battalion of the 8th Portuguese Line. But the odds were still very much in the French favour, and Birmingham's men were subject to the full force of the fourteen French cannon firing over the heads of their column. Major Birmingham was an ex-29th man, a veteran of that terrible day at Roliça, but even he could not stop his teenaged Portuguese recruits inching backwards, step-by-step, as the seven French battalions advanced confidently.

The battle was there to be lost at that moment. The French climbed closer to the plateau, and started to form into line on the flatter ground. Captain Thomas Lightfoot had command of the battered left wing, which appears to have fallen back towards the rest of the battalion prior to the attack. He had been joined by the whole of the 45th, under Lieutenant-Colonel Meade, and he now found himself second-in-command of the battalion, the senior captain being away with the light company. 'Meade being in conversation with General Spencer at some distance from the brow of the hill, and neither of them seeing the column which was fast approaching to the summit of the hill, I ran to the Colonel, and, telling him of it, asked him, at the same time, if I should take my detachment, and throw in a fire on the enemy's flank; which he instantly acceding to. I led them forward, and, placing them on a favourable site opposite to the flank of the column, I ordered them to commence firing. Being joined by Colonel Meade with the remainder of the regiment, the whole now poured their fire with great effect into the midst of the column, which fire was continued for about ten minutes, the 8th Portuguese Regiment (I suppose the same battalion that had previously come to the support of the left) also doing the same after our example.'

Next came the most controversial ten minutes of the battle. 'At length, General Leith, having come up from the right, charged the enemy in front, and the column went to the right about,' Lightfoot later recorded. 'Down it descended, sullenly and slow … pursued by us with shouts; but, having followed them to nearly the bottom of the Sierra, we again withdrew our troops, and resumed our original position. The Colonel, who was on horseback in the rear of the line all the time, now came up to me, and expressed his satisfaction.'[195] The term 'at length' may be entirely relative, since 5th Division accounts of the event read quite differently. At some point an aide-de-camp of Major-General James Leith arrived with news that Lieutenant-Colonel James Barns' brigade of the 5th Division was immediately following, and the fresh 9th and 38th Foot double-timed forward and met the tiring French column with deadly volleys and a bayonet charge. They flung the Frenchmen back down the hill, supported by the five companies of the 45th and the 8th Portuguese Line.

The part played by the 5th Division rankled with 3rd Division men for years to come, and broke out into verbal warfare in the British press in 1838. Picton and officers in his Fighting Third declared that their flank was never in danger; the 5th Division was equally adamant that they had arrived in the nick of time to drive the last French column from the summit. Captain Thomas Lightfoot recorded his views on the matter that year in response to a letter written by Sir John Cameron, who had commanded the 9th Foot in the 5th Division: 'To affirm that the 5th Division "saved the Right Brigade of the 3rd" on this occasion, or that the latter would have been "in a critical situation" if the former had not come up, is evidently going too far. For, had that division not come up, and had the enemy established his column on the top of the hill, he would still have had the 45th Regiment and the 8th Portuguese on his right flank, in readiness to charge, if necessary; and the former, at least, would have required but the word to have done it, as their comrades of the 88th Regt. had done before … If he did not do this, it was simply because the arrival of the 5th Division rendered it unnecessary.'

The 5th Division was new formation at the time of Busaco, having been formed only the month before, and no doubt its senior officers were keen to show that they had made an impression at the division's first action. But

Lightfoot was having none of it. 'But as the 5th Division did not, according to their own showing in Napier's History, pursue the enemy, but were prudently kept behind the rocks, lest the position should be retaken from them, they saw nothing of these troops in front of the pass, nor of the 45th Regiment and 8th Portuguese on the other side of the rocks, who were pursuing the enemy with shouts to the bottom of the hill, pouring in their fire continually upon him. They therefore concluded that they had, most miraculously, performed all the work themselves.'[196] Wellington later famously likened a battle to a ball, saying that it was full of interesting incidents that none of the participants could later put into chronological order, much less reconstruct a coherent story. Busaco was one of those days.

Lightfoot's letter home after the battle finishes with a description of the losses suffered by the 45th that morning. 'To give you an idea of the sort of fire the four companies sustained, we went into the field forty strong and upwards each company, and I can now muster only eighteen men in my company: the others suffered equally, one musters only fifteen. My Lieutenant was killed … To this I may add, that the whole four companies paraded afterwards, under my command, as one strong company, until an opportunity was offered, by our halt at Pombal, to equalise the companies.'[197] This suggests that the four left wing companies went into action about 180 strong, and suffered about a hundred casualties before breakfast.

But the verbal war was still many years in the future. The real war entered a lull; the French ceased their attacks on Picton's sector at that point – it was still barely eight o'clock in the morning – and a second assault took place about two miles to the north. There the French sector was commanded by the redoubtable Maréchal Ney, and upon hearing gunfire he assumed the French assaults against Picton were enjoying success. Ney was a man of action first and foremost and so he ordered his leading division under Loison to move off. The main highway in this part of the line climbed a long spur to reach the crest at the convent of Busaco. Loison's division puffed its way up the steep slope, wondering at the absence of troops on the crest. Little did they know that some 1,800 men of the 1/43rd and 1/52nd Light Infantry were lying in wait. As the French brigades approached the convent grounds, Brigadier-General Craufurd roared, '52nd! Avenge Moore!' and the two British regiments stood, fired a volley at point-blank range and charged with the bayonet. The French brigade turned and fled. Loison's other brigade fared no better, running into close-range fire from two artillery batteries to the south of Craufurd's men. Closer to the centre of the British line, a final thrust by one of Marchand's brigades met defeat at the hands of Pack's Portuguese brigade. The two sides occupied the rest of the day in sniping and skirmishing, and the French did not attack again.

The battle was over for the 3rd Division – Picton's first in the Peninsula. According to Ensign Grattan of the 88th, 'we had now leisure to walk about,

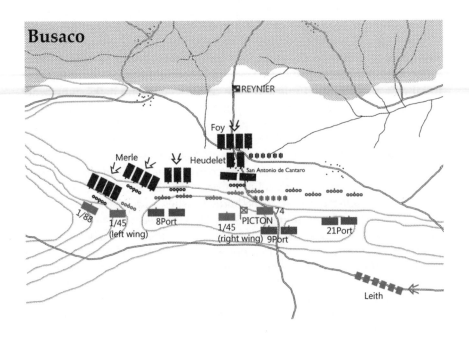

and talk to each other on the events of the morning, and look at the French soldiers in our front. They appeared as leisurely employed cooking their rations as if nothing serious had occurred to them, which caused much amusement to our men, some of whom remarked that they left a few behind them that had got a "belly-full" already. The rocks which had been forced by the three companies of the 88th presented a curious and melancholy sight; one side of their base strewed with our brave fellows, almost all of them shot through the head, while in many of the niches were to be seen dead Frenchmen, in the position they had fought; while on the other side, and on the projecting crags, lay numbers who in an effort to escape the fury of our men were dashed to pieces in their fall!'[198]

The losses in the 45th were considerable. Major William Smith, Captain Charles Urquhart, Lieutenant Ralph Ousely,[199] one serjeant and twenty-one rank-and-file were killed; Major William Gwyn, Lieutenants Alexander Anderson, John Harris, Ensign John Tyler (shot through in the shoulder), three serjeants and 106 rank-and-file were wounded, and twelve men were missing. Most of the casualties were in Major Gwyn's four companies, with the rest coming from the detached Light and No.1 companies. This was the highest loss of any battalion on the British side that day. With no majors left for duty, Captain Leonard Greenwell suddenly found himself second-in-command, quite a rise for a man who had ranked only eighth in seniority at Roliça. With Surgeon Boggie and both assistant-surgeons sick absent, an enormous load fell upon the head of newly-arrived Assistant-Surgeon

James Paterson, only just promoted from Hospital Mate. Paterson was a twenty-year-old from Strathaven in Lanarkshire, the son of a shoemaker, and had never been overseas before; to say that what he now faced was character-building is somewhat of an under-statement. Private John Fallawell, a 22-year-old from Worksop in No.2 Company had a dangerous wound that required the removal of his leg at the thigh; Private John Taylor had ribs broken in a musket-butt fight; Private Ben Thorpe had been shot in the chest. That was even before the other 110 casualties were considered.

Picton's division had received its first true baptism of fire. He wrote in his official report to Wellington: 'Your lordship was pleased to mention me as directing the gallant charge of the 45th and 88th regiments, but I can claim no merit in the executive part of the brilliant exploit which your lordship has so highly and so justly extolled. Lieut.-Colonel Wallace and Major Gwyn, who commanded the four companies of the 45th engaged on the occasion, are entitled to the whole of the merit; I am not disposed to and deprive them of any part.'[200] Wellington's official report of the battle was equally fulsome in praise: 'I beg to assure your lordship that I have never witnessed a more gallant attack than that made by the 88th, 45th, and 8th Portuguese regiments on the enemy's division, which had reached the edge of the sierra.'[201]

Busaco holds a significant place in Portuguese military history, for it was the first battle of the war in which their troops played a large part. They had behaved as well as any untried troops could, and importantly had even attracted Wellington's attention; five years later, he unsuccessfully requested their presence for the Waterloo campaign. Major Smith died before Marshal Beresford could consider placing him in command of a Portuguese regiment, although this fact was probably unknown to his fellow officers of the 45th. Of Smith's death, the Viscount Wellington reportedly said, 'Major Smith of the 45th regiment … was a gentleman of the most agreeable and unassuming manner. In him the Country has lost a most gallant officer. He was a hero – a second Charles the Twelfth of Sweden.'[202]

---

[185] The sick were detached from the column at Penacova on 22 September and sailed upriver to Coimbra.

[186] Wylly, p.171.

[187] ibid, p.169.

[188] This is based upon a casualty count of the various companies and who commanded them on the day of battle.

[189] 1928 Regimental Annual, p.259.

[190] ibid.

[191] ibid.

[192] One of which may have due to friendly fire.

[193] 1928 Regimental Annual, p.259.

[194] Campbell, p.173.

[195] 1928 Regimental Annual, p.265.

[196] ibid, pp.267-8.

[197] ibid, pp.268-9.

[198] Grattan, Vol. 1, p.59.

[199] Sadly, Ralph Ousely's staff education at the RMC had never been utilised.

[200] Wylly, p.173.

[201] Dalbiac, p.72.

[202] 1928 Regimental Annual.

Chapter 13

The Retreat to Torres Vedras

That night, both sides nervously watched each other's camp-fires. The morning of 28 September brought the sound of an army seemingly in retreat – the French opposite were no longer visible and seemed to be moving farther away. The men were jubilant – the day before had clearly been a victory, and they could look forward to an extra tot of rum in celebration, and a peaceful day cleaning their arms and accoutrements, and perhaps a snooze out of sight of the serjeants.

Lieutenant James MacPherson received a message that his great friend and fellow-sleeper John Tyler was mortally wounded and on his way to Coimbra, and not expected to live. He presented himself before Lieutenant-Colonel Meade and asked for a day's leave to see Tyler one last time; Meade was still furious about the absentee incident and with the other three either dead or mortally wounded, MacPherson was the only one left to punish. He flatly refused. The resourceful MacPherson then presented his story to Lieutenant-General Picton, who roared: 'What! Not let you go? Damn me, you shall go, and tell Colonel Meade I say so. D'ye hear, sir?'

Meade was flabbergasted, but could not countermand his superior; he muttered something about 'all discipline in the army has ceased' and waved MacPherson away.[203] So James went to Coimbra, where he found John Tyler more alive than previously expected, and the two shared an enormous breakfast. Tyler was a large man and a noted gourmand within the regiment, and could generally be relied upon to find a good meal just about anywhere.

On 9 November, in remote Fort George near Inverness, John and Mary Urquhart learned of the death of their son Charles, formerly captain in the 45th. He was the third of their sons to have been killed in the service of King George; the first had died on Jamaica and the second at Portsmouth. Two years later, the recently-widowed Mary applied for (and received) a £50 annual pension in her sons' names – slightly less than the average wage at the time. It was precious little for all her sacrifices.[204]

Back on the Busaco ridge, the rest of the battalion hoped for a good sleep, but they would not get one. They were kept awake all night and told to light as many camp-fires as possible, then put on the road at two in the morning; and marched fourteen hours over horrendous roads to end the day at the hamlet of Eiras, barely six miles (as the crow flies) from where they had started. Exhausted, they learned that the French were not beaten at all, but still marching on Lisbon, having flanked them to the north, and were perhaps a day's march behind. The brigade tramped through Coimbra late the following morning, and found themselves posted on a hill beyond the town as a rearguard whilst the rest of the army – and a large proportion of the population of Coimbra – passed southwards amidst rumours that a French Corps under Junot was snapping at their heels. It wasn't, it was several days away. The bridge across the Mondego was blown up nonetheless.

Whilst at Coimbra they learned that something almost unheard of had happened – Wellington had pardoned the four men on death row. 'Although the Commander of the Forces has long determined that he will not pardon men guilty of crimes of which these Prisoners have been convicted,' the pardon read, 'he is induced to pardon these men in consequence of the gallantry displayed by the 45th Regiment on the 27th inst. He trusts that this pardon will make a due impression upon the Prisoners, and that by their future regular and good conduct, they will endeavour to emulate their comrades, who have by their bravery saved them from a disgraceful end.'[205] Three of the quartet perished during the war or shortly thereafter – Edward Perrott was killed in action at the storming of Ciudad Rodrigo in January 1812; Joseph Freeman died of sickness in Portugal on 15 February 1813; and the irascible Thomas Horsley – who had robbed the captured French officer blind whilst awaiting his sentence at Celerico – died of consumption at the General Hospital on the Isle of Wight in August 1815. Joseph Norman fought on only to lose an arm at Badajoz, but survived to collect his Chelsea Pension and belatedly collected his Military General Service Medal in 1847.[206]

The rate of the retreat increased on good roads. The following day, 1 October, they stayed overnight at the convent at Pombal, where the monks, packing in anticipation of flight, threw open their provision stores and made the 45th very happy. Progress was slower by the time they reached Leiria the next day, despite having marched fifty-five miles in two days; the roads were jammed with fleeing locals. The 45th again found themselves quartered at a convent. Here things got out of control, as Private William Brown explained:

'I walked into the town, which I found in the utmost confusion. Most of the inhabitants had left the place, and the soldiers commenced the work of plunder. As I stepped into a house I met one of our men coming out with a bundle of dried fish on his shoulder, which he seems to regard as his own. On entering the place I found it to be a grocer's shop, in which were a number of soldiers very busy. One man had seized sack of rice, but it was so heavy he could not carry it, it would allow no want to participate with him, until another ripped the sack with a knife from top to bottom, when a general scramble ensued for the contents on the floor. A cask, containing butter, was surrounded by another squad, who, disagreeing about spoil, tore the cask into staves, and in the contest most of the butter was trodden underfoot. The happiest fellow I saw in the whole group, was won with his cap full of cayenne pepper, with which he seemed well pleased, and in secure possession, as nobody appeared to envy him of his prize ... In returning towards my quarters at the convent, a short distance from the town, I met a Portuguese leading a heavy laden ass. He had not proceeded far when he came in contact with two soldiers, who immediately seized the animal and led him away, while the poor peasant stood confounded and amazed; and when he saw his property at a considerable distance exclaimed, "Adeus, Adeus, pauvre borico!" So saying he turned himself around and walked away. Such is the fate of a country where war spreads its desolating wings. The inhabitants are robbed and plundered by friends and foes, and fall an easy prey to the victors and vanquished.'[207]

And so, for the first time in the brigade's experience, came the behaviour that would vilify the British Army in the aftermaths of Badajoz and Ciudad Rodrigo. Wellington learnt of it and immediately issued an order which suggested he knew the 3rd Division as the worst culprits. 'Major-General Picton is requested not to allow the troops of his division to enter any town unless necessarily obliged to pass through it, until further orders.'[208]

Thus the 45th were tramping routes last seen more than two years before during the advance to Roliça, but bypassing the towns. The roads behind them were becoming even more clogged with Portuguese fleeing from the advancing French. Rumours were rife in the ranks that they were bound for Lisbon and evacuation. The column was allowed to rest outside the beautiful village of Alcobaça and the 45th camped near the monastery, the largest in Portugal, where the officers of the division were treated to a fine dinner by the monks. They marched again in the evening of 5 October, took the wrong road and promptly got lost in the dark. The following day they bypassed around Caldas, Obidos and Roliça, taking a more leisurely ascent of the escarpment, past the Vimeiro battlefield and through the town of Torres Vedras in a valley cut through a mountain range, where they were astounded to see forts sited on all the surrounding mountain-tops, merely part of a chain of fortifications that extended from the Atlantic (some eight miles to the west) all the way down to the River Tagus, twenty miles to the south-east. The forts had been built by 10,000 Portuguese civilian labourers under the supervision of seventeen British, Hanoverian and Portuguese engineer officers. They halted there and the next day the rain came in bucket-loads, a torrential downpour that lasted for a week. On 11 October Captain Archibald McDonald, newly arrived in country for his second tour of duty, was appointed brigade-major to a new brigade assembling in the

1st Division under Major-General Sir William Erskine, a role that would take him away from the 45th for good.

The allied defences of Torres Vedras were one of the marvels of the war, indeed of any war. It was Wellington's secret weapon and the French had no idea they even existed. The lines were manned by men of the Royal Artillery and Royal Navy gunners in addition to Portuguese militia, as well as the regular divisions of Wellington's army.

The brigade moved four miles south to Turcifal, then marched south-eastwards on 13 October on hearing of a French attack through Sobral. They stood to on a hillside near the village of Patameira expecting a battle the following day, but ended it without seeing a Frenchman. On 19 October the brigade moved further east, to Cardosas, there being a general belief that a French attack on what was now being called the 'Lines of Torres Vedras' would only come between Sobral and the Tagus. But it did not come, and the men spent their days improving fortifications. At last they saw Frenchmen; but not as they expected, rather fifty or sixty deserters each day. On the northern side of the lines, Masséna's men were slowly starving. As if the scorched-earth policy enacted by the defenders of the lines were not enough, the Portuguese peasantry had taken everything of value in their flight behind the lines on the approach of the French. And the French had no need for supply trains, choosing as they did to live off the land. It allowed them to advance at a spectacular pace in fields of plenty, but ground them to an emaciated halt when the land yielded nothing.[209]

To make matters worse, a Portuguese militia force under Colonel Nicholas Trant had captured Coimbra back from the French on 7 October, massacring many of the French wounded, capturing the rest and cutting off a possible line of retreat. The 45th likewise felt the effect of all the exertions of the prior four weeks; it increased the number of incapacitated men in the battalion. On 25 October in camp near Cardosas the 45th could only muster 429 fit men, with 273 men on the sick list, although a number of these were the recuperating wounded from Busaco. They were sent down to Mafra, and later transported down to Lisbon by the commissary-general's department. Some thirty-one men had died since 25 September, presumably the twenty-two killed at Busaco plus another nine perhaps dead from wounds. Major Gwyn and Lieutenants Anderson, Harris and Tyler were all still recuperating in hospital at Lisbon. Major George Purdon Drew went home at about this time (shortly to retire from the army) and most pleasingly, Captain Leonard Greenwell succeeded to the late William Smith's vacant majority without purchase, handing over command of his beloved Light Company to the appropriately-named Captain Tom Lightfoot. We can only assume that the men were sorry to see him go.

The division appears to have been sent north-west at the beginning of November, since divine service was held at Cadeira (Sao Pedra da Cadeira) every Sunday morning; Picton's brigade attended at eight o'clock and MacKinnon's brigade at ten.

The winter came on, but still the French did not advance. By the start of November they had lost close to 5,000 men from starvation; hundreds of deserters had surrendered to the allies. On the night of 14 November, protected by a dense fog, they retired twenty-five miles to Santarem, looking for a better source of supply; the fertile Tagus valley seemed to offer more hope than the rocky Torres Vedras ranges. The fog did not clear until ten o'clock the next morning, and then the British were slow in realising they had gone and therefore taking off in pursuit. Wellington's troops did not catch up with them until 17 November. The following day the French were in their new fortified camp, and it was Wellington's turn to face a strong defensive position.

A Regular Brutus

In mid-November the 45th gained a new company commander with the arrival of Captain John O'Flaherty, a good-natured and ruddy-faced ex-militiaman in his early thirties from Ballyhaunis in County Mayo. O'Flaherty had endured a rough thirty-day crossing from England to the Tagus, and had occupied his time playing draughts with officers from other regiments, winning fifty Spanish dollars from an unfortunate ensign of the 52nd Light Infantry – the equivalent of about six weeks' pay.[210] The 45th moved down to Tagarro near Alcoentre about this time and it became their winter quarters. Leaving Major Greenwell in command, Lieutenant-Colonel the Honourable John Meade went down to Lisbon sick, and to the relief of the miscreants in the battalion, went back to England in December (ostensibly on two month's leave); he never returned to the Peninsula, preferring to further his Parliamentary career instead. Captain Henry Dabsac went home to Dublin and also never returned – he died there on 7 June 1811.

The men's red coats were by now a dull brick-red bordering on pale brown; their white cross-belts a dirty buff, or else replaced completely by un-coloured leather straps; their white 'trowsers' replaced with the blue-grey numbers organised by Lieutenant-Colonel Guard sometime before Talavera. Grattan of the neighbouring 88th described their appearance: 'As to ourselves, we might be rigged out in all the colours of the rainbow if we fancied it. The consequence was that scarcely any two officers were dressed alike! Some with grey braided coats, others with brown; some again liked blue; while many from choice, or perhaps necessity, stuck to the "old red rag". Overalls, of all things, were in vogue, and the comical appearance of a number of infantry officers loaded with leather bottoms to their pantaloons, and huge chains suspended from the side-buttons, like a parcel of troopers, was amusing enough … Quantities of hair, a regular brutus, a pair of mustachioes, and screw brass spurs, were essential to a first rate

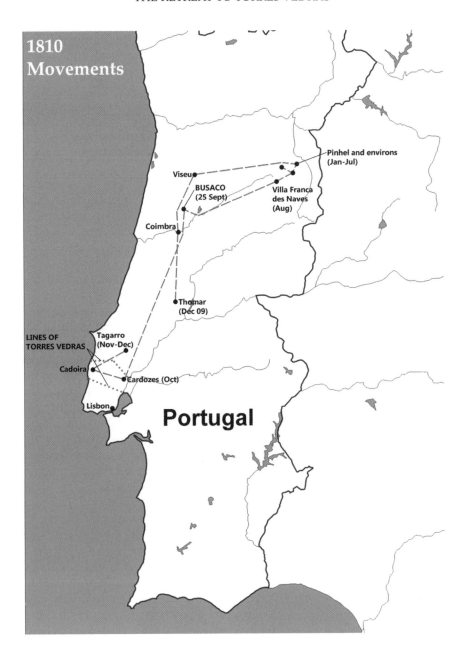

Count, for so were our dandies designated. The "cut-down" hat, exactly a span in height, was another rage; this burlesque on a chapeau was usually out-topped by some extraordinary-looking feather; while again, others wore their hats without any feather at all – and indeed this was the most rational thing they did. In the paroxysm of a wish to be singularly singular, a friend of mine shaved all the hair off the crown of his head, and he was decidedly the most outré-looking man amongst us, and consequently the happiest.'[211]

Wellington and Picton were both well-known for wearing civilian costume on campaign, and Wellington famously said he did not care what his men looked like, so long as they did their duty – or as Grattan observed, 'provided we brought our men into the field well appointed, and with sixty rounds of good ammunition each, (Wellington) never looked to see whether their trousers were black, blue, or grey'. It must have been exceptionally easy to tell a newly-arrived battalion, all pristine red coats and white trowsers, from a veteran one; the latter all dull-brown coats, trowsers of any colour and length, men with long hair and beards, commanded by officers sporting any outer-wear and headgear they chose, shaven heads and Zapata moustaches. There are many books on military uniforms of the era, but it is likely none of them capture the actual appearance of the veteran Peninsula infantryman of 1810.

Behind the lines the troops were bored, and it was trying Wellington's patience. He wrote from Cartaxo on 12 December that 'notwithstanding his repeated orders and the inconvenience which all the officers and soldiers have experienced from the practice of burning doors and windows, and the furniture and materials of houses, it still continues'. And then again, less than a fortnight later, on 23 December – 'officers of the army would not shoot the deer in the Royal or other parks without having leave to do so' One letter, written the day after New Year's Day, must have had him rolling his eyes: 'The officers and soldiers of the army are again warned that they have no more right to confine in a military guard an inhabitant of Portugal than they would have to confine one of His Majesty's subjects in Great Britain.'[212] And lastly: 'The Commander of the Forces is ashamed to acknowledge that the British troops have, in many instances, done more mischief to the country in this manner than had been done by the enemy.'[213]

In early December Picton established the brigade headquarters at Tagarro. Major Gwyn announced in late December that he had accepted a vacant lieutenant-colonelcy in the 2/89th Foot at Gibraltar and would not return to the 45th. Some of the officers went to Lisbon for Christmas to say goodbye to their gallant friend, but there was no cheer in that filthy city. Overflowing with refugees, economically drained by the war and lacking supplies (the bulk of those that arrived went to the army), the city and surrounding region was ravaged by disease over the winter of 1810-1811; somewhere between 40,000 and 50,000 Portuguese died. It was nearly two percent of the population. The number of sick men in the battalion decreased, down by a hundred men by Christmas Day. They were much better supplied than the French but still far from comfortable, living in makeshift huts and tents (usually just sheets strung between poles), no protection at all against the seemingly incessant rain. Rivers overflowed, and one accounted for Assistant-Surgeon John Mousdale, who accidentally drowned in December.

Wellington expected Masséna to retreat at any moment, but was also of the view that he might attack without warning, especially after French reinforcements arrived in late December. But both sides sat inert for the whole winter.

At divine service in the little square in front of the white-painted church in Tagarro on Christmas Day, the men of the 45th could look back at 1810 and be thankful that they had only fought one (albeit bloody) battle. Nonetheless, the battalion had lost 123 men during the year, the majority, as always, due to disease. The muster rolls also showed no men lost to desertion for the year, an extremely rare feat in the army at this time; unfortunately the second battalion in Nottingham had a poor year, losing thirty men.

[203] Wylly, p.177.

[204] Estimates and Accounts, Army, Naval, Civil List … 1817.

[205] General Orders, Vol. 2. p.172.

[206] WO116; Military General Service Medal Roll.

[207] Brown, pp.79-81.

[208] *Wellington's Dispatches*, Vol. 4, p.311.

[209] The French invasion of Russia in 1812 is a perfect example of this policy.

[210] 1932 Regimental Annual, p.236.

[211] Grattan, Vol. 1, pp.60-1.

[212] *Wellington's Dispatches*, Vol. 4, p.457.

[213] Supplementary Dispatches, Vol. 7, p.8.

Part V

1811

Chapter 14

The Advanced Guard of Infamy

The 45th was still at Tagarro on 23 January 1811, where only six company commanders were actually present with the battalion. Two days later at muster the battalion was starting to look healthy again, with 524 effectives and only 143 men sick. However, thirty-three men had been sent home since Christmas, the chronically sick and worn out, and those too badly wounded at Busaco to be of any further use on campaign. Captain Greenwell's Light Company was the strongest in the battalion with eighty-seven other ranks, and Captain Campbell's No.10, the weakest with only sixty-five rankers.[214]

On 23 February, while the battalion was still headquartered at Tagarro, something very odd happened. Richard Burke, one of the senior lieutenants, went missing; word later came back that he had deserted to the French. Wounded at Roliça, he was a veteran with six-and-a-half year's Army service. His company commander, Captain James Campbell, later had this to say about the incident: 'I do not know in what part of Ireland Mr. Burke first saw the light, but he had been sent in early life to Salamanca, to be brought up for the Roman Catholic priesthood. It was, however, I suppose, found that he was unfit for that calling; at least, I understand that he had never been ordained; and having married, some person had most unwarrantably taken it upon himself to recommend him for an ensigncy in the army, for which he was still more unfit than to be a priest, for he was both vulgar in looks and manners; but as he spoke Spanish, and some Portuguese, and announcing himself wherever he went as a good Catholic, he got on, though very ignorant and illiterate, famously, both with the priests and people of Portugal … having been sent off, in order to get him away from the regiment, with part of the 3rd Division's "advanced guard of infamy" – that is to say the soldiers' wives, whom it was found necessary to send to the rear, in consequence of the depredations they daily committed; these Amazons, headed by a well-known character, rose upon him with the most diabolical intentions, as some may remember, for the circumstance was much laughed at the time, and he only escaped from their clutches, by jumping out of a window, at the risk of breaking his neck.'[215]

One gets the impression that the soldiers' wives of the 3rd Division were as famous within the Army as their husbands – indeed, the term 'advanced guard of infamy' was coined by Picton himself – and the thought of a large party of them chasing one of His Majesty's officers out of a window is indeed comical. But the consequences of Burke's narrow escape from the Amazons were more serious. 'As soon as he disappeared, and that it was conjectured he had gone over to the enemy … Marshal Masséna finding him useless, he was altogether neglected, and having been left by the French, in their retreat, asleep in a hut, he fell into the hands of some of our light troops.'[216]

Burke was recaptured by a party of the 16th Light Dragoons on 8 March. According to a newspaper report, he fought like the very devil, was wounded, and pleaded insanity when captured. 'It was at once ascertained, that he had become deranged during his confinement. Upon this circumstance being made known to Lord Wellington, he, I understood, ordered him to be sent home, and I heard some time afterwards, that the unfortunate man died in a lunatic asylum in Ireland.'[217]

In April 1811 the *Cork Southern Reporter* supplied a very different view of the whole affair. 'In reality, [he] was taken by a French picquet of cavalry, which surprised him as he was taking a ride, in company with the Major of his regiment, [and] is returned to the British Army. He was separated from the Major, by having ridden to the top of one of those high hills with which Portugal so abounds, and ordered not to express a word. There was no message sent to the Commander in Chief, as reported: all the accounts Lord Wellington had, was a French prisoner having seen him at Massena's quarters. He took advantage of the confusion of the French Army on their retreat, and returned the first moment possible.'[218] But no amount of parochial support could save him. He was shown superseded on the Army List on 21 May, shipped back to await trial at Newport Asylum in England and disappeared from military history for some time. However there is no evidence that the trial ever took place, and Richard Burke was reinstated as a lieutenant in the 101st Foot in 1816, assuming his place in the lieutenant's list according to his original commission date of 14 November 1805. He immediately went on half-pay, the 101st Foot was disbanded in January 1817 and Richard stayed on the half-pay list until 1846, suggesting he died that year or early in 1847 – not earlier, as Campbell suggested. Was he the only British officer to desert to the French during the Peninsular War? Or had he been drunk? Or simply lost and unlucky? No court-martial was ever called to establish the facts. We will probably never know.

Pursuit and Skirmish

Captain David Lecky of the Grenadier Company was appointed to William Gwyn's vacant majority on 28 February but stayed on in Portugal, despite being technically on the strength of the second battalion as one of the junior majors. Lieutenant Bob Hardiman seems to have commanded the grenadiers for the next few months until the arrival of a replacement captain.

Picton's 3rd Division commenced campaigning for 1811 on 4 March. They occupied the ground that Masséna had recently pulled back from, but it was a mopping-up exercise since they were well removed from the main thrust of Wellington's advance. The initial movements of the French retreat had caused considerable confusion within the allied camp, and on 9 March Wellington's divisions were too widely scattered to press the French rearguard. Only the Light Division and Pack's Portuguese Brigade were available to follow the French; it took the 3rd Division a week to catch up, by which time the vanguard was near Pombal, eighty-five miles north of Lisbon. The British sent a small force of riflemen and *caçadores* into the town, which the French repulsed before retreating. The 45th took no part in the action.

The following day the pursuit of Masséna began in earnest. Wellington felt that he was close to the main body of the French and waited until he had three divisions in place before attacking Ney's advance guard at Redinha, five miles north-east of Pombal. Maréchal Ney had occupied an apparently vulnerable position, with a division on a plateau south of the village, and another to the north of the village on the far side of the Ancos River, linked by a narrow bridge. Wellington proceeded very carefully and put the Light, 4th and 3rd divisions into line (together with Pack's Portuguese) whilst the 1st and 6th divisions marched to their support. It was a day of manoeuvring rather than scrapping, in which the exposed French suffered heavily from allied artillery fire. At two o'clock in the afternoon the 3rd Division made two efforts to outflank the French line; twice the French retreated northwards just in time to avoid disaster, Maréchal Ney showing his customary skill at handling a rearguard.

The 45th, on the right-hand end of the entire allied line, suffered Lieutenant Hans Stevenson Marsh and six men wounded (mainly from long-range musketry duels between flankers) out of a total loss of about 200 men on each side for the day. On 13 March the French turned east, and began the long march back to Spain. Maréchal Ney was left behind at Condeixa, with orders to delay the British for as long as possible; however the 3rd Division advanced around the French left flank, forcing Ney to abandon Condeixa and retreat to Cazal Novo, five miles to the east. Wellington attacked the next morning; Marchand's division held a strong position on rising ground behind stone walls and concealed by fog. The Light Division came at the very much stronger French centre in the mist (losing nearly a hundred men doing so) whilst the 3rd Division attempted a turning manoeuvre on the right in order to rescue them. The French retired and formed a new line, and another flanking manoeuvre winkled them out of this position also, at which time they retired for the day. The 45th lost one man killed (Private Thomas McNamara), nine wounded and one missing out of a total British loss of 155 men.[219]

After a night march most of the French army crossed the Ceira River at Foz de Arouce (about 10 miles east of Coimbra) and camped on the heights above the village. Ney made the mistake of employing his divisions separated by a river rather than destroying the bridge (as he had been ordered by Masséna). Wellington's pursuit was delayed by heavy fog. The 3rd and Light divisions did not reach the Ceira until four in the afternoon on 15 March, and seeing the French arrayed in some strength decided to camp and wait for the rest of the army to catch up.

Wellington arrived just before dusk, and decided to surprise the French; the Light Division immediately attacked the French right and the 3rd Division their left. The French 39e Ligne broke, and attempted to cross the bridge; the way was blocked by French cavalry, so the infantry were forced to use a ford, and a number of Frenchmen were swept away and drowned; the regiment's eagle was lost in the panic, but later recovered by the allies and sent to London. Again the losses of the 3rd Division were quite trifling and the 45th lost only a single man wounded for the day.

The allies were now nearly 120 miles north of Lisbon and almost beyond the range of supply trains. Wellington therefore paused for a day to allow his supply convoys to catch the army. He resumed the pursuit with three divisions on 18 March, but found the French in a strong position on the Alva River. Another outflanking manoeuvre forced the French to abandon their new position. By this stage their morale was plummeting and the allies took 600 French prisoners on 19 March. The following day Wellington's army was across the Alva, but once again supplies were low.

On 21 March Masséna reached Celorico, close to the Spanish border and the French supply bases at Almeida and Ciudad Rodrigo. The logical thing for Masséna to do would have been to shift east to his supply bases, rest and re-fit. But Masséna had a reputation that was not based on rest and recuperation. He crossed the mountains between the Mondego and the Tagus rivers to occupy northern Extremadura in Spain, from where he hoped to launch a second invasion of Portugal – along the same terrible roads that had nearly ruined Gènèral Junot's original invasion in 1807.

Maréchal Ney wrote three letters of complaint over what he considered an absurd plan and was removed from command. The expedition lasted six days; Masséna's exhausted army struggled and starved in the mountainous terrain. The 3rd Division reached Maceira on 21 March, Celorico on the 26th and Guarda (the highest town in Portugal) on the 29th, where the British finally caught up with the French rearguard. Ney's replacement, Gènèral Loison, was caught almost entirely by surprise (whereas it is hard to imagine Ney failing to provide a rearguard action!) and ordered his corps to retreat without putting up a fight. The 3rd Division captured a fort on the left of the French position, and spent the day opposed (and unsupported) in the face of 15,000 retreating Frenchmen. Their reward was the half-cooked meals the fleeing French left roasting over camp-fires.

Sabugal

Maréchal Michel Ney, the man sacked by Masséna, was a man of heroic energy but deeply flawed by tunnel vision and a tendency to go to extremes; a classic case of all or nothing. But he was the greatest commander of a rearguard in Europe – as the 3rd Division had discovered at Redinha – and his loss to the French would prove disastrous.

André Masséna was a 55-year-old Italian (by birth) who had scrapped his way up from the ranks; as was often the way in French revolutionary armies, he had joined up as an ex-sergeant-major in 1792 and been catapulted to Général de Division in 1793. He was a general by instinct rather than learning, hated to read maps (or anything else), adored money and women above all else, but was invigorated by the spirit of Mars as soon as he was in sight of the enemy. Wellington never slept comfortably when opposed by the man.

March 1811 had been a bad month for Masséna. He had been pushed out of Portugal, fired his most capable subordinate, and then retreated along a line that suggested he had lost the ability even to get his subordinates to read maps or discuss the terrain with locals. And now he made one more mistake. His army was safely back across the Coa River by the end of March, but instead of logically continuing on to his supply base at Ciudad Rodrigo, Masséna decided to give his troops a few days' rest, spreading his troops out along the line of the river, assuming the allies would likewise rest at Guarda. But Wellington did not rest, spotted this weakness and pounced. Reynier's 2nd Corps was exposed at the southern end of the French line near Sabugal.

Under a cover of thick fog, the Light Division attacked across the Coa in the early morning of 3 April, thinking the supporting divisions (3rd Division on their left and 1st and 7th divisions in support) were coming on; in fact all three had stopped to await further orders, leaving the 'Light Bobs' (as they were now being called after their commander, Major-General Robert Craufurd) to deal with Reynier alone. The lights were 'rather heavily handled' and the 3rd Division eventually crossed the river in their support, to be obfuscated by rain and mist so heavy that Wellington could not see the action from his command post. Reynier slipped away whilst the British camped on the sodden ground having lost 150 men. The 45th lost two men wounded and one missing.

The Fighting Third

The actions of the preceding six months, from Busaco to Sabugal, had seen the 3rd Division at the forefront of almost every action. It was therefore no surprise that the rest of the Army started to refer to them as 'The Fighters', a nick-name that the division members eagerly adopted as their own. MacKinnon's brigade in particular was acquiring a reputation as trouble-shooters, ideal troops to have at hand in a tight spot. The others divisions had acquired nicknames as well, some more obvious than others:[220]

1st Division	The Gentleman's Sons
2nd Division	General Hill's Lambs
4th Division	The Observers
5th Division	The Dirty Division
6th Division	The Marchers
7th Division	The Invisibles
Light Division	THE Division

The 1st Division contained the Brigade of Guards; the 2nd Division unfailingly followed General Hill wherever he went; the 4th Division always seemed to be looking on the actions of the 2nd Division; the 5th always did more than its fair share of road-building and trench-digging; the 6th marched all over Iberia, rarely seeing action; and the new 7th Division had barely been seen by the rest of the army, despite being rumoured to exist. As for the Light Division, well, the sun shone out the back of their trowsers …

On 25 April the 45th were at a filthy village named Nave de Haver, six miles south of the frontier town of Fuentes de Oñoro. Quartermaster-Serjeant Francis Tinkler was discharged after fifteen years' service and his place was taken by Serjeant Lawrence Walsh from the Light Company. The battalion's effective strength on this date was 426 men, down by over a hundred in the last two months as the sickness rate increased again in the warmer weather. Twelve men were sent home in the month as unfit for further service.

Wellington had assembled the bulk of his forces on the Portuguese border in positions that blockaded the French garrison at Almeida, and settled down to starve the garrison out. He had 34,000 infantry (23,000 British and 11,000 Portuguese), 1,900 cavalry and forty-eight guns. Just across the border, Masséna had 42,000 infantry, 4,500 cavalry and thirty-eight guns, and a burning desire to restore his tarnished reputation. The French marched out of Ciudad Rodrigo on 2 May, watched by the Light Division, and by nightfall were in scrubby countryside somewhere between Gallegos and Espeja, about six miles east of Fuentes de Oñoro, shadowed by riflemen and King's German Legion dragoons every step of the way.

---

[214] WO12/5728.

[215] Campbell, pp.151-2.

[216] ibid, pp.152-153.

[217] National Library of Australia, 19th Century British Newspapers Online.

[218] National Library of Australia, Irish Newspapers Online.

[219] WO25/1275.

[220] Other names have been cited, such as the 7th Division being 'The Mongrels'. Those listed are based upon various sources.

Chapter 15

Fuentes de Oñoro

The road from Ciudad Rodrigo ran straight through the stone-walled village of Fuentes de Oñoro at the border, across a narrow stone bridge over the Dos Casas stream (a southern tributary of the Agueda), onwards towards Coimbra. Wellington had taken up a strong extended position on the line of the stream. A long line of hills and a ravine in front of the allied left effectively prevented any French attack on this part of Wellington's position, but the right was not as strong, being flat, open farmland. The village of Fuentes de Oñoro itself was a very defensible position, but there was little to stop an outflanking move to the south. It was a long way short from the steep rocky hillsides of Busaco. Not surprisingly, the bulk of Wellington's army was posted on the right. The left was held by the 5th and 6th divisions; the 1st and 7th divisions and a Portuguese brigade were stationed on the hills above Fuentes de Oñoro on the allied right, and the Light Division was in reserve.

The village itself was held by nineteen light companies detached from their parent battalions (2/24th, 2/42nd, 1/45th, 1/50th, 1/71st, 74th, 1/79th, 2/83rd, 1/88th, 2/88th, 1/92nd, 94th plus five KGL companies and two Portuguese companies) commanded by Lieutenant-Colonel William Williams of the 60th Rifles, short, stout and stentorian just as Colonel Guard had been. He had 460 men of the 2/83rd Foot posted at the top of the village in reserve. The line of the river was held by four rifle-armed companies from the 5/60th and one company from the 3/95th Rifles.

Present with this force was the 45th's Light Company under Captain Thomas Lightfoot, supported by his veteran serjeants Charlie Brittain, Will Raven, John Sproule and the newly-promoted Tom Wood, armed with the shorter light infantry muskets rather than the useless serjeant's pikes.[221] The village was a maze of narrow streets and seemingly identical stone cottages; they settled in positions amidst the rustic casas and stone walls, swatted the flies away and waited. It was a beautiful cloudless day, and getting hot.

Masséna made a frontal assault on Fuentes de Oñoro early in the afternoon. His II Corps made a diversionary attack on the allies whilst ten

139

battalions of Ferey's division of VI Corps attacked the village. The diversion came to nothing; but Ferey's leading brigade managed to capture some of the lower part of the village before being kicked out, and his second brigade arriving in support forced the allies back to the top end of the village. Wellington sent in three fresh battalions, including the 71st Highland Light Infantry, to reclaim the ground, Colonel Cadogan at their head, calling, 'My lads, you have had no provision these two days; there is plenty in the hollow in front, let us down and divide it'. Once upon the French the Colonel cried, 'Here is food, my lads, cut away'. There are very few accounts of this day's fighting in the village; it must have been horrendous, all close-quarters street-fighting and house-clearing. Ask any veteran which mode of combat he prefers least, and invariably will come back the answer: house-to-house. There were rumours of knots of troops entering houses for safety, only to be rooted out at bayonet-point; and entire sections being trapped in cul-de-sacs only to be fired on from all sides and virtually wiped out. The day cost Masséna 652 casualties, including 167 prisoners. The allies had lost 259 men – the 45th Light Company coming out relatively unscathed with only two men wounded and two men missing – but with the light battalion commander Lieutenant-Colonel Williams badly wounded and out of action.

Wellington fully expected a resumption of the attack the following day, but it did not come. Whilst both sides sniped across the Dos Casas, Masséna scouted the allied position, and finally discovered the weakness in Wellington's right flank – just one infantry battalion in the village of Poço Velho (two-and-a-half miles south of Fuentes de Oñoro), and a band of Spanish guerrillas at Nava de Haver, another two-and-a-half miles farther south.

Acutely aware of the threat to his right, Wellington moved the 7th Division – his newest and weakest division, comprising two recently-arrived British battalions, the Chasseurs Britanniques, the Brunswick-Oels-Jägers and five battalions of Portuguese troops – to Poço Velho, aided by a cavalry screen. He also called in the Light Division from the northern flank to a central position better able to support the south – and the men of that elite formation had fire put in their belly that night by the arrival of their old commander Major-General Robert Craufurd, back from sick leave in England. The 45th did not move at all this day, but oddly lost one man to desertion – Private William Hall of Captain Scott's No.2 Company.[222]

The brigade spent the day barricading the avenues leading to Pozobello and Fuentes, and temporary defences were constructed at the heads of the different streets, and trenches dug here and there as a protection against the cavalry attacks expected.[223] A private of the 71st who had fired 107 rounds the previous day found entertainment and everyday comforts in the activities of Saturday, 4 May: 'The French brought down a number of bands of music to a level piece of ground, about ninety or a hundred yards broad, that lay between us. They continued to play until sunset; whilst the men were dancing, and diverting themselves at football. We were busy cooking the remainder of our sausages, bacon, and flour.'[224]

If Boney Had Been There

The following day, 5 May, dawned cloudless and hot. Like Vimeiro, and Orthez, Toulouse and Waterloo to come, it was a Sunday. It surely came as no surprise that Masséna attacked Wellington's right flank in the morning. Several regiments of French dragoons clashed with British and King's German Legion Dragoons and the latter were forced back to Poço Velho. French infantry then appeared nearby – Marchand's division attacked the village, forcing two isolated battalions from the 7th Division to retreat back towards the rest of the division, although only after suffering 150 casualties, mainly after being caught in the open by cavalry.

The French attack in the south created a new threat to Wellington's position near the village. He formed a new line along the ridge behind Fuentes de Oñoro; from west to east, the 1st and 3rd divisions and Ashworth's Portuguese their left in the village, whilst the 5th and 6th divisions remained in their original extended positions on the old allied left. However the 7th Division were the problem, strung out on the plains to the south. Wellington's response was a tried-and-true one; send in the Light Division. The isolated allied cavalry conducted a skilful running retreat which held off the French long enough to allow the 7th Division to take up a new, stronger position, which repulsed a fresh French cavalry attack.

Meanwhile Craufurd and the Light Division arrived and shepherded the 7th Division back to the main allied line, taking up a new position on Wellington's right, during which time Captain Norman Ramsay of the Royal Horse Artillery achieved his famous feat of extracting his two surrounded cannon from the midst of a French cavalry squadron at sabre-point. The Light Division then reached safety in the part of the line held by the 1st Division. Although three French infantry divisions were now moving into place on the southern plains to threaten the east-west British line, Masséna decided to have them sit and wait until the village of Fuentes de Oñoro was in his hands. This was his biggest mistake. The French cavalry pursued the Light and 7th Division for three miles, and ended their run close to the 3rd Division. Although badly winded they were still a threat to the infantry. Captain James Campbell recalled, 'Lord Wellington, I have reason to believe, ordered the 45th regiment (then under the command of … Leonard Greenwell), such was his opinion of their firmness, at the battle of Fuentes de Oñoro, to receive in line, and without forming square, the enemy's cavalry then advancing in force towards them, if they should venture to charge. The experiment was not, however, made, for the French, I conclude, observing such a steady determined front presented to them, thought it wiser to retire, especially as they were at the time suffering severely from our cannon; but I have no doubt, as to what would have been the result, had they ventured to charge.'[225]

The attack on the village began two hours after dawn. Ferey's division drove the 71st and 79th Foot out of the lower village, but the 2/24th Foot came up in support, and was able to drive the French back to the river. But it was ugly warfare, bayonet and fisticuff fighting in the streets, perhaps the largest mass bayonet fight of the whole Napoleonic Wars.

As the French fell back they were reinforced by eighteen grenadier companies of Drouet's division in bearskin hats; most British observers assumed they were being attacked by the Imperial Guard, which of course was untrue, as they were far away in France. The bayonet-scrapping started anew, and the allies pulled back to the winding lanes and stone-walled barns on the high ground, and the grenadiers were unable to advance to the plateau beyond. Believing that he was close to success, Drouet sent in the rest of his two divisions; eight fresh battalions swamped the defenders of Fuentes de Oñoro, forcing them out of the village.

From his position overlooking the village, MacKinnon could see the distant French divisions on the southern plain, unmoving. But he could also see things in the village were amiss. He asked Wellington for permission to charge, and received permission in the affirmative in a response brought back by Sir Edward Pakenham. MacKinnon put his two left-hand battalions – the 74th and 1/88th – into motion, and asked the 45th to wait, and follow in support if needed. The two battalions formed up in column of companies,[226] the 74th on the left and the 1/88th on the right, and advanced on the double down the hill and into the Calle del Teso, where the wild Irishmen of the Connaught Rangers could no longer be restrained and hit the 4/9e Léger in the streets of the village with a shock. More merciless bayonet fighting ensued, and in a few minutes the French turned and fled. The 74th reached the village a minute later and drove the French down the hill to the stone church, the Iglesia de la Asunción, where many threw down their muskets and surrendered. Captain James Campbell later recorded the following: 'The 88th, supported by the 45th, was ordered to charge into it and drive out the enemy. They soon did so in the usual style of the 3rd division. But I shall ever think with pleasure, of the extraordinary eagerness evinced by the 45th to advance to the help of their old friends the Rangers, who on that occasion wanted none.'[227] With the loss of the village came the end of the battle. Masséna was unwilling to attack Wellington's position on the ridgeline while the village remained in allied hands.

The losses of the 45th at Fuentes de Oñoro were slight – three were killed on 5 May, three wounded and two taken prisoner, both captured during the Light Company's confused fighting in the confines of the stone walls and battered buildings of the village on 3 May. Allied casualties totalled just over 1,700; French casualties were more than 2,700. Wellington later famously said of the battle: 'It was the most difficult one I was ever concerned in, and against the greatest odds. We had very nearly three to one against us engaged; above four to one of cavalry; and moreover our cavalry had not a gallop in them, while some of that of the enemy was fresh and in excellent order. If Boney had been there, we should have been beaten.'[228]

During the night of 5 May, the allies were ordered to dig in. From the village of Fuentes eastwards to Freinada, the divisions commenced a four-mile long earthwork, designed to prevent Masséna making a flanking movement to the west to relieve Almeida. To the exhausted troops, a night of digging the hard Portuguese earth must have seemed like torture. But it was all in vain; Masséna remained in place opposite Fuentes de Oñoro until 8 May, when he withdrew his lines and retreated to Ciudad Rodrigo.

On the night of 10 May the French garrison of Almeida successfully broke through the allied blockade, destroying large parts of the defences as they did so. Sick of the bad news from Portugal, Napoleon had already decided to replace Maréchal Masséna with Maréchal Marmont, who had learnt of his promotion at Ciudad Rodrigo on 10 May. Two days later Marmont took command of the Armée de Portugal, effectively ending Masséna's military career; the wily old veteran never held field command again.

The 45th camped at the battlefield for a few days, and then returned to their previous cantonments at Nava da Haver, where they were joined by a new assistant surgeon, Charles Cook, an Isle of Wight native who had spent three years at St George's Hospital, London. Although not mentioned in the official correspondence or General Orders at the time, a commission was offered to a senior NCO from each battalion in MacKinnon's brigade as a reward for their valiant charge at Fuentes de Oñoro, and so Serjeant-Major Nathaniel Carter received an ensigncy without purchase in the 79th Highlanders, who had suffered so severely in the street-fighting in the village. Irishman Jim Yates from the Light Company took over as serjeant-major on 25 May.[229]

---

[221] Based upon WO12/5728.

[222] WO25/1275.

[223] Grattan, Vol .1, p.64.

[224] Joseph Sinclair, *A Soldier of the Seventy-First*, .Frontline Books, 2010. p.86.

[225] Campbell, p.208.

[226] Each company in two lines and one behind the other. So each battalion was between twenty-five and thirty files wide and twenty ranks deep.

[227] Campbell, p.257.

[228] Supplementary Dispatches, Vol. 5, pp.176-7.

[229] WO25/1275.

Chapter 16

First Siege of Badajoz

Badajoz was one of the strongest fortified towns in Spain, protected by a ring of modern fortifications, eight bastions, and five outlying forts, two on the northern bank of the Guadiana river. It had fallen to the French on 11 March, after a successful siege. The French immediately put 3,000 men under Général Philippon there as garrison. Marshal Beresford (now attached to the Portuguese Army) was clearing the French out of Extremadura, but was to besiege Badajoz as soon as he had enough artillery, in the hope that it would lure Soult out of Andalusia to raise the siege. It did, with bloody results.

After Fuentes de Oñoro, Wellington put most of his army into camp between Almeida and the Spanish border, and set out for Badajoz with the 3rd and 7th divisions to follow. They marched on 14 May and passed through Castelo Branco, Villa Velha, Nisa and Portalegre, reaching Campo Mayor (just north of Badajoz) on 24 May, having marched 150 miles in ten days. On arrival, they were moved up to invest the fortress.

The siege of Badajoz had actually begun on 6 May, but lasted for one week only before Marshal Beresford had been forced to lift the siege and move south to block Soult's first relief attack at Albuera. The battle had been fought by elements of the 2nd and 4th divisions, and had been a bloodbath. Of the 6,500 British troops present, 4,159 became casualties – a staggering 64 percent. The 1/3rd Foot lost 643 out of 755; the 2/48th Foot 343 out of 452; the 1/57th Foot 428 out of 647. It had been like the firefight at Talavera, only carried on for two hours, not twenty minutes.

The second British siege began on 19 May but was little more successful. Wellington had arrived in the south to take personal command; most of the battered army that had fought at Albuera now under the command of Rowland Hill remained in the south of Extremadura, watching the French, while Wellington directed the siege. Picton's men crossed the Guadiana at the ford above the town and entered the trenches on the left bank on 27 May. The 45th had their first taste of trench-digging on the night of 30 May, when 1,600 men of the 3rd Division were handed shovels and told to dig, whilst another 1,200 (including Captain Greenwell's Light Company) covered them. The batteries opened fire at nine o'clock in the morning on 3 June, but the allies had hopelessly inadequate siege material and artillery. The castle remained largely undamaged, and eventually the few engineers on hand admitted that there was no chance of making a useful breach in the walls.

Two abortive assaults were made by the 7th Division on 6 and 8/9 June without making any impression. Upon learning that Marmont and Soult were marching his way, Wellington lifted the siege on 10 June and on 17 June the 3rd Division went back into cantonments on the line of the River Caya at Campo Mayor. On 22 June the combined French armies discovered Wellington in his new positions and despite outnumbering him, decided not to attack.

On 25 June the 45th were at Campo Mayor and quite weak in numbers, mustering 393 effective men only, and 223 sick. The first siege of Badajoz cost the 45th two men killed in the trenches (Private William Chatwin on 6 June and Private George Dyer on 8 June) and seven wounded (one of whom, Private William McLean, died of wounds on 14 June). It also cost the brigade the services of Major-General MacKinnon, who went home to England sick for an extended period. Lieutenant-Colonel Alexander Wallace of the 1/88th became temporary brigadier in his absence.

Luddites

Whilst the first battalion had been fading away numerically in Spain, the second battalion had been building its strength at home. In April 1810, in a complete departure from its usual duty cycle of Nottingham-Mansfield-Derby-Leicester, the battalion marched south to Portsmouth and sailed across to Guernsey in the Channel Islands, to replace the second battalion of the 38th Foot who had been assigned to active duty in Portugal. Thus the second battalion was not 'at home' when the Luddite rebellion began in Nottingham in March 1811 – Luddites being men named after the mythical Ned Ludd, who was reputed to live in Sherwood Forest. Luddites tried to save their livelihoods by smashing industrial machines in textile factories. What had started as a few isolated attacks upon a new knitting-frame machine in the Nottinghamshire village of Arnold had turned into an insurrection spread primarily throughout the regiment's heartland counties of Nottinghamshire, Derbyshire and Leicestershire.

The detailed reasons are complicated, but in summary a combination of the war, the loss of continental markets to the English textile trade and the introduction of new knitting machines which could be operated by fewer less-skilled (and therefore lower-paid) workers all contributed to the creation of an unemployed underclass of some 20,000 men and women in a radius around Nottingham. Between March 1811 and February 1812 they smashed about 1,000 machines with a damages bill between £6,000 and £10,000.

At the beginning of December, the military were called out to protect factories. The Berkshire Militia were force-marched 140 miles from Ipswich to Nottingham, and were soon joined by the Derby and Chaddesden Yeomanry and Radbourne Militia, and then by the Scots Greys and 15th Hussars later in the month. A ten o'clock nightly curfew was imposed in the town of Nottingham on 5 December. *The Statesman* newspaper published an article under the heading 'Mass unemployment, insurrection and military occupation' on 15 December, stating that there were 20,000 stocking-makers out of employment. 'Six regiments of soldiers from different parts of the country have been sent into this town,' it advised, 'and 300 new constables have been sworn to keep the peace. But all this is of no avail as the practice of setting fire to corn and hay stacks, and breaking open houses still continues. Nine Hundred Lace Frames have been broken ... which cost £140 each; from twenty to thirty of them are destroyed in a night. The whole country, for twenty miles round, is full of these ruinous proceedings, nor can they be checked ... This town is now a garrison, and strictly under martial law. God only knows what will be the end of it; nothing but ruin.'[230]

On parade at Saint Peter Port on 5 July 1811, 232 second battalion men – more than half of those present – volunteered for service in Portugal, along with eighteen officers who had 'become effective' in the first battalion.[231]

The news of the victories at Busaco and Fuentes de Oñoro had raised the prestige of the Army abroad; militiamen who had volunteered into the line in 1809 and 1810 could feel they were volunteering to join a winning team. The second battalion stayed a total of fifteen months on the small picturesque island - in sight of the French coast – before the remnants sailed back to Portsmouth in October, and from there marched to new billets, firstly at Steyning in Sussex, and then Hailsham and Eastbourne, and finally at Horsham for most of 1812. Being a feeder battalion for a unit on active service in the Peninsula, there was no value in them marching them back up north; better to keep them near the south coast, where drafts could be shipped from ports such as Portsmouth and Deal. Thus they spent the first nine months of 1813 at Lewes and the last quarter at Blatchington. Weak in numbers and far from its traditional recruiting ground of Nottinghamshire and surrounding counties, the second battalion could only count on growing smaller, and sending increasingly smaller drafts to the active sister battalion in Spain.

The Half-Way Mark
The first battalion of the 45th was at Castelo Branco on Sunday 21 July where Major Lecky was in command, Major Greenwell having gone to Lisbon sick as a prelude to going home to England for nine months. Lieutenant John Tyler had found himself a new job as aide-de-camp to Lieutenant-General Picton. Adjutant Richard Jones Colley was about to go

Left: A serjeant of the 45th (Nottinghamshire) Regiment of Foot circa 1807.

Above: Sir Thomas Brisbane. Note what appears to be the 45th's Regimental Medal hanging around his neck.

Below: The rearguard action at the Casa de Salinas (seen here) on 27 July 1809 cost the 45th Lieutenant-Colonel Guard and another four wounded, two men killed and seven captured.

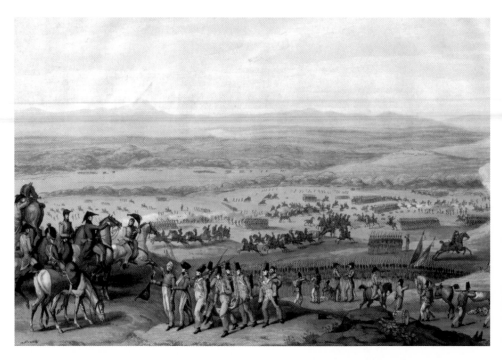

Above: A depiction of the Battle of Fuentes de Oñoro, as seen from the right of the position occupied by the 1st, 3rd and 7th divisions on 5 May 1811. (Anne S.K. Brown Military Collection, Brown University Library)

Below: British infantry attempt to scale the walls of Badajoz during the Peninsular War.

Above: Men of the 3rd Division during the attack on Badajoz Castle.

Below left: Lieutenant James Dawes Douglas, a 45th man who later commanded a Portuguese brigade.
Below right: Lieutenant Richard Hill of the 45th seen in later life.

Above: The Battle of Orthes, 27 February 1814, a painting by William Heath.

Left: As a Lieutenant in the 45th, James John Rowe wrote some graphic entries in his diary regarding his unit's actions.

Above: A memorial to Serjeant Major Robert Elliott, later commissioned in the 82nd Foot.

Right: Leonard Greenwell finally achieved his long sought-after promotion to lieutenant-colonel, in the 45th, on 19 May 1814.

General Thomas Picton, by the artist   Colonel William Guard.
Martin Archer Shee.

Left: A depiction of the General Service Medal awarded to the 45th's Private James Talbot. Note the 'Corunna' clasp.

Below: An illustration of the 45th's Regimental Medal.

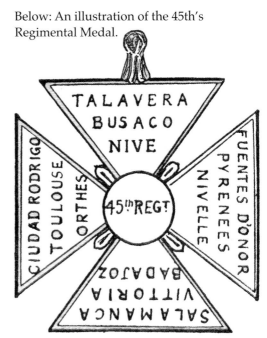

Left: The memorial to the Sherwood Foresters at Crich, Derbyshire. (Courtesy of D. Twigg, www.geograph.org.uk)

Below: As a lieutenant, Benjamin Geale Humfrey joined the 45th in 1811 – at which point he would have been referred to as a 'Johnny Newcome'.

home, having been put on the strength of the second battalion, to marry his sweetheart Sarah Lister, daughter of the Regimental Colonel.[232]

Why is 21 July important? It looked just like any other day on campaign. Except that (and they could not possibly have known it), the battalion had just passed the half-way mark in their Peninsula campaign. What did the battalion look like in July 1811 and how did it compare with the battalion that had landed almost three years earlier? They had fought in five major Peninsula battles, barely firing a shot in the first two and being only lightly involved in the fifth. However Talavera and Busaco had cost them 310 men. Of the forty officers and staff who arrived in August 1808, only thirteen were still present; Major David Lecky, Captains George Miles Milnes, John Cole, Thomas Lightfoot, James Campbell, John Robinson, and Lieutenants Bob Hardiman, Theo Costley, Edward Hackett, Charlie Barnwell, and John Tyler, Paymaster Marcus Dalhunty, Quartermaster Ed Thresher, and Surgeon John Boggie. The serjeant-major was the newly-promoted Jim Yates, Lawrence Walsh was quartermaster-serjeant, Campbell Kelly was paymaster's clerk, Joe Baker was armourer-serjeant and John Green the drum-major. The battalion had laid 334 men in Iberian graves (far more through sickness than in battle), lost sixteen deserters, and had sent 123 men home; nearly as many men combined as had sailed from Cork that July morning three years earlier.[233]

The muster rolls show a total of 749 privates were on the strength of the first battalion. Of the total complement, eighty-eight were in England, forty-five were prisoners of war, and 116 were absent in Lisbon (presumably sick); in fact 158 men, or a quarter of the battalion were on the sick-list. Some 192 men (or one man in four) had served for more than seven years, and thirty-five men had served for more than fourteen.[234] An analysis of the veterans reads like an archaeological stratum of the regiment's services. The two most veteran privates in the ranks were Thomas Crutchley and John March. Both had enlisted into the 45th in England in June 1793 whilst the regiment was on its first tour of the West Indies. Then came half-a-dozen men who had joined the 45th in late 1794 after its returned from the Caribbean in a skeleton state: John Bird, George Cunningham, Samuel George, Robert Jennings, John Quinn and Francis Reiville. Most veteran of all, perhaps, were the few remaining men who had been drafted into the 45th from other regiments on Dominica in 1795 and 1796 – Lawrence Boyle, Samuel Hitchings, Miles Morrison, James Taylor and Giles Thornby. However the eldest men in the ranks were two Irishmen, Privates Redmond Kilpeake and Thomas Wharton, at 56 and 55 years of age respectively. They were old enough to be the grandfathers of the youngest, Drummer John Murdagh, enlisted at sea off the Cape of Good Hope, who was still just 13. The veterans would have been lean, sun-tanned, with a working knowledge of Portuguese and Spanish (usually in a highly corrupted form), dressed in faded and patched red jackets, local trowsers (usually brown) and more often than not, locally acquired shoes or sandals.

By late July 1811 the 1/45th had a high percentage of veterans in the ranks, a low rate of desertion, a stable battalion staff, several officers attached to important staff positions, several commendations from Viscount Wellington for meritorious service, and a bullet-torn faded green Regimental Colour. It was a proud member of the Fighting Third. But late July was important for more than just being the mid-point of the 45th's service on campaign. By mid July 1811 the great unrecognised crisis in the Peninsular War had come and passed. Two French armies had assembled to invade Portugal for a fourth time, and indeed Wellington had concentrated his forces to meet them. But the French had withdrawn – it was the great unfought battle of the Caia, the hinge point of the Peninsular War.

Until July 1811 Wellington had always adapted his movements to his opponents: after that month the initiative 'passed insensibly to him'.[235] The silent crisis had involved several weeks of manoeuvring behind a substantial cavalry screen, for newly arrived horsemen had doubled the available British cavalry strength. New infantry battalions and artillery companies had arrived also, and for the first time Wellington could contemplate campaigning with a force strong in all arms. He had danced to the French tune for nearly three years; from late 1811 onward they would dance to his tune. Sir John Fortescue wrote that 'there was more reorganisation carried out in the allied army during the months of June, July and August 1811 that at any other period of Wellington's command'. He anticipated some big campaigns in 1812 and wanted to get his house in order beforehand, to reorganise his eight infantry and single cavalry divisions, plus some independent Portuguese brigades, bringing in newly arrived units and swapping others around to even out the distribution of experience.

What the French habitually referred to as 'the English Army'– in fact, four men in every ten were Irishmen, with only a solitary English divisional commander, the rest being four Scotsmen, three Irishmen and one Welshman – defended Portugal with 57,000 men. Across the border, but widely dispersed, were the armies of the Kingdom of Spain. The Army of Catalonia under Teniente-General De Contreras had just been destroyed at the siege of Tarragona, so was effectively *hors de combat*. As part of the reorganisation, the Spanish Regency appointed Joaquín Blake y Joyes (the son of an Irishman) Capitán-General of the combined Army of Valencia (under Teniente-General Charles O'Donnell, an Irish émigré) comprising nearly 25,000 men, and Teniente-General Freire's 16,500 strong Army of Murcia. In the south, Teniente-General Castaños, the victor of Bailén,[236] commanded the Army of Extremadura, 7,500 men operating mainly out of the Algarve region and in Andalusia. Lastly, far to the north, the Army of Galicia under Teniente-General Santocildes y de Llanos had 15,000 men to occupy the French in Asturias and Galicia.[237]

Thus the allies had about 121,000 men in the field, of which about 34,000 were British. However the French had over 350,000 troops in Spain, of whom more than 290,000 were present and under arms in late July. Maréchal Auguste Frédéric Louis Viesse de Marmont's Army of Portugal was the most immediate threat – nearly 39,000 men at Almaraz, less than 100 miles due east of the 3rd Division. Maréchal Soult's Army of the South had three corps (I, IV and V) totalling some 69,000 men under arms in the vicinity of Seville, and able to threaten the southern Algarve region of Portugal.

Elsewhere King Joseph's[238] Army of the Centre totalled more than 23,000 men in and around Madrid. Newly promoted Maréchal Louis-Gabriel Suchet (the victor of Tarragona) had over 43,000 men away over on the east coast, and newly-appointed Général de Division Dorsenne commanded a widely-dispersed 88,000 men in the north, head-quartered on Valladolid; lastly, Maréchal Étienne Jacques Joseph Alexandre Macdonald (the grandson of a Scots Jacobite) commanded nearly 24,000 men in faraway Catalonia.

In an unusually candid letter from his headquarters on 2 July 1811, Wellington complained to his elder brother, William Wellesley-Pole, 'I have 50,000 men, including every Portuguese I can get together, and artillery; and about 4000 cavalry, of which 3000 are British. The French have above 60,000 men, including 7000 cavalry, and not including artillery: but they don't like to attack us, and are now breaking up … I am waiting to see whether I cannot give one of them a knock: if I can't, I must then wait till Soult will undertake something to the southward, when I shall be able to try my hand on the north of the Tagus.'[239]

In this context can be seen the enormity of the task ahead. Wellington had to rely upon the Spanish tying various French elements down whilst he defeated them in detail. His immediate threats were Marmont and Soult, and it is these two who will figure largest in the campaigns of 1812 and beyond.

The Whipper-In Was Come

The state of discipline within the army occasionally drove Wellington to despair, and so he recommended to Viscount Castlereagh on 17 June 1809 that he create a regular provost establishment. 'All the foreign armies have such an establishment,' he advised.[240] Two weeks later he added, 'The appointment of Assistant Provost Marshals, I am sorry to say, is but too necessary'.[241] The corps of assistant provost-marshals eventually grew to twenty-four men, all hand-picked serjeants, who wore a red scarf around their right shoulder as identification.[242]

Serjeant Charles Smith of the 45th, a former stockinger from Loughborough in Leicestershire, was appointed one of these assistant provost-marshals in mid-1811. Assistant provost-marshal carried with it the pay and entitlements of the rank of ensign, although Smith remained a serjeant on the muster-rolls, and in the eyes of the officers. The duties of the provost-marshal were defined by an order from the adjutant-general dated 1 November 1811: 'The Provost Marshal has not the power of inflicting summary punishment for it unless he should see him in the act of committing it. If he should not see him in the act of committing it, he is directed to report the offence to the Commander-in-Chief of the army ... Their duty is, by vigilance and activity, to prevent those breaches which the Commander of the Forces is sorry to observe are too common, and to punish those they may catch in the fact.'[243]

Many of the assistant provost-marshals were undoubtedly honest and upright men, but the actions of a few of them soon made them the most-hated individuals in the Army. The 45th was not immune, as William Brown recalled:

'Next morning before marching, I had another proof of the mild discipline, and the tender regard with which we were treated by our superiors. Having been busily employed during the night, we were by daylight very fatigued, when the Provost-Martial chancing to pass, one of our men in a jocular manner, called to his comrades to cheer up, as they soon would have done, for the whipper-in was come. This was sporting with the lion's paw, and was overheard by the man of stripes himself, who ordered the wit to be instantly seized, and tied up to the next tree, where for his joke he received four dozen ticklers.'[244]

The two matters which caused Wellington more nail-chewing than any other during the war were the state of supplies and the state of the army's discipline. Officers at battalion level had no control over the former, but total control of the latter. For every forbidding, lash-loving martinet such as Robert Craufurd, John Frederick Browne and the Honourable John Meade, there was probably a clutch of officers with a more benign live-and-let-live attitude.

A study of the inter-officer relationships at battalion level might provide some clues as to where the 45th stood on such matters. We cannot know from this distance the intricacies of the leadership chain at the head of the battalion, but we can get some indication in an account written by James Campbell in 1840. Campbell served in the 45th from 1801 until his transfer to the 50th Foot in 1825 as a major and brevet lieutenant-colonel. His service in the 50th being short (he retired the following year), we must assume that the following was written with the 45th firmly in mind. 'In no regiment that I have ever had any thing to do with, have I yet found the link of responsibility perfectly kept up,' he wrote. 'For instance, the majors were not made answerable for the state of their respective wings. The captains were almost never interfered with by the majors, who were really little else than sinecurists: indeed, commanding officers in general, did not like their doing so; as they too frequently looked upon it as meddling with what did not concern them; and they too often rendered the captains also mere nonentities with their companies; managing all promotions, &c. between themselves and their adjutants.'[245]

His statements are worth dissecting. Campbell ultimately served under Majors Coghlan, Patton, Gwyn, Smith, Lecky, Greenwell and Lightfoot, seemingly as fine a group of field officers as produced by Wellington's army, and therefore his suggestion that they filled an office requiring little or no work for the salary sounds like a gross insult. However remembering William Smith's letter before Busaco ('and as apparently I might be spared from [the 45th] without inconvenience') we start to see the essence of Campbell's comment. For majors were lieutenant-colonels in waiting, and the rank of lieutenant-colonel was the first step on the ordered procession to general officer rank. Campbell also suggests these men were ruled by a string of dictatorial and micro-managing commanding officers, assisted by servile adjutants – a role which Campbell had once filled. But the biggest bar to discipline must have been the seeming emasculation of the company captains (and Campbell was one of them!) which raises the notion that the battalion was effectively held together by the subalterns and the senior NCOs taking direction from over-bearing lieutenant-colonels.

The fact that the company commanders of the 1/45th suffered a casualty rate of over sixty percent during the war proves that they were worthy of their country's respect, even if they could not obtain the same consideration from their commanding officers.

---

[230] National Library of Australia, 19th Century British Newspapers Online.

[231] Meaning that they had become amongst the senior in their rank and were therefore now officially attached to the first battalion.

[232] Richard and Sarah were married at St James, Westminster, on 28 October 1811.

[233] Based upon WO17/157.

[234] Based upon WO12/5728.

[235] S.G.P. Ward, *Faithful – The Story of the Durham Light Infantry*. Naval & Military Press, p.109.

[236] The first French defeat at the hands of the Spanish, on 19 July 1808.

[237] Based upon organization as shown in Appendix XVII in Volume 4 of Oman.

[238] As in Joseph Bonaparte, the kind-hearted but militarily inept older brother of Napoleon.

[239] *Supplementary Dispatches*, Vol. 7, p.176.

[240] *Wellington's Dispatches*, Vol. 4, p.434.

[241] ibid, p.455.

[242] And in a later era around their hats; hence the genesis of military police as red-caps.

[243] General Orders and Regulations, pp.250-1.

[244] Brown, pp.277-8.

[245] Campbell, pp.175-6.

Chapter 17

El Bodón

Foiled at Badajoz, Wellington decided to blockade the frontier fortress town of Ciudad Rodrigo. Sometime in late July Wellington sent his trouble-shooters – the 3rd and Light divisions – to commence the blockade. He was not strong enough to risk besieging the place, in the knowledge that if pushed the French could raise a much larger army to raise the siege.

The allies were completely in position on 11 August, the 3rd Division holding Carpio de Azaba, about six miles west of the fortress. Wellington had 45,000 men in an arc around Ciudad Rodrigo in mid-September. West of the fortress, on the River Azava were the 1st and 6th divisions; the 3rd Division were at El Bodón, eight miles south of the fortress; the Light Division was posted at Martiago, three miles south-east of El Bodón; and the 4th Division were at Fuenteguinaldo, another seven miles south-west of El Bodón. Strongly suspecting the blockade would provoke an eventual French response, Wellington picked out the latter place as a defensive position.

Two brigades of French dragoons and two brigades of light horse appeared south of Ciudad Rodrigo on 25 September, sent forward to reconnoitre the allied positions south and west of the town. Marmont wanted to know the location and strength of Wellington's forces which he assumed were on their way to besiege Ciudad Rodrigo. The cavalry broke through Wellington's cavalry screen and then found themselves in the middle of the 3rd Division, stretched out in four separate clusters over six miles of road. The first troops they encountered, posted on a plateau at the top of a steep slope, were part of Colville's brigade – the 1/5th and 77th Foot and the 21st Portuguese, together with a Portuguese artillery battery. The cavalry captured the guns, but Major Henry Ridge of the 1/5th (another of the army's 'valiant majors' like Gwyn and Smith who went on to renown) ordered his men to advance in line, firing three volleys of musketry as they marched. James Campbell of the 45th was witness to 'the splendid achievement of the 5th regiment, in the famous retreat of the 3rd division from El Bodón to (Fuente) Guinaldo, in which I saw that corps receive the charge of the French cavalry steadily and firmly; to my delight and astonishment, however, they in turn charged them, and drove them down the hill with considerable loss. The 5th and 45th were, perhaps, as steady under arms, and as well conducted regiments as any in the army; yet I have seen both led away at sieges, and upon other occasions, when opportunities presented themselves, like the rest.'[246]

The dragoons fled back down the hill, a rare example of cavalry being repulsed by infantry not formed in square. Colville's brigade then commenced a retreat towards Fuenteguinaldo, marching in square. The dragoons attacked it from three sides at once without success, eventually resorting to sniping from horseback at a distance using their carbines. Such weapons with their small calibre balls were generally of little use, but could still cause painful and inconvenient wounds; a private of the 3rd Division was wounded at El Bodón by a musket-ball which passed through his testes and scrotum, and through the back part of the opposite thigh. Carried to Sabugal, he remained under a doctor's care for a month, under very moderate treatment, 'and suffered little from inflammation, when he was sent to the rear nearly well'.[247]

Nearby British cavalry charged the disordered French, forcing them to retreat, winning some respite for the perspiring and retreating infantry. This brigade was joined by Lieutenant-General Thomas Picton himself with Wallace's brigade (1/45th, 74th, 1/88th, three companies 5/60th) near El Bodón and what was now nearly the whole division marched south-west to Fuenteguinaldo, Colville's brigade still harried by the French cavalry as they marched. William Brown left a graphic account of the events of that day:

'By this day's encounter the division had several killed and wounded; while at the same time the enemy carried off a quantity of our stores and baggage, together with the greater part of the women belonging to our brigade. Their co-mates, however, did not seem deeply affected at this circumstance. The same night when seated round the fire, an Irishman, who had lost his wife, being condoled with on the occasion, replied, "Faith, boys, I would not have cared a straw about it at all at all, but Jenny the b...h has got my pipe away with her!"'[248]

There was a sequel to this event, which Brown recorded sarcastically: 'When we had been a few days in quarters, the women, who were taken in the late affair at El Bodón, were escorted to our outposts by a party of the enemy's cavalry, and were thus again restored to their loving husbands.'[249]

The war between the French and the inhabitants of Spain and Portugal was one of unaltering spite and cruelty; this seems to have had no impact on the civility which existed between the French and the British armies, as the above example shows. MacKinnon's brigade lost only five men in the retreat from El Bodón, including Serjeant Michael Maloney from No.7 Company and four men from the 88th, all missing (most probably guarding the baggage and women) and presumed taken prisoner. The French harassment

El Bodón

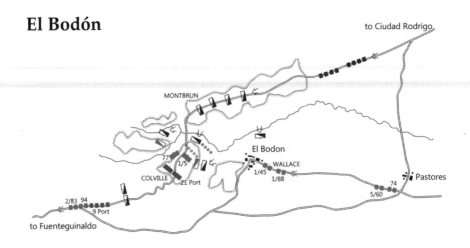

did not stop there, and continued the next day (26 September) over the border into Portugal. The 45th returned to the campsite near the tiny village of Fuenteguinaldo, a place which William Brown had nothing good to say about: 'Our brigade was quartered in a small, mean, dirty village; and being extremely crowded, our situation was very uncomfortable, while our allowance of bread was by no means calculated to improve it, being curtailed from 16 ounces to 8, and that of mouldy biscuit.'[250]

Marmont had 20,000 men over the Aqueda, with another 20,000 close behind. Wellington had less than 15,000 men around Fuenteguinaldo, and the Light Division not yet arrived. But Marmont was not Masséna; he was a more cautious creature altogether, and dared not risk an attack against what he perceived to be a prepared position. If only he knew it was a 'mean, dirty village' overcrowded with starving, grumbling troops, might he have been more daring?

Comings and Goings
The 45th were at Aldea de Ponte on 25 August with only 371 effectives in the ranks, the lowest figure since landing in Portugal three years earlier. Newly arrived was Captain Henry-Moore Herrick, the 26-year-old middle son of a minor Irish aristocrat from Cork, who took over the Grenadier Company but seems to have gone immediately on the sick list. Only three captains were on duty with their companies that day (Mills, Lightfoot and Campbell), the rest being in the hands of subalterns.

Three days later one of the oldest men in the battalion, Private Francis Finnistone – one of the true veterans of the Army, having served in the famous Black Watch with Abercromby in Egypt in 1801 – was discharged to the 12th Royal Veteran Battalion at the age of 51. Fifteen men had been discharged the previous month, many being men who had transferred from the Army of Reserve in 1804 for seven years' service, being at the end of their term of enlistment.[251]

A month later and camped at Fuenteguinaldo – about fifteen miles south-west of Ciudad Rodrigo, and less than ten miles from the Portuguese frontier – Major Lecky was still in command and the number of effective men was still low at 386 only, with 160 men sick. There were only nineteen officers present and on duty. However, recently landed at Lisbon was the transport *Orlando* containing eighteen officers and 226 men from the second battalion on Guernsey, who would swell the battalion back to something close to full establishment strength for the campaigns of 1812.[252]

The following evening Wellington evacuated Fuenteguinaldo, concerned that he was still outnumbered by Marmont and that his position perhaps was not as strong as the French seemed to think. By sunset on 27 September Wellington was concentrated around Alfaiates, about five miles inside Portugal, whilst MacKinnon's brigade performed advanced guard duties at the more comfortable town of La Albergueria de Argañán, just inside Spain. Poor Major Lecky had a violent attack of gout and was sent to the general hospital in the rear, leaving Captain Thomas Lightfoot temporarily in command until he was relieved by Captain George Milnes, returning from a bout of sickness in late October. Also returning from sick leave on 31 October was Major-General MacKinnon, back after an absence of five months; so Lieutenant-Colonel Alexander Wallace handed over the brigade and returned to his place at the head of his beloved Rangers.

Most welcome amongst all this sickness and absence was the party of drafts from Guernsey for the 45th who marched into Albergueria in mid-October. The 232 privates were distributed amongst the companies and the numbers shuffled to ensure all companies had a more or less equal muster. It was the first large draft the battalion had received since mid-1809.

Conducting the men were seventeen officers – the two most senior returning for their second tour of duty. Captains Alexander Martin and Brinsley Purefoy had gone home in late 1809 as their recent promotions had placed them at the bottom of the seniority list of captains and therefore technically on the strength of the second battalion. The promotion of David Lecky and death of Henry Dabsac had pushed them into the upper echelons of the captaincy list and allowed them to serve with the first battalion again. Lieutenants Francis Andrews and Hill Phillips were likewise back for their second tour, both having gone home in August 1809 for the same reasons as Martin and Purefoy.

The 'Johnny Newcomes' were lieutenants Benjamin Geale Humfrey, Benjamin White, John Metcalfe, Hugh Forbes, and Thomas Atkins; the ensigns were George Little, Richard Henry Hill, James Coghlan, James Dale, Charles Munro, James Stewart, John-Fitzwilliam Jones and George MacDonnell. The ensigns were mostly very young – Munro not yet 17, Hill 18, Stewart 19. In a parallel with the terrible wastage of young officers in the

First World War, these 'new boys' would unfortunately prove to be the 45th's lost generation. Of the fourteen unblooded officers, seven would ultimately be killed, six wounded, and only one – Hugh Forbes – survive the war unscathed.

To counteract the joy and novelty of the new arrivals was the sad news of Surgeon John Boggie's departure. He had been promoted to staff surgeon (working out of a general rather than regimental hospital) and was replaced by William Smyth, who had served with Boggie as an assistant-surgeon in the 28th Foot, which suggests Boggie recommended him as his replacement. Smyth was a 30-year-old Home Counties man with seven years' Army experience, and three years in the Peninsula, where he had patched the ruined 28th Foot after the bloodbath at Albuera.[253] He would need all of those skills and more to deal with the sieges of 1812.

Also departing was Quartermaster Edmund Thresher, having acquired a lieutenancy in the 2nd Royal Veteran Battalion. A long-serving ex-ranker, he was considered, in Army terminology, 'old and worn out'. Quartermaster-Serjeant Lawrence Walsh replaced him in December. Walsh was an Irishman from Limerick with a wife and adopted daughter at home.

Perhaps saddest of all was the departure of the popular Major David Lecky, so riddled with gout in his legs as to be almost incapable of service. He went home to recover his health but never returned. After his departure the battalion was commanded by Captain Lightfoot for a short time, and then by Captain George Milnes, who had been tenth in seniority at the landing in August 1808. A clutch of junior officers also went back to England, having 'become effective in the second battalion' as the muster rolls record it – another way of saying that promotions and departures had put them in the junior of their rank, and therefore properly belonging to the 2/45th. And so Captains John Cole and John Robinson, and Lieutenants Boys, Trevor and Sparrow departed.

The countryside held few charms for Major-General MacKinnon, who after an absence of four months, had a different perspective than the men who had seen the state of the country daily. 'The population of the country, through which the different columns of the enemy passed … one-third of this population, taken on average of the whole, has not returned; nor have the remaining two-thirds much increased the population of that country which has afforded them refuge … The houses left without inhabitants are daily going to ruin, being exposed, without repairs, to the savage of the elements and the still more relentless ravages of the soldiery, and even of the remaining inhabitants, who are made thieves either from natural inclination or from want … The fields … are now growing over with weeds, and will very soon return to their native heath … When I ask an inhabitant why he does not plant vegetables – "it would only be for the soldiers," he replies.'[254]

The 45th spent the remainder of the year at Albergueria, and the officers entertained themselves with horse races, concerts and theatrical 'events', especially those of the Light Division, which had a formidable reputation for pantomime. Other ranks took their leisure in the taverns of Albergueria and Alde da Ponte, the arms of local señoritas and the occasional acquisition of stray sheep for dinner, the men slipping out of camp at night armed only with bayonets and rumbling tummies. They needed to take care, since there were more dangerous predators than Hosiers in the area – wolves. The peasants complained about the disappearance of livestock (although from the presence of the wolves it seems the 45th may not have always been to blame) and so Picton issued an order that company officers were to call the roll several times each night.

For some, the local girls held too much temptation. Private William Brown was one so smitten: 'Fernando Silvero, in whose house my master was quartered, rented at a low rate a few acres of land; on which, by the industry of himself and two sons, his family were enabled to live in tolerable ease and comfort. Besides his two sons, he was the father of a lovely daughter named Rosa, the pride and joy of her parents. This pretty village maid was yet in her teens, possessing all that glow of health and beauty which innocence can bestow. The day I first beheld this charming girl, was that on which I first entered her native village. As I approached her father's house she stood on the threshold. When I drew near, and could discover the mildness of her countenance, and the graces of her person, new and strange sensations affected me. My mind was confused and flurried, a kind of trepidation shook my whole frame; I felt the crimson current mount my cheek, and when I essayed to speak my tongue refused its office. The contour of her face was oval; her complexion of that hue which is termed brunette, but inclining to a light olive. Her soft, moist, and cherried lips, when opened, displayed a case of teeth that rivalled the finest ivory; and the bloom that sat upon her cheek, which vied with the rose in beauty; and her dark sparkling eyes, with the black glossy ringlets which shaded her high and polished forehead, were enough to warm the heart of the most rigid ascetic.

'As a minute detail of the progressive intimacy that ensued between us, and which kindled in time to a mutual flame, might prove uninteresting, I will pass over the incidents of this endearing period. May it therefore suffice – in a short time I found her sentiments reciprocal with mine, and I basked in the sunshine of her smiles, and revelled in all the luxury of a chaste and genuine passion, "with joys that guilty pleasure never felt".'[255]

The fourth Christmas in the Peninsula was celebrated at the little church overlooking the square in the centre of Albergueria. The strength of the 45th on that chilly Christmas Day was 809 effectives (of whom 193 were sick). The battalion had lost sixty-two men during the year (nearly all to disease) and incredibly only two men had deserted, putting the 45th on a par with far more 'elite' regiments.[256] An even hundred men had been sent home (a third of these in January, mainly the convalescents from Busaco) but 232 had joined in October to bring the battalion up to something like full strength. They would need all their strength in the months to come.

---

[246] ibid, pp.208-9.

[247] Guthrie, *Lectures on Some of the More Important Points in Surgery*, p.44.

[248] Brown, pp.122-4.

[249] ibid, p.126.

[250] ibid, pp.125-6.

[251] Based upon WO25/1275.

[252] Based upon WO17/157 and WO25/1275.

[253] The 2/28th Foot had lost 167 men at Albuera.

[254] MacKinnon, pp.94-6.

[255] Brown, pp.115-7.

[256] By comparison the second battalion at home had lost two men to disease and nineteen men to desertion.

Part VI

1812

Chapter 18

Ciudad Rodrigo

On 4 January 1812 Major-General Henry MacKinnon wrote the final entry in his journal. 'At nine o'clock this morning my brigade marched from Aldea de Ponte, in Portugal, to Robledo, in Spain, the distance of twenty-six miles, through a continued wood of oak, we crossed the Agueda at the Ponte de Villan: in many places the snow was knee-deep, and continued to fall during the day, till two o'clock. The head of the column did but reach Robledo till an hour after dark, and the rear at midnight, leaving between 3 and 400 on the road; two died on the march, and several since of fatigue.'[257]

Captain Thomas Lightfoot agreed with his brigadier's assessment of the weather. 'We marched on such a day as I have never seen before; such a hurricane of hail, wind and snow, with such piercing cold as the wind rushed down the mountains, that men and animals lay promiscuously dead or dying on the road.'[258]

They reached Robleda at nine o'clock at night, where the officers at least enjoyed dry beds in warm cottages. The 45th camped at Zamorra (about eight miles south-east of Ciudad Rodrigo) from 6 January, the same day that Wellington and his staff arrived before the walls of Ciudad Rodrigo.

Captain John Jones of the Royal Engineers spent much time reconnoitring the city and described it as follows: 'Ciudad Rodrigo is built on a rising ground on the right bank of the Agueda ... the interior wall is of an old construction, of the height of 32 feet, and is generally of bad masonry, without flanks and with weak parapets, and narrow ramparts; the exterior ... is constructed so far down the slope of the hill as to afford but little cover to the interior wall ... and the French since they had been in possession of Rodrigo, had made strong-posts of three convents, one on either flank of the suburbs, and one in the centre, and they had also converted into an infantry post the Convent of Santa Cruz, situated just beyond the glacis on the north-west angle of the place.

'The ground without the place is generally flat, and the soil rocky, except on the north side, where there are two hills called the lesser and the greater Teson; the one, at 180 yards from the Works, rises nearly to the level of the ramparts, and the other, at 600 yards distance to the height of 13 feet above them … The difficulty of contending with a rocky soil, and the fear of delay in gaining possession of the suburbs, rendered an attack from the north most advisable.'[259]

On 8 January Ciudad Rodrigo was invested; and at dusk that day, a small fort containing fifty Frenchmen and three guns, was taken after an assault by the Light Division. The following day the 1st Division commenced the first parallel trench. Two days later it was the 3rd Division's turn; the 45th had to march eleven miles to the trenches, leaving at seven o'clock in the morning and being relieved the following day at one o'clock by the Light Division. The men of the 3rd Division waded across the freezing waters of the River Agueda to the east of Ciudad Rodrigo and after briefly stopping to warm themselves at some enormous fires which burned for their benefit, they filed into the trenches which ringed the ancient cathedral city.

The divisions of the army took it in turns to don their greatcoats and forage caps (over-sized berets that the men wore when off-duty) and to stand knee-deep in mud in the pouring icy rain at night, digging trenches around Ciudad Rodrigo. The French sneaked a howitzer into the garden of the convent of San Francisco and lobbed a few rounds onto the allied trenches; Private John Regan became the battalion's first casualty, killed on their first night of digging.

There was only one house in the neighbourhood, which was reserved for the wounded, so all men were obliged to sleep out, and the cold was intense.[260] On the first day digging, MacKinnon's brigade lost two men killed, seventeen wounded, and two men of the 60th Rifles deserted to the enemy.[261]

The 5/60th often filled its ranks by attracting foreign prisoners of war captured from the French; one understandable outcome of this strategy was that some would take the opportunity to return to their former employers when the right moment arose. The King's German Legion and Brunswick-Oels-Jägers also employed this technique (with similar results); in the Chasseurs Britanniques, a notional French Royalist émigré regiment, such desertion was rife.

A few nights later a stray shell fell amongst a digging-party of the 4th Division, blowing up thirty-one men in the resulting explosion; the ground was literally covered with dismembered arms and legs. The 3rd Division's duty roster had them digging again on 15 January.

Private William Brown was, as usual, in the thick of it: 'I was posted along with a young Englishman, who might be about my own age, with whom I lay close for some time, viewing the astounding scene; a scene which none but those that have been similarly situated, can form a just conception of. On each side were employed above fifty pieces of heavy cannon, the balls of which passed over our heads with a hideous noise, spreading death and devastation wherever they went; while the hissing bombs, as they winged through the air, and their subsequent explosions, the deafening roar of cannon, their gleaming flash, contrasted with the darkness of the night, the shouts of the parties at work, and the cries of the wounded, formed altogether such a scene as resembled more the works of devils, (if devils do fight, which is something problematical) than the works of men. While thus engaged, my companion started to his feet, at the same time swearing he would suffer to be shot, rather than be frozen to death, lying on the ground. We therefore rose, and after walking about some time, a volley of grape-shot fell amongst us, when my companion exclaimed; "Oh God! I am wounded; run for assistance to carry me off." Having brought up from the hollow a non-commissioned officer and two men, it was discovered the wounded man had received a shot in one of his knees, which had broken the bone, and shattered his limb considerably. He was accordingly carried away by the sergeant and one of the men, while the other, an Irishman of the name of Murphy, was left with me as a substitute for my former associate, who was scarcely gone, ere another volley of grape annoyed us, and my new companion fell to the earth exclaiming, "Ah! By Jasus, I am killed!" When assistance was brought, it was found that the ball had entered his head behind the left ear … The hour being at length expired, we were relieved from our perilous situation, and joined the companies in the hollow, which were withdrawn at daybreak.'[262]

Well Might Officers Be Proud Of Such Men

Artillery fire from the allied siege artillery gradually created two breaches – one large, one small – in the walls of the city. The Royal Engineers declared the breaches to be as damaged as they would get on 19 January, and so Wellington declared it was time to go in. Picton's 3rd Division drew the Great Breach and what seemed to be a weak part of the defences away to the right which might fall to an escalade, whereas the Light Division drew the Lesser Breach to the left.

The 45th ate their evening meals in silence on their camp-ground, then up-ended their camp kettles, took off their knapsacks and filed into the trenches in a manner that would have been instantly recognisable to an infantryman a hundred years later. As they marched, Lieutenant-General Picton addressed them. His exhortation to the Connaught Rangers was recorded: 'Rangers of Connaught! It is not my intention to expend any powder this evening! We'll do the business with the cowld iron!'

The artillery kept up a covering fire whilst the 3rd Division filled the sap in front of a hillock called the Small Teson. They watched and listened to artillery rounds falling on the distant Great Breach as officers checked their fob-watches. Captain James Campbell was present, and recorded that 'I was in the trenches with the 45th regiment, which was destined to lead the assault of the main breach. Whilst waiting for the hour fixed upon for this purpose, an order arrived from Sir Thomas Picton, to form a Forlorn

Hope. The officers commanding companies were therefore called together, and desired to bring to the head of the column, six men from each for the purpose. They soon returned, but to my surprise, unaccompanied by a single soldier, all of them declaring, that every man present volunteered for the pre-eminence, and they wished to know how they were to act, for that the oldest soldiers claimed it as their right. Well might officers be proud of such men, who could evince such a spirit with the breach, I may say, yawning for their destruction.'[263] But a whole battalion could not be the Forlorn Hope, and so twenty-five men under Lieutenant William Mackie of the 88th Foot were selected.

At seven o'clock on that bitterly cold night a bugle sounded and the assault began. More than 150 sappers commanded by Captain George McLeod and Lieutenant Thompson of the Royal Engineers led the way, each man carrying two bags filled with hay. In their trail came the Forlorn Hope. Among the handful of NCOs was Serjeant Jim Waite of the Grenadier Company, who unlike Mackie could not expect a promotion if he survived, only the recognition of his peers. MacKinnon led his brigade on foot immediately behind them, right-in-front (meaning the 45th leading) in column of companies. The companies took a few minutes to assemble once out of the trench and the way to the breach was long and straight, downhill and across a stream, uphill to the edge of the ditch (empty moat), where the sappers had thrown down the hay-bags to give the stormers something softer to land on, rather than a thirteen-foot drop.

The *fausse-braie*[264] on the opposite side of the ditch had also been breached by artillery fire and so formed a ramp of stones for the attackers to run up, over a rampart and onto the rock race of the Great Breach itself; and then the climb to the citadel ramparts. They were therefore visible for a long time before reaching the breach itself; the French were more than ready to give them a rousing reception. Picton advanced with them, at least as far as the ditch. Captain Alexander Martin, commanding the grenadiers of the 45th, requested permission to lead as he stood with his company at the head of the column. This request was very reluctantly acquiesced, and as there was no time to make any other arrangements, the battalion advanced rapidly, but compactly and in perfect order, towards the breach.

The outer edge of the ditch was soon reached. The 45th men jumped in upon bags of hay thrown there by the sappers. At that moment a very loud explosion took place, seemingly at the foot of the breach, which, providentially, the regiment had not then reached. This did not stop their progress, and the breach was ascended under a destructive fire from all points. To their horror they saw that the breach was completely cut off, and that there was no possibility of advancing or descending into the city.[265]

Captain Lightfoot's Light Company was ordered to ascend the breach, along with other light companies of the brigade. 'Here I was destined to lead a storming party with my company, preceded only by the Forlorn

Hope, consisting of ten files;[266] we quickly ascended the breach and such a slaughter commenced! The enemy had cut off the breach by a deep ditch and parapet. To descend into the body of the place was impossible, owing to the perpendicular depth of the fall from the ramparts, and the masses of ruins which lay scattered there.'[267]

However, the 45th had arrived slightly after two flanking battalions, the 2/5th and the 94th Foot, who had come up on their flank after running along the ditch from a southerly position. These lead battalions absorbed some of the French fire that would otherwise have come the way of the 45th. Captain Martin's Grenadiers were the lead troops of the main column. Captain Bob Hardiman and Lieutenant Hans Marsh pushed men across the ditch and up the rock-strewn breach. As he did so, Hardiman spied his good friend Will Grattan from the Connaught Rangers. 'What's that you have hanging over your shoulder?' he enquired of his friend. 'A little rum, Bob,' Grattan said, unslinging a canteen of the dark stuff. 'Well,' Hardiman said, 'I'll change my breath; and take my word for it, in less than five minutes some of the subalterns will be scratching a captain's arse, and there'll be wigs on the green!'[268] He swigged a mouthful of rum, shook Grattan's hand warmly, and continued up the rocky face of the breach. But the French gunners at the ramparts were still in action, and a few minutes later a discharge of grape-shot fired in enfilade took off the rear of Hardiman's head; he died instantly and sank to the ground where he lay face-up, with no visible sign of injury to those passing by.

Perhaps Lieutenant William Persse from No.2 Company stopped to recognise his friend, for he was hit in the front by grape-shot also and sank to the ground almost in a seated position next to Hardiman, stone dead. Captain Martin reached the top of the breach, was shot through the body and collapsed, but continued to exhort his men to advance even whilst prone, before passing out.[269] The leading troops cleared the ramparts, and MacKinnon directed the Connaught Rangers to advance to the right, and for the 74th to clear a French parapet on the left. As he led the 74th over the parapet, he yelled to his aide, Lieutenant John Beresford, 'Come, Beresford, you're a fine lad, we'll go over together!'

Captain James Campbell met General McKinnon in the breach: 'And though I tried, amidst the uproar, to make him understand how we were situated, and that we could not gain ground to the left, yet he seemingly did not understand me, and went on in that direction. Whilst thus situated, another and a most dreadful explosion took place, which shook the ramparts like a powerful earthquake, and destroyed General McKinnon and most of those who had followed him.' Campbell hit the dirt. 'Every man went to earth as they were rained upon by stones, bricks, timbers, body parts and mud. MacKinnon's scorched body was later found amongst the rubble on the glacis; Beresford was seriously wounded and died shortly afterwards. A party of men from the 88th, noticing the French artillery gunners still at their pieces and reloading for the next discharge, threw off their arms and accoutrements, and clutching only bayonets, clambered up to the ramparts and slew the artillerymen at their guns. Not one survived.'

Brigade-Major Wylde[270] suddenly appeared, 'coming greatly animated from the right, and pointing in that direction; all followed him with loud cheers, and I will venture to say, that he was the first man, who that night entered Ciudad Rodrigo. In their hurry in falling back from the breach, the French had not had time to remove a few planks laid across the cut to our right, and more were found on the other side; and thus by unflinching and persevering gallantry on the part of the leading brigade of the 3rd division, under a most appalling fire, the city was carried.'[271]

Captain George Milnes was hit leading the centre companies, and handed command of the battalion over to Captain Thomas Lightfoot, who recorded his recollections of the night in a letter home dated 20 February. 'The men fell in heaps; but in the meantime, the other troops having successfully scaled the walls to right and left, the enemy fled, firing as they went two mines between them and us, by which many were blown to atoms. We now let each other down into the interior of the place, and charged through the whole town, but the enemy had hid himself in the houses, to escape from immediate slaughter ... Four of my subalterns were killed ... I was near losing my leg, a ball having struck me just above the ankle, but was turned off by the spur of my boot, and left no more than a rent in my trousers.'[272]

Captain Bob Hardiman and Lieutenants Alexander Bell and William Persse were killed, as was one drummer (William Jordan) and fourteen rank-and-file, amongst them Private Edward Perrott, spared from the noose after Busaco by Wellington's forgiveness. Two more privates, Michael Kelly and James Butler, subsequently died of wounds. Two serjeants, two drummers and thirty-one rank-and-file were wounded.[273] A 3rd Division soldier was wounded during the assault of Ciudad Rodrigo by a ball which entered and lodged in the left side of the back. Left among the dead and dying at the field hospital, in the rear of the trenches, he was sent to the 4th Division hospital.[274] Here, under a treatment which included bleeding, starvation, and quietude, he gradually recovered.[275] He was one of the rare lucky ones. Lieutenant Ben Humfrey was knocked off a scaling ladder and fell heavily onto the rocks below, injuring himself badly. Lieutenant Hill Phillips was hit clambering up the breach.

Bob Hardiman's death hit the brigade hard; the men 'talked only of Hardiman' and were outraged that his body had been stripped down to his underwear in the drunken aftermath.[276] Young Alex Bell's demise prompted a touching obituary in March 1812: 'In the breach of Ciudad Rodrigo, in his 20th year, Lieut. Alex. Bell of the 45th regiment. The glorious circumstances attending his fate, together with the recollections that he has fallen in the service of his country, leaving behind him an unsullied reputation as a

gentleman and a soldier, are great alleviations to grief, and soften even the keen feelings of parental affliction in lamenting his irreparable loss.'[277]

But another loss touched the army even harder. Major-General 'Black Bob' Craufurd had been hit under the armpit near the base of the Lesser Breach by a musket-round fired from above him. The musket-ball was loose inside his rib-cage and could not be extracted. In agony, short of breath and bleeding profusely, he was stretchered away by a party of Light Bobs, exhorting his men to carry on. But he could not live long.

Victims To Their Folly
What happened after the storming is probably hard for those of us who have never faced death in battle to understand; it is even harder to excuse.

The usual *modus operandi* for Wellington's army had generally been to camp on the field of battle, never allowed to pursue a beaten foe for profit. But Ciudad Rodrigo was a new experience, for just over the ramparts lay a beaten retreating enemy and an entire city full of plunder. Freed of the shackles of the normally rigid camp discipline, the stormers ran amok through the streets of the ancient cathedral city. After the battle, a great part of the battalion had been got together by the officers' exertions in a large building in which they posted themselves immediately after the city had fallen. But while some watched one door, and all officers thought they had the soldiers secure and out of harm's way, almost all contrived to escape by another door, and the officers 'had nothing for it but to arm themselves with patience and resignation'.[278] That most of a battalion could escape almost unhindered out of one door actually beggars belief, and suggests that the NCOs did nothing to stop them. Were the officers and NCOs too shell-shocked to have any effect? Or were they sub-consciously recognising the age-old rule that a victorious besieging army had full rights to sack a captured fortress? Campbell later recalled seeing 'a party of these madmen, belonging to all the corps engaged, sitting round a table, in a large house, carousing, singing, cheering, and firing off their muskets. The windows were all open, so that we could see everything that was going forward, for the house was in a blaze about them. I called aloud, and did everything possible to induce them to come out, but all in vain; they neither listened to me, nor to several other officers who were equally exerting themselves to save them, and we even ran great risks of being shot by these idiots, who continued drinking, singing, firing and cheering, and in which delightful occupations, I saw that they were most cordially joined by some of the French garrison. This noise, however, and the reports of their muskets suddenly ceased; the roof of the building had fallen in, and they were all swallowed up amidst the ruins! These wretched men were, I conclude, returned by their regiments as killed in the assault of the fortress.'[279]

Private William Brown of No.4 Company was of course present, and recorded the night in his inimitable style: 'Numbers ... endeavoured to indemnify themselves by plunder. No sooner was the enemy disarmed than all seemed intent on having something for their trouble. The houses, which were in general shut up, were soon broken open, to the ruin of the terrified inhabitants who stood aghast while they saw their houses pillaged, and their property carried away by their friends and allies, the generous British. Some, more outrageous than the rest, proceeded even to greater extremities; by insulting the men and subjecting the wretched females to that, which to mention, would make humanity shudder, and wound the delicate ear of virtue. All order and subordination for the time being lost, I spent the early part of the night in rambling the streets, which were crowded by our men, many of whom were deeply intoxicated, and seemed as happy as if they had been all created dukes of the place. Others, again, more provident, or perhaps more covetous and rapacious, groaned under loads of spoil, which, to any but themselves appeared vain, as they were not able to carry them off.

'At last, getting amongst some of our company, I entered a house with them, the inhabitants of which were absent, having most probably fled from the horrors of the time. There not being sufficient room for us on the hearth, a fire was kindled in the midst of the apartment, around which we got seated, and being supplied with abundance of brandy and wine, which was brought up in large water buckets from a cellar immediately under, we all got as merry and happy as belted knights ... In the midst of all this preparation for festivity, the floor, which was composed of wood, gave way – when, as if by enchantment, the fire and all that was on it disappeared, and, like the baseless fabric of a vision, left not a wreck behind. All who were able made a scramble for the door, which having gained, they looked back with astonishment on the sudden change of affairs. Those that were left on the floor, insensible to the danger they were in, were seized by the heels and dragged out, their heads corning thump on the steps as they descended the stairs.'[280]

No doubt there were more than a few sore heads on 20 January 1812. There were no punishments inflicted on the day after, since the Army could not possibly flog everyone. Wellington was not impressed, but eventually found time for some plaudits; Captain Milnes and the temporary engineer Lieutenant John Metcalfe were mentioned in Wellington's dispatches after the action, where 'they distinguished themselves not less in the storm of the place than they had in the performance of their laborious duty during the siege'.

Thomas Picton gave the Grenadier Company of the 45th one hundred guineas[281] for their share of the night's work, and expressed the hope that the men would do him 'the honour to drink to the future success of the third division'. The Army suffered nine officers and 169 other ranks killed, seventy officers and 748 wounded, and seven missing on the night of 19 January; how many were lost in the drunken aftermath is not recorded.

Forbes and Kempt

Thomas Forbes was born in Newe, Aberdeenshire on 7 August 1774, the fourth son and fifth child of the Reverend George Forbes of Leochel. He was related by marriage to Lieutenant-Generals Andrew Leith Hay and James Leith. He joined the army as an ensign in the newly-formed 80th Foot in 1794, transferred to the even newer 100th Foot and then the 37th Foot in 1796. He married Miss Eliza Stewart of Pittyvaich during a leave of absence from Gibraltar in October 1799 and eventually had six sons – George, John, Charles (died at the age of nine), Michie (died aged three), Thomas (died a few months old) and Michie Stewart. In October 1808 he obtained Francis Frye Browne's vacant majority in the 45th and joined the second battalion in Mansfield. He served as George Purdon Drew's second-in-command until he said farewell at Christmas 1811 and travelled out to Portugal to join the first battalion as the only major and new commanding officer, in lieu of the departed David Lecky. He arrived just after Ciudad Rodrigo as someone virtually unknown to the remaining captains in the battalion – Milnes, Lightfoot, Mills, Campbell and Herrick.

The officers of the Coldstream Guards (in the 1st Division) arranged to take the body of Major-General MacKinnon to Espeja for burial.[282] His journal was published in England a few months later, with all proceeds to go to the care of his two infant sons. His brother and fellow Coldstream Guards officer Daniel (at that time on leave in England) would later be one of the senior officers defending the chateau of Hougoumont at Waterloo.

'Black Bob' Craufurd lingered for four days and died at two o'clock in the morning of 24 January. His body was carried to a spot under the Lesser Breach by the serjeant-majors of the 1/43rd, 1/52nd, 2/52nd and three battalions of the 95th Rifles, and buried later that day. Wellington declared his loss 'a bitter blow'.

The 45th returned to Zamorra where on 25 January they had an effective strength of 474 other ranks but 248 men on the sick-list. 'Died since last return' numbered twenty-eight men, presumably the seventeen men killed or died of wounds immediately after the action, plus perhaps some of the wounded who had perished a few days later. The following day they were put in motion southwards, and three days later reached their old cantonment of Albergueria.

Mackinnon's old brigade passed to the newly promoted Major-General James Kempt on 8 February. Kempt was a 47-year-old Scot with a lean face and a lazy right eye, having a 'passion for road-making and pretty women', an experienced infantryman who had been one of the heroes of the Battle of Maida in 1806. His early career had been stuttering – commissioned as an ensign in the 101st Foot in 1783, becoming a lieutenant in August 1784, placed on half-pay when the regiment was disbanded the following year; then a similar process as captain and major in the 113th Foot, which was disbanded in 1795. He served in recruiting at Glasgow but was reduced to half pay for a third time in 1796. His lucky break came in 1799 when, as a lieutenant-colonel unattached, he was appointed aide-de-camp to Sir Ralph Abercromby, then commanding the troops in North Britain (Scotland), whom he accompanied on the Helder campaign and later to Egypt. In 1803 he became aide-de-camp to General David Dundas, commander-in-chief of the Southern District in England, and then purchased the lieutenant-colonelcy of the 81st Foot, with which he went to the Mediterranean in 1805 and fought at Maida. The following year Kempt was assigned as quartermaster-general in Canada, and was promoted colonel in 1809. He transferred to the staff of Viscount Wellington with the local rank of major-general in 1811.

Southwards they kept marching, and every man soon guessed their destination – Badajoz. For Badajoz was the fortified city that guarded the main road from Madrid to Lisbon, and the place that had frustrated Wellington eight months before. Unfinished business remained there. But the battalion was sick again, losing twenty-three men to disease in February, and in their camp on the River Tagus, the men were impatient to get the next phase of the campaign over with.

The vacancies caused by casualties from Ciudad Rodrigo needed to be filled, and a clutch of promotions in early March settled the matter. Lieutenant Charles Barnwell was appointed adjutant in place of the departed Richard Colley; Richard Hill, James Coghlan, James Dale and Charles Munro were all promoted to lieutenant without purchase; and most interestingly, the battalion's own Serjeant-Major James Yates and Serjeant-Major George Golland (from the 5th Foot) were handed ensigncies without purchase, possibly as a reward for the division's performance at Ciudad Rodrigo. Yates's promotion bucked the trend of non-commissioned officers being moved out of their own regiment upon promotion, and perhaps tells us something of the character of the man that he was able to step up to the role. Also new was Ensign William Hunt, a nineteen-year-old from Little Dalby in Leicestershire who had been serving as a volunteer with the 61st Foot in the 6th Division.

Ciudad Rodrigo earned the army's commander a new title; the Earl of Wellington.

---

[257] MacKinnon, pp.98-9.

[258] Wylly, p.195.

[259] Jones, pp.96-7.

[260] MacKinnon, p.99.

[261] ibid, p.99.

[262] Brown, pp.134-6.

[263] Campbell, p.208.

[264] A *fausse-braie* was a rampart built in the middle of a ditch to make crossing it more difficult.

[265] Campbell, pp.204-6.

[266] Originally twenty-five men according to Campbell, but perhaps down to only ten men by this stage.

[267] Wylly, p.198.

[268] An archaic Irish saying that means there'll be fisticuffs over the vacancies.

[269] Wylly, p.197.

[270] Captain William Wylde of the 87th Foot, Brigade-major to MacKinnon's brigade.

[271] Campbell, pp.205-6.

[272] Wylly, pp.199-200.

[273] Many wounded were left unrecognised and unattended amongst the dead.

[274] At Aldea Gallega, some ten miles away.

[275] George James Guthrie, *Lectures on Some of the More Important Points in Surgery, Oxford University*, J. Churchill, 1846, p.36.

[276] Hardiman had been sending his pay home to his sister Belinda all campaign; cut off from his support through death, she applied for a pension in distressed circumstances.

[277] *Gentleman's Magazine*, March 1812.

[278] Campbell, p.207.

[279] ibid, pp.207-8.

[280] Brown, p.140-3.

[281] About £400 a man in today's terms.

[282] A bicentennial plaque was unveiled on 23 January 2012 in Espeja in honour of Major-General MacKinnon. He also has a memorial plaque in St Paul's Cathedral.

Chapter 19

The Place is Ours

The order to march came on 8 March; and the following day they crossed the Tagus on a bridge of boats near Villa Velha, bound for Elvas by way of Portalegre. By 14 March the Light and 3rd divisions were concentrated near Elvas, about ten miles west of Badajoz. Two days later they crossed a pontoon bridge four miles west of Badajoz and once again went into the trenches.

The city of Badajoz stood on a point of land at the union of the rivulet of the Rivellas with the Guadiana, the former a tributary stream, meandering round the south-east of the fortress. A rocky height, thirty metres above the level of the river was topped by an old Moorish castle which stood above the other works, and overlooked the junction of the Rivellas with the Guadiana. The fortifications of the castle consisted of a wall without ditch or counter-scarp; regular curtains and bastions, ten metres high; in many parts the wall was nearer fifteen metres high, owing in part to the inequality of the ground. There were two outworks on the left of the Guadiana, one called La Picurina, the other a fort named Pardaleras, situated between the lower Guadiana and the fort of Picurina. On the right bank of the river was the hill and fort of San Cristobal.[283] The garrison comprised over 5,000 French troops commanded by Général de Division Armand Philippon, a 50-year-old fire-eater who had risen from the ranks. With stronger defences, more than three times as many defenders as Ciudad Rodrigo and an extremely able commander, Badajoz would be a tough nut to crack.

On the wild, wet and windy night of 17 March selected parties of men from the 3rd, 4th and Light divisions commenced digging parallels in front of the fortress. Wellington (every so often remembering that he was born an Irishman) wrote, 'We are getting on well with our operations here, although the weather is very bad. The soldiers swear we shall succeed because we invested on St. Patrick's eve, and broke ground on St. Patrick's Day.'

The following morning Private William Brown was in the trenches, laying out breakfast for his master (probably Lieutenant Costley) when a shell landed on the rampart and covered officer, servant and breakfast with mud. Both men crawled out of the mire unharmed, but the breakfast was lost to nature. Digging continued in the pouring rain later on 18 March and all through the following night; in thick fog just after lunch on 19 March about 1,500 Frenchmen made a sortie out from the fortress, whilst forty French dragoons raced around the flank and made their way to the British depots in the rear. The cry '*A sortie! a sortie!*' was heard up and down the allied lines.

The trench guard retired in the face of French assaults at both ends of the parallel, but rallied as troops picked up muskets or shovels with which to beat the French back. Most of the French were grenadiers armed with hammers and nails, intending to spike the allied guns. Vicious hand-to-hand fighting ensued for some time (during which Lieutenant Ben White of the 45th was conspicuous) but the French eventually retired, not before the British had lost 150 killed and wounded; Private John Handford of 2 Company was the only man of the 45th killed; the commander of the Royal Engineers, Lieutenant-Colonel Richard Fletcher was also amongst the wounded. The French cavalry had been stalled before they had chance to ransack the depot.

As the attackers retired, French artillery on the ramparts opened up on the British pursuers; a cannonball took off the crown of a 45th man's shako 'as neatly as if it had been done with a knife' without removing the hat from his head. The heavy rain recommenced immediately after the sortie and continued for eight days. The men in the trenches wondered whether they were digging a new river, since they seemed to be moving earth to make room for more water.

On 22 March Lieutenant John Metcalfe was assigned to be assistant engineer at the siege, on account of their being insufficient Royal Engineer officers present to undertake the works. On 23 March many of the works the men had constructed were so sodden that revetments were caving in and the earth ramparts could not be persuaded to take any form. The French continued to bombard the diggers throughout. Private John Ryan of No.9 Company was killed on 22 March, and three men on 24 March – Privates Henry Bailey, William Long and Robert Wilson. Wilson, of the Grenadier Company, had a premonition of his death on the morning he died and was reluctant to go to the trenches, telling all around him he would not return. Another grenadier detailed to cooking duties offered to go in his place, and Wilson gratefully exchanged. But after a day's cooking, whilst Wilson was serving hot meals to grateful diggers in the trenches at dinner-time, a shell burst at his feet, cutting him in two.[284] Private Sam Pepper of No.9 Company was far luckier, being glanced by a cannonball, but somehow survived more badly bruised than broken.

The allied guns were finally in place and commenced bombardment of the fortress at eleven o'clock in the morning of 25 March. The French guns returned fire briskly, and the men of the 45th entering the trenches at dusk had to endure a barrage that cost them five men killed and four wounded.

Later that night 500 men of the Light and 3rd divisions – including the flank companies of the 3rd under Captain Lightfoot – assaulted the outlying Fort Picurina, which they took in under an hour but at the cost of over sixty percent casualties. The guns of the fort had been silenced, but the attackers faced a barrage of musketry as they toiled up the steep scarp, and used their ladders like bridges to cross the ditch. Major-General Kempt released his reserve, a hundred men of the 2/83rd with perfect timing, and they arrived just in time to gain entry at the only damaged part of the defences. The whole affair had lasted twenty minutes at the cost of 319 allied troops; Captain Lightfoot was slightly wounded and Privates Thomas Chapman, Joseph Dobbs and Michael McGrath of the Light Company were killed.[285]

On 26 March the first of the 'Johnny Newcomes', Lieutenant Thomas Atkins, a former officer in the North Yorkshire Militia was killed in the trenches, and 20-year-old Private William Russell of No.9 Company lost his right leg to a shell-blast. In the period 18 March to 26 March Captain Thomas Lightfoot, Lieutenants Francis Andrews, Hans Marsh and John Metcalfe were all wounded. The 45th lost one officer and thirteen other ranks killed; and five officers, two serjeants and 45 other ranks wounded, plus three men missing, almost without firing a shot in anger except for a brief tussle during the French sortie.

Captain James Campbell was appointed brigade-major to Kempt's brigade on 28 March, a fitting reward for a talented young officer. As brigade-major he was effectively the senior staff officer in the brigade, conveying Kempt's orders to the battalion commanders, and receiving and distributing orders to the brigade from headquarters.

The digging continued. Major-General Kempt was ever-vigilant when on duty, frequently calling out to the toiling men, 'Work away, boys. There's one above sees all!' Private Patrick Dunn of No.3 Company was killed in the trenches on 29 March; the period 31 March to 3 April cost the 45th one officer killed and a serjeant and two men wounded.

The officer was another 'Johnny Newcome', Lieutenant Ben White, who was sitting reading a book in the trenches with his friend Lieutenant Edward Cotton of the 88th when a shell struck his head. Poor Lieutenant Cotton was unscathed, but so covered with White's blood and brains that it was thought he had been frightfully wounded. Captain James MacCarthy, 50th Foot, was an assistant-engineer attached to the 3rd Division. 'Several council were held and opinions expressed,' he wrote, 'when General Picton, feeling assured of the inaccessibleness of the breaches – which was afterwards proved correct by the severe losses the 4th and Light divisions sustained – proposed an escalade of the castle, and explained his plan, undertaking the performance thereof with his division, and not meeting with the acquiescence anticipated, he retired to his camp to await the official orders.'[286] Picton felt slighted; fortunately for the army, his plan was agreed to, for the breaches were not accessible.

Then The Place Is Ours

Orders came down from Wellington's headquarters on 5 April; the attack was close. The Light Division was to attack the breach on the flank of the bastion of Santa Maria; the 4th Division the breach in the bastion of La Trinidad; and the 5th Division was to carry the bastion of San Vicente on the west side by escalade. Picton had prevailed, and the 3rd Division was to capture the castle by escalade and then fall upon the rear of the breach defenders. The orders had specific instruction for the division. 'The attack of the Castle to be by escalade ... The troops for the storm of the Castle, consisting of the 3rd Division of Infantry, should move out from the right of the first parallel at a little before 10 o'clock, but not to attack till 10 o'clock.' They were to cross the River Rivillas below the broken bridge over that river, and attack that part of the castle which was on the right, and in the rear of the great battery firing on the bastion of La Trinidad. Once in possession of the castle, parties were to be sent to the left along the rampart to fall on the rear of those defending the great breach in the bastion of La Trinidad, and to communicate with the right of the attack on that bastion.[287]

By late on 6 April all was in readiness. Picton explained his arrangements and gave his orders to his assembled brigade and battalion commanders, then pulled out his watch and said, 'It is time, gentlemen, to go,' before adding emphatically, 'Some persons are of opinion that the attack on the castle will not succeed, but I will forfeit my life if it does not'. The men of the 3rd Division waited in the trenches for the signal. One concession to the horrors ahead was a relaxation of the dress-code, and so the men were without their knapsacks, jackets open, neck-stocks off, shirt collars unbuttoned, trousers rolled up to the knee, long haired and bearded from weeks on campaign, their bronzed faces upturned to the parapet, waiting for the signal. It came at twenty-five minutes past nine; Captain MacCarthy was allotted the onerous task of leading the 3rd Division to its place in the trenches, and found himself on the wrong end of Picton's temper, as the General asserted that MacCarthy was leading them in the wrong direction. 'Drawing his sword, [he] swore he would cut me down. I explained, and he was appeased.'[288]

Luckily for all MacCarthy brought the head of the division to the right spot in the first parallel, into which Picton led his men on foot. Senior officers clambered down into the trenches, and the men of the 3rd Division followed them, taking twenty minutes to form up and move forward in one solid mass, with the 45th in front, the 88th and 74th in close support, then followed by the 9th and 21st Portuguese Line under the command of Colonel José Joaquim de Champalimaud, then the second British brigade under Colonel James Campbell at the rear, the 2/5th, 77th, 2/83rd and 94th. They advanced to the River Rivillas undetected, but some French fire-balls (an early form of flare) lit up the night sky, and the 3rd Division froze. The French on the ramparts had below them the sight of 4,000 men formed approaching the castle. The stormers let out a yell of defiance, and all hell was let loose. Within seconds every French gun that could be brought to bear against them was firing.

When the division had advanced some distance from the trenches, with Picton at its head, along with General Kempt, Colonel Burgoyne of the Royal Engineers and staff, the enemy's fire increased considerably. Captain MacCarthy was walking between General Picton and General Kempt when Picton stumbled and dropped, wounded in the foot. 'He was instantly assisted to the left of the column, and the command devolving on General Kempt, he continued to lead it with the greatest gallantry. On arrival at the mill-dam (extremely narrow) over which the troops were to pass, streams of fire blazed on the division; the party with ladders, axes, etc. which had preceded, were overwhelmed, mingled in a dense crowd, and stopped the way.'[289]

Private William Brown was one of the ragged stormers of the 45th. 'The point at which we descended into the ditch was between two bastions, from both of which we experienced a most dreadful fire of musketry, while from the body of the wall the enemy continued to pour, by means of boards placed on the parapet, whole showers of grenades, which they arranged in rows, and, being lighted with a match, the whole was upset, exploding amongst us in the ditch with horrid destruction. Coils of rope, in a friable state, strongly impregnated with tar, pitch and oil, were likewise employed by the enemy as a means of annoyance, which completely answered the purpose intended by scorching and scalding numbers in a dreadful manner … The ladders, by some mistake, were not brought up in time, and the period passed while waiting for them I shall never forget.'[290]

Ten minutes into the assault, all was chaos. The ladders had been delayed. When they at last arrived, Captain John McCarthy and Brigade-Major James Campbell laboriously raised five ladders on the mound of rubble against the wall, and both men arranged the troops on them as best they could; four of the ladders with troops on them and an officer on the top were broken near the upper end, and men tumbled back down into screaming heaps.[291] The fifth ladder had no officer, but a private of the 45th at the top was shot in the head as soon as he appeared above the parapet, and tumbled backwards to the ground; the next man, Corporal Michael Kelly of Captain Milnes's No.7 Company, shot the French defender (presumably manically trying to reload) and instantly sprang over the rampart. However the French were well-prepared; each man had beside him eight loaded muskets, whilst enormous pikes with crooks attached to them were distributed amongst the defenders for the purpose of grappling with the ladders. The broken ladders were replaced by fresh ones, and more ascending troops started to make headway.

Private Brown's story corroborates much of the above, for he says the following: 'Our men rushed up the ladders with the greatest impetuosity, but when near the top the whole broke down, and all that were on them were precipitated on the points of their comrades' bayonets, by which many received their death. We were then ordered to unfix our bayonets and sling the firelocks on our shoulders, which being done and a number of ladders brought, we immediately began to ascend. The ladder I chanced to be on was laid to the bottom of an embrasure, in which were a number of the enemy ready to receive us, and in front of them stood an officer with a pistol in each hand ready cocked. On the ladder a Grenadier officer of our Regiment preceded us, who, when his head was nearly on a line with the enemy's feet, was fired at by the officer in front. Missing the contents of the pistol he instantly gave his opponent a back-slap across the legs with his sabre, who fell over into the ditch. Our officer then leapt into the embrasure, cutting down all that opposed him, and was immediately followed by the men, who became directly masters of the rampart. The enemy retired beyond the court of the Castle to a gateway that communicated with the town, where a number of prisoners were taken.'[292] The grenadier officer was probably Lieutenant Hans Stevenson Marsh, commanding in Captain Martin's absence.

One of the first officers of the 45th to make the ascent up the ladders was Lieutenant James MacPherson, closely followed by Lieutenant-Colonel Hercules Pakenham, the younger brother of Major-General Edward Pakenham. With armed Frenchmen up ahead, and a staff officer waving a sword inches from his posterior, no pressure on young MacPherson! He arrived to within a few rungs of the top, where he discovered that the ladder was about three feet too short. He called to those below to raise the ladder more perpendicularly whilst he pushed it away from the wall at the top. The men below brought it nearer at the base; but as MacPherson wobbled around on the top section, he saw a French soldier point a musket against him, and before he could take evasive action, the Frenchman fired. The musket-ball struck a Spanish silver button on his waistcoat, which broke in half; the ball ricocheted and glanced across his chest, breaking two ribs. He suddenly found it difficult to breathe; the fractured part of one rib pressed in upon his lungs so as to constrict respiration. Wavering at the top of the ladder, Pakenham tried to push him to one side to pass him, but was also severely wounded at this moment. Then the ladder broke; and below was a *chevaux-de-frise*[293] of bayonets. Pakenham, taking the hand of the wounded MacPherson, said, 'God bless you, my dear fellow, we shall meet again'. But MacPherson rode the ladder down, and somehow descended to the ditch in safety, then fainted. When he awoke he found himself attended by two of his men, one supporting his head upon his knees, and the other holding a cup of hot chocolate to his lips. MacPherson tried to rise, and in so doing the fractured bone which had been pressing on his lungs was pushed back into place, and he could breathe again. Still unsteady, he mounted another ladder, but in the interim the walls had been now gained; climbing over the ramparts in great pain, he ran towards the tower from which he had seen the French flag waving for three weeks. It is appropriate that MacPherson tells us what happened next – the most famous moment in the regiment's history – in his own words:

'I at length found my way to the tower, when I perceived the sentry still at his post. With my sword drawn, I seized him and desired him in French to show me the way to the Colour. He replied, "Je ne sais pas." I upon this gave him a slight cut across the face, saying at the same time, "Vous le savez a present"; on which he dashed his arms upon the ground and, striking his breast, said, as he raised his head and pointed to his heart, "Frappez! Je suis Francais!" his manner at the same time indicating that the Colour was there. I could not wait to provide for the safety of this brave fellow, so I called out loudly for a non-commissioned officer to take charge of him, so that he should not be hurt. One stepped forward, when, giving him instructions to protect the gallant soldier, I ascended the tower; but my precaution was vain, for I afterwards discovered that the noble fellow was amongst the slain.'[294]

MacPherson tore the French flag down. For lack of anything else, he took off his red jacket, and hoisted it on the staff as a substitute for the Union Jack.

Down on the ramparts, Major Henry Ridge of the 5th Foot – one of that fine strata of fighting field-officers within the Army to which Majors Gwyn and Smith had so conspicuously belonged – erected a ladder at a low point in the castle wall, and upon a second ladder being placed by Lieutenant Thomas Cranch of the 5th, the two swarmed up over the parapet, followed by their men. The castle was won; the increasing numbers of troops following them drove the French in a desperate hand-to-hand conflict through the castle gates into the town. But almost every other assault on the town had failed, and Wellington was worried.

Then an officer rode up at speed – it was Lieutenant John Tyler of the 45th, Picton's personal aide-de-camp. 'Ah, Tyler, well?' enquired Wellington. 'General Picton has taken the castle, my lord,' said Tyler. 'Then the place is ours,' remarked Wellington. 'Return to General Picton and ask him to keep possession of the Castle at all hazards.'[295]

Tyler hastened back to find Picton, who had been hit in the groin at the foot of the ramparts and lay insensible and unrecognised for twenty-five minutes. Coming to, he hauled himself to his feet and roared his men on. Although wounded, he had already ordered parties to the left, along the ramparts, to fall on the rear of the Frenchmen defending the Great Breach, and to communicate with the right attack on the bastion of La Trinidad. But

Badajoz

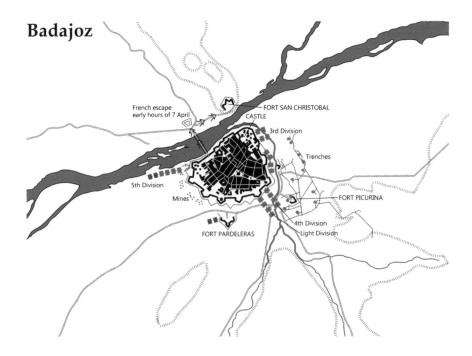

the French closed and barricaded the gates communicating with the ramparts, and forcing these barriers took time. The French made a desperate attempt to retake the castle, and in the vicious hand-to-hand fighting, the gallant Major Ridge of the 5th was killed. Captain MacCarthy cited seeing Lieutenant Sam Macalpin of the 88th Foot as the first officer to enter the citadel (where he was immediately killed) but reported that the 3rd Division were masters of the castle by midnight:

'It was indeed delightful to hear our buglers upon the wall near the citadel sounding the animating "Advance!" to proclaim their success and accelerate the distant troops; which consoled the wounded and ameliorated their pangs. One bold bugler, as soon as he mounted the wall, determining to be first – when sounding the "Advance" – was killed in the act of blasting forth his triumphal music. Numbers of heroes fell on both sides. At the castle the bodies of the English and French laid upon each other; but General Picton's division conquered, and was established before twelve o'clock in the citadel, which commanded all the works of the town, and in the town.'[296]

Elsewhere, the other divisions had been powerfully resisted. The attack on the main breaches was showing little success. The defenders employed musketry, grape-shot, hand grenades, bags filled with gunpowder, and every possible form of destructive missile short of boiling oil to drop on the heads of the attackers. With over 2,000 casualties and nothing to show,

179

Wellington ordered the remainder to retire just after midnight and reform for a second assault.

James Leith's 5th Division had been more successful to the south and west. They carried San Vicente bastion by escalade, and then moved across town towards the Great Breach. With two points of entry – the castle coupled with the presence of the 5th Division in the streets – the French became convinced that it was useless to continue the struggle. They concentrated in the centre of town, leaving parties of volunteers as virtual suicide squads to face the British troops taking them in rear, then broke and fled across the bridge over the Guadiana into Fort San Cristobal. When the stormers mounted the Great Breach the second time they found the ramparts abandoned. Badajoz had fallen.

Butcher's Bill

'During the night the moans, prayers, cries, and exclamations of the wounded fully expressed the degrees of their agonies, in the varieties of acuteness and cadence of tone, from the highest pitch in the treble to the lowest note in bass. Some of the wounded were, undoubtedly, raving mad, violently vociferating dreadful imprecations and denunciations; others singing; and many calling the numbers of their regiments – as, "Oh, 45th! Oh, 74th! Oh, 77th!" to attract their comrades to their aid. Many of the fallen heroes received additional wounds during the night. ... At daybreak the wailings of the wounded had been either silenced by death or subsided by the exhaustion of the survivors; and the thunder of the guns having ceased on the previous night, was succeeded by a solemnity which now was more awful to us than the raging of the battle.'[297]

Captain Henry-Moore Herrick, the newly commissioned Ensign George Golland, Ensign George McDonnell, Serjeant Henry Badcock, Corporals Mark Atkins and John Torphy and fifteen men were killed; Lieutenant-Colonel Thomas Forbes, Captains James Campbell, John O'Flaherty and Thomas Lightfoot (who commanded the light companies of the division), Lieutenants James MacPherson, Francis Powell and James Reynett, Ensigns Charles Munro, James Dale and James Stewart, eight serjeants, one drummer and sixty-five men were wounded.

Nineteen-year-old Ensign John-Fitzwilliam Jones was seriously wounded and his wound appeared mortal. Ensign Charles Munro was still only 16 years of age.[298] Beneath one of the ladders lay the body of a corporal of the 45th – whether Mark Atkins, John MacLerane or John Torphy, history doesn't relate. He had been wounded at the breach and fallen forward on his knees and hands. In the noise, darkness and confusion, the foot of a ladder had been placed on his back, and the weight of the men ascending the ladder had squashed him like a bug, forcing blood out of his ears, mouth and nose. Miraculously neither the Light nor Grenadier Companies had suffered a single fatality in the assault, although both had plenty of wounded.

The location of the regimental hospital is unknown, but was more than likely a commandeered house near the breach. Whatever it was, it must have been a charnel-house. Surgeon William Smyth had gone home for health reasons a few weeks before and assistant-surgeons Charles Cook and Harry Radford were overwhelmed. Private William Westrage of the Light Company had his left arm amputated and his left leg removed at the thigh, a lengthy operation that was also performed on his friend Private Pat Stanton and Corporal John Watson. Private Joe Norman of the Grenadier Company, miraculously pardoned after Busaco, had thrown himself into the assault to win back his reputation, and paid for it at the cost of his left arm; he was also shot through the body. Privates Francis Bursling, William Cavenagh, John Costellow and John Keatley also had arms removed. Private Thomas Crutchley of No.7 Company, one of the old men of the battalion at 43 years of age, was hit in the left chest and left thigh but survived. Private Charles Cawley was shot in the right arm and left shoulder; the latter ball was extracted but the former was lodged too deep and left where it was, always a dangerous action in the days before antiseptics and penicillin. But Cawley would survive for a long time yet. Then there were those such as John Clarke and William Crowder who suffered serious wounds falling from ladders, Crowder with a hernia that would trouble him for life. The suffering did not end in the days after the battle – the teenaged Ensign John-Fitzwilliam Jones died there on 18 July after enduring fifteen weeks of agony.[299]

The Army had lost five generals wounded – Picton and Colville commanding the 3rd and 4th divisions respectively, plus Kempt (wounded early in the action, hit in the leg, a wound that would trouble him for life), Harvey and Bowes amongst the brigadiers. The Fighting Third had lost over 600 officers and men in one night. Lieutenant-Colonel Alexander Wallace of the 88th assumed temporary command of the 3rd Division, and Major Thomas Forbes of the 45th became a temporary brigadier. It had been a horrendous night for the allied army; fifty-two British officers had been killed and 203 were wounded, 602 other ranks killed and 2,138 wounded. Portuguese losses totalled 730. In terms of casualties, it was amongst the half-dozen bloodiest battles involving the British Army during the Napoleonic Wars.

The next morning, Wellington surveyed the carnage at the Great Breach. Around him, some 2,500 men either stared blankly at the sky, cried for their mothers or gasped in silent agony. Wellington found himself with tears in his eyes, and tried desperately to control himself on the approach of General Picton. 'I bit my lip and did everything I could to stop myself for I was ashamed he should see it, but I could not.'[300] Picton, acting ever the flint-hearted soldier for the benefit of those nearby, blurted out, 'Good God.

What's the matter?' Wellington, who was to famously burst into tears after reading the casualty list after Waterloo, plainly brought his emotions under control. He needed to, because down in the town, other events were unfolding that required his attention.

The Demons of Rage

It should come as no surprise that the aftermath of Badajoz was similar to the madness that followed Ciudad Rodrigo, only worse.

Private William Brown was as horrified as before: 'When the garrison surrendered, leave for two hours was given us to go to the town, camp or wherever we pleased, but the town was universally preferred. All rushed to the gate that communicated with it, which caused a deal of noise and squabbling. for the enemy had built up the gateway as a means of defence, leaving only a narrow passage through which but one man could pass at a time. They all, however, got to the town soon enough for the poor inhabitants, who were by many of our men shamefully and barbarously treated. There was not, I believe, a house in the whole town that was not ransacked from top to bottom – murder, rape and robbery were committed with the greatest impunity … I proceeded along the street, in which were exhibited every crime that could render man contemptible and disgrace human nature. At last arriving at the ground of the preceding night's encounter, a very different scene presented itself from that which I had just left. There lust and rapine were perpetrating every crime, and at the moment trampling upon every principle sacred and civil, moral and religious; at that very instant were the demons of rage ruining everything good and virtuous, destroying the properties and violating the rights of every family and of every habitation. But here reigned a still and solemn silence; not a sound was heard, not a voice arose to disturb the awful pause, save the faint groans of the wounded and dying … Amongst the slain I saw many of my comrades and associates, with whom I had travelled many a long and weary mile. Some with whom I was intimately acquainted, and with whom but yesterday I had conversed freely, now lay stretched in their gore.'[301]

This dismal behaviour carried on all night and all the following day. In desperation, Wellington drafted this curt note from his tent on the evening of 7 April: 'It is now full time that the plunder of Badajoz should cease.' And lest anyone think he was not serious: 'The Commander of the Forces has ordered the Provost Marshal into the town, and he has orders to execute any men he may find in the act of plunder.'[302]

Lieutenant James MacPherson found himself called up before the wounded General Picton in the early morning of 7 April, and presented to the General the French flag he had taken down from the Castle the previous night. 'Sir,' Picton said, 'I congratulate you on your gallantry and thank you; this night you have allied your fate to mine.' He warmly shook

MacPherson's hand. 'There is a hand will never forsake you; from henceforth your promotion shall be my look-out.' Picton would not accept the flag from the young officer. 'No,' he said, 'take it to Lord Wellington, and show him what the 3rd Division can do.' MacPherson demurred, claiming he was in too much pain, but Picton insisted. MacPherson accordingly presented the flag to Wellington himself; the commander-in-chief thanked him and invited him to dinner. Unfortunately his wound prevented him from accepting the invitation.[303]

[283] Grattan, Vol. 1, pp.238-9.

[284] Brown, pp.145-6 and WO25/1275.

[285] WO25/1275.

[286] McCarthy, pp.167-8.

[287] *Wellington's Dispatches*, Vol. 9, pp.32-3.

[288] 1909 Regimental Annual, p.21.

[289] ibid, p 22.

[290] Brown, pp.149-50.

[291] ibid, p.22.

[292] Brown, pp.151-2.

[293] A hedge of bayonets stuck point upwards in a timber board.

[294] Wylly, p.212.

[295] ibid, p.213.

[296] McCarthy, p.176.

[297] 1909 Regimental Annual, p.26.

[298] Statistics based upon returns of wounded in official despatches, and from a study of WO25/1275.

[299] Hall, p.317.

[300] Rory Muir, Wellington: *The Path to Victory*, 2013, p.457.

[301] Brown, pp.154-9.

[302] General Orders and Regulations, p.18.

[303] Wylly, p.216.

Chapter 20

Salamanca

The 3rd Division camped in the shadow of Badajoz for a few days and marched north-westwards on 12 April through Campo Mayor and Arronches, bound for Portalegre. Pressing on, they crossed the Tagus at Villa Velha on 16 April and reached Castelo Branco the following day. On 21 April they passed through Sabugal and turned east, crossing the frontier near their old stomping-ground at Albergueria and camped in the vicinity. For the first time since landing in 1808 the number of effectives was outnumbered by the sick; on 25 April the 45th had 315 able-bodied men in the ranks and 323 in hospital. The death toll since 25 March had been forty-two men, about half of whom had been lost at Badajoz and the rest died of wounds or sickness. The battalion badly needed new officers but gained only two, 17-year-old Ensign Ralph Smyth Stewart from Edinburgh, and Captain Greenwell returned from England. With Forbes commanding the brigade, a new commanding officer was expected daily from England, Lieutenant-Colonel Henry Ridewood.

Whilst in and around Albergueria the battalion patrolled, drilled and romanced. The village had been desecrated by the French, as Private William recorded: 'It was also found to have undergone the fiery ordeal of the enemy, who had laid it completely in ruins, while the whole of the inhabitants were fled to the mountains. On perceiving the devastation and ruin that had been committed, I flew to the dwelling of Fernando Silvera. What my sensations were, may be more easily imagined than described, when I found all ruined, the inmates fled, and no one near that could inform me when, or in what direction they retreated. The walls were dismantled of the roof, and divested of all the doors and windows; and when I passed the threshold I found the furniture broken and destroyed, the shattered pieces of which lay strewed on the floor.

'As I stood on the once happy, but now deserted and desolate hearth, contemplating the foul outrage that had been committed on innocent and harmless people, I heard footsteps in the passage, and to my ravished and enraptured view, my dearest Rosa entered, who, when she beheld me,

184

exclaimed, "Mina Gulliame!" and in a moment we were in others arms. When the emotions this unexpected meeting had raised were somewhat subsided, the lovely girl informed me that upon the approach of the enemy, her parents, with a number of their neighbours, retired to a sequestered spot, about two leagues distant, where they had then been ten days; but having heard of the retreat of the enemy, and the subsequent advance of the British, she, in company with a few belonging to the village, had come down to ascertain the truth of what they had heard.'[304]

In mid-May the battalion's current station was listed as noted as being Renadoes, possibly modern Rendo, about ten miles west of Albergueria. Ensigns Henry Middleton and John Trumball Ray arrived there conducting fifty-three men from the second battalion, replacements sorely needed given that the battalion sick-list still hovered above 300 men. Ray was a 20-year-old Londoner who had served as a volunteer at Badajoz and gained his ensigncy by dint of the large number of vacancies after Badajoz.

The hero of the hour, Lieutenant James MacPherson, was still looking for promotion. Lieutenant-Colonel Henry Ridewood wrote a letter to the adjutant-general's office on 12 May, asking that 'Lieutenant MacPherson ... was among the first, who mounted the Walls, and although wounded, at the time, in the most gallant manner, climbed up the Flag staff, and struck the French Colour, which he afterwards, presented to the Earl of Wellington. Lieutenant MacPherson has I believe, been recommended, by the General of the Division, to the Commander of the Forces in this Country, that his name may be submitted to His Royal Highness for promotion, which I trust renders any more I could say in his favour, unnecessary.' It was to no avail as MacPherson was destined never to serve as a captain in the 45th.

Some 10,000 men under Lieutenant-General Sir Thomas Graham had been left to hold Badajoz; news had arrived that Maréchal Marmont had pushed past Ciudad Rodrigo into Portuguese territory at the head of 35,000 men, which had triggered this forward advance. However Marmont had retired upon Salamanca and both armies settled down to prepare for the next phase of the campaign.

On 13 June the army crossed the river Agueda near Ciudad Rodrigo, and arrived in front of Salamanca four days later, splashing across fords on the River Tormes above and below the town and encamped where the army was concentrated on the height of San Cristobal, some five miles north of the ancient university town. The battering trains accompanying Wellington's army were brought to bear on the modest forts surrounding Salamanca; the first attempt to carry them by escalade failed, despite them having been damaged by the bombardment.

Marmont used the delay to concentrate 36,000 men. By 20 June the two armies were facing each other in battle array, but other than a few skirmishes, inactivity reigned. On 24 June Marmont crossed the Tormes at Huerta, ten miles east of town and just beyond the British right flank, driving in the King's German Legion cavalry as he did so. Wellington sent the recently-returned Lieutenant-General Thomas Graham with 12,000 men across a bridge upon his right, and Marmont re-crossed the river and fell back. On 27 June the allies captured the last of the French forts in front of Salamanca. Realising that the town was lost, and after destroying the works at Salamanca, Marmont retreated north-east towards Tordesillas on the river Duero. Wellington pursued for fifty miles and by 2 July both armies were facing each other on opposite banks of the Duero, neither strong enough to attack the other.

Picton and Pakenham

The 3rd Division suffered a seemingly irreparable loss on 28 June; Thomas Picton was so completely struck down with fever caused by the eruption of his Badajoz wound that he had to be invalided home. Picton's loss was keenly felt.

A serjeant of the 45th later wrote that 'General Picton, or "Old Picton" as we used to call him, was always very well liked by the division: he was very strict, sometimes in particular about any little bit of plunder that the men would sometimes pick up; and he used always to be talking about how wrong it was to take from the poor people because the countries happened to be at war. He used to have the men flogged when they were found out: but when he flogged, many others took life; so our fellows always thought "Old Picton" a very kind general. Besides this, the men always thought he had their welfare at heart; for every soldier in the division knew that if he had anything to complain of, "Old Picton" would listen to him, and, if he could, set him right. As to his fighting, I always thought that it was he who made the third division what it was in moments of excitement, when the fiery temperament of his nature was called forth, his whole countenance betrayed the overwhelming influence of passion; and he then gave utterance to a storm of bitter reproofs, but what he ordered them to do; and I really think, if the general had placed himself in the thickest fire we were ever in, that, so long as he remained, his division would have stayed with him to a man.'[305]

His place was taken by Major-General the Honourable Edward Michael Pakenham, a 34-year-old Irish aristocrat with experience in the Irish Rebellion, Canada and the West Indies; he had tasted as much action as any man that age could reasonably have been expected to savour. He was also Wellington's brother-in-law, being a younger brother of Kitty Wellesley. His friends called him 'Ned' but his troops called him nothing at all, having had little or no time to get to know him. Wellington considered him no genius, but an officer of uncommon reliability. A man was not awarded the command of the 3rd Division lightly.

From 3 July until 12 July the 3rd Division was quartered near some fords on the south side of the river at the village of Pollos, about five miles west of Tordesillas, where the French 7th Division under Général de Division Jean-Guillaume-Barthélemy Thomières held the northern bank. The Spanish summer was extreme, with an officer recording that the thermometer in his tent did not drop below ninety-four degrees Fahrenheit for two days, and that the temperature in the sun was 110 degrees, making his sword hilt too hot to handle. To combat the heat troops from both armies bathed and mingled in the same stretch of river, little knowing that one division would destroy the other in just over ten days' time.

The relationship between French and British soldiers in off-duty moments throughout the war was invariably cordial. Each respected the other, despite the fact that in recruitment, training, supply and motivation the two armies were as alike as apple and fish.

The Frenchman was a conscript, potentially from nearly any class of society, the Briton a volunteer and almost always from the labouring classes. Basic training in the French Army was as much about indoctrination into the Emperor's way of conducting war as much as learning the basics; whereas a British recruit could expect to be flogged if he failed to adhere to the minutest drill requirement. Any Frenchman doing well on the battlefield could expect to be rewarded with the coveted *Legion d'honneur* medal, his regiment extolled in the Emperor's famous Bulletins, and after many years' service, ascent to the famous *Garde Imperiale*; for the redcoats there were no medals, no mentions in despatches to anyone below officer level, and a discharge to a garrison battalion if one was lucky.

Any Briton who was 'gone for a soldier' was just that in the eyes of the public at home – gone. In the days before a mass postal service and with high rates of illiteracy, the daily lives of these men was a complete mystery to their families left at home, and many men just disappeared completely, their last resting places unknown to their kin.

Any Frenchman falling into the hands of the enemy sincerely hoped that enemy wore a red coat. Spanish and Portuguese guerrillas invariably showed little or no mercy to captured French soldiers, usually in retaliation for isolated French atrocities against civilians across the Peninsula. This lack of mercy usually involved torture, and even capture by Spanish troops did not guarantee a fair ministration. But to be a captive of the British Army ensured good treatment and the likelihood of sitting out the war in Scotland or the Midlands.[306]

On 17 July, Marmont, freshly reinforced by 8,000 men with another 10,000 allegedly on their way, crossed the river and moved southwards towards a rendezvous with King Joseph marching from Madrid. The allies followed and for three days the two armies manoeuvred across open country in plain sight of each other, often not much more than a musket-shot apart. Three days later both were in sight of Salamanca again, and Wellington crossed the Tormes leaving the 3rd Division guarding the north bank to the east of the town. The night of 21-22 July was the worst the men of the battalion could remember, with violent thunderstorms and sheeting rain all night long. The troops gave up all hope of digging trenches, as they filled faster than they could be dug. No-one was sure whether the storm was a good omen, or ill.

Salamanca

The morning of Wednesday, 22 July dawned cloudless and fair, but the men of the 45th were drenched and exhausted, covered in mud, tattered and bearded from ten weeks on campaign. The one thing they needed least was the singular thing that they were about to experience. There were twenty-six officers and 416 other ranks present and fit for duty, but only three company captains available. Sometime in the morning they were formed up and marched through the streets of Salamanca, then turned left across the old bridge at noon and marched two miles south to the village of Aldea Tejada, arriving between one and two o'clock. The rest of the army was somewhere to the south-east, hidden in rolling yellow farmland and behind rocky flat-topped hillocks. Somewhere out there also was Marmont's French army, which had been handled with cool efficiency in the perambulating manoeuvres of the past ten days.

Maréchal Auguste Frederic Louis Viesse Marmont was the youngest of Napoleon's marshals, having reached the rank at the age of 35, as well as perhaps the most urbane and intelligent. But he was prone to fits of depression and carelessness in the heat of the moment, and carried an enormous chip on his shoulder; he never felt truly appreciated, and his vanity craved much appreciation. This would later fuel his decision to become the first marshal to defect to the allies in the dark days of 1814.

He now planned to flank Wellington to the south-west, cutting the road to Ciudad Rodrigo, and sent his divisions across a plain to the west. Although he was tactically sound, here Marmont's characteristic carelessness kicked in. The divisions were allowed to string out too far apart, leaving a large gap between the French left and the rest of the army. Wellington famously saw the gap whilst eating lunch in a farmyard on some heights, threw his chicken leg over his shoulder and put his army into motion.

Captain James Campbell was with the 3rd Division staff when Wellington approached. 'It might have been near two o'clock, when Lord Wellington, followed by some of his staff, galloped up to where the 3rd division was posted; and calling for Sir Edward Pakenham, he gave him certain orders in a very few impressive words, and Sir Edward's reply was quite in character.'[307] Captain Tmomas Lightfoot recorded the meeting between Pakenham and Wellington in a letter written the day after the battle. 'His Lordship's orders to Lord Pakenham in our hearing were: "Pakenham, you will carry that height where the enemy's left is posted by storm, and when you have gained it, go at them, hard and fast, with the bayonet." "Yes, my Lord," cried Pakenham, "that I will, by God!" and galloping off, placed himself at our head.'[308]

Given that the heights in question were two and a half miles away and partially concealed by intervening ground, the exact tenor of what was said might have been only half-remembered; but Lightfoot commanded the 45th Light Company on the day, and was probably at the front of the division and therefore in a position to hear what was actually said. The 45th's camp kettles were in an instant overturned, and packed on the mules, which started for the rear. The division was soon under arms, and moved off rapidly in open column, right in front, the 45th leading. Sir Edward Pakenham, 'in his quick decided manner', pointed out the direction they were to take to Captain James Campbell, and asked him tell Colonel Wallace of the 88th regiment, being in temporary command of the brigade, 'to move on with as much rapidity as possible, but without blowing the men too much'.[309]

Pakenham spent a little time fussing over the formation of the division because it was his first day in command during an action and he wanted to make a good impression. He arranged Wallace's brigade into a column of companies[310] and placed them on the left flank; the 45th in the lead, the 88th in the centre, and the 74th at the rear. To their right marched James Campbell's 2nd brigade, two battalions of the 5th leading, then the 94th, and the 2/83rd at the back. On their right tramped the 8th Portuguese brigade, four battalions of the 9th and 21st Portuguese Line. The left and front of the formation was covered by light infantry and riflemen from the 60th Foot; two artillery batteries walked on the left flank, and two light cavalry brigades covered the right flank. It must have been quite some spectacle – 7,000 men marching across the Spanish farmland in the bright sunlight, headed to meet the advancing tip of a French division as yet unseen. They soon descended into a small valley, and having brought up their left shoulders a little, pushed on at a quick pace, but in excellent order, to the right, allowing the sides of the valley to conceal their movements. The whole of the left flank of the column was covered by a cloud of sharpshooters, composed of light infantry companies, and riflemen of the 5/60th Rifles.

After moving a considerable distance in this order the head of the column, by bringing up the right shoulder, began to ascend the hill, on the top of which they expected to find the enemy still extending to their left. Having fairly outflanked the French left, the whole formation formed line, and with Sir Edward Pakenham in front, hat in hand, and the brigades advanced 'in beautiful style, covered by our sharpshooters, the right of the first line admirably supported by the left brigade'.[311]

The brigades were in line facing east by this point, Wallace's brigade in the lead, with the 45th on the right. Captain Thompson's brigade of Royal Artillery had unlimbered and was delivering a cannonade over their heads into the waiting French lines, Thomières' 7th Division clearly seen on the wooded ridge of the Pico de Miranda ahead. The French were out-numbered eleven battalions to seven.

The advance stopped as Major-General Pakenham rode along the line, addressing the troops as extra serjeants came forward to help guard the colours. Waving his hat, Pakenham then advanced the line into the French. As they approached, the long British first line – which easily outflanked the more compact French column – bent inwards at the wings to envelope the 'Parleyvoos' with a withering series of volleys taken front-on and in enfilade. James Campbell appreciated Pakenham's skill. 'The enemy's skirmishers and ours now set to work, yet we did not wait for their indecisive long shots; but advancing still rapidly and steadily, our right soon came into contact with their left, which had opened a very heavy and destructive fire upon us, and which would have lasted long enough had the brigade been halted to return it, but it was instantly charged and overthrown. It was now evident to us all that Sir Edward Pakenham knew how to handle Picton's division. But at this critical moment some of the enemy's cavalry charged in turn, and most gallantly, the right flank of the 45th regiment, but a well directed fire from the 5th, which had been brought up, so as to be close at hand, removed all apprehensions in that point, and the enemy's infantry were quickly pursued, chiefly by Colonel Wallace, at the head of the 88th whose impetuosity was found most difficult to restrain.'[312]

Private William Brown's account of the French cavalry charge suggests that it was more serious than Campbell recollected: 'As our brigade was marching up to attack a strongly posted column of infantry, a furious charge was made by a body of cavalry upon our Regiment, and, not having time to form square, we suffered severely. Several times the enemy rode through us, cutting down with their sabres all that opposed them. Our ranks were broken and thrown into the utmost confusion. Repeatedly our men attempted to reform, but all in vain – they were as often cut down and trampled upon by their antagonists. At length, however, the enemy was driven off by some squadrons of our cavalry, who came up in time to save us from being totally destroyed. Numerous and severe were the wounds received on this occasion. Several had their arms dashed from their shoulders, and I saw more than one with their heads completely cloven. Among the rest I received a wound, but comparatively slight, although well aimed. Coming in contact with one of the enemy he brandished his sword over me, and standing in his stirrup irons, prepared to strike; but, pricking his horse with my bayonet, it reared and pranced, when the sword fell, the point striking my forehead. He was, however, immediately brought down, falling with a groan to rise no more.'[313]

The cavalry went on to put the 1/5th Foot in Campbell's brigade to temporary flight before being charged and dispersed by one of the light cavalry brigades attached to the 3rd Division, Portuguese dragoons under the command of Benjamin d'Urban. At some stage during the French cavalry attack, Lieutenant Hans Marsh's grenadiers on the right flank wheeled to face the horsemen and delivered a telling volley at close range, which caused the dragoons to retire. 'Well done, 45th,' Major-General Pakenham said as he rode past. The division continued to advance and, though in motion and still exposed to a heavy fire, order was soon restored in the ranks. With Sir Edward Pakenham still in front, they were ready for another dash at the enemy, who were trying to reform on a gentle height, a short distance in front. 'But how truly inspiring the scene had now become, and how "beautifully the practice" of Major Douglas's artillery was telling among the French! Another charge was intended; the French would not, however, stand, and retired in tolerable order, but most severely galled by our sharpshooters, who were close at their heels. They then took up another position, in which they were reinforced by a large body of their troops, and many guns, which opened on us.'[314]

A little later a French officer picked up a musket and attempted to shoot Pakenham; the piece either misfired or was not loaded, and so he picked up another. Corporal Pat Cavanagh of No.3 Company, a ten-year veteran of the regiment, stepped out of the ranks and coolly shot the French officer dead, but was hit and killed by a French sniper at virtually the same time. Leonard Greenwell, who had experienced the luxury of having a horse since his elevation to major eighteen months earlier, was on horseback leading the light companies of the 3rd Division, a target too large to ignore; at least that is what the French *tirailleur*[315] who lined him up in his sights thought. Major Greenwell was hit by a musket-ball that passed through both arms and his body. He fell from his horse, and was carried helpless to the rear. The ball could not be extracted from his left arm and remained there for life.

The French reinforcement behind Thomières' rapidly dissolving division was General Clausel's division, who were charged by the British heavy cavalry – 3rd and 4th Dragoons and 5th Dragoon Guards[316] under the command of Major-General John Le Marchant – before they could inflict any damage on the 3rd Division. The charge pushed so many already shaken men of the French 7th Division into the waiting arms of Pakenham's men that the division virtually ceased to exist. As the French fled, a private of the 45th chased a French soldier with his bayonet. As a last resort the Frenchman threw away his musket and endeavoured to escape by climbing one of the scrubby trees on the Pico de Miranda. For his trouble, he received the bayonet 'in that portion of his person which should never be presented to either friend or foe'.

Maréchal Marmont was severely wounded by a shell early in the battle, and command devolved upon Général de Division Jean Bonnet, who was likewise wounded within minutes. The third in line was the ever-dependable Bertrand Clausel, and he held his ground on the right and right

Salamanca

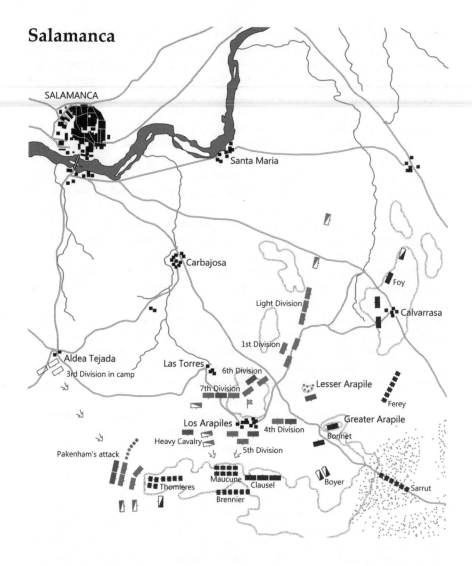

centre with considerable obstinacy. The work of the 3rd Division being largely done, the 4th and 5th divisions, supported by the 1st, 6th and Light divisions, attacked the French in echelon from the right, and the action raged round the Greater Arapile hill in the centre, which the French still held.

Pack's Portuguese brigade attacked the rocky height in vain, losing 386 men in ten minutes, and French artillery in the second line was posted far enough in advance to shell the allied line. Pack's failure gave Clausel time to take the offensive. He advanced upon Lieutenant-Colonel Cole's 4th Division, which gave way, whole battalions streaming to the heights at the rear. Wellington hurried forward Henry Clinton's 6th Division, and after an ugly half-hour – in which the 11th and 61st Foot lost more than two-thirds of their men as casualties – the allied ascendancy was restored at this point. Clausel abandoned the Greater Arapile and, covered by Foy's division, retreated on Alba de Tormes in the gathering darkness. The allies were too worn out by the days of marching and fighting to pursue beyond the river – the very thing Lieutenant James Dawes Douglas had bemoaned in 1808.

The losses of the 45th in the battle – indeed, of the 3rd Division in total – were relatively modest. One corporal (Cavanagh) and five rank-and-file were killed or died of wounds. Lieutenant-Colonel Forbes, Major Greenwell, Captain Lightfoot, Lieutenant Coghlan, Ensign Ray, one serjeant and forty-four other ranks were wounded. The 3rd Division lost 563 men, slightly less than ten percent of the starting strength. By comparison, the two French regiments opposed to them lost seventy-seven and eighty-two percent. The total allied loss amounted to 7,264, out of some 46,000 engaged, of which the British casualties were 694 killed, 4,270 wounded, and 266 missing.

News of the victory caused celebrations at home on a scale not seen since Trafalgar. The *Nottingham Journal* reported on 4 July 1812, 'We have seldom witnessed a more general and gratifying scene of rejoicing than was exhibited in this town on Monday and Tuesday last, on account of the brilliant series of glorious and happy tidings which reached us last week, in such rapid succession from the Continent. Large fires were seen blazing in the streets, with sheep and oxen roasting before them, guns firing, bells ringing, music playing, public dinners in all parts of the town, tea parties for the females, fireworks, illuminations, etc. The streets were crowded. There were on the whole 20 to 30 sheep roasted, and four oxen were roasted in the Market Place besides sheep, and distributed with a liberal proportion of ale.'[317]

---

[304] Brown, pp.160-2.

[305] Robinson, pp.379-80.

[306] At peak, there were more than 30,000 Frenchmen in British prisons, and 12,000 Britons in French prisons.

[307] Campbell, p.224.

[308] Wylly, p.224.

[309] Campbell, p.224.

[310] That is, each battalion in a column half a company wide by twenty ranks deep; so the brigade would have been about twenty to twenty-five files wide by sixty ranks deep, but with gaps between companies. It permitted rapid deployment to line by wheeling the companies by ninety degrees.

[311] Campbell, pp.224-5.

[312] ibid, pp.225-6.

[313] Brown, pp.176-7.

[314] Campbell, p.226.

[315] *Tirailleur* means literally 'shooter'; a French light infantryman in skirmish order.

[316] These units were fighting their last battle in their old-fashioned bicorne hats; in a few months' time they would get the brass helmets still worn by Household Cavalry units today.

[317] National Library of Australia, 19th Century British Newspapers Online.

Chapter 21

Madrid

Ensign James John Rowe was a scholarly 16-year-old from East Down in Devon, the eldest son of a modest landowner, and a student at the Royal Military College at Great Marlow. He was gazetted ensign in the 45th without purchase whilst still a student on 19 December 1811, but stayed at the college in order to receive his certificate on 13 July 1812. He left a narrative of his service in the Peninsula which is valuable for its depiction of a typical young officer's journey to join his regiment on active service:

'I did not expect or wish to return again to College, for my Regiment was actively employed under Lord Wellington in Portugal. I longed to see service; and I had already had eight months leave from my Regiment. In due course I received an order from the War Office to join the 45th at Blatchington, Sussex, the 2nd Battalion being there in barracks ... I collected all traps,[318] and set out for Brighton per Coach, where I arrived on the 1st of September early in the morning. I breakfasted at the Stein Hotel, and set out in a post-chaise for Blatchington in time to save my distance for the Monthly Report. I arrived at Seaford about 1 p.m., and immediately called on the Commanding Officer in barracks about a mile distant, and reported my arrival, having also a letter of introduction to Captain Bishop. I sought his protection knowing no other Officer then present. He received me with the thoughtless confidence, generosity and bonhomie of a West Indian, and found few obstacles to our acquaintance which immediately commenced under favourable omens... and among the collection of Officers I now called my brothers no one more congenial to my taste than Bishop [a Creole of respectable birth and education of Barbadoes, of which island his father-in-law General McLean was Governor][319] ... On Sunday the 20th Sept. having returned from Church I was suddenly called by the Commanding Officer, Colonel Le[c]key, and he apprised me of an order he had just received to send a detachment of men to the 1st Battn. in Portugal, wishing to know if I desired to go, recommending secrecy in my preparatory measures, fearing desertion, and telling me they would march Wednesday morning. This was short notice, & I little prepared; but I hesitated not a moment in accepting the proffer, though from having so lately joined and juniority I was entitled to respite. I immediately wrote home a bulletin of the good news, & commenced operations ... We were forthwith embarked on board H.M. frigate *Melpomone*, then a troopship, in barges from the Fleet in Spithead ...The gale moderating, we sailed next morning at daybreak, soon cleared the Needles, and bade a long Adieu to Albion's cliffs. We had very heavy weather all the way to Lisbon, and in consequence parted off the Lizard, and made the passage in eleven days. We saw the coast of Spain on October 9th, weathered Cape Finisterre, and having fair weather and a fine breeze made the Rock of Lisbon easily on the 11th.'[320] The frigate also conveyed 120 drafts for the 45th from the 2nd Battalion.

On arrival in Lisbon, the new officers were quartered in a house normally occupied by Captain Brinsley Purefoy of the 45th, who was at the time commanding the Troop Depot at Belem. After nine days in 'this broiling hovel' they were ordered to march for the Army, and set out for the market-place in the company of Lieutenant James Miles Milnes, 'to assist us with his local and colloquial powers'. Their aim: to purchase that most desirable of assets for any new officer in Portugal – a mule. 'Captain Bishop purchased one I had marked out, a sturdy bright-eyed little animal about 11 hands, for a hundred dollars.'[321]

Captain Purefoy was by no means one of a small rump of British officers at Lisbon; in fact the rump had swelled to a considerable size, which caused some enmity amongst the officers in more dangerous positions, and weakened the leadership at the front. Captain James Campbell later recalled the time, and the circumstances of their return to service: 'In Portugal especially, we had often far too many officers at such stations – for instance at Lisbon, or rather Belem, Coimbra, &c. where it was well known many of them staid [*sic*] so long, that Lord Wellington had often to give them very broad hints, that it was high time they should remember that their regiments were in presence of the enemy.'[322]

Campbell stuck his tongue firmly in his cheek for the finish to his description: 'The mule or horse had very likely soon to be sold, from want of food and people to look after them, so that the good things brought up being consumed, the temporary campaigner again fell so sick, that it became indispensable for him to revisit an hospital station, to recruit his health and replenish his supplies.'[323]

The following day Rowe's detachment was sailed from Belem, past the fleet of Royal Navy men-of-war that was permanently stationed in the Tagus to guard Lisbon. They passed the famed Lines of Torres Vedras at four in the afternoon and landed at Villa Franca at six.

'We entered Spain ... The tall straight swarthy Spaniard, in the fantastic yet elegant mountain costume, shows a conscious superiority of heart, blood, and aspect over his neighbour of Portugal, and takes peculiar care to convince the stranger of it by independent mien, and haughty carriage.'[324]

The capital of independent mien and haughty carriage laid many days mule-ride away, and the 45th were on their way to see it.

Just before the battle, the new commanding officer, Lieutenant-Colonel Henry Ridewood finally arrived. Ridewood was 40, from Horsham in Sussex, a veteran on his third tour of duty in the Peninsula, having previously served with both battalions of the 52nd Light Infantry in the now-famous Light Division. He was the stepson of Major William Molesworth Madden, another 52nd man who had distinguished himself in the storming of Seringapatam in 1792. Henry had served in the 52nd Foot for nineteen years, distinguishing himself at the capture of Ceylon, Ferrol and the campaign in Denmark. He was accompanied by his 20-year-old wife Charlotte (nee Murray; they had been married eleven months) and his manservant, Private George French, a former card-maker in his mid-forties from Dursley in Gloucestershire, who transferred from the 52nd Light Infantry into the 45th in order to continue serving Ridewood.

Captain James Leslie, a former adjutant to the second battalion also arrived for service. With Majors Forbes and Greenwell and Captain Lightfoot wounded, Captain John O'Flaherty suddenly found himself second-in-command. Lieutenant James Miles Milnes was promoted to captain on 23 July, in place of the long-absent Edward Scott, who went on half-pay in England. Newly-arrived Lieutenant Donald McLeod went sick and was left behind when the army followed the beaten French; he was to die at Salamanca on 28 August.

The French, now commanded by Général de Division Bertrand Clausel, an expert manoeuvrer, retired to the south-east towards Albe de Tormes, whilst Foy's 1st Division was roughly handled by the superb King's German Legion cavalry – always Wellington's most reliable horsemen – at Garcia Hernandez on the day after Salamanca. Then they turned north for Valladolid, bound ultimately for the great castle of Burgos. The allies reached Valladolid on 30 July, where they captured seventeen cannon and 1,100 Frenchmen, as well as 'liberating' a large quantity of French stores; they would need the stores in the days ahead, for Wellington reversed the direction of the advance and turned the army south-east, towards Madrid and the incumbent King Joseph Bonaparte. The troops were elated – was the war almost over?

However, the 100-mile march in the merciless Spanish summer heat did much to curb their ardour. The exhausted troops arrived in front of Madrid on 12 August to find the last remaining French troops[325] walled up in the Buen Retiro, a star-shaped fort next to the main bull-fighting ring near the centre of town. The 3rd Division was ordered to attack from the north and the 7th Division from the south, and the garrison surrendered on 14 August – only the 7th Division suffered any casualties in the assault, and they were very slight. The hoard within the palace grounds was immense – 189 cannon, 3,000 barrels of gunpowder, 20,000 stand of arms, 7,000 bayonets,

3,000,000 rounds of ball cartridge and – most embarrassing of all for the French – two Eagles.[326]

The allies officially entered Madrid on 15 August; the 3rd Division led the way, the 45th in front, their band under bandmaster Serjeant Joe Morgan playing *The British Grenadiers*.[327] The citizens of Madrid gave Wellington's army 'joyful acclamations and benedictions'; they too thought the war almost over. Plied with as much free food and drink as they could hold, the men of Wellington's army turned from troops to tourists, wandering about Madrid in large groups, gawping at the regular exhibitions of fireworks given at the Plaza Mayor, the fountains on the Paseo del Prado, the *calles* full of brightly-coloured stuccoed houses.

Wellington felt a need to regularise their habits and appearance as demonstrated by this order from 13 August: 'The Commander of the Forces requests that the Soldiers may not be allowed to walk about the streets of Madrid, unless regularly dressed in their uniforms with side-arms. Those going to work, or on fatigue, in their fatigue dresses, will of course be under the orders of Officers or of Non-commissioned Officers. In case any Officers are desirous of seeing the Palace, they are requested to apply, at the entrance, for some of the servants of the household to attend them.'[328]

The men struggled with the new currency and the conversion between Portuguese reis and Spanish dollars. They knew that 20 reis made one vinghtem (about 2 pence) and that 40 reis were one real villon (about 4 pence); but now they had to remember that 800 Portuguese reis made one Spanish dollar, which was more or less the equivalent of four shillings and sixpence. Most gave up on the maths and concentrated on the fact that the local red wine was cheap and plentiful. Some of the 45th attended the public execution of a nobleman, an *afrancesado* (who had fraternised with the French administration). He ascended a scaffold, then after much praying, was seated in a kind of throne with backboard; a bag was placed over his head, a chain wrapped around his neck and through two holes in the backboard, and after a wrench of the chain, strangled to death. The troops also went to a bullfight, which seemingly impressed none of the hardened veterans.

Private William Brown wrote: 'In the centre was the arena, or scene of action. It was surrounded by a railing six feet high – light being admitted from the top of the building, which was open. To witness the exhibition a vast concourse were assembled amongst whom were a number of our officers and men. The most of the latter, however, I dare say were greatly disappointed; for soon after the commencement of the entertainment, or rather the disgusting spectacle, many of them rose and left the place. Imitating their example, I went home to the convent in which our regiment was quartered, completely disgusted with the cruelty displayed, and even with the puerility of the thing; itself, for in reality the picadores, matadores, and what not, ran little or no danger whatever.'[329]

But despite the comforts of the big city, the battalion was withering away. On 25 August the 45th could only show twenty officers, twenty serjeants, sixteen drummers and 247 other ranks effective – the lowest total for the entire war – with six officers and 377 other ranks sick. Some forty men were sent home during August, the most in any single month of the war.

On 29 August, Wellington puffed out his chest and issued the following proclamation to the Spanish people: 'SPANIARDS! It is unnecessary to take up your time by recalling to your recollection the events of the last two months, or by drawing your attention to the situation in which your enemies now find themselves … you are reminded that your enemies cannot much longer resist; that they must quit your country if you will only omit to supply their demands for provisions and money, when those demands are not enforced by superior force. Let every individual consider it his duty to do every thing in his power to give no assistance to the enemy of his country, and that perfidious enemy must soon entirely abandon in disgrace a country which he entered only for the sake of plunder, and in which he has been enabled to remain only because the inhabitants have submitted to his mandates, and have supplied his wants.

'Spaniards! Resist this odious tyranny, and be independent and happy. WELLINGTON.'[330]

With this morale-boosting verbal hoorah behind him, Wellington set out northwards on 1 September to further discomfit the scattered army of General Clausel, taking the 1st, 5th and 7th divisions, two brigades of heavy cavalry and some Portuguese brigades with him, but – and most head-scratchingly bizarre – only two cannon. His most reliable troops, the Light, 3rd and 4th divisions, were left behind as the garrison of Madrid under the overall command of Lieutenant-General Rowland Hill. But Clausel would not be drawn into battle and by more adventurous manoeuvring, lured the allies into the ancient castellated town of Burgos.

The place lay more than 130 miles to the north of Madrid, and took seventeen days to reach, so that the allies could not lay siege to the French garrison cooped up in the castle there until 18 September. In the first week of the siege of Fort St. Michel they lost nearly 700 men; in October he learnt from Lieutenant-General Hill in Madrid that combined French armies under King Joseph and Maréchals Soult and Suchet were approaching the Spanish capital. Since there was no way that three divisions could defend the capital against maybe 70,000 Frenchmen, Wellington decided to lift the siege of Burgos and retire south. The allies marched away on 21 October; in the last four weeks of the siege he had lost 1,000 more men for no gain whatsoever. It was Wellington's least impressive exploit of the entire war; nonetheless whilst there, and because of Salamanca, he learned he was now the Marquess of Wellington.

Spaniards in the Ranks

In October Major Leonard Greenwell, still suffering from his incapacitating Salamanca wound, went down to Lisbon and then home for the second time. Lieutenant Hill Phillips, discomfited by his injury at Ciudad Rodrigo, went also, destined never to return.[331] The battalion received a fresh batch of officers from home around the same time, all Irishmen: Captain (brevet Major) John Massy Stacpoole, Lieutenant Philip Stopford Cosby, and Lieutenant Edward Francis Moore. Stacpoole was the younger son of a well-to-do Dublin family whose patriarch was a former officer in the Royal Horse Guards; he had served in the Inniskilling Dragoons for some years and had two elder brothers who were or had been captains in the Royal Navy.[332] Cosby was from an eminent County Cavan family, and Moore was a teenager from Carlingford in County Louth.

Famine was rife in Spain and Madrid suffered as much as any other place, probably more due to bearing the burden of so many allied soldiers. Lieutenant-Colonels Ridewood of the 45th and Trench of the 74th organized a daily dinner for about 200 inhabitants 'who, without this rescue, must have perished'. It is unclear where the food for this compassionate gesture came from, and whether the officers and men of the 3rd Division were required to sacrifice a percentage of their rations in order to make it happen.[333]

The health of the battalion on 25 September had improved only slightly with the sick list down to four officers and 291 men. In October four more officers arrived – Captain Alexander Anderson (back for a second tour), Lieutenant John Forbes, Lieutenant Daniel Stewart and Ensign Averel Lecky.[334]

At about this time, and in accordance with Wellington's approval of the notion, the 45th recruited some Spaniards into the battalion – thirty-two in all suggested by the muster rolls. The experiment was a disastrous failure. True, the battalion effective numbers were still very low (377 on 25 October) but the morale of the men received no boost whatsoever by the acquisition of a clutch of non-English speaking peasants, all but one of whom deserted or died within four months. Twenty-four deserted on one single day, 16 November; Privates Santiago Aslargo, Jose Torrecellos and Santos Garcia at least lasted until 25 January 1813 before French Leave,[335] giving Private Francisco Elkey the distinction of being the sole Spaniard left in the ranks. Elkey deserted just before Vitoria on 18 July 1813, re-joined on 17 October and (after tasting British military justice) went sick in France and was finally struck off the roll in March 1815.

Our Situation Truly Miserable

To the utter despair of the inhabitants, the allies evacuated Madrid on 31 October. The French re-occupied the city the following day. The 3rd

Division started on the road north-west across the mountains towards Aravelo, before turning south-west and marching across flat, featureless farmland through Fontiveros, before turning west to Alba de Tormes, which they reached on 7 November.

The night after the 3rd Division left Madrid, the troops passed through a forest, which was found to be full of pigs; so many pigs were slain in the woods by marauding troops that the lives of the staff and other officers of the division attempting to stop the slaughter were in peril. The French were astonished at the noise and assumed that the allies had chanced upon a French patrol.

The 3rd and 4th divisions crossed the ford at Alba de Tormes and camped at Calvariza de Ariba, only about three miles from the Salamanca battlefield, where white skeletons still dotted the yellow plain. As was often the case during the war, most of the company officers were sick or absent, and the companies largely in the hands of the subalterns. On 11 November the battalion was in Salamanca itself, where it received a back-log of pay.

However it seemed that Maréchal Soult was up to his old tricks and threatening to cut the allies off from Ciudad Rodrigo, so the allies resumed the retreat on 14 November. The 3rd Division was last to march, forming the rearguard. The next few weeks were the worst the 45th experienced in the entire war. As ever, Private William Brown left a graphic and lengthy account of the debacle:

'It was now our sorrows commenced; the rain that had begun early in the morning descended in torrents. When we gained the road it was completely cut up by the numerous baggage and the whole army which preceded us, for on this memorable retreat our division formed the rearguard. We were not long in this puddle, which was nearly knee-deep, ere the majority were barefoot. To add to our distress the enemy's cavalry came furiously upon both our flanks, and annoyed us considerably with a smart fire from their carbines, until a body of cavalry came to our assistance, who kept the enemy at bay, while we moved off as well as we could. Having dragged through this slough of despond until long after dark, we filed to the right and encamped in a wood at a short distance from the road. The ground destined for our quarters during the night was low and flat, and when we stepped over the ditch that surrounded it, we were immersed to the knees in water. This was, to be sure, more pleasant than the mud we had marched in all day, yet it bore a very cheerless aspect when we reflected that it was our bed for the night.'[336]

The following day, 16 November, was the day that most of the Spanish recruits deserted; given the above, one can perhaps understand why. Hatchets for cutting wood had been thrown away in the retreat, so the men tore branches from the trunks of trees and laid on the ground, but as everything was soaked and the rain still continued to fall in torrents, no-one could get a fire started. Opening their knapsacks, each man, for his own comfort and the public good, contributed something to the fire. William Brown gave one shirt, three brushes and a button-stick.[337]

The rearguard passed near the battlefield of Salamanca, and saw a sight that broke their (hungry) hearts: 'On the morning as we passed the bridge of Salamanca we saw the Tormes choked up with the stores that had been thrown over the bridge, that they might not fall into the hands of the enemy … But so anxious were our rulers that none of it should fall into the hands of the French, that we were prohibited from touching any part of it.'[338]

The incessant rains turned the line of march into a quagmire. The next morning at daybreak they moved on, passing through many oak-woods, the acorns of which 'were picked up by officers and men and eaten with as much relish as if they had been the greatest dainties'. In the afternoon they encamped in a wood, but were scarcely halted before the French cavalry made a furious attack, so they went to ground until after dark. They then obtained leave to lie down on the ground, 'from which numbers never rose again'. On the morning of the 18th they were aroused long before morning from their watery beds to commence another day of hunger, hardship and fatigue.[339]

The pursuing French were never far behind. 'I was roused from my reverie by the sudden and quiet advance of a large body of cavalry. A number of poor fellows who were lying around me vainly flattered themselves that it was the last of our rear-guard advancing; but overhearing their language and the-oft-repeated "sacra votre" [sic], I dropped my knapsack, darted into a thicket, and in a moment after I heard the screams and cries of the poor men I left on the ground, who, I make no doubt, were by the enemy butchered in cold blood.'[340]

They reached Ciudad Rodrigo on 19 November. 'Many men who had been under General Moore during the disastrous retreat to Corunna, avowed they had undergone more fatigue and suffered greater privations on the retreat from Madrid than they had ever done the whole of their lives,' Brown later wrote.

The army was then put into cantonments on the frontiers of Spain, and the brigade was quartered at Fuenteguinaldo. Captain Tom Lightfoot wrote home from there on 22 November. 'Our sufferings on the retreat have almost broken the men's hearts. Judge of our situation, exposed constantly to the inclemency of the season, in the dreary month of November, marching by day over a country literally under water, and bivouacking by night in fields of mud, occasionally manoeuvring in front of the enemy in ploughed ground up to our knees in puddles; then wading rivers rushing in torrents from the mountains; at night endeavouring to keep alive by kindling large fires, fearful of lying down to sleep, lest our limbs should afterwards be stiff with cold. From these circumstances, and sometimes nothing to eat, we have been compelled to leave a great number of men on the roads who became unable to march. The people of England will no doubt be greatly disappointed on this occasion, but it is less wonderful that we were compelled to retreat from Madrid than that we ever arrived there.'[341]

The worst part of the retreat was on a par with the privations suffered by Moore's men on the road to Corunna, albeit for a shorter period. The battalion lost twenty-one men to desertion during the period of the retreat, almost all of them the suddenly unenthusiastic Spanish recruits. The musters show thirteen men died; twelve men appear to have been taken prisoner during the retreat, and one, Private John Faulkner, reported as missing. Once the desertion figures are added in, the battalion suffered a total loss of forty-seven men during the retreat, almost as many as at the great battle of Salamanca, whilst barely firing a shot in anger.[342]

Four months after the great victory at Salamanca, Wellington's army was exhausted, cold, starving, and broke. Most men were barefoot and clothed in rags. It felt like defeat. The worst conditions on the retreat had lasted only four days, but the army had fallen apart in a way that the French Army, used to subsisting off the land, never would. Wellington was ropeable; he issued an order from Freneda on 28 November that upset virtually every officer in the army.[343]

'GENTLEMEN ... I must draw your attention in a very particular manner to the state of discipline of the troops. The discipline of every army, after along and active campaign becomes in some degree relaxed, and requires the utmost attention on the part of the general and other officers to bring it back to the state in which it ought to be for service; but I am concerned to have to observe that the army under my command has fallen off in this respect in the late campaign to a greater degree than any army with which I have ever served, or of which I have ever read. Yet this army has met with no disaster; it has suffered no privations which but trifling attention on the part of the officers could not have prevented, and for which there existed no reason whatever in the nature of the service; nor has it suffered any hardships excepting those resulting from the necessity of being exposed to the inclemencies of the weather at a moment when they were most severe ...

'But I repeat that the great object of the attention of the General and Field Officers must be to get the Captains and Subalterns of the regiments to understand and perform the duties required from them, as the only mode by which the discipline and efficiency of the army can be restored and maintained during the next campaign.'[344]

On the one hand, the officers were right to feel aggrieved by the suggestion the army had not suffered any hardships other than 'the inclemency of the weather'; the 45th had 47 empty spaces on the muster roll to prove it. To balance that view, the army had behaved poorly during the retreat; Spanish citizens had been robbed mercilessly, often at gunpoint, and bands of men had detached themselves from their regiments on forage and plunder expeditions, many to be taken prisoner. But things did not get any better at Fuenteguinaldo. The 45th remained eight days in this town, during which time they suffered much from the want of food and blankets. They were quartered in the dark cell of a chapel, the walls of which were cold, damp and clammy. 'This was very uncomfortable lodgings to men worn out with fatigue and hunger; while our fare was still very scanty, and we had no means to procure any more than what was served from the stores. But indeed, though our pockets had been full of money it would have been to little purpose, for everything was scarce, and what was to be had was at an extravagant price. Bread sold at one dollar per pound and salt went for half as much, while everything else was in proportion.'[345]

One regiment in the division, however, habitually ate better than the rest. This was the green-clad 60th Foot, and Captain James Campbell tried to reconcile the difference in culinary approaches between British and continental troops. 'The comfort in which the men of the 5th battalion 60th regiment [who were chiefly Germans] lived upon service was very striking, when compared with the wretched diet of the generality of British soldiers,' he wrote. 'It seemed to be settled amongst themselves, that every man of the mess of the 5th battalion 60th, had to carry something, that is say – highly-spiced meats, such as sausages, cheese, onions, garlic, lard, pepper, salt, vinegar, mustard, sugar, coffee, &c.; in short, whatever could add to or make their meals more palatable, nourishing, or conducive to health. As soon as the daily allowance of beef was issued, they set to work and soon produced a first-rate dinner or supper, which were often improved by certain wild herbs which they knew where to look for.'

He contrasted this to the culinary skills of his own men: 'Day after day they boiled their beef, just killed, in the lump, in water, which they seldom contrived to make deserving the name of soup or broth. This and their bread or biscuit was what they usually lived upon.' Campbell also lamented the fact that the thoughts of his countrymen were 'too often directed to ardent spirits and to the means of procuring enough of it; for though a certain allowance, usually of rum, was issued daily, this was not sufficient to satisfy their longings for more. And it was always known when the rum was about to be given out when we heard a shout in the camp, and from many voices a cry of "turn out for rum".'[346]

We get a vivid glimpse of what the 45th looked like at this time from Brown: 'The whole of my garb at this time consisted of my red jacket, which, during part of the retreat, had no sleeves, having been torn to tatters amongst the bushes and briers; but which deficiency I had since made good, by stitching to the precious article the legs of my only pair of stockings, the colour of which were light blue, forming a fine contrast with the jacket, which by tear and wear was approximating to, a dark brown. My trowsers, which once belonged to a Frenchman, I picked up in the Retiero at Madrid. They were originally black, but had so often been mended with patches of divers shades, that it could not be distinguished. As for a shirt, ah pauvre homnio! –he had none. A tag of what was once a shirt, hangs down before and behind, having much the resemblance of a que [sic], and the whole so stiffened with nits, of so shining a quality, that anyone at a little distance might have thought it richly embroidered with silver lace … Shoes and stockings I had none, having left them far behind on the deluged plains of Leon but which were soon replaced by new ones, received as a gift from the Marquis Wellington, who generously bestowed upon every individual of the army, a pair of shoes, in consideration of the arduous service in which we had lately been engaged. This was the second pair I had received in the manner; his lordship having been graciously pleased to order, upon the capture of Badajoz, a pair to each man engaged at that place; but for all this, our situation at this period was truly grievous. We were but meagerly fed, and as has been already mentioned, most wretchedly lodged.'[347]

The chilly sojourn in the squalid village of Fuenteguinaldo did not last long and at the beginning of December the brigade marched fifty-five miles north-west to winter quarters at a cluster of villages in beautiful countryside south-east of Lamego. Once there the starving troops were supplied with copious quantities of food and their back-pay, in an effort to raise morale. Soon after arrival at this place, on 8 December, the 45th gratefully received more officers and men from the second battalion, those who had sailed from Portsmouth at the end of September – Captain James Bishop, Lieutenant Robert McGibbon, Ensigns James John Rowe, Robert McKenzie and forty-nine other ranks. Bishop was a 20-year-old creole born on Barbados, the son of an eminent island family with eight years' active service behind him; Rowe the diarist from East Down in Devon and McKenzie an 18-year-old Highlander from the remote crofting hamlet of Skerray on the north coast of Scotland. Some two or three weeks earlier several other officers had joined from home – Lieutenant William France Reynett and Ensign Thomas Andrewes, Reynett being the 23-year-old younger brother of Captain James Henry Reynett. With them was the battalion's new surgeon, William Reynolds, fresh from the second battalion, ending a nine-month period during which the 1/45th had no senior surgeon in the field. In December, 26-year-old ex-North Devon militiaman and former Royal Marines subaltern Lieutenant Joseph Douglas joined from England and Lieutenant John Forbes left, having only been with the battalion for two months. Lieutenant-Colonel Alexander Wallace of the 88th who had commanded the brigade since Kempt's wounding at Badajoz was invalided home, and the brigade seems to have been commanded

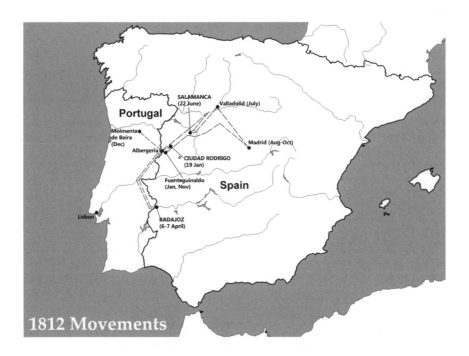

temporarily by Colonel John Keane, a 31-year-old Irishman and former commander of the 60th Rifles.

The brigade celebrated Christmas Day at the little church in Leomil and reflected on a year of constant campaigning. Since 4 January 1812 they had reduced two fortresses, fought in the most celebrated victory of the entire war so far, captured the capital of Spain, and enjoyed its distractions – then (and completely against the run of play) been forced to retreat back inside Portugal in the worst conditions available to memory. During the year the battalion had lost 185 men dead, forty-one men to desertion (almost all of them the pointless Spaniards) and seventy-three men had been sent home as unfit for further service – almost 300 men, compared to the 382 fit men available for duty on Christmas Day.[348] The battalion's dead and discharged since August 1808 outnumbered the men fit for service by about two to one.

A whole raft of officers took the opportunity to go home at this time, two subalterns after only a month in the country and both suffering terribly from ague. George Milnes's wife had died in Lisbon at the end of February, the news reaching him lying still wounded on his sick-bed before Badajoz. For the other ranks, there was no such relief – they were there until worn out, or too badly wounded to carry on, or for the duration. In September, in Madrid, it had appeared as if that duration would be short; but in December, back inside Portugal, it began to dawn on them that the war might have a few years yet to run.

318 Traps was British army slang at the time for what today officers would call 'kit'.

319 Not quite accurate; in fact Lieutenant-General Fitzroy Grafton McLean married Bishop's widowed mother in 1814.

320 1935 Regimental Annual, pp.206-8.

321 ibid, pp.208-9.

322 Campbell, p.119.

323 ibid.

324 ibid.

325 King Joseph and his main garrison had left some days earlier.

326 Each French regiment received one golden eagle from Napoleon to adorn its colours. The loss of one was considered catastrophic.

327 And possibly a piece named *The Spanish Call*. At some stage during the war the 45th was quartered near a convent; at certain set times each day an instrumental call, sounded from within the convent walls, was plainly audible to the troops. It was discovered that this call was played to summon the Sisters to meals. When the 45th moved on, the Mother Superior of the convent presented the Regiment with the music for their call, as a token of appreciation for the exemplary behaviour of the troops during their stay. Later it was played by the successors of the 45th, the Sherwood Foresters and later the Worcestershire and Sherwood Foresters, and currently by the Mercian Regiment. It is played before formal Mess Nights to notify officers to assemble.

328 General Regulations and Orders, Vol. 4, p.210.

329 Brown, p.182.

330 *Wellington's Dispatches*, Vol. 9, pp.380-1.

331 Phillips transferred to the newly raised 13th Royal Veteran Battalion on 25 January 1813, along with Brinsley Purefoy and James Yates.

332 The eldest, George, had died as a prisoner aboard a French ship in the West Indies in 1796.

333 1932 Regimental Annual, p.231.

334 It is unclear whether this officer was related to Lieutenant-Colonel David Lecky, but hailed from the same country, Derry.

335 British Army slang for 'scarpering' or similar.

336 Brown, pp.183-5.

337 ibid, p.186.

338 ibid, p.186-7.

339 ibid, pp.187-8.

340 ibid, pp.188-92.

341 1914 Regimental Annual, pp.14-5.

342 WO25/1275.

343 It was addressed to brigade commanders and above in the first instance, but read by all once a leaked copy made its way into the British newspapers.

344 *Wellington's Dispatches*, Vol. 9, pp.574-7.

345 Brown, pp.192-3.

346 Campbell, pp.105-7.

347 Brown, pp.193-5.

348 The second battalion in Sussex had lost five dead and seventeen deserted for the year.

Part VII

1813

Chapter 22

Moimenta da Beira

The New Year found the 3rd Division billeted in numerous villages south-east of Lamego. The Right Brigade[349] under Colonel John Keane was comfortably dispersed; the 1/45th under the command of Major Thomas Forbes was at Moimenta da Beira, the 74th under Lieutenant-Colonel the Honourable Robert La Poer Trench at Sarzedo, the 1/88th under Captain Robert Nickle and Pakenham's divisional headquarters were at Leomil, and the companies of the 60th Rifles under the command of Lieutenant-Colonel John Forster Fitzgerald at Paradosa. The Left Brigade, under Lieutenant-Colonel James Campbell of the 94th Foot, was dispersed at Ferrarin, Villars, Adabares and Fonte Arcada. The most junior brigade, the Portuguese under Major-General Manley Power, was to the north at Granja Nova. Such arrangements were typical during the winter months in the Peninsula, whilst both sides waited for 'campaign weather' with the coming of spring.

Despite the beauty of their surroundings, January 1813 was a bad month for the battalion. Some fifty-two men died during the month, the highest of any single month in the war. Weakened by their recent exertions, many men succumbed to a local fever – William Brown was one so affected. 'We had not been long in quarters when a most malignant fever made its appearance amongst us, by which in a short time numbers were swept away. The nature of the disease being so fatal and contagious, men could not be got to attend the sick, and it was found necessary to take the first for duty. By this expedient, I was compelled to attend one of the wards in hospital; which duty I managed above three weeks, but was then seized with the distemper. My head was immediately shaved and blistered, but being insensible, and in a high brain fever, I tore the plaster off, and threw it out of the window. Another was directly applied, while my hands were secured down by my sides; in which state I lay several days. Six weeks elapsed before any symptom of recovery appeared, at which period I was so weak and emaciated I could hardly walk across the room. While here, I had an opportunity of being present at the opening of several men who had died of this disease. It was observed, that the lungs were thickly covered with small black spots, resembling grains of gunpowder; and of all that died, their face in a few hours after, assumed a dark livid hue.'[350]

To exacerbate matters, newly arrived Surgeon William Reynolds died of typhus on 3 February, leaving the battalion without a surgeon yet again. He had been senior surgeon to the regiment since John Boggie's departure in August 1811, but had served in England until late 1812 before joining the 1/45th in the field. Alas his field service tenure was to prove short, leaving the ever-toiling assistant-surgeons Charles Cook and Henry Radford to deal with the sickness that carried away another thirty-five men in February. On 25 March Surgeon Richard O'Connell was appointed from the 43rd Foot. He was a 'coarse Irishman' and seemingly not well-liked by the men, at least not by William Brown.[351]

The number of fresh men from England was drying up. The first battalion had received drafts totalling 370 men in 1808, 242 men in 1809, four men in 1810 (when the battalion spent much of the year in cantonments and behind the lines), 232 men in 1811 but only 102 men in 1812. A draft of thirty-five men[352] had volunteered for service abroad at Mansfield on 25 January, but there were no more suitable men at the home depot. For all across the United Kingdom, as the war in Spain and Portugal entered its sixth year, the flow of new recruits had become a thin trickle. In an effort to reinvigorate recruitment, Whitehall gave the militia regiments a prod; in March 1813 the volunteering of men from the Nottinghamshire Militia into regiments of the Line recommenced. It appears that the men were permitted to enter the Foot Guards, and any regiment of the Line except the 60th; but no men were allowed to enter the 43rd, 51st, 52nd, 68th, 71st, or 85th Regiments of Light Infantry, or the 95th Rifle Regiment, unless he was specially fit for service, and not less than five feet five inches, or more than five feet ten inches in height; and no man was permitted to join the Foot Guards who was not five feet seven-and-a-half inches in height, or upwards. For every fifty men who volunteered from the militia, a free commission in the Line was offered to a militia officer.[353] It was a good enough idea. By way of proof, Richard Jones Colley, Robert Dawson, Joseph Douglas, John O'Flaherty, Francis Powell, Brinsley Purefoy and John Evans Trevor had all been militia officers before volunteering into the 45th, good officers all; and Powell had received his commission for free after bringing with him ninety-nine militia volunteers. But it did not produce many more recruits for the battalion in 1813 – Britain was running dry.

Whilst cantoned in this picturesque countryside, the brigade, like every brigade in the Army, drilled and trained; there would be no more repeats of the Burgos debacle. Under the watchful eye of Lieutenant-Colonel Ridewood, Major Forbes and Serjeant-Major Elliott, the ten companies square-bashed and repeated David Dundass' eighteen movements[354] until the actions became automatic; then they marched across country twice a week, just as Wellington had ordered. When off-duty, the officers went hunting – the Standing Orders of most regiments declared, 'every facility will be given for the pursuit of hunting, shooting, fishing, or other manly exercise, compatible with the due performance of duties' – and the men played football. All ranks needed to be wary of the local wolves, who took sheep and small children with impunity.

They say a change is as good as holiday, and some things changed for the better. On 1 March the army received its first supply of bell-tents, the first ever issued to British soldiers, and these were distributed at the rate of three per company; twenty snoring privates packed in like sardines per tent it is true, but infinitely preferable to lying out in the rain. Blankets were also provided. The old cast-iron camp-kettles were put into storage at Oporto and replaced with new, lighter tin models. But best of all were the new uniforms to replace the threadbare 'red rags'.

On 27 April a private of the 45th, Thomas Sisson, wandered into the camp of the 15th Hussars at Thomar, having apparently escaped from French custody at Madrid. He reported that there was 'much French cavalry in that city, but that the French are retiring to the Ebro'. He was given to Colonel Charles Fane of the 2/59th (2nd Nottinghamshire) Foot to escort back to the 45th. It is unclear in what action he had been taken prisoner. Sisson[355] may not have been the most reliable eye-witness (he deserted in April 1814) but no doubt his news was welcome to the Earl of Wellington, who was in the final stages of planning his campaign for 1813. The French were retiring north, closer to their depots in France.

Major-General Edward Pakenham was transferred to command the 6th Division on 26 January,[356] and Major-General Charles Colville assumed command in the absence of Thomas Picton, who had been gone more than six months. Colville was a Scotsman, a 42-year-old from Dundee who had distinguished himself in Egypt and the West Indies, recently returned from England where he had been recuperating from a Badajoz wound.

On 25 March the brigade finally received a new commander in the shape of Colonel Thomas Makdougall Brisbane, a 39-year-old keen amateur scientist and astronomer from Ayrshire. Thomas was the son of a Scots family of ancient lineage. He had attended both the University of Edinburgh and the English Academy in Kensington, but despite his strong scientific leanings, a military career was his calling.

In 1789 he was commissioned ensign in the 38th Foot, which he joined in Ireland and struck up a long friendship with a fellow subaltern, Arthur Wellesley; he and Wellesley had represented 'All Ireland' in a cricket match against the Garrison at Phoenix Park in Dublin in 1792. From 1793 to 1802 he served with the 38th and 69th Foot in Flanders, the Leeward Islands and Jamaica. He went home in 1803 but when the 69th was ordered to India, he went on half-pay in Scotland due to ill-health. It gave him time to indulge his interest in astronomy, and in 1808 he built the second observatory in

Scotland at the rear of his estate. In 1810 he was promoted to colonel and elected a fellow of the Royal Society, and in 1812 at his good friend Wellington's request, his health being much improved, he was promoted local brigadier-general in Spain.

So Healthy, So Strong

On 5 May, Wellington wrote to Earl Bathurst that he had never seen his army 'so healthy or so strong'. The army had increased in numbers by 25,000 men since the beginning of December, due to a combination of fresh regiments from home, drafts and returned convalescents. On 25 April the number of sick men in the 45th had fallen to 161, precisely half the number it had been six months earlier.

A batch of new men had arrived during the month, thirty-five privates conducted all the way from Portsmouth by Captain William Hardwick and Lieutenant Colin MacDonald.[357] Hardwick, 41, was a bachelor from London who had joined the Army at the relatively advanced age of 33 in 1804 in response to the invasion threat. MacDonald was a teenager from Inch in Lochaber.

Lieutenant-General Sir Thomas Picton[358] re-joined the army and took over command of the 3rd Division on 1 May. Whilst at home, he had recuperated for a while 'taking the waters' at Cheltenham, bought himself a large country pile at Tywi near Carmarthen, and got himself elected to Parliament as the Tory member for Pembroke. Of his return, Lieutenant John Tyler of the 45th said, 'I was much surprised one afternoon by hearing a kind of low whisper amongst the men of my regiment, who were at the time amusing themselves in a variety of different ways. This whisper was quickly increased to a more general commotion, as they all set off in the direction to which their attention had been drawn, at first walking, and then running a kind of race, as each tried to distance the others in first reaching the point of their destination. For a while I was quite at a loss to account for this sudden movement; but at length I discerned at some distance several mounted officers riding slowly towards our quarters. Curiosity led me to follow the men; but long before I could reach the spot, the approaching horsemen were surrounded by the soldiers, who had now collected from all directions, and were warmly greeting them with loud and continued cheers. As I came nearer, I soon recognised General Picton. Many of the men were hailing him with most gratifying epithets of esteem, one of which in particular struck me: this was, "Here comes our brave old father!" The general seemed much gratified, and smiled upon them with a look of unaffected regard. I was not forgotten or unnoticed. His eagle eye in one moment was fixed upon me, and holding out his hand, he observed, "Ah! My young friend; what! You come to meet me too?" Nearly the whole division collected before he reached his quarters: and thus surrounded by his delighted soldiers, he returned to lead them on again to a still more splendid career of victory.'[359]

Major-General Colville moved back down to a brigade command. Everywhere the men of the 45th looked there were signs that the winter break at Moimenta could not last much longer: fresh cavalry regiments, more artillery than they had ever seen, new equipment, new uniforms, large drafts of men from home. The command to be in readiness to move came on 11 May, and the move order itself came five days later.

The brigade marched north-eastwards, through some lovely mountainous country and camped at the war-ravaged village of Trevão (Trevoes); the next night they camped in a wood at São João de Pesqueira. Early the next morning they crossed the River Douro in small boats surrounded by 'wild woody mountains'. On 20 May they halted at the ancient cathedral town of Vila Flor, where Picton issued a memorandum stating that he was 'much gratified at finding himself again at the head of a Division, which has signalized itself on so many occasions, and which has never failed of complete success in anyone of the important enterprises it has been employed upon. From a continuance of the same spirit, good humour and unanimity, the Lieutenant-general confidently anticipates equally brilliant results during the operations of the present campaign.'[360]

The same day Ensign James John Rowe was appointed an orderly ADC to Picton, a temporary capacity which he would occasionally serve in the coming campaign. The following day the 3rd Division camped together for the first time at Bornos, and the brigade arrived at Vimiosa on 24 May and halted for two days to allow the 5th Division to catch up. The retreating French had obligingly left 16,000 rations behind, which were enjoyed by all, especially the bread. The weather was good and the marching healthy; on 25 May the battalion had the smallest sick-list since they had rested at Pinhel in February 1810. The number of effectives was back up to 488 men, still a long way short of establishment, but about average for Wellington's army at this time. A typical day's march started at four o'clock in the morning, with thirty minutes rest every four hours, and camp was set at about five in the evening.

On 27 May the 3rd Division crossed the Spanish frontier by fording a rivulet near Alcanices. Although they did not know it at the time, they had left Portugal forever.

On 29 May they heard the deep rumble of French cannon in the distance, and cheered; the French outposts were less than three miles away. Two abortive attempts were made to cross the rapidly flowing River Esla, costing a few cavalrymen lost drowned. The army camped for two days whilst the engineers constructed a pontoon. By 1 June they were at Zamora on the River Duero (the Spanish leg of the Douro). Officers and men guessed that their destination was Burgos, presumably to resume the siege abandoned the previous October. On 4 June the officers of the division briefly celebrated King George's seventy-fifth birthday before marching twenty miles to Lamota; it was an especially auspicious day for Colonel

Brisbane, since clusters of senior officers were usually promoted en masse on this day, and he was in the next tranche to be elevated to major-general.[361]

Brigadier-General Brisbane carried with him everywhere a pocket sextant chronometer and an artificial horizon, which he used to take altitudes of the sun and thus work out the exact time at every rest halt. The men viewed him as what we might call today a 'Nutty Professor'; Wellington, ever pragmatic, used him as the army's official time-keeper. At Toulouse, in April 1814, Brisbane visited the famous observatory and was gratified to find that his fob-watch agreed with the official chronometer to within five seconds.

Notwithstanding his eccentricities, Brisbane made a positive impression upon his new brigade – Captain James Campbell developed a strong respect for the man. 'How differently were Sir Thomas Brisbane's kindly feelings evinced for those placed under him. No officer commanding a corps was allowed, under any pretence, to keep his men unnecessarily under arms, especially after a march. As soon as the soldiers reached their cantonments, or ground of encampment, they were ordered to be instantly dismissed, and allowed to go into their quarters or tents to take off their accoutrements, knapsacks, etc. so that they might as soon as possible recover from the fatigues or the march; for keeping men standing, after being heated, till they became chilled, was always found to be injurious to their health.'[362]

The creaky commissariat waggons averaged twelve miles per day whereas the troops averaged twenty; and so on 8 June the men were placed on half-rations. The following day it started raining, and did so for five days. On 14 June they were at Topia, due north of Burgos, and still headed north-east; they were now farther inside Castile than they had ever been, but now knew Burgos was not their destination, since the French had destroyed the works there and retreated. Forced to live off land that the retreating French had stripped bare, the men starved. 'The country had been exhausted by the enemy during their retreat, so that no hope could be entertained of a supply in that quarter, while our prospects in regard to the stores that were following us were equally dark,' William Brown wrote. 'By the 16th our stores being completely exhausted, we had to subsist on what we could pick up in the fields where we encamped. The bean fields, which were very numerous in that part of the country, were now our only resource. The stalks were torn up by the roots, and carried in armfuls by our men to the camp, but not having come to maturity, nor indeed half-grown, the hulls, leaves and tender tops of the straw were boiled and devoured with the greatest avidity. Such was our fare for five days preceding the Battle of Vitoria.'[363]

The army crossed the Ebro on the 16th and 17th, the artillery being lowered and crossed by ropes. Once across the Ebro, the 3rd was joined by the 6th and 7th divisions as well as a large contingent of Spanish troops, and the encampment was larger than the men of the 45th had ever seen before, over 20,000 men. Then followed several arduous days of marching, twenty to twenty-five miles each day, along boggy roads made deeply rutted by wagons and gun-limbers. On 20 June the column stopped at the village of Subijana Morillas. Most in the ranks would have preferred one big battle and the possibility of plunder afterwards to sitting in Spanish fields eating bean roots; they were not to be disappointed.

[349] So-called since Keane was the senior brigadier; this would reverse with the arrival of Colville on 1 May.

[350] Brown, pp.201-2.

[351] William Brown was particularly vitriolic towards him, even though in his autobiography he mistakenly attributes O'Connell's presence to an earlier period, 1810-1811. Brown's view may have been coloured by the fact they were both chasing the same señorita.

[352] Just enough men to replace the battalion's losses to sickness alone in February.

[353] Lowe, p.40.

[354] General Dundas wrote a drill-book outlining eighteen basic manoeuvres for infantrymen in 1808.

[355] Sisson was one of the draft who had joined the battalion in October 1811 and had been assigned to No.9 Company.

[356] Evidently many of the 3rd Division were sorry to see him go.

[357] Based upon WO25/1275.

[358] Picton had been knighted at Carlton House on 1 February 1813.

[359] Robinson, pp.177-8.

[360] Wylly, p.239.

[361] Brisbane was promoted, although he did not receive confirmation for some weeks.

[362] Campbell, p.192.

[363] Brown, pp.204-5.

Chapter 23

Vitoria

Wellington's plan for the day was ambitious and certainly not consistent with his image as a defensive commander. His army was to form four columns of attack, the Left Centre Column (under Lieutenant-General Lord Dalhousie) comprising the 3rd Division and the 7th Division. The official orders for this column read that 'the 3rd Division, followed by the 7th Division, will move at daybreak and will proceed by the village of Anda, and thence (turning to the right) towards the village of Los Guetos, on the road from Anda to Vitoria. On approaching Los Guetos this column will throw out detachments to the right towards Nanclares, to put itself in communication with the detachments of the column marching upon that village.'[364]

As at most of the battalion's major battles, the officer corps of the 45th was well under strength at the time. Ridewood had eight captains present, but no majors. Luckily Lieutenant-Colonel Ridewood had a clutch of supernumerary officers on hand to plug the gaps – Captains Anderson, Bishop and Leslie, and Lieutenants Rowe, Stewart and Hunt. Just before the battle, volunteer John Connell Edmonds, a 19-year-old Wexford native, was given a vacant ensigncy without purchase and joined the officers' mess.

The bugles sounded at one in the morning on 21 June, and the 3rd Division was on the road by three, marching north-east and ascending a hilly range in a rainstorm. After twelve miles through heavy roads they were informed the enemy were in position about four miles from the spot in which they halted during a heavy fall of rain accompanied by thunder and lightning. They ascended a hill for about a mile, when they saw on the left the camp of the Guards and their columns in line of march, on the right the Light Division already engaged in a brisk cannonade.

Here a superb view struck their sight – the whole field of Vitoria in one panorama, the town in the centre enclosed by an amphitheatre of rugged and wooded mountains; columns of smoke rising from artillery, and soon the running fire of *tirailleurs*. It was now obvious they would soon have battle, and accordingly they halted a few minutes to make arrangements.

216

Men fixed their flints and bayonets, officers quit their horses, and blankets were stretched on hedge-stakes and poles for bearers.

Lieutenant James John Rowe, the 19-year-old subaltern in Captain O'Flaherty's No.1 Company, left a diary of the battle which is valuable for being written immediately after the action: 'I, tho' already nearly done up by the morning march and cloaked up in rear of the column, was at once obliged to quit mule cloak & sickness, leaving all care and fear behind to mingle in the fray. Thus with two sticks of chocolate in haversack over my shoulder and sword in hand we advanced briskly; and for the last mile went into the field double-quick to gain a bridge over a deep stream. This soon warmed me, and brought me entirely to myself.'[365]

Many accounts of Vitoria have the 3rd Division marching at dawn; as can be seen from the above account, the division's march started much earlier and was more arduous than is generally recognised. Spurred on by Picton, they advanced down out of the hills, through the village of Mendoza with the light troops of the division in front, followed by Brisbane's brigade (the 45th leading), then Colville's brigade, then Power's Portuguese brigade; Lord Dalhousie's 7th Division followed somewhere behind.

Captain James Campbell of the 45th, still brigade-major to Brisbane's unit, provided this account of the early movements of the 3rd Division: 'To my surprise, and I believe that of Sir Thomas Brisbane and many others, we met with no opposition in passing the Zadorra … Whilst the troops were passing this, in a military point of view, formidable object, over some very narrow bridges, I again went on some distance and even in front of our light troops, to ascertain, if possible, what might be before us, for by this time Lord Hill was sharply engaged considerably to our right, and we began strongly to suspect that the French still intended to be for once patient and to deceive us; so much so, indeed, that I every instant expected to see their masses and cannon crown the rising ground just before us, prepared to attack us whilst still embarrassed in the passage of the deep, high-banked, but narrow river. I very soon observed on the more distant heights a few vedettes, whose attention seemed entirely attracted to their left, in which direction the firing had greatly increased … Sir Thomas therefore (for I know not what had become of Lord Dalhousie and the 7th Division) with his usual impetuosity, pushed his light troops, cannon and columns, rapidly for the unoccupied heights, of which he got possession without firing a shot, and before the enemy seemed to be aware of their importance; or else they had erroneously calculated that the natural difficulties we should encounter at the Zadorra would either greatly delay or perhaps deter us altogether from advancing in the direction we had taken.'[366]

Another version of events has it that an aide-de-camp galloped up, looking for the 7th Division, which had not yet arrived at the Zadorra; the

ADC made the mistake of demanding of General Picton whether he had seen Lord Dalhousie. 'No, Sir, I have not seen his lordship, but have you any orders for me, Sir?' Picton enquired. 'None,' replied the aide. 'Then, pray, Sir, what are the orders you do bring?' 'Why,' answered the aide, 'that as soon as Lord Dalhousie with the 7th Division shall commence an attack upon that bridge, the 4th Division are to support him.' Picton drew himself up to his full height and said to the astonished aide-de-camp, 'You may tell Lord Wellington from me, Sir, that the 3rd Division under my command shall in less than ten minutes attack the bridge and carry it, and the 4th Division may support if they choose!'[367] He then rode to the head of Brisbane's brigade, and with the cry of 'Come on, ye rascals! Come on, ye fighting villains!' led them in motion towards the bridge. If Rowe's account is correct the brigade had already marched sixteen miles along muddy roads before ten o'clock in the morning, yet still they surged forwards, energized no doubt by a burst of adrenalin activated by the distant sounds of musketry and cannon fire.

Private William Brown in his autobiography (written in 1829) described the action in a manner that suggested he had recently finished reading Napier:[368]

'Being ordered to move forward, we descended the heights and advanced across the plain in the direction of the enemy. On gaining the river side, it was found to be unfordable by reason of the strength of the current and the depth of water. This was a very unfortunate circumstance, for we were now sorely galled by the enemy's cannon shot from the heights, and annoyed by the fire of their light troops stationed on the opposite bank. We then moved to a bridge, some hundred yards higher up, but which was found barricaded with wood. From an isolated hill in front of the chain of heights, and about two hundred yards from the bridge, the enemy kept up a heavy cannonade, mowing down our ranks, and literally making lanes through our columns. The bridge being found impassable, to ford the river was once more attempted; but all our efforts in this proving of no avail, orders were given to counter-march and force the bridge. We had not space left for this evolution, so that the column got into confusion. This was a dreadful moment. From the enemy's cannon the shot flew quick, our men fell fast, and nothing less than total destruction seemed inevitable, when a round shot from the French struck the barricading and threw the planks of which it was composed to a considerable distance. Our troops, like lions pursuing their prey, immediately rushed on the bridge, and, without any orders being given, cheering as they went, flew up the road, climbed the height, and neither stopped nor stayed until they were on the summit and in possession of the enemy's redoubt, who, in their flight, left behind four pieces of cannon and a quantity of arms and ammunition.'[369]

Rowe's version of the advance from the bridge was written more conservatively and from less distance in time. He has it that on reaching the bridge they found it blocked up, a battery throwing shot and shell over it, then they attempted to ford. The Light Company succeeded, and the battalion forced the bridge. Only two shells pierced the column, and did little damage. 'It was now near 10 a.m. The Light Division rapidly advancing on our right driving in the enemy's Advance after crossing the river advancing in close columns a Brigade of Cavalry formed to charge us, but a few exceeding well-directed shots of artillery sent them about. We then gained a considerable height under a hot fire from the retiring enemy. Here we had a momentary glance of nearly the whole field.'[370] Rowe's description that 'the battalion forced the bridge' strongly suggests that the 45th was at the head of the brigade (which as senior regiment, would have been quite customary) and presumably was the first unit across to the south bank, whilst the light infantry of the division waded across at the ford. Having command of the knoll of Arinez, Picton sent the 88th and the 74th to capture the adjacent village. Captain James Campbell told of the desperate struggle in Arinez: 'They quickly brought forward a large body of troops of all arms, to recover what they ought never to have lost. A desperate struggle ensued, especially in a village just behind the heights, and which ought to have been guarded with the utmost care by the French, being an important point in their position; but Sir Thomas Brisbane, with his brigade, after a severe contest and by turning their left with his right regiment (viz. the 1/45th) had got full possession of it, and the fate of the battle was thus, I may say, in a moment decided, for their centre being forced, the wings, especially the left, had also to give way, and to my delight I beheld, at this critical moment, our old and often tried friends, the Light Division, coming up in our own style upon our right, carrying all before them. When we had repulsed the enemy, who had fought very gallantly, from the village, and were again advancing upon them in the usual manner of the 3rd Division, Lord Wellington rode up to us, followed by his staff; and he knew well how to profit from what had been, at least to us, so unexpectedly accomplished.'[371]

The Connaught Rangers had captured the village at bayonet-point, whilst the 45th had flooded around the western side to link up with the Light Division, who had come up in support. The French fell back and took up a second line, vigorously defended and more vigorously attacked. The brigade lost many men in gaining a village under a fire of *tirailleurs* and flanked by artillery. The Portuguese on their right made a fine charge: 'The enemy were cool and obstinate. They retired on a third line, slowly; but were soon turned.'[372]

This was fast, fluid warfare on vast open plains, very different to the ponderous formation battles on cramped fields such as Waterloo or Talavera. The French took up this third line close to the main east-west high road, probably somewhere between Arinez and Gomecha. The 45th, in reserve, were used to charge the French 103e Ligne – apparently suffering very few casualties whilst doing so – and the French soon retired. 'The chief point now was the High Road to Vitoria, which was gained by great bloodshed and open fighting, advancing in lines wherever the field would allow. The artillery of the French were now verging on the great Road to our immediate left. Several in their haste upset in the hedges and ditches.'[373]

The French line had been cut in two by the 3rd Division, causing them to fall back in confusion across the great plain. They formed a north-south line to the west of the city of Vitoria, bolstered by 75 pieces of artillery.

Wellington formed six brigades into line for a massive advance,[374] and also brought up seventy guns under Lieutenant-Colonel Alexander Dickson; and at four o'clock the greatest artillery duel of the entire war commenced. The British and Portuguese troops had never heard such a cannonade, and were allowed to lie down as the French cannonballs carved furrows through the fields; however, as was customary the officers remained standing. The French artillery fire slackened after a time and the allied line advanced just before five o'clock, the ten companies of the 45th marching in column of companies in more or less the exact centre of the allied first line, with a Portuguese brigade on each flank.

Ensigns Ray and Edmonds clutched the tattered colours and joined in the chorus of *The Young May Moon*, the regimental marching song, just as the men had sung that first day in action at Roliça. The line of columns advanced slowly, as some thirty French cannon were still in action, and allied diversionary attacks on the flanks had not yet completely developed. The brigade advanced to a copse (located probably to the south-west of the village of Ali) and found the French deployed in their line, supported by their seventy-five cannon. A shell exploded beneath Lieutenant-Colonel Ridewood's horse, but he somehow rode the ruined creature to ground level and calmly assumed command on foot.

The Grenadier and No.1 Companies were detached to join Lieutenant Humfrey's Light Company as skirmishers to clear a mass of French *tirailleurs* from a hedge before advancing into the copse. Lieutenant-Colonel Ridewood brought the rest of the battalion forward on the double, but paid a price for his boldness. He received a wound in his left arm, but brandishing his sword over his head, exclaimed, 'Never mind this, my lads, I will lead you on to glory!' Dashing across the field their progress was arrested by a high hedge, whilst the enemy kept up a destructive fire from a neighbouring field. 'At this moment the balls flew as thick as hail, one of which struck my breastplate, which prevented any further injury. At the same time, my comrade, while standing conversing with me, received one in the very centre of his forehead. He fell at my feet and expired without a groan. He was a native of Ireland, a brave soldier and had seen much service.'[375] But the gallant Ridewood was down. 'I was pulled from behind by the belts, and on turning round, I was ordered by the Adjutant to go and

Vitoria

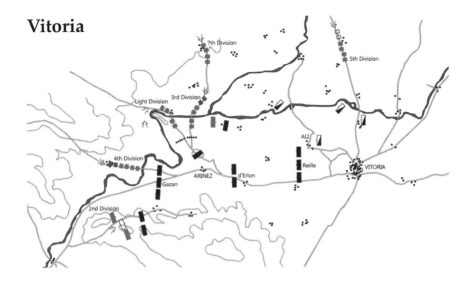

assist in carrying off the Colonel. Three others being ordered on this duty, we found our gallant commander apparently lifeless, stretched upon the green sward. In addition to the wound in his arm already mentioned, a musket bullet had entered his breast, from which flowed fast a crimson stream. Having taken a blanket from one of our knapsacks, we laid our expiring commander upon it, and in the silence of grief conveyed him to a neighbouring farmhouse, where a surgeon attended, who, when he had examined the wound, pronounced it mortal.'[376]

The location of the farmhouse in question was probably on the edge of the village of Ali, close to the copse. Private George French arrived at the farmhouse and took over the care of the grievously wounded Colonel Ridewood.

Whilst the balls flew 'thick as hail' new recruit 16-year-old Private Francis Womack of No.3 Company received a musket-ball wound in one of his arms; a ball passed through his shako, another hit his knapsack, a third carried away his canteen, and both his right- and left-hand men were shot down and wounded. However after six o'clock, a brigade of Highlanders came down out of the northern mountain range and skittled the French left flank, just as General Graham's corps captured the bridges and villages behind the French right rear.

The French in Vitoria were outflanked and beaten; all that remained was to retreat whilst there was still chance. Captain (Brevet-Major) Thomas Lightfoot was wounded yet again commanding the light companies of the brigade, and so command of the battalion devolved upon Captain John O'Flaherty, which was to Lieutenant James John Rowe's advantage. 'Our

Major Lightfoot received a wound commanding the Light Companies. The command devolved on the Captain of the Company I was attached to, which I succeeded to in course. The pass gained, the enemy filed cooly to the rear, but soon commenced a rapid retreat under a galling fire of artillery. A scene of confusion now occurred. The enemy's artillery, blocked up by accidents and upset in the High Road, was abandoned. Their infantry stood no longer. After a few shots the town of Vitoria [simply walled] was evacuated. It was now about 5 p.m. Some brilliant charges took place near Vitoria on our left. Our Hussars suffer much from the weight of the French Cuirassiers.'[377]

The French cavalry formed one last line of resistance. Captain James Campbell, on horseback, was well placed to witness events. 'Their cavalry suddenly appeared before us, presenting a firm and most imposing front. Our cavalry – I think they were all light – had now got in front of us, in considerable force; it was therefore evident, that an important moment in the battle approached; and as Sir Thomas Brisbane was anxious to see how our cavalry would accomplish a charge, which we concluded must be made, I most willingly went on with him some distance before his brigade, still advancing in column. Our cavalry went on bravely to the attack, but the French did not wait to receive it: on the contrary, they advanced boldly, rapidly, and in fine order, to meet our people. The shock was severe. But I soon saw, and I believe so did my general, that it was high time for us to be off to the infantry, for I must confess that the battle of Marengo flashed across my mind at the instant.' Marengo was a battle in 1800 that the advancing Austrians assumed they had in the bag, until counter-attacked by Bonaparte's reserve late in the day. 'We soon rejoined the brigade, when commanding officers of corps were requested to keep them well in hand, and ready, if necessary, to form squares. .But the French seemed to have accomplished what they had in view; that is to say, to cover the retreat of their discomfited infantry.'[378]

Totally Knocked Up
In fact, the French army virtually disintegrated. In their haste, they caused a massive traffic-jam on the road eastwards through Salvatierra; all the artillery was abandoned. In desperation, virtually everything was left behind. The 45th advanced rapidly three miles beyond the town through scenes of rapine and plunder, for the heavy baggage of the French Army was here stopped – all the waggons of the Commissary-General, some carriages (among them Joseph Bonaparte's) – in short all the material of the French army, save two field-pieces. 'The plunder of coin and valuables was inconceivable,' Rowe wrote. 'We halted about 7 p.m., and bivouacked. A perfect market soon opened. A Guard posted near the road stopped several bags of doubloons and dollars who the officer at hazard of his life conveyed

to Headquarters. The most acceptable plunder to me was bread wine and brandy and other necessaries. I had, however, two mules, some goats, and some little articles I bought of the soldiery. I was so exhausted and weak I was glad to sleep beside a watch-fire - the night was very cold, I had no cloak. More somniferous comrades had their pockets pickt.'[379]

Lieutenant Rowe was too ill to take full advantage of the sudden good fortune of the victors. The 3rd Division had been on the move for sixteen hours, and had marched more than twenty-five miles in addition to fighting a major battle. No doubt many men of the division were as exhausted and weak as Rowe.

Wellington rode into Vitoria, and posted the Life Guards there as a provost-guard. But his army went on a loot binge. Charles Oman rightly recognised that the plunder masked a failure to complete the victory. 'If the prisoners were fewer than might have been expected, material captured was such as no European army had ever hands on before, since Alexander's Macedonians plundered camp of the Persian king after the battle of Issus,' he wrote. Some 151 guns, 415 caissons, and 100 artillery wagons were taken. Probably no other army had ever lost all its artillery save two solitary pieces. The baton of Jourdan, as Marshal of the Empire, delighted the Prince Regent when it arrived in London. 'A few thousand extra prisoners – the total taken was only about 2,000 – would have been more acceptable tokens of victory,' Oman lamented.[380]

The plunder 'represented the exploitation of Spain for six long years by its conquerors'. The military chest containing millions of Francs recently received from France for the payment of the army was found unopened, as were the finest Italian pictures from the royal galleries in Madrid. The largest hindrance was a large mass of French and Spanish civilians, 'women and children, dead horses and mules, absolutely covered the face of the country, extending over the surface of a flat containing many hundred acres'. These camp-followers joined the victorious soldiery in the plundering; the battlefield turned into chaos for several hours. But in the defence of the private soldiers, we have seen that they started the battle having eaten nothing but bean roots for five days – and their pay was undoubtedly months in arrears. For example, the troops who fought at Buenos Aires in July 1807 received their pay for that quarter in March 1808. Men who fought at Roliça and Vimeiro (August 1808) received their pay for that period in October 1809. And men who fought at Talavera received their pay in February 1810, seven months after the battle. Survivors of Busaco waited four months, those of Badajoz eight months, men at Salamanca waited six months – and so on. Therefore pity the poor victors of Vitoria who had not eaten a decent meal in six days, nor seen a shilling in six months and it becomes easier to understand why they acted as they did – they behaved almost exactly as penniless starving people would have done anywhere when suddenly faced with a vast hoard of loot. The difference was they were British soldiers, and therefore confined by a set of rules that made few allowances for normal human (as distinct from instructed) behaviour. Had Sir Thomas Brisbane allowed his men to follow and pick up the boxes of money which could have been gathered, they might have enriched themselves to a very great extent. But he waylaid the stragglers and made them disgorge their plunder, and next morning had three such piles of dollars as enabled him to give five dollars to every soldier belonging to his brigade.[381]

Five dollars roughly equated to slightly more than one guinea, or about a month's pay for an average private (before stoppages). Individuals made away with all manner of loot – to quote one account, 'poodles, parrots and monkeys were among the prisoners' – some of which had more military value than commercial, since almost the entire staff-paperwork of Joseph's army had fallen into allied hands.

Understandable as it may have been irresistible to penniless and starving men, the plundering completely destroyed any chance of a rapid pursuit of the French. As after the retreat from Burgos, Wellington was fuming. He wrote to Earl Bathurst a week later: 'We started with the army in the highest order, and up to the day of the battle, nothing could get on better; but that event has, as usual, totally annihilated all order and discipline … The night of the battle, instead of being passed in getting rest and food to prepare them for the pursuit of the following day, was passed by the soldiers in looking for plunder. The consequence was, that they were incapable of marching in pursuit of the enemy, and were totally knocked up. The rain came on and increased their fatigue, and I am quite convinced that we have now out of the ranks double the amount of our loss in the battle; and that we have lost more men in the pursuit than the enemy have; and have never in any one day made more than an ordinary march. This is the consequence of the state of discipline of the British army. We may gain the greatest victories; but we shall do no good, until we shall so far alter our system, as to force all ranks to perform their duty.'[382]

It was the same problem Captain Douglas had identified and lamented upon after Vimeiro; that a victorious British army was inherently incapable of pursuing a defeated enemy. No allied troops moved at all during the morning of Tuesday, 22 June. Despite finding himself with his own company, Lieutenant Rowe was nonetheless assigned mop-up duty. The troops remained halted till 2 p.m. on that day, at which point Rowe was sent with a detachment over the field of action to pick up and secure the wounded or stragglers. He retraced the ground the 45th had been over, and found several dead. 'All the wounded were conveyed to neighbouring houses, but numbers of wounded Frenchmen remained still on the field. He assisted as many as possible, and conveyed them to the road, where waggons waited to take them to hospitals.'[383]

364 Wylly, p.242.

365 1936 Regimental Annual, p.207.

366 Campbell, pp.238-40.

367 Wylly, p.245.

368 William Napier published the first volume of his *History of the War in the Peninsula* in 1828.

369 Brown, pp.206-7.

370 1936 Regimental Annual, pp.207-8.

371 Campbell, pp.240-1.

372 1936 Regimental Annual, p.208.

373 ibid.

374 With seventy cannons in between and another five brigades in a second line; it was the most Napoleonic moment of Wellington's career.

375 Based on the casualty rolls, this would appear to have been Private John Mahony of No.4 Company.

376 Brown, pp.210-1.

377 1936 Regimental Annual, p.208.

378 Campbell, pp.242-3.

379 1936 Regimental Annual, pp.208-9.

380 Oman, Vol. 6, p.441.

381 Brisbane, p.23.

382 *Wellington's Dispatches*, Vol. 10, p.473.

383 1936 Regimental Annual, p.209.

Chapter 24

Murder Will Out

Sir Thomas Picton constantly considered that the 3rd Division never received its fair share of recognition in Wellington's official dispatches. 'The 3rd Division had again the principal part of this action, and I may well say, covered itself with glory, having contended during the whole day against five times our numbers and fifty pieces of cannon,' he wrote on 27 June. 'But, notwithstanding this great disparity of numbers, we bore down everything before us, during all which we were so situated as to have the eyes of all the army fixed upon us. Our loss was certainly great; out of 5,600 men we lost 1,800 in killed and wounded.'[384]

The main problem was the brief mention of the part of the 3rd Division in Wellington's official dispatch. As was often his way, he tried to please everybody by mentioning everybody, but in his usual abbreviated style, so that nobody received much in the way of column inches. He also wrote it from his own point of view, and no commander can ever have seen everything. Picton was of the view that, 'The official dispatch is a most incorrect relation of the circumstances of that memorable event ... Upon the whole the Division has not had its proportion of credit; but its operations were in view of the whole army, and murder will out in the end.'[385]

Despite Picton's rantings and the heavy casualties in the 3rd Division, the 45th got off relatively lightly. Four rank and file were killed and Lieutenant-Colonel Ridewood, Lieutenants Reynett and Little and new boy Ensign John Edmonds, five serjeants and sixty-one rank and file were wounded (with all four officers listed as 'severely').[386] The 74th lost similar numbers, whereas the 88th lost 215 men, one suspects mainly in their aggressive attack on the village of Arinez. Total losses in Wellington's army were 740 killed, 4,174 wounded and 266 missing; the 3rd Division's share was almost 1,400 men.

Initially it looked as if Lieutenant-Colonel Ridewood would not last the night, but in fact he rallied and endured nearly three weeks of agony tended by Surgeon O'Connell and Paymaster Dalhunty, as well as his faithful manservant Private French. Shortly before his death, he wrote out his resignation from the army. No doubt he also wrote a last letter to his step-father in Horsham, who had at one time five sons serving in the Peninsula – William, Captain 52nd Foot, killed at Badajoz; Wyndham, Lieutenant 43rd Foot, severely wounded at Badajoz; Monson, Lieutenant 43rd Foot, wounded at Vimeiro; Edward, Lieutenant 95th Rifles, as yet unwounded; and Henry, 45th Foot, mortally wounded at Vitoria. If he wrote a last letter of all, it was almost certainly to his heavily pregnant wife Charlotte, anxiously waiting for news in Lisbon. Henry died on 11 July. Soon after, Charlotte delivered a daughter, Henrietta, the couple's only child.[387]

Viva Los 'Engleses'

At eight o'clock on the morning of 23 June, the army moved forward again; the 3rd Division was to follow the French to Salvatierra. Wellington needed to restore order in Vitoria, and sent picked men to undertake that task, including Private William Brown. 'Thirty men from each regiment of the division were ordered for this affair, and the first for duty being taken, I was included in the number. We were immediately sent to our destination, which was two leagues distant. Our route lay along the road which the enemy in their flight had taken, the preceding evening. It was now blocked up by cannon, ammunition waggons, and other carriages, which they had abandoned in terror, and by which we now encountered considerable difficulty in passing. On entering the town we remained on the streets while arrangements were making concerning our quarters, during which we experienced a most hearty welcome from the inhabitants, who, assembling around us, displayed the greatest enthusiasm, and rent the air with shouts of, 'Viva los Engleses !' A number of young women began the bolera, in which they assumed all the lascivious attitudes, and went through the most voluptuous movements, for which that dance is noted. The music they had was a pipe and tabor, which was played by a fellow very fantastically dressed, and the orchestra he performed in, was one of the waggons left by the enemy.'[388]

But this *joie de vie* masked a darker side to the proceedings. 'This burst of joyful mirth and gladness, formed a striking contrast with the desolation and ruin that prevailed in the place, every thing bearing the marks of recent warfare. Many of the houses were defaced; what was once the enemy's baggage still lay and obstructed the passage in the streets, where were strewed many of their slain, on which the Spaniards vented their fury and revenge, by mangling the lifeless and inanimate bodies.'[389]

The 3rd Division followed in the wake of the fleeing French amidst scenes of carnage and devastation; abandoned carts, dead horses, and desperately wounded men left abandoned in the road, and as a result, the pursuit was slow. They joined the rest of the allied pursuers, some 40,000 men camped in a field near Salvatierra as it poured with rain all night long,

227

without tents as they baggage had not kept up. The following day was miserable – the army marched over horrendous boggy road all day, then were treated to a hailstorm as they tried to make camp at dusk, being battered by hailstones the size of musket-balls.

They marched twenty-four miles on each of the following two days, reaching the Great Road to France late on 25 June. En route they repaired bridges destroyed by the French, and found communication with the locals impossible since none of the Spaniards attached to the division spoke Basque. On 26 June the division passed Pampeluna (Pamplona) and were cantoned at villages named Villava and Huarte, about two miles from the town. San Sebastian and Pamplona were the last two French occupied cities between Vitoria and the border, but the French had allowed the citizens of the latter place to leave of their free will, and many did so and entered the allied camp for safety.

The following day the 3rd and Light divisions were ordered to march fifteen miles south to Tafalla, where General Clausel's division (which had not been at Vitoria) was believed to be, threatening to attack the forces besieging Pamplona. They marched over a mountain and arrived to find that Clausel had disappeared somewhere to the south-east, so they marched eastwards to Caseda, then Sanguesa, movements designed to prevent Clausel joining the main French field army now stationed in the Pyrenees.

Scum of the Earth

Wellington sent an aide, Captain John Freemantle of the Coldstream Guards, home with the Vitoria dispatches, carrying with him a battalion pennant of the French 100e Ligne regiment and the baton of Marshal Jourdan, which had been taken in the action. The baton was laid at the feet of His Royal Highness the Prince Regent. On 3 July, the Prince Regent reciprocated in kind: 'You have sent me, among the trophies of your unrivalled fame, the staff of a French Marshal; and I send you, in return, that of England.'[390]

Field-Marshal was a rank generally reserved as a reward for geriatric officers or members of the royal household. At 43 years of age Arthur Wellesley became the youngest non-royal field marshal in British history. Little did he know that his army at Vitoria also contained fifteen future field-marshals, an event unrivalled in British military history. But for the collapse of discipline at the end, Vitoria might have been his finest hour, even counting Waterloo. The plundering actions of his army irked him for weeks, and led to a vitriolic turn of phrase that is repeated in his memory more than any other, even today. In a letter from Huarte in Spain to Henry, Earl Bathurst on 2 July 1813, Wellington wrote the most-quoted phrase of his life: 'We have in the service the scum of the earth as common soldiers; and of late years we have been doing every thing in our power, both by law and by publications, to relax the discipline by which alone such men can be kept in order. The officers of the lower ranks will not perform the duty required from them for the purpose of keeping their soldiers in order; and it is next to impossible to punish any officer for neglects of this description. As to the non-commissioned officers, as I have repeatedly stated, they are as bad as the men, and too near them, in point of pay and situation, by the regulations of late years, for us to expect them to do any thing to keep the men in order. It is really a disgrace to have any thing to say to such men as some of our soldiers are.'[391]

His opinion did not change with time. On 4 November 1813, he declared in a conversation with Philip Henry, Fifth Earl Stanhope, 'I don't mean to say that there is no difference in the composition or therefore the feeling of the French army and ours. The French system of conscription brings together a fair sample of all classes; ours is composed of the scum of the Earth, the mere scum of the Earth. It is only wonderful that we should be able to make so much out of them afterward. The English soldiers are fellows who have enlisted for drink – that is the plain fact – they have all enlisted for drink.'[392]

But not all men had enlisted for drink. As part of Wellington's remedy for distancing the non-commissioned officers from the other ranks ('and too near them, in point of pay and situation,' as he had bemoaned on 2 July) he had long planned to implement a senior NCO rank within each company, something between serjeant and serjeant-major. He hoped to create something akin to the aura held by NCOs in the Guards. In regiments full of upwardly mobile young officers generally as interested in the social scene as soldiering, the NCOs truly were the backbones of their regiments and possessed a superiority widely recognised within the army. Happily Horse Guards agreed with Wellington and issued this directive in the euphoric weeks after the great battle of Vitoria: 'The Commander-in-Chief commands ... that in all regiments of infantry, whose services are not subject to limitation, the pay of the Serjeant-Major shall henceforth be raised to three shillings per day, and that ... one serjeant in each company of battalions of the above description ... shall be called the 'Colour Serjeants,' and that they shall bear above the chevron the honourable badge of a regimental colour supported by two cross swords. It is His Royal Highness's pleasure, that the duty of attending the colours in the Field, shall at all times be performed by these serjeants.'[393]

And so, on 25 July 1813, the first colour-serjeants were appointed in the 45th – the most deserving serjeant from each company. There were three Englishmen, Pete Robins, Charlie Brittain and Tom Wood; and five Irishmen, Pat Mitchell, Martin Hyland, James Nixon, Hugh McTeague, and Pat Bray. Interestingly, there do not seem to have been any appointments in numbers 2 and 9 companies. Given the appointment occurred only a month on from Vitoria, we must assume these were men who had not disgraced themselves in the aftermath of that battle. 'Colour-serjeant' was a title (an 'honourable appellation') not a rank; such men still counted as serjeants for administrative purposes and could be demoted back to the ranks as easily as any other NCO; and the award was only open to men 'whose services are not subject to limitation' – in other words, to those enlisted for life.

The first batch of colour-serjeants in the 1/45th was a very experienced group indeed. The average age of the new appointees was 31 years and nearly all had been in the Peninsula since the landing in August 1808. All had been in the army more than seven years, but time in rank varied between seven months (McTeague) up to nearly eight years (Brittain). Unless they would go on to the rank of quartermaster-serjeant or serjeant-major (only one would, Pat Mitchell, quartermaster-serjeant in 1821) this was probably as high up in the Army hierarchy as they could aspire. Given their humble origins (Bray was a blacksmith, Hyland a wheelwright, Brittain a framework-knitter, Wood a weaver, the rest 'labourers', a catch-all term for no occupation) the three chevrons with colours and crossed swords above must have made their wearers very proud men.

[384] Wylly, p.249.

[385] ibid.

[386] Based upon WO25/1275 and casualty report in *The Times*.

[387] Based upon correspondence in WO42/39.

[388] Brown, pp.219-2.

[389] ibid.

[390] National Library of Australia, 19th Century British Newspapers Online.

[391] *Wellington's Dispatches*, Vol 10. pp. 495-6.

[392] His men thought rather better of him. As Captain Kincaid of the Rifles famously said, 'as a general action seemed now to be inevitable, we anxiously longed for the return of Lord Wellington ... as we would rather see his long nose in the fight than a reinforcement of ten thousand men any day.'

[393] General Orders, Horse Guards, 6 July 1813.

Chapter 25

The Frontiers of France

In anticipation of future events, Wellington issued orders from Iruta on 9 July, reminding the army that the country in front of them was the enemy's, and the commander of the forces was particularly desirous that the inhabitants be well treated, and private property be respected.[394]

Maréchal Nicolas Jean-de-Dieu Soult replaced the ineffectual Maréchal Jourdan on 12 July, organising the remaining French divisions into a single Army of Spain. Soult was 44 years old, grim-faced, short and stout, an organiser and disciplinarian rather than battlefield leader; he had proven himself an excellent civil administrator in Spain but his great weaknesses were plundering and indolence. He was from the Tarn region is southern France, less than 200 miles from the allied front line, and therefore probably had some local knowledge to bring to bear.

The hungry defenders of Pamplona ventured out on 15 July looking for forage. The 3rd Division was briefly engaged in a skirmish, and forced the French back into the fortress whilst being bombarded by the town's artillery. Being relieved in front of Pamplona by some new Spanish divisions, by 18 July the 45th was at Olague, surrounded by 'romantic woods and forests' in the picturesque Lantz Valley about ten miles north of Huarte, where all the villages looked more French than Spanish; unsurprising, given that they were barely more than ten miles from the French border. The battalion was relatively healthy, with a small sick-list, although ten men were sent home during the month, some perhaps convalescents from Vitoria. Captain Thomas Lightfoot returned from his wound and assumed command, at least in the absence of Majors Forbes and Greenwell.

On the same day, Maréchal Soult advanced his reorganised army across the frontier with a view to raising the siege of Pamplona. What followed in the next week were the most confused and least-understood battles of the Peninsular War, usually lumped together under the collective term 'Battles of the Pyrenees'. The 3rd Division and the 45th took little part in them. Two French columns advanced south; the western column surprised an encampment of the 2nd Division near the Pass of Maya, and a sanguinary rearguard action (especially by one wing of the 92nd Highlanders, who lost over 400 men to short-range musketry fire in an hour) temporarily stalled General d'Erlon in a rugged mountain pass. Fifteen miles to the south-east, the second column under Generals Reille and Clausel advanced along two narrow ridges in thick fog, where a day of confused but less bloody fighting ended with Lieutenant-General Lowry Cole retiring his 4th Division towards Pamplona to avoid encirclement. Picton heard about the fight during the night, and ordered the 3rd Division immediately to arms; they marched at four o'clock in the morning of 26 July, seven miles through 'desperate passes and defiles' to Zubiri, but too late to participate in any action. During the afternoon the 3rd and 4th divisions retired, and the 3rd took up an entrenched position on rising ground at Gorea (Gorraiz), four miles from Pamplona.

The two French columns took up position on a ridge north of the city on the stormy evening of 27 July. Cole and his 4th Division defended the parallel Heights of Oricain to their south, with Pack's 6th Division due from the west, the 3rd Division holding the right flank at Huarte, and a Spanish division in reserve in front of Pamplona itself. On 28 July – a beautiful sunny morning – the French columns blunted themselves against the British line along the ridge (a day Wellington later described as 'bludgeon-work') with about 2,000 losses on either side; but the 3rd Division at Gorraiz was unengaged. Sir Thomas Brisbane, with his brigade in reserve behind the Egues River valley near Huarte, recorded his recollections of the day years later: 'The enemy were considerably exhausted by ascending the mountain, and were so vigorously attacked by the fourth division, that they were completely routed with immense destruction. My brigade was so delighted with the gallant conduct of the fourth division that they gave them three cheers, which immediately brought down upon us eight battalions of the French whom we were keeping in check across the ravine, thinking that we were going to attack them; but the action was merely partial. The French solicited a flag of truce, which was granted, and the following day was occupied in burying the dead.'[395]

Despite the cheering, the Fighting Division must have been chagrined to be reduced to the level of observers and grave-diggers. The following day the 2nd and 7th divisions arrived to bolster the allied line, and both sides licked their wounds, although there was some skirmishing between the lines. During the action a young French major led a small party of his men in what was a virtual banzai attack in front of a picquet of the 88th, running screaming across open ground yet completely unsupported by his regiment. The Rangers shot the officer and a few men down before they retreated; they re-appeared later under a flag of truce to collect the officer's body. Wellington rode through the 3rd Division camp this day and was heard to remark that 'nothing but a spirited pursuit now remains to complete the victory'.

The following day, 30 July, the allies did just that between Sorauren and Gorraiz. The 45th participated in the advance of Brisbane's brigade against

Foy's Division. The 45th lost one officer wounded – Lieutenant Ben Humfrey, whose right hand was mangled by a shell-burst – and seven men wounded in the actions this day; one of whom, Private John Straw of the Light Company, lost his left leg at the thigh.

Lieutenant Rowe, however, managed to find some humour in the events of the day. 'We advanced through the woods, cut off 500 of Parisian Young Guard[396] – the finest fellows I ever saw. Many fell dying of fatigue; the generality were intoxicated … Our men were completely equipped with French clothing, all new and in high order, ours greatly in want. Our soldiers changed everything but the shreds of their red jackets on the field with their prisoners – the most extraordinary comical scenes I ever witnessed.'[397]

So ended the second Battle of Sorauren, or as the men called it, the Battle of Pamplona. The French retired across the Pyrenees and back into France, fighting a number of minor actions en route, none of which involved the 3rd Division. Brisbane's brigade marched to Roncesvalles, with the 45th (resplendent in French shirts, trowsers and shoes to go with their 'red rags') in the lead, where they camped on the mountain top in thick fog 'destitute of everything but tents and our half-rations'; then to the Pass of Maya, where their campsite was surrounded by the unburied bodies of men killed on 25 July. After this horror and discomfort Lieutenant Rowe and the 45th finally moved on to a pleasant spot on 8 August. 'The most interesting wild romantic country now presented itself, and I never felt more gratified in rural contemplation,' he wrote. 'Fancy, wild herself, cannot paint the various scenes of wooded height and broken glen, obtruding rock and rushing torrent, roads cut through rocks and hills, some overhanging foaming floods. We pass the remains of this delightful month in the charming Valley of Bastan … I shall ever look on this scene with pleasure, so suited to my taste, a lovely climate and simple remarkably fine rustics, its inhabitants the handsomest race I ever saw, and living in the first ideas of primitive simplicity.'[398]

On 31 August whilst on reconnaissance the 45th experienced a twenty-minute hailstorm with stones the size of hen's eggs, which pelted the men exposed on a ridge-line to the point of injury, and terrified even the hardened veterans in the ranks. The battalion occupied Ariscon (Arizkun), marched to Echellar on 2 September where the battalion glimpsed distant views of San Sebastian, and back to Ariscon a week later. At Ariscon they sat out the rest of the month, frustratingly only four miles from the French border – but not quite there yet. Lieutenant-General Picton obtained leave to go to England on health grounds once again, so Major-General Brisbane commanded the division temporarily until Major-General Colville returned from the 6th Division on 8 September.

An Officer Well Qualified to Succeed

Wellington wrote to Colonel Torrens from Lesaca on 11 August 1813: 'Some days previous to the death of Lieut. Colonel Ridewood, of the 45th regiment, who died of the wounds he received at the battle or Vitoria, he signed his resignation, which I understand has been transmitted by his widow to the office of the Commander in Chief ... Although I believe it is not usual for His Royal Highness to accept the resignation of officers on their death bed, and moreover that the Lieutenant Colonel did not purchase his commissions, I am induced, from the very favourable opinion which I entertained of his services and merits as an officer, and from the knowledge that his family have been left but scanty means of support, to recommend the question to the Commander in Chiefs kind attention, and to express a hope that, at all events, his widow may receive a liberal provision ... I avail myself of the opportunity to recommend Brevet Lieut. Colonel [Henry] Craufurd, of the 9th Regiment, as an officer well qualified to succeed him in the 45th Regiment. He has been many years in the service, has frequently commanded the 9th Regiment on important occasions, and has always distinguished himself.'[399]

Charlotte Ridewood received a Royal Bounty of £200 per year in addition to her late husband's pension. Major (Brevet Lieutenant-Colonel) Henry Craufurd was a Scotsman from Greenock, who had commenced his military career in the 81st and 98th Foot before purchasing a captaincy in the Glasgow Fencibles in 1792. In 1799 he was placed on half-pay and gained an appointment in the 9th Foot, with whom he served in Flanders and at Cadiz.

He purchased a majority in the 9th Foot in August 1804 and commanded the second battalion of that regiment for three years before joining the first battalion in Ireland in 1808. He served at Roliça and Vimeiro, commanding the 9th at the latter action, before being part of Sir John Moore's Corunna expedition. On returning to England he served in the disastrous Walcheren expedition.

He returned to Portugal in March 1810 and had been second-in-command of the 9th Foot at the time of Wellington's recommendation. The Honourable John Meade may have also had some influence in the appointment, since Meade and Craufurd had served together as subalterns in the 9th Foot in 1799.

Major Craufurd was gazetted lieutenant-colonel in the 45th on 26 August; unfortunately he was killed leading the right wing of his old regiment in the abortive daytime assault on the breach at San Sebastian five days later. He was due to leave for Olague and the 45th the next day. The battalion had just lost their fifth commander in action without even knowing it. The freshly arrived Major Thomas Forbes assumed command, and secured the vacant lieutenant-colonelcy without purchase on 7 October. To fill the gaps created, Thomas Lightfoot acquired the vacant majority,[400] Theo Costley the vacant captaincy, and Henry Middleton the vacant lieutenancy.

Ariscon was a bucolic spot; a pretty village of chateaux and farmer's cottages, surrounded by golden fields of maize and orchards. Whilst at Ariscon in September the battalion received some new officers and men from the second battalion – Captain Thomas Hilton, Lieutenant William Berwick, Ensigns James Reid and Edmund Hesleden, conducting a draft of twenty-five recruits.[401]

Thomas Hilton was a 24-year-old from Leigh in Lancashire, the middle son of landed gentry; his entire career until joining the 45th had been with the 6th (Inniskilling) Dragoons, and he was still learning to fight on foot – so somewhat surprisingly took over the Light Company[402] in place of the newly promoted Lightfoot. Berwick was a 19-year-old Irishman, Hesleden a 24-year-old from Barton-upon-Humber in Lincolnshire, and Reid an 18-year-old Edinburgh lad with his first year of service just under his belt. Lieutenant Edward Moore went home about this time, and Surgeon O'Connell was appointed to the staff; so Charles Cook received a well-deserved promotion to surgeon on 9 September. Major George Miles Milnes also returned for his second 'tour', having recovered from his Ciudad Rodrigo wound.

San Sebastian finally fell and the 3rd Division was ordered to march west on 7 October, where they took up a position which allowed them to watch the 1st Division's attack at La Rhune. Each day thereafter brought sharp skirmishes, none of which involved the 3rd Division. Brisbane's brigade took up residence at Zugarramurdi, about ten miles south-west of St-Jean-de-Luz, 250 metres above sea level and exactly one mile from the French border. From the hill behind the town, one could easily see the Bay of Biscay.

Zugarramurdi was not a pleasant posting. It rained almost incessantly, and when it wasn't raining it snowed. The campsite was on the downhill side of the village, and in the rain was like sleeping in a river. Food was short and the men were on constant outpost duty as they were so close to the border.[403] Still, the battalion was healthy, with (on 25 September) 449 effectives and only 144 men sick. To increase their chances of staying this way, Assistant-Surgeon Richard Lloyd (a graduate of St George's Hospital in London) arrived in late October. He was a Welshman from Cardiganshire who had served in the Walcheren expedition in 1809, and had been serving as hospital mate at Lisbon for the past two years.

---

[394] *Wellington's Dispatches*, Vol. 11, pp.169-70.

[395] Brisbane, p.24.

[396] Rowe probably means the Parisian National Guard – the Young Guard was not engaged in this theatre.

[397] 1936 Regimental Annual, p.211.

[398] ibid, p.212.

[399] *Wellington's Dispatches*, Vol. 10, pp.627-8.

[400] Lightfoot had been twelfth in seniority on landing in August 1808; at the time of promotion to major he was second.

[401] Based upon WO25/1275.

[402] Light infantry duties were the most complex of all infantry tasks. Light infantry had to learn to fight in open order as well as in regular formations, and were highly trained.

[403] Outpost duty was undertaken by picquets, each picquet consisting of one corporal and six men.

Chapter 26

Nivelle

On 31 October the starving French garrison of Pamplona surrendered, and the Spanish divisions employed in the siege were free to join the allied field army. There was now no reason to stay on the Spanish side of the Pyrenees. The rainy, snowy and occasionally hailing sojourn at Zugarramurdi was about to end. On 4 November Wellington was seen on the hill above the village, studying the distant French fortifications through a telescope. On 8 November Hill's corps (the 2nd Division and the Spanish divisions) arrived in the valley of Bastan, and the army was concentrated.

Captain James Campbell, brigade-major of the first brigade of the 3rd Division, was called for in the afternoon of 9 November 1813 and they met in an 'awful kind of cavern, with the torrent rushing through it at Zugarramurdi,[404] in which he gave me directions for bringing down the Division to where it was to remain until the hour should arrive for its advance, under Sir Charles Colville, against the line of the Nivelle'. He was to bring down, as soon as it became dark, the Fighting Division.

At the appointed hour, the bugle sounded for the troops to get under arms, and in twenty-five minutes more, the Right Brigade, followed by the other two, commenced the descent down the mountainside from their billets uphill of Zugarramurdi, ordered watch where the placed their feet in the dark. The baggage was to remain and to follow by another circuitous road in the morning. After some hours of hard work, they found themselves at Zugarramurdi, through which the division passed, and at about one o'clock in the morning the brigades were ordered to camp for the night on a meadow under the 'canopy of heaven, and until the hour for assaulting the redoubts and entrenchments arrived … When day dawned our army, to the right and left of us, was seen moving in most perfect order to make combined attacks upon the enemy's entrenchments.'[405] Secrecy was vital, and preparations almost had the air of a big First World War attack about them.

Soon after midnight, the army (having fallen in without signals by trumpet or drums), began to descend the Pyrenean mountains by moonlight, by the passes of Maya, Zugarrimurdi, Echalar and Irun. Before dawn several divisions were concentrated at the foot of the heights in the plains of Zarta and Anhou, preparatory to the attack to be made at the daybreak. The baggage remained on the mountains, the tents left standing and fires burning to deceive the enemy. This grand movement was made with a quietness and secrecy almost incredible. 'So profound a stillness prevailed,' Commissary Daniel recorded, 'that at Zugarrimurdi, while six thousand troops were passing under arms, their silent march was truly impressive'.

The allied army was formed in three corps; on the left flank, by the sea, Lieutenant-General Sir John Hope with the 1st and 5th divisions; on the right flank, in the Valley of Bastan, Lieutenant-General Hill's command. In the centre, between Maya and Echalar, more than half the army under Marshal Sir William Carr Beresford[406] – the 3rd, 4th, 6th, 7th and Light divisions. At 90,000 men and ninety-five cannon, it was the largest army Wellington had yet fielded, and afforded him yet another chance for a grand gesture.

Commissary Daniel was present with the forward troops: 'At length a grey streak, the Harbinger of day, appeared in the east, and almost instantly a cannon posted on the heights of Le Rhone was fired: this was the signal for a general attack, and all our columns rising from their ambushment, moved forward, when the French [taken by surprise] were seen running to their posts in all directions.'[407]

Major-General Sir Thomas Brisbane was suitably impressed by the view from horse-back. 'This action presented one of the finest military spectacles that ever was witnessed. As we had a considerable extent of plain to pass after descending from the Pyrenees, and being near the centre of the army, I could see nearly the whole of it. Corps marching and forming into lines, columns, and echelons, such a scene was seldom presented in any action, which the fineness of the day contributed not a little to enhance.'[408]

At some point during the morning, the 45th crossed the border and entered 'the sacred kingdom' (as the men sarcastically called France) and in so doing left Spain forever. The French were in entrenched positions along an arced twelve-mile front extending from in front of Saint-Jean-de-Luz on the coast, all the way to a height on the east bank of the River Nivelle, which generally ran in the French rear. A bridge across the Nivelle near the eastern end of the French line – the Bridge of Amotz – was the 3rd Division's target for the day.

The Light Division accomplished the day's first major task, ejecting the French from their defensive works on the Lesser Rhune by eight o'clock. Cole's 4th division stormed a redoubt in front of Sare and captured it in less than fifteen minutes. Lieutenant James John Rowe of No.2 wrote in his diary that night: 'Now the most superb sight of the kind conceivable presented itself. The 4th and Light divisions surprised the enemy's camp on

La petite Rhune, before they had time to strike a tent, and were pursuing them headlong down the mountain, the Sixth and Second on the right descending from the Pass of Maya, while the Guards attacked St. Jean-de-Luz. About 10 a.m. the action became general, and continued without intermission till dark, the enemy disputing obstinately every inch.'[409]

Brisbane's brigade advanced down the Harrane valley and captured the bridge at Amotz by eleven o'clock, which cut communications between the French left and centre. French resistance in this part of the line was generally feeble. 'Owing to some delay that took place,' William Brown wrote, 'the morning was well advanced ere we reached the enemy's outworks, which were a line of forts and redoubts upon a plain. Having passed these without molestation, we moved on to the main position, which was about half a mile to the rear of these works and situated on a height, strongly entrenched along the sides, with redoubts on the summits. Dashing through the Sorre, which by the bye was no great cordial on a frosty morning, and, surmounting the abatis which the enemy had laid on the slope of the height on which they were posted, our troops drove them from their double row of entrenchments, and in a few minutes after established themselves in the redoubts.'[410]

Sir Rowland Hill's corps erupted from the valley of Bastan, and the 6th Division from the pass of Maya, marching against the French left-hand division of Count d'Erlon. A cannonade which sounded like thunder, was heard at intervals on the allied far left, where Sir John Hope with the 1st and 5th divisions was pinning down the French left near Saint-Jean-de-Luz. With the bridge in hand, Colville was ordered to take the 3rd Division two miles down the road to the village of St Pée, thus cutting the French line in two. About noon the French main camp, said to be capable of containing 25,000 men, was set fire to and burned in a few minutes.

Clausel placed some troops in a redoubt which was assailed by the Right Brigade under Colonel Keane,[411] with Brisbane and Power's Portuguese in support. This brigade lost 355 men in a short time, with Lieutenant-Colonel Thomas Lloyd of the 94th dead – he was shot, fell from his horse, staggered, threw his sword away and exclaimed, 'It's all over with me!' before collapsing – Lieutenant-Colonel Hugh Gough[412] of the 87th wounded, and many German riflemen of the 60th *hors de combat*. But the redoubt was carried, along with an entire battery of artillery, and the French line cut in two.

Lieutenant Rowe recorded an event that was probably funnier later than it seemed at the time: 'The whole were in full retreat by 2 p.m., carrying away nearly the whole of their artillery, blowing up some caissons of ammunition. A strange instance of panic occurred. Our Brigade, after entering a fort, were formed in close column to move forward, when an alarm spread that some shells were alive, and a little loose powder flashing off the whole made a sudden rush outwards and spread a hundred yards in every direction, all looking on with dismay.'[413]

Nivelle

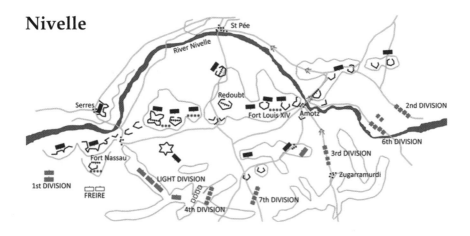

Punctured all along his line, Soult retired northwards towards Bayonne in confusion. Brisbane's brigade lost only one man this day, a wounded private of the 45th. The allies lost 3,250 men, 800 of them Spanish. French losses were 4,350, including more than 1,200 prisoners and fifty-nine cannon. No-one could agree on a name for the battle; Hope's men called it the Battle of Saint-Jean-de-Luz; Hill's right column, the Battle of the Valle de Bastan; the 3rd Division, the Battle of St Pée; the 4th Division, the Battle of Sare; the 6th Division, the Battle of Anhou. Wellington, who had the final say, opted for the name of the river at his enemy's back – Nivelle. The battle was a resounding success, the least known and understood of Wellington's battles. He had manoeuvred more than 90,000 men from three nations over a twelve-mile front and defeated an entrenched army utterly, with minimal loss of life. Many twentieth century generals, equipped with modern communications, would have been happy to have achieved as much. Wellington himself considered Assaye and Nivelle his greatest achievements, even after Waterloo.[414]

The 45th camped in the woods near St Pée the night after the battle, their first night on French soil. Due to the sounds of distant explosions of mined bridges blowing up, the men could not rest well. It rained heavily and all the next day,[415] and in the absence of their baggage, the men slept in the mud. Major-General Brisbane spent the day of 11 November camped under the boughs of a tree. The baggage came up the next morning and the division moved off after ten, and camped at Arrauntz that night, six miles north and within sight of the River Nive. There it rained incessantly, and despite the tents, the troops were exceedingly miserable. A week later the officers were allowed to quarter in the town, but not the other ranks, who remained waterlogged.

Later in the month new officers arrived, along with one old face. New ensigns Armar Lowry, Lambert Brabazon Urmston and George Croasdaile appeared from England, along with the recuperated Major Leonard Greenwell. With them were nineteen privates who had sailed from Portsmouth in October.[416] Lowry was 22 and from an eminent County Tyrone family; Urmston a 19-year-old descendant of an ancient Norman-Irish family from Chigwell in Essex; and Croasdaile a 16-year-old from Bray, just south of Dublin. Sadly, Captain and Brevet-Major George Miles Milnes left for good, having been back with the battalion for only two months – he had gained a regimental majority in the 10th Royal Veteran Battalion, then serving in Canada. Perhaps his wound had curtailed his mobility and forced his move to a less strenuous posting. Lieutenant Edward Francis Moore, completely incapacitated by fever and ague, was sent home to recover his health and did not return. Major Greenwell assumed command of Colville's converged light battalion, confirming his status as the pre-eminent commander of light troops in the 3rd Division.

The Greater Rascal

One morning in late October, Captain James Leslie awoke in his tent to find that his portmanteau, which he used as a pillow, was missing. Amongst other things, it had contained forty guineas in gold; plunder perhaps from the French baggage-train at Vitoria. He immediately put his company in marching order, grilled them and reported the matter up the line. The adjutant-general was not impressed. 'His Excellency considers this case such an instance of the hardened combination of the individuals, as well as their immediate comrades, to screen dishonesty, and impede the course of justice, that I have received the Field Marshal's commands to direct, in resistance of such a system, that the suspected soldiers, as named in the margin, together with the company or companies to which they may belong, be required to stand under arms for eight hours every day till further orders. His Excellency may he possibly influenced by your further reports on this subject, to be addressed to me every eight days.'[417]

No.3 Company stood under arms for two days, but nobody bleated. With no clues as to the thief, Lieutenant-Colonel Forbes ordered that the tents of the company be removed and the ground below them dug up. Beneath one tent five guineas were found, and the entire tent-company put on a charge. The men pleaded innocence until it was remembered that two of their number were absent, being man-servants to subalterns. Both were later found dead drunk in the camp. Placed under guard, each started to argue with and accuse the other in front of Serjeant-Major Elliott, and more guineas were found in their clothing.

A few days later both were up before a general court-martial, where the 'greater rascal of the two' saved his skin by giving evidence against the other. Thus, on 6 December 1813, Private James Kelly of No.3 Company, a seven-year veteran of the regiment, was hung (probably from a convenient tree) at Arrauntz, the only man of the 45th to receive this sentence during the war. The battalion would have been formed up in hollow square, with the No.3 Company drummers Will Gladwin and Joe Strike beating a tattoo as Kelly, dressed in a white shirt and with a GUILTY sign hanging around his neck, was led to the gallows and blindfolded. The only two officers present with the company, Captain James Leslie and Ensign John Edmonds, would have supervised the execution party, assisted by Serjeants Pat Mitchell, Will Smith and John Weir. Had it been required, a provost-marshal would have administered the coup de grace with his pistol. After Surgeon William Smyth pronounced him dead, the body would have been carried three times around the place of execution, 'in order to render the example the more striking, and to impress the greater terror on the minds of the spectators'. The 'greater rascal', Private John Hernon, also a seven-year veteran, received 700 lashes. The battalion was forced to watch both punishments.

One afternoon a private of the 88th was discovered coming out of a house with a ball of worsted yarn. The provost-marshals nabbed him, and after the most cursory of questionings, the man was dragged to a clearing, placed on a cart whilst a rope was strung around his neck, and hanged from a tree whilst the brigade watched on in horror. His body was left swinging for a day as a warning to others.[418] The reader may recollect that the provost-marshals (and their assistants) were given, by the order of 1 November 1811, *carte blanche* to inflict punishment for any offence they had witnessed with their own eyes. Wellington had issued his order about respecting the lives and property of French citizens on 9 July, and on every occasion showed that, by jingo, he meant it.

Commissary John Daniel described it thus: 'About this time some severe and painful examples were made in order to preserve the strictest discipline and a due observance of the orders issued upon our entering the French territory, which strictly prohibited every thing which might subject the inhabitants of the country to unnecessary inconvenience, The Spanish army, however, resolved to have some revenge, and shewing a determination not to submit to the severe discipline imposed on the British and Portuguese troops, was sent back into the Pyrenees for the present.'[419] General Longa's Spanish troops had behaved execrably since entering France, exacting revenge for six years of occupation upon the hapless population, and so Wellington had no option but to send them home again. General Morillo's veteran brigade, always the pick of the Spanish forces, was kept with the allied field army.

Sir Rowland's Battle

Bayonne was Wellington's next target, but a difficult one. The city was the most powerful military base in south-western France and surrounded by fortifications. It was connected to a good road network and could be re-supplied from the north bank of the Adour River. The River Nive snaked more or less south-east from Bayonne. The French defences, in addition to the garrison itself, extended from the sea near Biarritz across five miles of marshy country to the Nive.

With the rain teeming down, Wellington sat and pondered his next move. His army was weaker after the loss of the Spanish divisions, and the French were extremely strongly posted. But Napoleon himself settled the matter on 8 December; for on that day, news arrived of the catastrophic French defeat in far-off Leipzig, and Wellington knew that if he knew, the French troops opposite him did also.

Early on 9 December, General Hill's corps crossed the Nive from west to east and advanced across high country towards Bayonne from the south-east, as three French divisions in that area retreated without much resistance. General Hope pushed the 1st, 5th and Light divisions up from Saint-Jean-de-Luz and tackled the French outposts in a day of inconclusive fighting.

Early on 10 December, Hope's outposts were attacked, a battle which saw the Light Division holding off four French divisions at Arcangues. The 5th Division, with Hope leading, eventually restored the balance. The 3rd Division was unengaged on the first day, holding the bridge at Ustaritz, and on the second day arrived too late to help Hope's counter-attack. Lieutenant James John Rowe was much more observer than participant: 'We moved down to the banks before daylight. When the alarm was given, the tirallade from the banks as far as seen was beautiful. A few shots of round and grape cleared the approach for the pontoons, which were soon laid and the old bridge repaired. This allowed the Sixth Division to cross with some cavalry. General Hill, having crossed at Cambo, drove the left of the enemy in on the works of Bayonne. The action was warmly contested at the walls. Marshal Soult, repulsed on the right, passed the whole of his force through Bayonne, and attacked General Hill.'[420]

All was quiet on 11 and 12 December, and then the following day Soult turned his full force upon General Hill's corps, on the east bank of the Nive. The 3rd Division was still guarding the bridge from Ustaritz, miles from the action, as Hill fought virtually unaided (especially by Wellington) all day. Brisbane's and Keane's brigades had been double-timed towards the sound of the guns, but arrived too late to be any use; Hill had already defeated Soult at the battle of St Pierre. It was probably his finest hour. The 3rd Division had not fired a shot on any of the five days, nor taken a single casualty. Thus, none of the division's regiments gained the battle honour 'Nive'.[421]

On 14 December the 3rd Division crossed the Nive and resumed its old billets in Arrauntz. In true military mix-up fashion, they re-crossed the following day at Ustaritz and marched to Yatzu (modern Jatxou), where they stopped for three days, then marched to Urcuray near Hasparren on 19 December, to link up with the 2nd Division and keep an eye on a French

242

division lurking near that place. Maréchal Soult retired north yet again; as at Albuera in 1811, he had shown himself a master at getting his troops to the battlefield in either an advantageous position or array (or both), but had absolutely no idea what to do with them once on the field. His divisional commanders were left completely to their own devices in the thick of the action, which in the days before radio communication, was courting disaster. Wellington probably micro-managed more than was strictly necessary, but at least his divisional commanders always knew exactly what they had to do.

As for higher level formation commanders, Wellington had four – Rowland Hill, William Beresford, Thomas Graham and John Hope. The victorious battle of St Pierre had repaid Wellington's trust in the rosy-cheeked country gentleman Hill; Beresford was still a much better motivator than tactician; Graham a lion, but at 65 years of age and with failing eyesight, possibly unfit for further service; Hope was 'the most efficient officer in the army' and brave beyond compare, but often too involved with the leading elements to see the bigger picture. Wellington always evaded officially naming a second-in-command, but the Army universally recognised Hill as the man.

The Moral Effect

At Urcuray the men were wakened before dawn every day and put at the alarm-posts; they were well inside France now, and Soult's men were close by. Six-man picquets patrolled constantly, a wearying task given that it rained virtually every day in December, and a dangerous task given the ability of the French to use local knowledge to their advantage. Lieutenant Rowe was unimpressed. 'Our troops suffered more from this harassing work and bad weather in bivouacs than during all the previous campaign,' he wrote in his diary. 'Here we lost a great many by the activity of General Harispe, who constantly attacked our picquets and foragers ... We now form the extreme right, and having confined the enemy beyond the Adour remain cantoned some weeks, the enemy's posts close to ours, through which we had often communication and in consequence lost a great number from desertion, which had occurred but in one solitary instance since their arrival in the Peninsula in 1808.'[422]

The brigade lost a dozen men in December and January, one man in the 74th, six men in the 88th, and five in the 45th. It was more than in any other single two-month period of the war, not counting the ridiculous affair with the Spanish recruits. Most disappeared into the French countryside but one, Private James Fox of the 45th, re-joined the regiment in Ireland on 25 July 1817! The relative lushness of the countryside, and the warm welcome from the inhabitants was probably mainly to blame. Captain James Campbell visited Sir Thomas Brisbane and said, 'Sir, there are about 300 Frenchmen at our advanced post; are we to let them in?' Brisbane replied, 'We are not

1813 Movements

making war against the French inhabitants, only against the French army, therefore allow as many of them to come in as possible'. They sold off what they had brought with them to the brigade, and were promptly paid. They went home and told their friends and countrymen how they had been received, and the brigade never went without afterwards. 'I remarked to Sir Thomas Picton, that the moral effect we had produced here upon the people was more important to us than any battle we had gained. We paid for everything in the same manner as we do in England.'[423]

Wellington's policy was clearly paying off. Brisbane, keen to discover his landlord's opinion in general respecting local affairs, dined with him. 'He informed me that not only the French officers, but also the French soldiers had told the French inhabitants not to quit their houses, but to remain at home, as they had nothing to fear from the British army.' As they approached and entered their towns they were received with the waving of handkerchiefs. 'I never heard a complaint from any inhabitant against our soldiers,' Brisbane wrote.[424]

Given these conditions, it was easy to become complacent. Captain James Bishop was reminded that there was indeed a war on when he was taken prisoner by a picquet of the French 21e Chasseurs à Cheval on New Year's Eve whilst commanding a foraging party in the valley of Macaye. The entire six-man party of officers man-servants also became prisoners – Serjeant Charles Oats and Private Jeremiah Bowers of No.2 Company, Private Sam Cowan of No.1, Private Tom Chandler of the Light Company and Privates Eleazor Grenan and Richard Oakland of No.10. Two mules were also taken by the French, and one went missing – Lieutenant Rowe's prized acquisition from Lisbon.[425]

The 45th celebrated Christmas at the little church at Urcuray, where there were twenty-six officers, twenty-six serjeants, seventeen drummers, thirty corporals and 464 privates available for duty. During the year the first battalion had lost 117 men dead and seven to desertion, and had sent twenty men home. The second battalion on the south coast of England had lost two dead and twelve to desertion. The end of the war was close, but how close no-one could say. There were those who placed their money on being in Paris at Christmas 1814.

[404] Zugarramurdi was (and still is) famous for its caves.

[405] Campbell, pp.244-6.

[406] Beresford was a field-marshal in the Portuguese army.

[407] Daniel, pp.255-6.

[408] Brisbane, p.25.

[409] 1936 Regimental Annual, p.214.

[410] Brown, pp.252-3.

[411] Although Keane was less senior than Brisbane, he held temporary command in lieu of Colville, who was senior to Brisbane, and thus it remained the Right Brigade. Such was the way of seniority.

[412] Later Viscount Gough, one of the most famous British soldiers of the Victorian era.

[413] 1936 Regimental Annual, p.214.

[414] Assaye was a bloody assault against a numerically far superior native army in India in September 1803, which was won by sheer bravado and luck as much as skill.

[415] It is astounding how many of Wellington's victories were bracketed with either torrential downpours or thunderstorms; Salamanca, Vitoria, Sorauren and now Nivelle. Such conditions followed Quatre Bras and preceded Waterloo also.

[416] Based upon WO25/1275.

[417] *Wellington's Dispatches*, Vol. 7, p.79.

[418] Brown, p.263-4.

[419] Daniel, p.266.

[420] 1935 Regimental Annual, p.215.

[421] Although this developed into a controversy in later years, as we shall see.

[422] 1936 Regimental Annual, p.215.

[423] Brisbane, p.32.

[424] ibid.

[425] 1935 Regimental Annual p.215 and WO25/1275.

Part VIII

1814

Chapter 27

Orthez

Hasparren was a pleasant if chilly cantonment for the regiment, high up in the Basses-Pyrénées department. France was so very different to Spain; the wine and food more plentiful, the natives friendlier and more accommodating. The south of France had never been particularly fond of Napoleon, and many of the locals (known as Haspandars) were closet monarchists, patiently waiting for the day when the Bourbons would return. They treated the British more as liberators than invaders. Communication was at best tenuous, since many Haspandars spoke Basque or Occitan rather than French.

On 5 January, Lieutenant-General Sir Thomas Picton re-joined his old 3rd Division. On 7 January Brisbane's brigade sent out a picquet to flush out some French advance elements near the town, when Picton rode forward for the first time. The 45th was lying down at the head of Sir Thomas Brisban's brigade, which was concealed behind a height ready for an intended attack. The enemy was posted at a bridge on the right bank of a brook, and occupying a few houses close to it.

Opposing sentinels were within ten yards of each other, when, to the delight of the regiment, in the words of Campbell: 'Up rode their favourite chief; in an instant, and under strong and general impulse of feeling which could not be suppressed, they to a man stood up and gave him three hearty cheers, which were immediately responded to by the 74th and 88th Regiments, thus discovering where they were to the French. "Well, 45th, you have let the enemy hear you, you may now if you please, let them feel you," was Picton's smiling reply; and at the same instant he ordered the attack; which I need scarcely say was completely successful.'[426]

Although history tends to portray him as a stony-faced disciplinarian, no divisional commander within the allied army was as popular with his men as Picton. The only man to have rivalled him was 'Black Bob' Craufurd, another stern, plain-spoken individual, although his particular brand of reverence tended to waver along with his moods. One can view this as a lesson in necessary character-type for high command, but the assumption unravels when one considers Sir Rowland Hill, almost the polar opposite of these two men; balding, rosy-cheeked, softly-spoken, almost a country rector in appearance and manner, but just as revered by his men and respected more by Wellington. It only proves that high command was as much about chemistry as inspiration and perspiration.

The 45th remained at Hasparren until the middle of February. Picquet duty was constant, and Private William Brown tells us of the daily fraternisation with the French: 'Each alternate day we were on duty, nearly the one half of our number being on picquets at the outposts, which were pushed out in advance to the very teeth of the enemy, a small stream, over which a man might leap with ease, being the only boundary between our sentinels and theirs. There we stood upon the opposite banks, and conversed with as much freedom as if we had been the greatest friends, and intimately acquainted for years.'[427] Brown also echoed a sentiment that would have found purchase in any modern conflict. 'Indeed the cordiality that subsisted between us was very surprising and pleasing, and at the time I thought it a pity that so many men, who had no umbrage at each other, should be led by the nose, and made to butcher one another, merely for the sport and aggrandizement of a few.'[428]

In late January Lieutenant James John Rowe was ordered home as the recently-promoted Rowe found himself 30th in seniority in a list of 36 lieutenants, and therefore bound for duty with the second battalion. 'Our Regt. marched down to St. Jean de Luz for new clothing and appointments. I remain[ed] there one day ... and obtain[ed] my long-lost box and bag of comforts with the regimental stores in the Castle.'[429] Rowe confirms that the 45th, like many of the regiments in the army, received the new pattern uniform at Saint-Jean-de-Luz – a better cut of jacket, blue-grey 'trowsers', and new shakos similar to the Portuguese model, with a low crown and false front. They could at last shed the outfits stolen from French prisoners after Nivelle. The old stove-pipe shako was gone forever, and the men were now outfitted in the uniform that would be made famous by their comrades at Waterloo eighteen months later.

The weather improved by mid-February, and a new campaign season was imminent. The 3rd Division marched eastwards on 14 February, through Bonloc and Saint-Esteben, arrived at Saint-Martin-d'Arberoue the following day, then Masparraute, Garris and Saint-Palais on 18 February. There they found the French had destroyed the bridge over the River Bidouse. The British had to wait two days for it to be repaired, and then camped some four miles beyond it. They marched north-east, and on 24 February the light companies of Keane's Right Brigade suffered a rebuff and considerable losses at Sauveterre-de-Béarn trying to clear the French off the bridge over the Gave d'Oleron. They crossed the bridge, but the French blew it up and left them stranded on the wrong side of the river; they had to swim back across to retreat, in which panic Ensign Thomas Fair of the

94th was drowned. Wellington resolved the crisis by crossing the 2nd, 6th and Light divisions over a pontoon bridge upstream and falling on the French left, at which point they gave up the town.

The situation was unfortunate in that it was avoidable – Picton's orders were to demonstrate in order to hold the French in place whilst Wellington crossed, not to attack unsupported. For herein was Picton's one great weakness. No man in the British Army could be relied upon to march to the sound of the guns so much as Sir Thomas; and yet no officer was so casual in the interpretation of orders. As he had done at the bridge at Vitoria, Picton over-shot a direct order and caused fifty-four needless casualties. This same behaviour would have tragic consequences at Toulouse.

The rest of the 3rd Division crossed the bridge the following day, camped near Salis-de-Béarn, and crossed the Gave de Pau at a ford on a bend in the river at Bérenx. The 45th were marching in the rear of the 3rd Division, and as they advanced down the riverbank towards Orthez, they passed the Marquess of Wellington on a small hill, a telescope to his eye, watching the distant French. Seeing no troops following behind the 45th, he grabbed Lieutenant Charles Munro of No.2 Company (serving as adjutant in the absence of the wounded Lieutenant Barnwell) by the arm, and said, 'Get on the other side of this hill, or the enemy will see that there are no more troops across and be down on us'. Munro did as he was ordered, but luckily no French appeared.[430] Maréchal Soult had concentrated his forces on a ridge-line just north of Orthez, and Wellington hastened to get all of his divisions (bar Hill's) across the Gave de Pau at daybreak on 27 February. The first big battle of 1814 was taking shape.

Imagine if you will, a battle in which French troops occupy a ridge-top in line, waiting for the advancing British columns to approach. Such a reversal of traditional roles was the Battle of Orthez. The action began just after half-past eight in the morning, when Cole's 4th Division climbed heights at the western end of the French ridge, attacking the village of Saint Boès. Meanwhile, the Light Division advanced up another spur, through the site of an ancient roman camp, and halted whilst the 52nd Light Infantry went on ahead to assist the 4th Division, who had been rebuffed at the village. Wellington's plan was to hit the French line hard on the left with the 4th and 7th divisions, and pin their centre down by a demonstration in their front by Picton's 3rd Division, with the 6th Division in support; several miles to the east, Hill, Wellington's only truly trusted independent commander, was to cross the river on the other side of Orthez and threaten the French left flank and rear.

Picton arrayed his division on the plain near the river and split it into two. The Right Brigade under Keane and the Portuguese would climb the central of the parallel spurs, whilst Brisbane's Left Brigade would climb the right. The enemy appeared well-sited and confident on the ridge-line; 'the dispositions made by the French at Orthes, were … superior to what we usually met with', in the view of the brigade-major, Captain James Campbell. Brisbane's brigade was to advance up a long crooked spur to the main crest. The path was narrow, only wide enough for the battalions to advance in column, with swampy declines and wooded ravines to either side. But before they could advance, there were some Frenchmen in a ravine to be disposed of. James Campbell was on hand. 'Seeing a body of cavalry assembling behind the [French] infantry, with which we were more particularly engaged, I pointed them out to Sir Thomas Brisbane, who took such steps as he thought necessary in case of their venturing to charge us, impolitic as it was, with such a large force to contend, with, it was evident that there was nothing for it, but to detach some companies into the ravine, to drive out the French skirmishers, who invariably took in flank the 4th division, in the several gallant attempts successfully made on the narrow tongue of land, by the regiments composing it, to get forward. I conclude Lord Wellington saw how the two divisions were situated, and sent a considerable part of the light division to our support, and to clear the ravine.'[431]

Brisbane's brigade was then able to advance along the spur. They were under fire from French artillery on the ridge-line, with six light companies of the division (under Lieutenant-Colonel Greenwell) in front, then the 1/45th, then the 1/88th and 74th in turn. The 6th Division was to advance in their support, several hundred yards to the rear. Yet it would be some time before Clinton's 6th Division could arrive, and Picton dared not attack unsupported. There was a lull of nearly two hours as Picton's three brigades waited for their supports to form up, all the time under artillery fire. Finally half an hour before noon, the 6th Division was in position, and the order to go was given.

Private William Brown recorded one of the most detailed accounts of Orthez from any participant: 'We dashed forward ... at double quick time, and soon got under cover of the heights on which the enemy were placed. Being thus screened from the destructive fire of their cannon, our General halted, and after drawing us up in close column by regiments, he seemed to get into a kind of quandary, and appeared not to know well what to do. In the meantime the enemy advanced to the brow of the hill, and continued to pour volleys of musketry upon us, until the Adjutant-General, who was a most gallant officer, came galloping from the left, exclaiming, "Good God, General Brisbane, what stand you there for like an old woman, while the Brigade gets cut off. Form line and send out the 45th a-skirmishing!"'[432]

The adjutant-general was none other than Major-General Edward Pakenham, the former temporary commander of the 3rd Division, and one is struck by the genuine respect felt for him by men of the division. His death at New Orleans less than a year later, after reluctantly assuming a command he did not wish for and let down on all sides by inferior officers, seems all the sadder.

Two companies were left with the colours, the remaining eight ascended the hill and were sent forward in open order, including William Brown's No.4 Company, 'but were received in such a manner as I had seldom before experienced. We were but a mere handful of men, a skirmishing party, opposed to a dense column of infantry, supported by artillery and cavalry; the bullets flew as thick as hail, and literally tore up the ground from under our feet. Thirteen men of our company alone fell within a few yards of each other on the brow of the hill; notwithstanding, our men continued to press on the enemy, who, after a dreadful conflict and carnage, gave way, when we got possession of a ditch which we kept until the Brigade advanced in line.' It was hot work. Suddenly they were reinforced by several light companies from the division. 'We now advanced at double quick, and, giving three cheers, charged the enemy's light troops and drove them from a ditch in a parallel line with the one we had just left. In turning round the angle of the ditch, one of our company, before he had time to front the enemy, received a shot in the hip and fell on the bank exclaiming, "Blast my limbs! I would not have cared a damn if I had got it anywhere else, but now people will say I was running away and got shot in the arse!"'[433]

The brigade manoeuvred from column to line as they approached the ridge-line, under cover of the skirmishers. Brisbane then ordered the advance. At the commencement of the movement the 45th was drawn up in line, partly hidden by a hedge. The bugles sounded the recall, and the Light Company men – amongst them Lieutenant James MacPherson, detached from his No.10 Company – came scampering back to form in the rear. As the files opened to let them through, one or two of the enemy's *tirailleurs* had followed them nearly to the line, and MacPherson was anxious to see all the men through before he himself retired. He was about to effect his own retreat but saw one of the enemy's sharpshooters, within twenty yards, raising his piece to take a deliberate aim at him. He left us with his own description of events: 'I saw the man taking a deliberate aim at me. What to do I did not know. I could not get at him before he could fire, while to run would have been equally useless – I should then be shot in the back; for I knew that he was one of those picked men who never missed anything – in fact I could think of nothing else to do but stand fire. The fellow was a confounded long time taking his aim, as if determined to make sure of his mark; so I put myself in an attitude – by presenting my right side to him, putting my arm straight to cover me, and screwing myself up as small as possible – but I can assure you I felt smaller than I looked, as I thus stood like a target to be shot at by a fellow that could hit anyone of my buttons that he pleased. At last – bang went his piece, and I felt in a moment he was all right. I did not fall, but staggered a few paces backwards, and then felt very much inclined to reach my soldiers, some of whom had seen the whole affair without being able to render me any assistance. My right arm was rendered unserviceable and I felt confident that the ball had entered my body, but I was uncertain whether or not it had found its way out. I staggered towards the line, but must have fallen, had not a brave fellow named Kelly[434] – an Irishman and one of our crack shots – seeing that I was hit, run forward to support me. As soon as I felt his friendly grip round my body, I mustered fresh strength, although bleeding profusely both inside and out.

'Kelly commenced a dialogue, observing, "By me sowl, Sor, you're badly wounded, sure". I felt very faint, but replied, "Yes, Kelly, I think so; feel if the ball is out". Kelly watched its course, and then, placing his hand upon my loin, where it should have made its exit, exclaimed, "No, by me sowl, then it isn't; and you're spaking yet. But where's the man that did it?" Without at the moment any feeling of revenge towards him whom I then thought my destroyer, I pointed in the direction from whence he had fired; and there, on the very same spot, stood this daring fellow, deliberately reloading to have another shot at my assistant or to finish me. But Kelly quitted hold of me for a moment, and I saw his unerring gun raised to his shoulder; the French soldier was unmoved – Kelly fired and he fell dead.'[435]

The brigade advanced to within a hundred yards of the French line and commenced firing rolling volleys. It was deadly work, that hot afternoon at Talavera all over again, and the French showed no signs of retiring. The good reasons for having the fresh 6th Division in close support are illustrated by William Brown. 'Our party got on a height from which we had a complete view of the dark masses of the enemy in column, one of which was advancing to the point we were on, while their officers, with hat in hand and loud huzzas, encouraged their men to advance,' he wrote. By this time his company was greatly diminished in number, nearly the one-half having been killed or wounded, 'and would in all probability have been obliged to give way, but a staff officer came up at the critical moment and encouraged us to stand our ground, as we would be relieved in a few minutes by the troops that were advancing'. The reinforcements were two brigades of the 6th Division, which had been kept in reserve, formed immediately in the rear, 'when we retired filing through their line, which advanced and encountered the enemy on the summit of the height, when a most desperate and sanguinary conflict ensued. Our troops, when at a distance of a very few yards, fired a volley and instantly charged, pushing with the bayonet their adversaries downhill, who fled in the greatest haste and consternation.'[436]

The 45th at this time, it must be remembered, were eight companies in open formation, facing several French battalions in line formation on a ridge-line. Without support, they had no chance of clearing the enemy before them. The arrival of the formed 6th Division allowed the battalion to fall back behind cover, and be witness to the men of the 6th employing the standard British practice of volley and charge to clear the crest.

Serving in the Light Company was a corporal named Robert G. Grier, a tallish 24-year-old from Limerick. On any muster roll of the battalion he appears as simply R.G. Grier. He was in fact a former officer of the 1st Foot (The Royals) who had gotten drunk in the hours before the storming of Badajoz and had been left behind insensible in the trenches. Rather than being cashiered (or worse) for cowardice, he had been quietly removed from the regiment, and then enlisted as a private in the 45th at Lewes in September 1813. According to Lieutenant Charles Munro, Grier 'behaved with the greatest gallantry on several occasions, and at Orthes shot a French Grenadier through the head, and had his own arm shattered at the same time by the Frenchman. Our adjutant having been wounded a short time before, I acted as adjutant at Orthes, dismounted from my horse, and sent Grier on his back to the rear. I never saw Grier or my horse afterwards. As we advanced at daybreak in pursuit of Soult, I had not an opportunity of inquiring about my horse. Grier died in hospital of his wounds, and my horse no doubt fell into the hands of the hospital staff. Grier was a splendid soldier, and would no doubt have been restored to his rank in the Army had he lived. So you see that getting drunk before the enemy is not always cowardice, although doubtless it looks very like it.'[437]

Grier was almost certainly a pseudonym, since no officer named Grier served in the 1st Foot in this period.[438] And he did not die, as Munro thought, but survived to be discharged as a serjeant in 1816 – not as a restored officer. And so Munro lost his horse, a nag with a story attached. He had bought the horse in question from Lieutenant James MacPherson for a hundred dollars, and as money was scarce, he had to give MacPherson a draft for a hundred dollars on the army agents in London. MacPherson was shot through the body at Orthes, and left for dead on the field, so Munro congratulated himself that although he got the horse he would not have to pay for it; and that the draft for the hundred dollars would be buried along with MacPherson in his pocket. However, on the burial of the dead next day, MacPherson showed some signs of life, was taken to the General Hospital at Orthes, recovered from his wound, was invalided to England, and got the hundred dollars in London.[439]

The ridge being cleared of the French, two companies of the 88th Foot were left behind to guard the divisional artillery. A regiment of French cavalry – the 21e Chasseurs à Cheval – saw the opportunity and charged down the main road at them, sabreing many unlucky Rangers. But the other eight companies were just over the crest, came up, formed a rapid firing line, and gave the chasseurs a volley, emptying 150 saddles. By this stage, General Hill had crossed the river east of Orthez and the French were in danger of being attacked behind their left flank; they retired to a secondary position about two miles north of Orthez, but Wellington's six divisions were bearing down on them.

The arrival of several battalions of French conscripts from Toulouse did absolutely nothing to bolster the French cause; they dropped their muskets and fled at the first shell-burst, whereupon many of their better-trained

Orthez

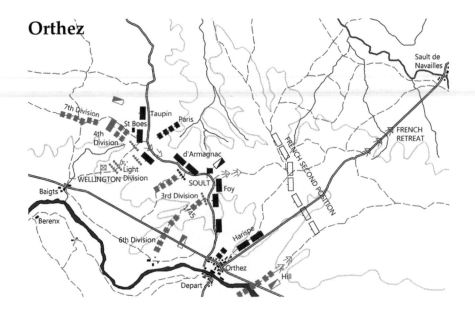

comrades swiftly followed suit. The retreat was well-ordered up to a point – and then the British cavalry were finally let loose. 'Their retreat was soon converted into a ruinous and disorderly flight in which they were charged by our cavalry, making dreadful havoc among them,' William Brown reported. 'Many of their soldiers threw away their arms and thousands were taken prisoners, besides a number of cannon. The pursuit was continued until night, when our Division encamped in a field by the roadside.'[440]

Officially the French lost 1,366 prisoners out of a total loss of just over 4,000 men; however, this figure does not include supporting services or the Toulouse recruits, so William Brown may be right when he infers there were over 2,000 captives. As usual, the Commissariat failed the victors again after the battle. 'For my own part I had fired 250 rounds of ball cartridge,' Brown later wrote,[441] 'by which my shoulder at night was as black as coal. The consequence was the men were so fatigued, that when encamped they either could not, or would not pitch the tents, but threw themselves on the ground exhausted. We were, however, ordered to set them up for our own welfare, which was at last, with manifest reluctance, complied with, for few entered them, but sat or lay round the fires although it was a keen frost. Notwithstanding the toil and peril we had been exposed to during the day, there was no bread for us at night; we were therefore obliged to put up with the carrion that was served to us for beef, which we frizzled over the smoky fire, and, having swallowed it, composed ourselves to sleep on the cold, frozen ground.'[442]

The 45th had suffered severely in the attack. Lieutenant John Metcalfe and fourteen other ranks were killed; Captain James Leslie subsequently died from his wounds. The indestructible Lieutenant James MacPherson was shot through the body, but would pull through. Lieutenant Ralph Smyth Stewart had been shot through the neck from above; the wound would cause his right shoulder to ride higher than his left for life, making it impossible for him to put a standard uniform jacket on.[443]

The 3rd Division losses were seventy officers and 730 other ranks out of an allied total of nearly 2,000. Once again the Fighting Division had lived up to its reputation. One high-profile casualty was the Marquess of Wellington himself; a spent musket-ball had hit the pommel of his sword, driving into his thigh.

Bruised but very much alive, Wellington had won another offensive battle, his sixth in a row. It is a pity his reputation is mainly founded on five defensive actions at Vimeiro, Talavera, Busaco, Quatre Bras and Waterloo, which were ultimately in the minority. Major-General Sir Thomas Brisbane had dinner with Wellington in Paris in 1815, and asked him the difference between his methods and those of his opponents. 'I heard the Duke at his own table in Paris ask, "What is the difference between Soult and me?" A general pause ensued, when his Grace said, "I will tell you the difference. I often bring my army into an infernal scrape, but it always gets me out of it. Soult often did the same for his army, and then he was left by it."'[444]

---

[426] Campbell, p.85.

[427] Brown, p.264.

[428] ibid.

[429] 1936 Regimental Annual, p.216.

[430] Wylly, pp.261-2.

[431] ibid, pp.250-1.

[432] Brown, p.267.

[433] ibid, pp.267-8.

[434] Probably Private William Kelly of the Grenadier Company.

[435] Wylly, pp.264-5.

[436] Brown, pp.268-9.

[437] 1914 Regimental Annual, pp.297-8.

[438] The 1812 Army List for the 1st Foot does contain a captain who was dismissed that year; however the individual does not appear on the Peninsula Roll Call.

[439] 1914 Regimental Annual, p.298.

[440] Brown, pp.269-70.

[441] The average soldier was supplied with sixty rounds, so William Brown suggests that he was re-supplied three or four times during the action. This seems unlikely.

[442] Brown, p.270.

[443] WO25/775.

[444] Brisbane, p.30.

Chapter 28

Toulouse

The night of 27 February was frozen and unpleasant, but the following day was worse. The bugles sounded at daybreak and when the men of the 45th awoke they found themselves in a dreadful state with cold. Most were so benumbed all over they could scarcely move. 'My gaiters, which to ease my ankles I had thrown off the previous evening, I now left behind me, they being as stiff as boards with lying in the frost all night,' Brown wrote. 'When about to march, the animating shout of "Turn out for rum" was heard, which soon re-echoed from all quarters. Owing to the severity of the night, the Commander-in-Chief had been pleased to order an extra allowance of this vivifying liquor, which was accordingly received by us while standing in the ranks, and under its animating influence we marched off in pursuit of the enemy … When we got upon the road a most horrid spectacle presented itself. Our cavalry, on the preceding evening, had at this spot charged the already routed and flying enemy, who now lay thickly strewed on the road, which was nearly blocked up with the dead and dying. Many of them had received dreadful wounds from the British sabres. Arms, accoutrements and baggage lay in promiscuous heaps or were strewed on the ground.'[445]

The provost-marshals were busier than ever the deeper the army marched inside France, to the sadness of Brown: 'As we passed along through this havoc of bloodshed and horror, an appalling sight of another description met our eyes, which was as follows: His Excellency, the Commander-in-Chief of His Britannic Majesty's Forces in the Peninsula and France, Generalissimo of the Allied Armies in the Peninsula, Field Marshal Arthur Wellesley, the Most Noble Marquis of Wellington, Duke of Ciudad Rodrigo, Lord Talavera, and Count Vimiera, Knight of the Most Noble Order of the Star and Garter, &c. &c. &c., in his wisdom, thought proper at this time and place, to cause a man of our division, and of the 5th regiment, to be hanged by the neck until dead, dead, dead. The poor fellow was apparently dead enough, and hung suspended from a tree on the road side as we passed; in order, as I suppose, to greet our eyesight, and cheer our hearts, after the fatigue of the preceding day, and by way of encouragement to strain every nerve in future. What the man's crime was I never learned, but doubt not it must have been enormous – perhaps the taking of a loaf of bread, when he was in danger of being starved to death for want of provisions, which ought to have been served to him from the stores; and which, get or not get, he and all others would be charged with. Or, perhaps, he had the audacity to lift a ball of worsted yarn.'[446]

The 3rd Division marched to Saint-Sever that day, in concert with the 4th and 6th divisions, the Hussar Brigade and the reserve artillery, and endured a horrible night of rain and sleet. The following day they crossed the River Adour, where some skirmishes (not involving the 3rd Division) were fought against the French rearguard at Air-sure-l'Adour. Soult had destroyed all the bridges across the river, and combined with the damp season (it snowed the night of 2 March) and the generally swampy nature of the countryside, movement was slow and supply difficult. Wellington called a temporary halt. Soult was struggling to hold together a disintegrating army, as many deserted the colours to go home or surrendered themselves to the allies, although there was no doubt a hard core who would fight to the bitter end.

The advance did not re-commence until 15 March, and the 3rd Division was directed up-river to Barcelonne-du-Gers, and then Tarsac, by which time the allied army was advancing eastwards. Most could guess that Soult was falling back on Toulouse, still some seventy miles to the east. The 3rd Division was diverted south and on 19 March arrived at Vic-en-Bigorre, where General Comte d'Erlon's division was acting as a rearguard whilst Soult retired on Tarbes.

In an affair fought mainly by light companies and sharpshooters, fighting one-man battles with French skirmishers in vineyards, the 45th lost one man wounded and the 74th and 88th a handful more, although the 60th Rifles lost forty-one men. If Nivelle had been a First World War battle fought a hundred years ahead of its time, Vic-en-Bigorre was a Second World War skirmish, an action fought entirely by individuals in open order. 'Besides the 5th battalion 60th, a battalion of Portuguese cacadores and our light infantry companies, whole regiments, (and here we felt the want of knowledge of light infantry movements in all corps) only retaining some companies in reserve and for support, were engaged as sharpshooters,' James Campbell recorded. 'They were, however, constantly pushed forward upon the French, and recommended not to throw away their fire in long shots, but rather, as much as possible, to endeavour to close with them; and if a halt was any where perceived in any part of the advancing skirmishers a staff officer was invariably sent to the point to ascertain the cause. The French, therefore, invariably gave way, and in their confused retreat they became exposed, in running from one enclosure to another, to the fire of our troops. After driving them for a considerable distance before us in this style, the coming of night stopped our career, but had we stood and fired, as usual upon such occasions, this brilliant feat of the 3rd division would never have been heard of.'[447]

The brigade pursued the French to Tarbes, a beautifully sited town with snow-capped mountains behind. They marched into town with the band playing, and were so well-received by the locals that it was easy to forget this was the land of their enemies. '[The French] fell back upon Tarbes, a handsome town, and extremely neat and clean. As we passed through this place, the inhabitants stood on the streets; with pitchers of wine, and pressed us to drink, to which we were nothing loath. From this place every inch of ground was contested by the enemy, who destroyed all the bridges as they went along. Not a day passed without skirmishing, and some of it very severe. But all their efforts were of no avail; Soult, with his dispirited army, was compelled to retreat across the Garonne, when, owing to heavy and incessant rains, our army was put into cantonments.'[448]

One almost gets the impression that the allies received more support from the French population than their own army. The French withdrew from the vicinity of Tarbes during the night of 20 March. The 3rd Division followed the next few days in dreadful weather, north-east to Plaisance-du-Touch, west of Toulouse, at which place they arrived on 28 March. On 25 March (when the battalion was at Samatan) the battalion had only 318 men under arms, with 204 men sick (many of them the wounded from Orthez) and sixty-five on command.[449] At the start of April, Lieutenant George Morgan arrived from home – the last officer to join the battalion during the war.

By the end of March the 3rd Division was at Cugneaux on the River Garonne, about six miles from the city. During the evening of 31 March orders came down that an attack could be expected from the French in the morning. The 45th were under arms at three o'clock in the morning of 1 April but it was a false alarm, and the men were dismissed. They moved back to Plaisance-du-Touch and the following day marched twelve miles north to Grenade, where Wellington kept his headquarters. The weather was still execrable, and the night of 4 April saw such storms that all the rivers flooded. The allies were trying to build pontoon bridges across the Garonne by which to transfer several divisions across to the eastern bank, but the rain was hampering any progress. So did the French. They floated barges full of giant rocks and loose timbers down the river to destroy any bridges that might be appearing. The rain stopped on 6 April but the rivers were still too swollen. The 45th were placed on bridge-duty, standing guard over the Royal Engineers and sappers and miners.

The Bridge-Builder

Lieutenant-Colonel Forbes had long harboured an interest in bridge-building – in fact one gets the impression a budding career as a civil engineer was cut short by the army. But at Toulouse he got an opportunity to combine both interests; it is entirely possible that volunteered the 45th for this duty. The pontoon bridge was finished early on 8 April and the Spanish Division crossed over to the eastern bank. The 45th were ordered to help the engineers dismantle the pontoon bridge during the evening of 8 April (as it was to be moved up-river), and orders were given to take up the bridge, which was, packed upon a number of waggons, and conveyed along the right bank of the river, until within a short distance of Toulouse.

'Notwithstanding the toil we had undergone, we were ordered to get on our knapsacks and accompany the waggons on their route,' Brown recorded, 'which, when at their destination, were unloaded, and the bridge once more laid across the river, and left in charge of a party belonging to the light division. We then marched off and joined our brigade, which was lying in front of Toulouse, close to the enemy's lines. When we arrived at the camp, being completely exhausted, I threw myself on the green sward, but had been only a few minutes at rest, ere I was called out on fatigue. This was another bridge I was to assist in throwing over a ditch we had crossed when entering the field, in which we were encamped ... Colonel Forbes, who had been some time our commanding officer, had got so enamoured of engineering, that he appeared determined not to leave even a single cart rut without a bridge ... As such gentlemen's wishes generally amount to positive orders, we commenced; and under his directions, by sunset, had finished a passage, which he was pleased to pronounce sufficient for the whole army to pass; but it was neither used by the army nor himself.'[450]

The pontoon bridge was re-laid two miles up-river and the Light Division crossed. With these troops across the river, battle was imminent, and Lieutenant-Colonel Forbes realised he had blundered in allowing his battalion to become the bridge-guard. He wrote frantically to Captain James Campbell, brigade-major to Sir Thomas Brisbane: 'The idea of his remaining in the rear in command, even of such a regiment as the 45th, and though employed upon an important duty, was intolerable. Almost every hour I received a letter from him, urging me to represent to Sir Thomas Brisbane how unhappy he and his regiment felt, at being left in such a situation; and entreating that he might be allowed to give up his post to some troops more in the rear, or to detachments coming up to join the army. His impatience was for some time laughed at; but at last I had the pleasure of sending him orders to abandon his post, and to replace himself and his regiment at the head or the Right Brigade of the 3rd Division. He came up just in time for the battle of Toulouse.'[451]

The army was ordered to close up around the city, and the 45th joined the division in the evening; marching through the camp with their band playing and Lieutenant-Colonel Forbes at their head.[452]

Toulouse

The town of Toulouse is seated on the right bank of the River Garonne, over which there is a handsome stone bridge of seven arches, which (together with the suburbs of the town on the left banks of the river), had been fortified and barricaded against assault. On the east side of the river the Languedoc canal formed a crescent encircling the town, being cut along the margin of the suburbs. It fell into the river about half a mile below the great bridge. The banks of this canal were for the most part lined with batteries or breast-works, every road or pass enfiladed, and all the bridges over it barricaded and fortified. In addition to these, the range of heights to the east contained a chain of redoubts and other field-works, capable of affording cover to fifty thousand men with a hundred pieces of cannon, and all the houses on the heights being loop-holed for light infantry.[453]

The battalion was put into motion just before sunrise on the 10th, a little after seven in the morning. Advancing along the east bank of the Garonne, the brigade came upon an outpost of Frenchmen garrisoning the farm of Petit Gragnague. Despite Picton's order to 'demonstrate' against the enemy, he chose to go in all guns blazing, and detached three companies from each of the 45th, 74th and 60th Rifles under Major Thomas Lightfoot of the 45th to clear the farm and outbuildings.

House-to-house skirmishing continued for upwards of an hour. Private William Brown and five comrades from No.4 Company were sniping from a window when something fell on the floor, emitting smoke. Assuming it to be an unexploded shell, they all bolted for the only door. Once outside they realised it was in fact Private David Evans' shako. He had stuffed it full of cartridges, and when coming in contact with the flashing pan of his musket, it had exploded. Evans had lost all his hair and looked 'like an old ram when singed by a cook'.[454]

The French eventually retired from Petit Gragnague and fell back to a redoubt that guarded the bridge at Pont Jumeaux across the Languedoc canal. Picton decided to attack the redoubt at Pont Jumeaux at two in the afternoon. The Right Brigade, under the command of Major-General Brisbane, was ordered to leave the plantation in which they had been hidden, and to attempt to force a passage over the canal, by means of a bridge situated near its junction with the River Garonne. The bridge was covered by an extremely strong redoubt in front, and artillery on each flank. Sir Thomas Picton personally directed this attack. 'The artillery attached to Sir Rowland Hill's corps, perceiving the intention of Sir Thomas Picton, opened a heavy fire across the river; but unfortunately they struck down some houses which had served to protect the light troops of the division, and this left them exposed to the incessant shower of grape which was kept up by the enemy,' Picton's biographer later wrote. 'The works which Sir Thomas Picton was now about to attack had been prepared with the utmost skill and care; everything that art could devise to render them impregnable against assault had been done; but it was not until the counter-scarp had been gained that General Picton discovered the formidable nature of the defences.'[455]

With Brisbane at their head, the brigade formed up on the south side of the plantation. The light companies of the brigade, under Major Thomas Lightfoot, formed the first wave, in open order. These comprised, from right to left, the 45th (under Captain Tom Hilton), the 88th (under Captain Robert Nickle), the 74th (under Captain Donald Macqueen), and the three companies of the 60th Rifles. The redoubt they had to attack was an inverse U-shape and only about 50 yards wide, approached across a flat field – requiring a converging line of attack, therefore there was not the room for all battalions of the brigade to form line; so Brisbane compacted the battalions into a shallow column. Five companies of the 45th were to form the right flank of the advance and five companies of the 74th (under Captain and brevet-Major James Miller) the left; whilst three companies of the 88th formed the third line. The remaining companies of the 45th, 74th and 88th stayed in the plantation as a tactical reserve.[456] On a signal from Major-General Brisbane, the light companies advanced across open ground towards the redoubt, which was in fact an earthen rampart surrounded by a ditch which guarded a single stone bridge across a canal. As the six companies advanced the French artillery on the far side of the bridge opened up with a salvo and they broke into a slow run as the cannonballs looped over, bounced and in places knocked men aside like skittles. At a distance of about 100 from the redoubt, the French muskets started popping and men dropped all along the ragged line of attack. When they arrived at the ditch they realized that they did not have sufficient ladders to affect any sort of escalation, and so after milling around without making any impression, most light company men went to ground to snipe at the French defenders. Some went around the flanks and down to the canal bank in the hopes of finding an unguarded rear entry to the redoubt, but none existed, and these men found themselves sniped upon by French *voltiguers* on the opposite bank.

With the light infantry prone in the ditch, the French shifted their fire to the thirteen advancing companies now looming through the smoke. The French artillery had the range by now, and the compact masses of formed infantry made a more effective target than the loosely formed skirmishers. The cannonballs did great execution in the ranks of the 45th and 74th. Urged on by their officers, the companies broke into a jog when within a hundred yards of the redoubt. Strangely, the French infantry inside had not fired – yet. But when it came it was terrible.

The simultaneous volley cut down 100 men in the advancing column, and the formations shuddered, slowed for a second and then ran harder. Men stopping to snipe at the French were urged onwards by serjeants and officers. At fifty yards another French volley did even worse damage, and those in the lead who were still on their feet bolted to the ditch and jumped in. But many stopped to shoot back at the French, and the action became one of individual firing-at-will – the French, however, were secure behind their ramparts, whilst the 45th and 74th were completely exposed. With the *fantassins* (infantry) within the redoubt occupied by the British troops at their front, the French artillery was able to devote all its attention on the advance of the supporting 88th, a mere three companies who received the artillery's full attentions. The 88th lost thirty-six men killed and fifty-six wounded out of about 150 who participated in the attack.

The 45th and 74th continued firing from the ditch and their exposed position in front of the redoubt. But without scaling ladders, or any other means of gaining entry, it was hopeless. It seems the only man who actually made it inside the redoubt was Private Pat Connor of the Light Company of the 45th, who plunged in amongst the bristling bayonets of the French, yelling 'Hurrah! Ye buggers, hurrah!'[457] The bugles sounded the recall, and back they went. Lieutenant-Colonel Forbes was riding at the rear of the 45th during the retreat, when a cannonball hit him in the back and passed straight through him. The commander's curse continued: Guard, Smith, Ridewood, Crauford and now Forbes. The French had long endeavoured to relieve them of Gwyn and Greenwell also, but somehow both had miraculously survived. Ensign Edmonds and then Lieutenant Douglas both went down whilst carrying the King's Colour. But Private Connor was captured unhurt, not killed, and so survived to return to the 45th a few days later. Captain Alex Martin, the lover of all things zoological and botanical, fifteenth in seniority at Roliça, led the 45th from the field. He had probably never imagined himself commanding the regiment on a battlefield.

It was an action eerily similar to the fruitless assault on the American ramparts at New Orleans nine months later. It cost the 45th Lieutenant-Colonel Forbes and ten men killed; eight officers, eight serjeants and sixty-four rank-and-file wounded, and five men missing.[458] Earlier in the day another cannonball had neatly removed Major-General Brisbane's hat without touching a hair on his head. '[It] spun me round with irresistible force, and knocked me flat on the ground,' Brisbane recalled. 'I was so confused with the violence of the concussion, that I deemed it prudent to send for the officer next in command to be near me, and to take the command of the brigade in case of necessity. While in this state of confusion I was shot through be left arm by a musket-ball, when the blood, flowing profusely from the wound, immediately relieved my head, and restored me to my senses. This is perhaps a rare instance where a musket-ball has proved beneficial to an individual, and even rendered him medical assistance when absolutely requisite.'[459]

The action now transferred to other parts of the field. Lieutenant-Colonel Forbes's body still lay in the open. Some men of the 45th afterwards obtained leave to carry it off, and gave it a soldier's grave. Command of the brigade devolved upon Colonel John Taylor of the 88th, 'who had, however, only to lead off the remnant of the troops, and establish them in their former position, where Picton and his division were condemned to remain inactive, listening with intense anxiety to the thunder of battle, which had now broke forth with renewed fury on their left'.[460]

Wellington later caustically commented that the 3rd Division had sustained losses 'in consequence of General Picton having exceeded his instructions'. To the west, Hill had harried some French outposts but the fighting was not serious. In the east, Beresford's corps had started the day well behind schedule. General Freire, commanding a Spanish division, sent his men to assault the Heights of Calvinet without British support – they gained a momentary foothold in a road cut, but were counterattacked and sent into headlong retreat.

After some delay, the 4th and 6th divisions under Beresford reached their start line after a long southerly march, with the 6th Division leading. These divisions advanced up the slope from the south and fought their way to the top of the Heights despite bitter resistance, in which the 42nd Highlanders (The Black Watch) lost 414 men. Wheeling northwards, they captured two redoubts and began rolling up the French defences. The redoubts were lost to a counter-attack but finally captured again after bringing the 4th Division forward. With the Heights lost, Soult withdrew his troops behind the town's fortifications.

Soult decided to pull out of the town after he spotted allied cavalry moving up the Toulouse-Carcassonne road, his only route of escape. The French withdrew from Toulouse at nine o'clock that night.

The battalion went into bivouac that night in and around a large empty chateau about 500 yards behind Petit Gragnague. In faraway Paris, the former Emperor of the French had abdicated six days earlier; but the news had not yet reached Toulouse. On Easter Sunday Napoleon Bonaparte was contemplating an action that awaited him in the morning; the signing of the Treaty of Fontainebleau between France on one side, and representatives from the Austrian Empire, Russian Empire and Kingdom of Prussia on the other. The men who survived Toulouse could console themselves with the fact that they had survived this final day. They were far luckier than the 1,300 or more men who died that day – British, Portuguese, French and Spanish – who thus fell on the very last day of the war.

An Unnecessary Battle

Fortescue described Toulouse as 'the most unsatisfactory action that Wellington ever fought and the worst managed'. Toulouse was also the 3rd Division's only failure on a battlefield. Total allied losses were nearly 600 killed and over 4,000 wounded. Commissary John Daniel saw many melancholy scenes in the camp after the battle. 'I joined the brigade just at the time the 45th regiment were burying poor Colonel Forbes,' he later wrote, 'whose body they had obtained leave to bring off from the spot where he fell, in front of the fortified bridge over the canal. The Colonel had a presentiment of his fate from the time that the regiment received orders to join the division yesterday; and as soon as it was known that a battle would be fought he became visibly depressed, and could not divest himself of the idea that he was doomed to fall. We were all much grieved to see the melancholy by which he was depressed as he rode round the camp last evening, as though he was taking a last farewell of his regiment. He left a widow and family in England to lament his fall.'[461]

The 391 casualties in the 3rd Division (most of which had been inflicted within a ten-minute period) plainly swamped its medical resources. 'All the houses and cottages here were full of the wounded of the 3d division,' Commissary Daniel recorded. 'We entered one where poor Little of the 45th was dying – the scene was very distressing. The brigade went into bivouac behind a large empty chateau, orders having been given for the tents and baggage to continue in the rear. I remained with them until about 10 o'clock, and then returned to the baggage camp. Barnwell's servant having been widowed, I endeavoured to find him out at the hospital, in the ruins of a large deserted chateau, where a most shocking scene presented itself. Several of the poor fellows were dead, and others dying, while the wind whistling round the turrets of the mansion, seemed to mock the moans of these poor victims of fame, who were extremely destitute, and in most of the rooms had no other light but what the moon afforded, which served to increase the horror of the scene. I went to my tent greatly discomposed in mind: the camp-fires of our left column were glimmering over the field of battle on the heights, lighting many a sad and tragic scene.'[462]

Lieutenant-Colonel Forbes ought to have been eligible for a military burial involving a funeral party of 300 men, but the above suggests he was buried fairly quickly after the action and without much fuss.[463] Today there is a sepulchre to him in St Andrew's Church (now the Musée Historique) in Biarritz[464] and a commemoration pillar near where he fell, which was restored in the early twentieth century by the Sherwood Foresters.

Toulouse was also the most unnecessary battle Wellington ever fought. The following day, Monday, 11 April 1814, the Treaty of Fontainebleau was signed in Paris.[465] The treaty was ratified by Napoleon two days later; he was no longer Emperor, and the Napoleonic Wars were over.[466] The joyful news reached Wellington late on 12 April. He immediately sent an emissary to Soult, who had also heard, and an immediate suspension of arms was called, the armistice officially confirmed by Soult on 17 April. The war was over, and the fact was common knowledge amongst the soldiery on Wednesday, 13 April 1814.

News travelled fast across the Channel. On 14 April 1814, The Nottingham Journal trumpeted an advertisement: 'Public Dinner at Thurland Hall, Nottingham – There will be a dinner on Monday, the 18th inst., at Thurland Hall, to celebrate the late glorious news and the downfall of a great Tyrant, who has been a curse of the human race, and the cause of all the misery and bloodshed that have desolated the civilised world.'

445 Brown, pp.271-2.

446 ibid, pp.272-3.

447 Campbell, p.252-3.

448 Brown, pp.274-5.

449 WO17/157.

450 ibid, pp.277-80.

451 Campbell, p.127.

452 1926 Regimental Annual, p.232.

453 Daniel, pp.312-3.

454 Brown, p.281.

455 Robinson, pp.309-10.

456 In the absence of any detailed documentation concerning the assault, and in fact several contradictory sources, this battle-array is all my supposition, but seems logical given the limited space available in which to channel the attack, and the actual casualties incurred.

457 Brown, p.287.

458 Wylly, pp.274-5.

459 Brisbane, p.27.

460 Robinson, p.332.

461 Daniel, pp.323-4.

462 ibid, pp.324-5.

463 Lieutenant-Colonel Forbes was later re-interred at the Guards Cemetery at Bayonne.

464 The same memorial also commemorates Lieutenants John Metcalfe and George Little.

465 Napoleon had in fact already abdicated on 7 April.

466 For now at least.

Chapter 29

What Fine Fellows

Soult had evacuated Toulouse on the night of 11 April and the allies entered it as liberators early the following day. Wellington entered in triumph that morning at about ten o'clock. He was met at the gate by the local authorities, civil and military, headed by the Mayor and commandant of the national guards, and escorted down the main street to Place Capitole, a large building of white stone from which flew the white banner of the Bourbons; curiously it waved over a bust of the Emperor Napoleon, which they had either forgotten to remove or had not had time to take down. Every window and even the house-tops around the square were crowded with well-dressed females, crying 'Vive le Roi!' and 'Vive les Bourbons!' National guardsmen with the white cockade and colours paraded the streets, and in the square two regiments of British cavalry were drawn out to receive Lord Wellington with due honours. 'About half past 9 o'clock our old general Sir Thomas Picton rode across the square with laurels in his hat: he was greeted as he passed, and shortly afterwards, the approach of Lord Wellington being announced, the cavalry trumpets were sounded and swords drawn.'[468]

Sir Rowland Hill with his 2nd Division then marched over the great bridge and through the town, to keep an eye on the remains of the French Army which had gone in the direction of Ville Franque, about twenty miles distant. 'The rest of our army encamped on the field of battle, our division spreading along the banks of the canal. I pitched my tent on a grass plat near the river, and close to the ruins of some houses which had been burnt during the action. At one o'clock in the afternoon dispatches arrived from Paris by an officer, who as he passed through the town to Lord Wellington's quarters, announced the news of peace; and shortly afterwards the following particulars being made public and proclaimed throughout the town, soon reached us in the camp, where they created the most lively sensations.'[469]

The news of the Emperor's fall arrived too late in Bayonne, where the French commander conducted a sortie on the night of 14 April, resulting in over 800 casualties to the 1st Division; 142 allied soldiers, mostly Guardsmen, died in a war that was already over. The 3rd Division was put under arms on 17 April and marched just after sunrise, bound for Ville Franque. Rumour was rife; had the news of peace been erroneous? Nine miles outside Toulouse, whilst the troops were lounging in a field during a break in the march, a carriage flanked by French Lancers and British Light Dragoons whizzed past, with a white flag riding before it. The troops buzzed with excitement. So, the news was true. The Division camped at Bassieges (Baziege) that night, and all men put white cockades on their shakos. The men expected to carry on the same road the following day, but were halted, and learnt of Soult's agreement to the armistice. On 19 April they marched back to Toulouse, and the following day marched to their peacetime cantonment down-river at Grenade.

On 25 April the battalion had only 279 effectives on parade, the second-lowest total for any month of the war. This low effective strength may in fact have allowed the 1/45th to dodge a bullet; for the Duke of York had written to Wellington on 14 April – barely two days after the news of peace – suggesting fourteen battalions to be despatched to aid the war effort in North America,[470] including long-serving Peninsula regiments such as the 3rd, 5th, 9th, 27th, 29th and 40th Foot (to which the 5/60th Rifles were later added). All were to be completed to strengths of between 800 and 1,000 men with recently forwarded recruits. With a gross strength of less than 600, somewhat fewer than 300 left standing for active duty and only limited numbers of men forthcoming from the second battalion, the 1/45th (even as veteran as it had become) was presumably excluded as a viable component of the force.

On 19 May 1814, Leonard Greenwell finally achieved his long sought-after promotion to lieutenant-colonel in the regiment (although he had been lieutenant-colonel in the Army since 17 August 1812). He had been born the third son of Joshua Greenwell Esq. of Kebblesworth in Durham, and as younger sons often did, entered the Army as an ensign in the 45th Foot on 7 August 1801. He moved through the ranks steadily; lieutenant in September 1802, captain in April 1804. He had served in South America and since the landing in 1808. He had been wounded more often than any other man in the battalion.

The 3rd Division was joined at Grenade on 25 May by a party of men released from French prisons – ex-prisoners or war, some were men not seen for nearly five years. Their experience had no doubt been similar to the news of peace as recorded by a British prisoner at Clermont: 'It was on Sunday, April 10, 1814, at half-past ten at night … Napoleon had abdicated the throne of France. Immediately we burst open the prison-doors and entered the town, where we found the inhabitants assembled, with music and dancing and illumination, the greatest joy being manifested by all classes; and as we mixed with the people we were often saluted and congratulated, now that peace was proclaimed, on our approaching return to our own country. About midnight the National Guards requested us to return to our abode, which at length we consented to do so.'[471]

Still travelling from Blois, where he had been moved after the Prussians captured Nancy in February, was an almost unrecognisable Colonel William Guard, aged and worn-out from four years in captivity. No doubt he would have barely been able to recognise the men of his own battalion, with so few remaining being veterans of 1809.

A few days later the battalion lost its last man on campaign. Private Thomas Waplington died of sickness on 3 June.[472] Then it was ordered to march about ninety miles to Bordeaux, through charming untouched countryside and in perfect weather. Each night the men were billeted on the locals who could not have been more hospitable if they tried. The men struggled with the thought that these people had been the enemy until only very recently, and contrasted the experience unfavourably with the often sullen reception they had received in Spain. They reached passages on 9 June, where the Army officially bade farewell to the Portuguese regiments, 'the fighting cocks of the Army' as Wellington had famously dubbed them.

Four days later the 45th was at Blanquefort, where the newly titled Duke of Wellington made his final inspection of the 3rd Division. 'Observe this regiment – how well they look!' the great man whispered to Major-General Brisbane as he rode within ear-shot of Lieutenant-Colonel Greenwell. 'They have been with me the whole time. They have gone through everything – what fine fellows!'[473]

Indeed, they had gone through everything. The 1/45th was just one of three British battalions to have served in the Iberian Peninsula continuously from 1 August 1808 until departure in July 1814;[474] the two others were the 1/40th (2nd Somersetshire) and the green-clad 5/60th (Royal American) Regiment of Foot. The force that Wellington commanded in 1813 and 1814 has been described as Britain's finest-ever overseas army, and the 1/45th was one of the most experienced battalions therein. They had never let their leaders or comrades down; but it was time to go home. The Duke of Wellington issued what was effectively his farewell to the army in a General Order dated 14 June 1814: 'The Commander of the Forces, being upon the point of returning to England, again takes this opportunity of congratulating the army upon the recent events which have restored peace to their country and to the world,' he wrote. 'Although circumstances may alter the relations in which he has stood towards them, so much to his satisfaction, he assures them that he shall never cease to feel the warmest interest in their welfare and honour; and that he will be at all times happy to be of any service to those to whose conduct, discipline, and gallantry, their country is so much indebted.'[475]

Sometime at the end of the month the battalion marched down river from Bordeaux to Pauillac and boarded transports for home. Some were destined to be left behind – Lieutenants Thomas Parr, Will Berwick, Dan Stewart and Colin MacDonald, as well as Paymaster Dalhunty were still on command in Spain and Portugal, along with two serjeants and five privates, probably to shepherd the nine serjeants, two drummers and 109 privates left behind sick in various hospitals. Eleven privates were also 'on command' in France in various roles and capacities. Of the thirty-nine company serjeants with the battalion, three were still at Lisbon, three were in England, six had been left behind sick in France, and two – Charles Smith and James Parkington – were assigned to accompany a new expeditionary force of two divisions under Lieutenant-general Lord Hill destined for North America,[476] having been appointed assistant provost-marshals.

It says something of the 45th that two of its best NCOs had been selected to enforce discipline on an expedition in which the battalion was not engaged. However by the end of the Peninsular War, the provost-marshals had made themselves the most detested men in the Army and most chose to return to another regiment rather than their own. This might have had something to do with Parkington's actions, for he never went to North America, and was discharged in Ireland on 24 December 1814; but we know that Smith went to Canada, where he received a commission as an ensign in the 7/60th Foot stationed in Quebec. Evidently he took Private George Hewitt with him as a manservant. Smith ended up on half-pay on the reduction of the 7/60th in 1817.

The 45th sailed in a small flotilla of transports superintended by HMS *Rolla*, accompanied by the 83rd Foot, one company of the 74th Foot and a batch of convalescents. After an uneventful journey they dropped anchor in Cork Harbour on 22 July and started disembarking the following day.

Ireland Again

'But what a contrast did the appearance of the regiment form, to that which it made six years antecedent, when embarking at this very port for Portugal,' William Brown wrote of their arrival at Cork Harbour. 'Then it consisted of eleven hundred stout young men,[477] glowing with health, and animated with the vigour of youth. Now, less than three hundred formed the skeleton ranks, few of whom but had been wounded, many oftener than once and none that were not more or less worn with fatigue and disease.'[478]

What would the crowd that lined the quayside at Monkstown on 23 and 24 July 1814 have made of these conquering heroes? Behind the band, probably playing the regimental march, *The Young May Moon*, would have marched two ensigns carrying the tattered and bullet-holed colours held aloft on (in the case of the Regimental Colour) a makeshift staff. Anyone familiar with the regiment in 1808 would have struggled to identify any of the officers at all, and in any event only four returning officers had embarked with the battalion six years earlier. Three of the drummers – John Murdagh, John Mahoney and Michael Carthy – were teenagers who had

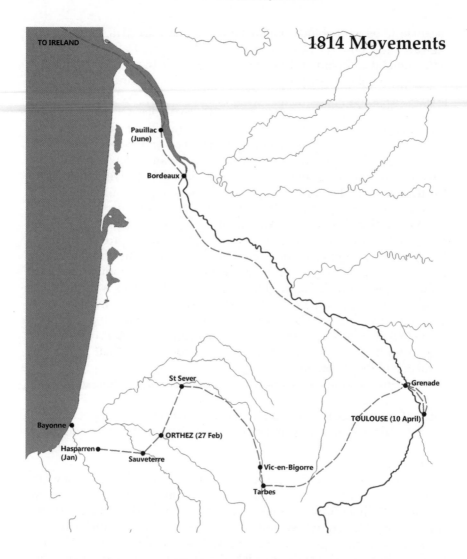

1814 Movements

TO IRELAND

Pauillac (June)

Bordeaux

St Sever

Grenade

TOULOUSE (10 April)

Bayonne

ORTHEZ (27 Feb)

Hasparren (Jan)

Sauveterre

Vic-en-Bigorre

Tarbes

seen six years' foreign military service and therefore could probably barely remember Ireland. Behind followed a column of impossibly tattered, lean nut-brown men, many with long hair and beards, with white Bourbon cockades on their battered shakoes, laughing and tossing about foreign words at random,[479] some unrecognisable even to loved ones. Long-abandoned wives and children ran expectantly along the column, looking for men not seen, in some cases, for almost exactly six years. Wails told of husbands not returned.

They marched into the new barracks at Cork where in succeeding days they were given new uniforms and equipment, and arrears of pay; in many cases, a considerable sum of money. They were then granted leave for eight days[480] in which to spend it. According to that muster roll (25 July 1814), the battalion contained 184 men with seven or more years' service, and twenty-one with fourteen years or more under the colours. Considering the total strength of the battalion (including those left sick or on command in France and Portugal), this meant that nearly one man in three had served for seven years or more. Few regiments in the army could boast this saturation of veteran soldiery within their ranks.

In early September the battalion – boosted by returned convalescents to a strength of 760 other ranks – marched for Enniskillen via Fermoy, Mitchelstown, Roscrea and Cashel. The 45th were home (at least, home to a third of them) in Ireland. But many had had their fill of the Army. Those who had rushed to join up in 1808 and had signed on for seven years could at least start counting the days until discharge. But for those who had enlisted for unlimited service, the options were to keep serving until worn out – or to desert.

The 45th stayed at Enniskillen from October 1814 onwards. Lieutenant-Colonel Greenwell went on extended leave, and with the senior major David Lecky also absent, command devolved upon the junior major, Hugh Stacpoole, elder brother of Captain John Massy Stacpoole. Hugh Stacpoole had never seen service in the Peninsula, and found himself commanding ten veteran captains and upwards of 500 suntanned hard-cases who had traded fire with the 'Parleyvoos'.[481]

Reduction

In September 1814 the second battalion was cantoned in William Guard's old home-town of Exeter, weak in numbers, the ranks filled with worn-out veterans, boys and malingerers.

In early October, Captains Alexander Martin and Alexander Anderson and Lieutenants James Reynett and William Berwick sailed from Cork across to Plymouth Dock, where the second battalion was due to be disbanded on the 24th of that month. They returned a few weeks later with ten serjeants and the remaining 142 fit men to be integrated into the first battalion, after which the 45th (no longer the first battalion!) had a strength of fifty-four serjeants, twenty-two drummers and 836 other-ranks.[482]

The arrival of the former 2nd Battalion men necessitated a reorganisation and shuffling of ranks. John Sproule was reduced to colour-serjeant on 25 February 1815 and 29-year-old former Royal Marine Sam Wallis, from the 2nd Battalion, was made serjeant-major in his place. After three and a half years as quartermaster-serjeant, Alex Adie was reduced to serjeant on 24 November 1815 and the job given to Michael Maloney from the second battalion instead. Paymaster's clerk Campbell Kelly was reduced to private in March 1815 and never again regained his rank up until his discharge in 1825; we can only assume some irregularity in his conduct over pay was to blame. Again, the role was given to a 2nd Battalion man, Daniel Harwood. The feelings of these veterans, forced to relinquish coveted and more highly paid positions to men who had sat out the war at home, were never recorded. But it seems logical to assume there was considerable cause for friction.

A mere handful of returning prisoners of war arrived back with the battalion in November; again, so very few in comparison with the number lost during the war, especially at Talavera. Many missing men were struck off the roll, never to be seen again, their fate unknown to this day.

The addition of the 2nd Battalion men allowed the regiment to discharge a clutch of worn-out veterans. Those who had been wounded or suffered some other disability queued up at Chelsea or Kilmainham for a pension, whilst the able-bodied took their home transportation disbursement and disappeared back into civilian life. Many discharge papers have been lost, so the circumstances of those without pension papers remain somewhat of a mystery, and will probably remain so forever.

In December the veterans of Buenos Aires and the Peninsula enjoyed their first Christmas at home since 1805. Private William Brown recalled the time fondly. 'In Enniskillen, the regiment remained five months, which time, though it was winter, passed on very pleasantly. Provisions were cheap and turf was served in abundance for fuel, enabling us to keep good fires, at which we passed the long winter evenings in an agreeable and comfortable manner, very different from that we had been accustomed to for some years past.'[483]

---

[468] Daniel, pp.329-30.

[469] ibid, pp.331-3.

[470] The so-called War of 1812 was in its third year of protracted bickering along the border between the USA and Upper Canada.

[471] *Prisoners of war in France from 1804 to 1814, being the adventures of John Tregerthen Short and Thomas Williams of St. Ives*, Cornwall, 1914.

[472] WO25/1275.

[473] Wylly, p.281.

[474] Three King's German Legion battalions also shared this distinction.

[475] General Orders and Regulations, pp.311-2.

[476] This expeditionary force did not sail, at least not as originally formed; the two divisions were to be commanded by Clinton and Kempt.

[477] Actually more like 900, but Brown hadn't been there at the time.

[478] Brown, p.298.

[479] For example: 'whopper' for large woman, 'padre' for priest, 'vamoose' for hurry.

[480] A little more than a day's leave for each year of active service!

[481] Slang for the French.

[482] Wylly, p.282.

[483] Brown, p.318.

Chapter 30

Forgotten You?

Lieutenant James MacPherson, the hero of Badajoz, was still a subaltern when the war ended; so little prospect did he place on advancement that leaving the Army seemed the only course. Then, one day in early April 1815, he was walking along Pall Mall in London, when he saw Lieutenant-General Sir Thomas Picton coming in his direction, accompanied by a gaggle of senior officers. Suspecting he would not be remembered, MacPherson prepared to pass by unnoticed, but Picton seized him by the arm and whispered, 'Damn it, sir, are you going to cut me?' MacPherson, no doubt embarrassed in front of a group of high-ranking staff, bowed and replied, 'No, sir, any officer who served under Sir Thomas Picton would be proud in the honour of being recognised by him. But I thought you might have forgotten me.' Picton was incredulous. 'Forgotten you? No, no, sir, I have not forgotten you. Come with me, sir.'[484]

He then took MacPherson home with him, and made out a personal application to Horse Guards for a company for his young friend. 'Lieut. MacPherson served seven years as a Subaltern officer in the 45th Regiment, he was personally engaged in every Battle, Siege & Skirmish, which took place in the Peninsula, from the Battle of Talavera, to that of Orthez. Lieut. MacPherson was wounded on mounting the Ladder at the assault of the Castle of Badajos, & notwithstanding, was one of the first to get into the place, & actually struck the Enemy's Colour, which he had the honour of presenting to the Duke of Wellington. He was engaged in every affair from the Siege of Badajos to the Battle of Orthez, where he was wounded through the Body & Arm, & his life for several months despaired of.'[485] This produced the usual official reply that there was 'at present no vacancy'.

Picton could not accept this and called personally upon the commander-in-chief, the Duke of York; and within a week MacPherson was gazetted captain in the 2nd Garrison Battalion, dated 25 April 1815.

The closeness of MacPherson's brush with death is well illustrated by the above description, and Munro's assertion that the man had been left for dead on the field of Orthez. In those times of relatively primitive

275

surgery, we must assume that MacPherson's recovery was nothing short of miraculous. By 1815 he may well have considered himself bullet-proof, un-killable; his later career in Ceylon is so full of daring deeds that it certainly suggests MacPherson believed himself to be so. But in reality MacPherson's primary motivation seems to have been an ardent desire for advancement; presumably being unable to meet the cost of purchased commissions, he sought promotion on the battlefield instead. So instead of leaving the army, this chance encounter with Picton seems to have set MacPherson on a different path, one that would define the rest of his career.

The Bourne From Whence No Traveller Returns

The *Nottinghamshire Guardian* of 13 January 1871 noted the death of Peninsula veteran William Crowder. It started that 'Death is rapidly thinning the ranks of the veterans in this locality, there being but one or two of the "Old Boys" left in the town, the others having one after another taken their last march to that "bourne from whence no traveller returns".'[486] The same paper also recorded the death of veteran George Cook on 9 February 1877 and said, 'By the demise of the old veteran we believe the last of the gallant 45th who were sent out from the county of Nottingham to do battle in the Peninsula is gone from our midst.'[487]

George may have been the last 45th veteran left in Nottingham, but was not the last of all. Probably the longest-survivor of the other ranks was Private Charles Cawley. This snippet appeared in *The Times* on 15 December 1884: 'Mr Charles Cawley has just died at Crossflints, near Bingley, at the age of 101 years. The deceased was an army pensioner, and had served in the 45th Regiment of Foot. He went through the Peninsula campaign, and was present at the sieges of Ciudad Rodrigo and Badajoz, and was twice wounded on the field of battle.'[488]

Chelsea pension records show that Charles Cawley (sometimes spelt Colley) was discharged on 23 February 1816, but did not apply for a pension until 23 March 1852. Perhaps the musket ball that had remained in his arm after Badajoz was causing him too much pain and incapacitation in his old age. Curiously, although they had abundantly deserved it, neither Charles Cawley nor George Cook ever applied for the General Service Medal.[489]

Research has shown that Cawley would probably have been eligible for Roliça, Vimeiro, Talavera, Fuentes de Oñoro, Ciudad Rodrigo, Badajoz, Pyrenees, Orthez and possibly Corunna too – nine clasps. Perhaps both Cawley and Cook lived too remotely to hear about the medal or maybe they did not wish to be reminded of those hard years.

The last of the officers was Lieutenant Charles Munro. He was placed on half-pay in May 1817, and so, because not otherwise employed, commanded the 1st Regiment of English Lancers in the service of Venezuela in the War of Independence in South America. In 1818 he commanded a division of the Colombian Army under that celebrated patriot, General Simon Bolivar at the Battle of Agnotmar. He married Amelia Browne in 1817, and they had eight children, one a son (Gustavus Francis) who attained the rank of major-general. In 1848 Charles succeeded his father as 9th Baronet of Foulis-Obsdale. Lady Munro died in 1849 and Sir Charles married again, to Harriette Midgley of Yorkshire. Sir Charles Munro died on 12 July 1886, at ninety-one, at Southport, Lancashire, where he had resided for several years. It was very nearly seventy-eight years to the day since the 45th had sailed out of Cork Harbour bound for Portugal. Lady Munro survived him by five days. He was not the longest surviving Peninsula officer – that person is generally acknowledged as being Captain James Gammell of the 59th Foot, another Nottinghamshire regiment, who died in Bath in September 1893, aged ninety-six – but he came close.

The number of the regiment did not even outlive Munro. The 45th (Nottinghamshire – Sherwood Foresters) Regiment, as it became in 1866, granting Colonel Guard his wish, linked with the 95th (Derbyshire) Regiment and as we have seen, became the numberless Sherwood Foresters (Derbyshire Regiment) in 1881. Today they are the 2nd Battalion, The Mercian Regiment (Worcesters and Foresters) – the fact that Worcester and Sherwood Forest are 120 miles apart makes it clear that this was a marriage of administrative convenience for the Army, not historical relevance.

Or was it? Memories of the 45th climbing that hill at Roliça in support of the 29th (the old Worcesters) may have lingered long enough for the connection to seem natural.

By 1887 they were all gone; the 45th, the Hosiers, the Fire-Eaters, the Old Stubborns, every last one of them – the unlucky Colonel Guard; those valiant majors, Gwyn, Smith and Greenwell; that jacketless hero, Jimmy MacPherson; the exemplary soldier and forlorn-hoper, Serjeant Jim Waite; six-times-wounded Jim Nixon; the boy born in the regiment, Tom Griffiths. Had they lived fifty years later, many of these men might even have earned the Victoria Cross. All that was left was William Brown's nearly forgotten autobiography, and the medals, the objects of desire for General Service Medal collectors everywhere, crowded with clasps representing days of stubbornness on Portuguese hillsides and nights of stomach-turning terror on the ramparts of ancient Spanish citadels. But it is too easy to forget that the medal was not awarded until 1847, denying the many veterans who had died before that year a place on the honour rolls or in the museum cases.

On 27 September 1910 a telegram was received at the headquarters of the 1st Battalion, Sherwood Foresters. It was from a Colonel Mesquita commanding the 8th Infantry Regiment of the Portuguese Army, and it simply read: 'The Commandant and Officers 8th Infantry Regiment transmit congratulations to 88th and 45th Regiments of the British Army on the centenary of the battle of Busaco, in which they distinguished themselves in a celebrated bayonet charge.'[490]

Philip Hugh Dalbiac's *History of the 45th* was published in 1902, and the reading of it may have inspired the commander of the 1st Battalion of the Sherwood Foresters, Lieutenant-Colonel Henry Carmichael Wylly, to celebrate Badajoz Day (6 April) when stationed in Hong Kong in 1903; the Trooping of the Colour was observed nearly every year until the centenary, which was celebrated on the regimental cricket-ground at Hyderabad in India on 6 April 1912. The regiment's facings were reverted from white to the traditional dark green in 1913, the same year that the old colours were laid up in Nottingham Castle.

After a lapse due to the First World War, the Badajoz Day ceremony was revived in 1922 and is still observed to this day by the regiment's successors, the 2nd Battalion, Mercian Regiment; a scarlet coatee is flown from the regimental flagpole on this date, as well as atop Nottingham Castle. It was raised amidst full military ceremony on 6 April 2012 to celebrate the 200th anniversary.

As Captain James Campbell said of the assault at Ciudad Rodrigo: well might officers be proud of such men.

---

[484] 1923 Regimental Annual, p.8-9.

[485] Robinson, pp.395-7.

[486] National Library of Australia, 19th Century British Newspapers Online.

[487] National Library of Australia, 19th Century British Newspapers Online.

[488] National Library of Australia, 19th Century British Newspapers Online.

[489] Former Private James Bowers, blind, illiterate and living in Edinburgh, also did not apply, even though he had served in all the actions between 1808 and 1811. More remarkably neither did William Wragg, although living as an in-pensioner at Chelsea Hospital where talk of such things would have been hard to ignore.

[490] 1911 Regimental Annual, p.14.

Bibliography

General Sources – Periodicals

The London Gazette online.

The Times online.

18th Century British Newspapers online. National Library of Australia.

19th Century British Newspapers online. National Library of Australia.

The House of Commons Parliamentary Papers (HCPP) online, National Library of Australia.

The Monthly Army List. London: various years.

The Naval and Military Magazine. London: T. Clerc Smith. Various years.

The New Annual Register, or General Repository of History, Politics and Literature. London: G.G. & J. Robinson, various years.

The Royal Military Chronicle or British Officers' Monthly Registers and Mentor. London: J. Davies, various years.

The United Service Journal and the Naval and Military Magazine. London: Henry Cole Byrne and Richard Bentley, various years.

General Sources – Reference

Nafziger, George. *Collection of Orders of Battle.* Available online.

General Sources – British Army

Baker, Anthony. *Battle Honours of the British and Commonwealth Armies.* London: Ian Allen Ltd, 1986.

Burnham, Robert and McGuigan, Ron. *The British Army Against Napoleon.* London: Frontline Books, 2010.

Burnham, Robert; McGuigan, Ron; Muir, Rory; *Inside Wellington's Peninsular Army, 1808 – 1814.* Barnsley: Pen & Sword, 2007.

Coss, Edward. *All for the King's Shilling.* Norman, University of Oklahoma Press, 2010.

Fortescue, Hon. J.W. *A History of the British Army.* Five volumes. Uckfield: The Naval and Military Press Ltd (N&M), 2004.

Haythornthwaite, Philip. *The Armies of Wellington.* Brockhampton Press, 2000.

James, Charles. *The Regimental Companion: Containing the Pay, Allowances and Relative Duties of every Officer in the British Service.* Three volumes. London: T. Egerton, 1811.

Mockler-Ferryman, Major A.F. *Annals of Sandhurst; A chronicle of the Royal Military College from its Foundation to the Present Day*. London: William Heinemann, 1900.
Mullen, A.L.T. *Military General Service Medal Roll 1793-1814*. Uckfield: N&M reprint, 1990.
Page, F.C.G. *Following the Drum: Women in Wellington's Wars*. London: Deutsch, 1986.
Philippart, John. *The Royal Military Calendar, or Army Service and Commission Book*. Five volumes. London: A.J. Valpy, 1820.
Reid, Stuart. *Wellington's Officers, Volume 1*. Leigh-On-Sea: Partizan Press, 2008.
Reid, Stuart. *Wellington's Officers, Volume 2*. Leigh-On-Sea: Partizan Press, 2009.
Reid, Stuart. *Wellington's Officers, Volume 3*. Leigh-On-Sea: Partizan Press, 2011.

General Sources – Peninsula War
Gurwood, John (Ed). *The Dispatches of Field Marshal the Duke of Wellington: during his Various Campaigns in India, Denmark, Portugal, Spain, the Low Countries, and France*. (12 volumes). London: Parker, Furnivall, and Parker, 1847.
Supplementary Dispatches and Memoranda of Field Marshal Arthur, Duke of Wellington, K.G. Arthur Wellesley (12 volumes). London: J. Murray, 1860.
General Regulations and Orders for the Army. Adjutant General's Office, Horse-Guards (5 volumes), 1809-1813. London: T. Egerton, 1811-1814.
Gurwood, John (Ed). *The General Orders of Field Marshal the Duke of Wellington ... in Portugal, Spain, and France, from 1809-to 1814: And the Low Countries and France, 1815*. London: W. Clowes & Sons, 1832.
Edwards, Peter. *Talavera: Wellington's Early Peninsula Victories, 1808-9*. Ramsbury: Crowood, 2005.
Hall, John A. *A History of the Peninsular War: Volume VIII – The Biographical Dictionary of British Officers Killed and Wounded 1808-1814*. London: Greenhill Books, 1998.
Jones, John T. *Journals of Sieges: Carried on by The Army under the Duke of Wellington in Spain during the Years 1811 to 1814* (3 volumes). Uckfield: N&M reprint 2004.
Oman, C. *A History of the Peninsular War. I. 1807-1809. From the Treaty of Fontainebleau to the battle of Corunna. II. Jan.-Sept. 1809. From the battle of Corunna to the end of the Talavera campaign. III. Sept. 1809-Dec. 1810. Ocaña, Cadiz, Bussaco, Torres, Vedras. IV. Dec. 1810-Dec. 1811. Masséna's retreat, Fuentes de Oñoro, Albuera, Tarragona. V. Oct. 1811-Aug. 31, 1812. Valencia, Ciudad Rodrigo, Badajoz, Salamanca, Madrid. VI. Sept. 1, 1812- Aug. 5, 1813. The siege of Burgos, the retreat from Burgos, the campaign of Vitoria, the battles of the Pyrenees. VII. August 1813 to April 14 1814. The capture of San Sebastian, Wellington's invasion of France, Battles of the Nivelle, the Nive, Orthez and Toulouse*. Oxford: Clarendon Press, 1903. Greenhill Books reprint.
Reid, Stuart. *Wellington's Army in the Peninsula 1809–1814*. Osprey Books, 2004.
Weller, Jac. *Wellington in the Peninsula*. Barnsley: Frontline Books, 2012.

Regimental Histories
Burton, Frank E. *The 45th: 1st Nottinghamshire Regiment, the Sherwood Foresters. Their Honours and Medals*. Article from Regimental Annual.
Cannon, Richard. *Historical Record of the 31st, or the Huntingdonshire Regiment of Foot; Containing an Account of the Formation of the Regiment in 1702, and of its Subsequent Services to 1850*. London: Parker Furnivall and Parker, 1850.
Cannon, Richard. *Historical Record of the 74th Regiment (Highlanders): Containing an Account of the Formation of the Regiment In 1787 and of its Subsequent Services To 1850*. London: Parker Furnivall & Parker, 1851.

Cannon, Richard. *Historical Record of the 88th Regiment of Foot, Or Connaught Rangers: Containing an Account of the Formation of Regiment in 1793 And of its Subsequent Services to 1887*. London: William Clowes and Sons, 1838.

Dalbiac, Colonel P.H. *History of the 45th First Nottinghamshire Regiment*. London: Swann Sonnenschein And Co., 1902.

Danielle, David Scott. *Cap of Honour: The 300 Years of the Gloucestershire Regiment*. Stroud: Sutton Publishing Ltd, 2005.

Everard, Major H. *History of Thomas Farrington's Regiment, Subsequently Designated the 29th (Worcestershire) Foot, 1694 to 1891*. Worcester: Littlebury & Company, 1891.

Lowe, A.E. Lawson. *Historical Record of the Royal Sherwood Foresters, or Nottinghamshire Regiment of Militia*. London: W. Mitchell & Co., 1872.

Paton, Glennie and Symons. *Historical Records of the 24th Regiment from its Formation in 1689*. London: Simpkin, Marshall, Hamilton, Kent & Co., 1892.

Sapherson, Alan (Ed). *Volunteer Regiments of England, Scotland and Wales, 1806*. Leeds; Raider Books, 1989.

Verner, Willoughby. *History and Campaigns of the Rifle Brigade, 1800-1813*. Naval & Military Press reprint (2 volumes).

Wylly, H.C. *History of the 1st and 2nd Battalions the Sherwood Foresters (Nottinghamshire and Derbyshire Regiment)*. (2 volumes). London: the regiment, 1929.

The Sherwood Foresters, Notts & Derby Regiment Regimental Annuals 1909-1938.

First-hand Accounts

Brown, William. *The Autobiography, or Narrative of a Soldier*. London: J. Paterson, 1829.

Campbell, James. *A British Army, as it was, - is, - and ought to be*. London: T. & W. Boone, 1840.

Daniel, John Edgecumbe. *Journal of an Officer in the Commissariat Department of the Army: Comprising a Narrative of the Campaigns Under His Grace the Duke of Wellington, in Portugal, Spain, France, & the Netherlands, in the Years 1811, 1812, 1813, 1814, & 1815; & a Short Account of the Army of Occupation in France, During the Years 1816, 1817, & 1818*. Published by the author, 1820.

Grattan, William. *Adventures with the Connaught Rangers: from 1808 to 1814*. (2 volumes). London: H. Colburn, 1847.

MacKinnon, Henry. *A Journal of the Campaign in Portugal and Spain, Containing Remarks on the Inhabitants, Customs, Trade, and Cultivation, of those Countries, from the Year 1809 to 1812*. London: printed for Charles Duffield, 1812.

McCarthy, James. *Recollection of the Storming of the Castle of Badajos*. London: W. Clowes and Sons. 1836. Spellmount reprint, 2011.

Robinson, Heaton Bowstead. *Memoirs of Lieutenant-General Sir Thomas Picton, G.B.C. &c. including his correspondence: from originals in possession of his family*. London: R. Bentley, 1836.

Sinclair, Joseph. *A Soldier of the Seventy-first, from de la Plata to Waterloo 1806-1815*. London: Frontline Books, 2010.

National Archives

WO12/5726 to WO12/5730 – Pay-lists and Muster Rolls for 1/45th Foot 1807 to 1814

WO17/157 – Monthly returns for 45th Foot, information kindly supplied by Andrew Bamford.
WO25/1275 – Muster-master General's Index of Casualties &c.
WO25 – Commission Books
WO25 – Field Officer Service records 1809
WO25 – Half-pay Officers' records 1829
WO25 – Retired Officers' records
WO25 – Surgeons' records
WO42 – Officers' Wills
WO65 – Army Lists
WO100 – Medals and Awards
WO116 – Chelsea Pensioner records
WO117 – Long Service Pensions
WO119 – Kilmainham Pensioner records.

Index

INDEX

286